RISING INDIA IN THE CHANGING ASIA-PACIFIC

Strategies and Challenges

RISING INDIA IN THE CHANGING ASIA-PACIFIC

Strategies and Challenges

Ganganath Jha
Vibhanshu Shekhar
Editors

PENTAGON PRESS

Rising India in the Changing Asia-Pacific: Strategies and Challenges
Ganganath Jha and Vibhanshu Shekhar (*Eds.*)

ISBN 978-81-8274-589-6

First Published in 2012

Published by
PENTAGON PRESS
206, Peacock Lane, Shahpur Jat
New Delhi-110049
Phones: 011-64706243, 26491568
Telefax: 011-26490600
email: rajan@pentagonpress.in
website: www.pentagonpress.in

Printed at Avantika Printers Private Limited.

Contents

Part II
MULTILATERAL INSTITUTIONS IN THE ASIA-PACIFIC: A ROAD AHEAD

Part III
INDIA AND SOUTHEAST ASIA

Part III
INDIA AND EAST ASIA

PART IV
INDIA AND THE SOUTH PACIFIC

About the Contributors*

A.N. Ram is former Secretary, Ministry of External Affairs, Government of India.

Amita Batra is Associate Professor at the School of International Studies, Jawaharlal Nehru University, New Delhi.

Amit Singh is Research Associate at National Maritime Foundation, New Delhi.

G.V.C. Naidu is Professor at the School of International Studies, Jawaharlal Nehru University, New Delhi.

G. Venkat Raman is Assistant Professor in Indian Institute of Management, Kozhikode.

Ganganath Jha is Professor at the School of International Studies, Jawaharlal Nehru University, New Delhi.

Hariyadi Wirawan is the Dean at the Department of Political Science, University of Indonesia, Jakarta, Indonesia.

A. Lakshmana Chetty is former Director at the Centre for Southeast Asian & Pacific Studies, Sri Venkateswara University, Tirupati.

Manmohini Kaul is Professor at the School of International Studies, Jawaharlal Nehru University, New Delhi.

Pranav Kumar is Assistant Professor in Motilal Nehru College, Delhi University, New Delhi.

Rabindra Sen is Professor at the Department of International Relations, Jadavpur University, Kolkata.

Rajaram Panda is Senior Fellow at the Institute for Defence Studies and Analysis, New Delhi.

The views expressed in this book are personal views of the editors and contributors. They do not reflect the views of the institutions which the writers are affiliated with.

Sarika Malhotra is a journalist.

Tridib Chakraborty is Professor at the Department of International Relations, Jadavpur University, Kolkata.

Varun Sahni is Vice-Chancellor of University of Jammu, Jammu.

Vibhanshu Shekhar is Research Fellow at the Indian Council of World Affairs, New Delhi.

Y. Yagama Reddy is Director at the Centre for Southeast Asian & Pacific Studies, Sri Venkateswara University, Tirupati.

Introduction

Vibhanshu Shekhar and Ganganath Jha

> "A change is coming over the scene and now Asia is again finding itself. We live in a tremendous age of transition and already the next stage takes shape when Asia takes its rightful place with other continents."[1]
>
> **Jawaharlal Nehru**, Asian Relations Conference in 1947, New Delhi.

Today, the Asia-Pacific stands on the cusp of a momentous shift, stirring intense debate and discussion among the academia and the policy-makers alike. Along with a revolution in the nature and dynamics of economic integration, the region is enjoying enormous swelling in its politico-strategic significance at the global level. Moreover, the region offers what ASEAN Secretary General, Surin Pitsuwan, calls 'the world's largest business space.' The region is more integrated than ever through cooperative activities and a plethora of institutional networks built around ASEAN. While the Asia-Pacific is emerging as an important player in global governance discourse, countries of the region are emerging as stakeholders and drivers in the success stories of the region. The multilateral engagement has undergone significant transformation in terms of geo-political outlook, agenda and mandate of institutionalized cooperation in the region. In fact, the idea of cooperation has never ever been so powerful and profound in the near history of the Asia-Pacific. The signing of the India-ASEAN FTA in goods and India's greater economic integration with the region further testify to the logic of shared prosperity.

The processes of cooperation in the Asia-Pacific are being driven not only by the prospect of collective prosperity, but also by the growing fear of 'strategic uncertainty, great-power rivalries and shared vulnerability.' As China and India have emerged as Asian powerhouses, the Asia-Pacific has become a battleground where each of them is utilizing its strategic resources and influence to its advantage. There is a greater degree of Chinese assertion in Asia coupled with efforts to prevent the emergence of any alternative power centre in the continent. The rise of China has been entwined with a sense of fear and an uncertainty as to whether it is a peaceful or conflict-prone process.[2]

Challenges are emanating both from within the state and without. The momentum of development generated over the years in Asia has come under severe stress, warranting initiatives and policies of the pan-Asian scale. The spiralling level of inflation, food crisis, energy crisis, and global financial meltdown are just some of those challenges which the countries in Asia cannot address unilaterally. The global economic crisis of 2008 brought home the point that both India and ASEAN are stakeholders and important players in the peace and prosperity in the region.

Defining the 'Asia-Pacific': A Nebulous Construct

Before laying out the evolution and expansion of India's strategic engagement in the Asia-Pacific during the last twenty years, it is important to define the geographical canvas of the book. The question arises as to what constitutes Asia-Pacific and whether there is any definitive geopolitical boundary of the region. The answer is 'no' and every country seems to have its own definition of the region. ASEAN has identified the Asia-Pacific with the ASEAN Regional Forun (ARF) and therefore the canvas changes with the entry of new members in the forum. India does not seem to have any water-tight definition of the Asia-Pacific. Australia's definition of the Asia-Pacific during the early 1990s did not include India but now does after the first decade of 21st century.

The region of Asia-Pacific remains an abstract notion and a context-specific, country-specific, and time-specific construct. In other words, the geo-political boundary of the region has been constantly changing, often reflecting the strategic priorities of the countries, organisations or actors trying to define it. Different pan-Asia-Pacific international organisations have varied in the number of members indicating divergent preferences of constituent countries, or rather dominant member-states. The Asia-Pacific Economic Cooperation (APEC) has 21 members, the ARF has 27 members and the Economic and Social Council of Asia and the Pacific (ESCAP) has more than 50 members. While the APEC includes Thailand and Vietnam as its members, it does not include the intervening space of Cambodia and Laos. The admission of Russia into the APEC in 1997 is understood as a product of US concession to Russia after opposition to its entry into NATO and under pressure from China, Japan and South Korea. While Australia under the Labor leadership of Bob Hawke and Paul Keating did not consider India as a part of the Asia-Pacific during the 1990s and opposed Indian membership in APEC, the same country under the similar Labor leadership of Kevin Rudd acknowledged India as an important player in the Asia-Pacific while floating a new Asia-Pacific Community in June 2008. Moreover, though not included in the ARF at the time of its inception, India was admitted to the Forum two years later, highlighting expansion in the approach of Association of Southeast Asian Nations (ASEAN) towards Asia-Pacific regionalism. Similarly, while India was included in the ARF in 1994, Pakistan was not admitted into the ARF until 2004. Despite not being located in East Asia, both Australia and New Zealand are members of East Asia Summit.

The Asia-Pacific as a regional entity still remains a 'nebulous construct' reflecting an expanding geo-political canvas with an indeterminate membership and criteria. Moreover, the region is experiencing parallel processes of community-building with different core areas and overlapping boundaries, emerging out of divergent strategic priorities and foreign-policy face of constituent countries.[5] Dennis Rumley identifies four different scales of community-building processes in the Asia-Pacific '(a) an overarching Pacific Rim or Pacific Basin concept which is an Asia and Pacific concept; (b) a less inclusive Asia-Pacific Economic Cooperation (APEC); (c) the scale of the Western Pacific states; and (d) a regional concept, which is exclusively Asian'.[6] Echoing similar vagueness, the former foreign minister of Singapore, Tommy Koh, while delivering a speech at the Asia-Pacific Community Conference, held in Sydney in November 2009, highlighted two distinct processes of community building within the region – East Asia community building and Asia-Pacific community building.[7] While ASEAN+3, EAS and ARF are ASEAN-driven processes, the APEC is an essentially US and Australia-driven cooperative initiative. These parallel processes also indicate a growing elasticity of geo-political boundaries, and the expansion of ASEAN-driven integrative processes. What differentiate these organisations and these cooperative processes are their geo-political canvas, the fulcrum of their activities, and their different composition. Given the ever-changing canvas of the region, the book identifies the "triangular geographical space between India, Japan and Australia covering eastern South, Northeast, Southeast Asias, island countries in the Oceania, and Australia and New Zealand as the region of Asia-Pacific".

Altered Geopolitics of the Asia-Pacific

Two important developments characterise the altered politico-strategic landscape of the Asia-Pacific in the twenty-first century. These are (a) the rise of China and India as important strategic players, and (b) the emergence of new power-configurations in the region.

Ronald Tammen and Jacek Kugler predict a Sino-US conflict in the future using the power-transition theory.[8] The theory postulates 'wars occur at the global level when a dissatisfied challenger sees an opportunity to take on the pre-eminent international leader'.[9] On the other hand, David Kang argues that the rise of

China has prompted Asian states to 'bandwagon', thereby, further consolidating China's strategic positioning in the region.[10] A few other scholars hint at the possibility of other Asian powers joining hands to balance the destabilizing outcome of the rise of China.[11] Mearsheimer states,

> If China continues its impressive economic growth over the next few decades, the US and China are likely to engage in an intense security competition with considerable potential for war. Most of China's neighbours, to include India, Japan, Singapore, South Korea, Russia and Vietnam, will join with the US to contain China's power.[12]

The rise of China has coincided with the rise of India as an important strategic player in the Asia-Pacific during the first decade of the twenty-first century. With its sustained economic growth, enhanced strategic presence in East Asia, long-standing 'China-threat' theory and a great power posturing, the perception of countries about India has changed from one of an insular South Asian hegemon to an important strategic player with the material capability of altering the balance of power in the region; C Raja Mohan characterises India as 'a swing state'.[13] India's altered strategic profile can be seen from the nature of its strategic engagements both bilaterally with select Asian players as well as multilaterally.

India has already signed strategic partnerships with Australia, Indonesia, Japan, Singapore, South Korea and Vietnam with wide-ranging defence and security cooperation agreements. While India and Japan signed the Global Partnership in April, India and the US signed the civil nuclear energy cooperation in July 2005. The Indian entry into the EAS during the same year was an outcome of its growing strategic ties with select ASEAN players, its changing geo-strategic profile in the Asia-Pacific, and its increasingly close relations with two important global players in Asia-Japan and the USA.

China initially opposed the idea of forming the East Asia Summit, then tried to scuttle India's entry into the grouping. In the face of failure, it decided to take over the agenda of the EAS by proposing to hold the summit in Beijing. The Chinese diplomatic offensive has invited varied responses from different countries in the region. The formation of the EAS is, in fact, the manifestation of ASEAN's policy of engaging with the major players in the region. ASEAN's unequivocal declaration of holding the annual EAS summit within the region was a response to the Chinese offer of holding the second summit in Beijing.[14] An important manifestation of the balance of influence can be seen in the form of Japan's favourable disposition towards India – Japan's support of India's participation in the EAS, Indo-Japanese maritime exercises, former Prime Minister of Japan Shinjo Abe's idea of establishing an arc of freedom and democracy along the outer rim of the Eurasian land mass, and subsequent proposal to set up a Quadrilateral Initiative.

On the other hand, the ASEAN countries find themselves interacting with China in a potentially unstable geo-political atmosphere. The rise of China and its growing strategic influence has brought Southeast Asia to the vortex of a great power rivalry with major global players – China, India, Japan and USA scrambling. While China faces what Robert Kaplan calls 'a blunt geographic wedge' from India in the Bay of Bengal and Indian Ocean and Japan in the East China Sea and western Pacific, it finds less formidable a challenge to its expansion in its sphere of influence in the Southeast Asian maritime corridors stretching from the South China Sea to the Strait of Malacca. The most apt example is an escalation of strategic hostility in the South China Sea. Moreover, China faces territorial disputes in the South China Sea with four ASEAN players – Brunei, Malaysia, the Philippines and Vietnam. Though Indonesia signed a strategic partnership with China in April 2005, and a maritime security cooperation agreement in 2008, there exists a lurking fear regarding China's strategic ambitions and policies towards the region. What further complicates the issue is the somewhat sudden nature of this rise, leaving very limited time and space for the region to respond to this mega development.

The first decade of the twenty-first century has seen the resuscitation of an 'Asian Century' discourse that entails importance of East Asia in global economics and the rise of China and India as new dynamos of global economic growth.[15] Wallerstein highlights the growing significance of East Asia in the areas of production, commerce and finance and argues that the region's importance is set to grow as the dollar tumbles down further.[16] As stated by the President of European Central Bank, Jean-Claude Trichet, the Asia-Pacific, representing roughly half of the global population, contributed around 37 per cent of global GDP in terms of Purchasing Power Parity (PPP), and roughly 40 per cent of global growth came from Asia in 2007.[17] While floating his 'Asia-Pacific Community' in June 2008, Kevin Rudd, the Australian Prime Minister, underlined the strategic importance Asia is going to carry in 2020–45 per cent of global GDP, one-third of global trade and 25 per cent of global military spending.[18]

Rising India's Responses to the Changing Asia-Pacific

With the increasing international recognition, rising India has seen growing synchronisation of drivers of India's rise and thrusts of India's eastward engagement. The engagement has metamorphosed into an expression of a rising power with global ambitions in the specific regional context of the Asia-Pacific, which as two distinct characteristics. First, the Asia-Pacific is increasingly becoming the hub of global economic and strategic entrepreneurship. Therefore, economic integration and acquisition of strategic resources, primarily energy sources, are prudent and beneficial policy options for a rising power in the region. Second, the region is gradually drifting toward uncertainty and instability, and the most important factor in inducing this uncertainty is the sudden and uncertain nature of the rise of China with which India has shared approximately fifty years of hostility. As India expands its strategic influence in the Asia-Pacific, it faces an enormous challenge from the growing power and influence of China. Such a perception has pushed an emerging power like India towards consolidating its strategic presence in the region by building strategic partnerships, developing naval strength, and infiltrating the ASEAN cooperative processes. Besides building strategic partnerships and developing an Asia-wide focus, India has followed the principle of ASEAN-centrality in its eastward engagement in the twenty-first century.

The Look East policy has been trying during the last five years to grapple with its new status and strategic ambitions, responding to prevailing uncertainty in the regional structure of power and China's growing threat, and at the same time, retaining its benign image. Moreover, the second phase of the policy has seen enormous expansion in terms of the geographical canvas of the policy. The Look East Policy (LEP) covers not only the ten ASEAN countries but also the Northeast Asian countries and countries of Oceania. The growing expansion in the outlook of the LEP has led to ASEAN being the nucleus of the policy with other regions and sub-regions forming the outer rims.

The expansion in the geographical canvas of the LEP and its significantly expanded scope of engagement have transformed the policy into what scholars characterize as a revived form of 'Nehruvian Asianism.'[19] The rising global profile of Asian players, including India, makes the statement more reflective of current international politics. In his speech in New Delhi in November 2007, Pranab Mukherjee reiterated the importance of the LEP in the 'resurrection of that vision of Pan-Asian regionalism.'[20]

Therefore, there is an urgent necessity for both India and ASEAN to steer the region towards prosperity and face challenges together. The challenges facing the two players are immense and they can, if not addressed effectively and in time, not only badly affect their prospects of development but also jeopardize the overall environment of peace and security in the Asia-Pacific. Three types of challenges can be identified – (a) facilitating cooperative engagement among them, (b) ensuring their strategic interests, and (c) retaining their geo-strategic significance in the case of altered politico-strategic landscape of Asia.

Structure of the Book

This proposed book is an effort to outline the emerging contours of the changing politico-strategic landscape of the Asia-Pacific, changing dimensions of India's eastward engagement, with special reference to its relations with ASEAN and various challenges the engagement currently encounters. The book, divided into five sections, deals with different dimensions of *realpolitik* in the Asia-Pacific and what new changes and challenges meant for India and ASEAN as they together enter into the second decade of twenty-first century and third decade of India's LEP.

The book is divided into five sections. The first section deals with different dimensions of politico-strategic changes taking place in the Asia-Pacific and their impact on the policies and strategies of India and ASEAN. The second section outlines various aspects of ASEAN cooperative processes and the scope for long-term cooperation between India and ASEAN at these forums. The third section of the book focuses on different aspects of strategic and economic cooperation between India and Southeast Asia. Underscoring the expanding geographical canvas of India's Look East Policy, the fourth and fifth sections of the book highlight different tenets of India's security, cultural and strategic engagement with East Asia and South Pacific. The strategic priorities of Japan and Australia, given their growing importance in India's strategic engagement, have been discussed in detail.

ENDNOTES

1. Cited in I K Gujaral, "Lands of the Asian Miracle," *The Hindu*, 10 August 1996.
2. Thomas J. Christensen, "Fostering Stability or Creating a Monster?: The Rise of China and U.S. Policy toward East Asia," *International Security*, Vol. 31, No. 1, Summer 2006, pp. 81-126.
3. Christophe Jaffrelot, "India's Look East Policy: an Asianist Strategy in Perspective," *India Review,* Vol. 2, No. 2, April 2003, pp. 35-68, 46; Prakash Nanda, *Rediscovering India: Evolution of India's Look East Policy,* New Delhi, Lancer Publishers & Distributors, 2003.
4. "Asian Economic Integration: Towards an Asian Economic Community," Speech by Pranab Mukherjee, Minister for External Affairs, Government of India At the High-Level Conference in New Delhi, Ministry of External Affairs, 12 November 2007, http://meaindia.nic.in/speech/2007/11/12ss02.htm
5. David Camroux, "Asia . . . whose Asia? A 'Return to the Future' of a Sino-Indic Asian Community," *The Pacific Review*, vol. 20, no. 4, December 2007, pp. 556–58; Dennis Rumley, "The Geopolitics of Asia-Pacific Regionalism in the twenty-first Century," *The Otemon Journal of Australian Studies*, Vol. 31, 2005, p. 7.
6. Ibid, p. 7.
7. Tommy Koh, 'Australia's Asia Pacific Community Proposal: Some Issues for Discussion', Conference on the Asia-Pacific: A Community for the twenty-first Century, Sydney, 3-5 December 2009, http://www.apc2009conference.org/userfiles/Koh.pdf.
8. Ronald L. Tammen and Jacek Kugler, "Power Transition and China-US Conflicts," *Chinese Journal of International Politics*, Vol. 1, No. 1, 2006, pp. 35-55.
9. Ibid, p. 39.
10. David C. Kang, 2003. "Getting Asia Wrong: The Need for New Analytical Frameworks," *International Security*, Vol. 27, No. 4, Spring 2003, pp. 57-85.
11. John J. Mearsheimer, *The Tragedy of Great Power Politics*, (New York: W.W. Norton, 2001),

p. 4; Ronald L. Tammen, "The Impact of Asia on World Politics: China and India Options for the United States," *International Studies Review*, vol. 8, 2006, pp. 570-76; C. Raja Mohan, "India in East Asia," *Australia-India Strategic Lecture Series 2007*, Lowy Institute for International Policy, Melbourne, 21 February 2007, http://www.lowyinstitute.org/Publication.asp?pid=548

12. John J. Mearsheimer, "The Rise of China will not be Peaceful at all," *The Australian*, 18 November 2005, http://mearsheimer.uchicago.edu/pdfs/P0014.pdf
13. C. Raja Mohan, *India in East Asia*, op. cit.
14. Mohan Malik, "The East Asia Community and the Role of External Powers: Ensuring Asian Multilateralism is not Shanghaied," *Korean Journal of Defense Analysis*, Vol. 19, No. 4, Winter 2007, p. 34.
15. Kishore Mehbubani, *The New Asian Hemisphere: The Irresistible Shift of Global Power to the East*, (New York: Public Affairs, 2008); David Scott, "The twenty-first Century as Whose Century?," *Journal of World-Systems Research*, Vol. 13, No. 2, 2008, pp. 96-118; Immanuel Wallerstein, "East Asia and the World: The Decades Ahead," No. 157, Birmingham University, 15 March 2005, http://fbc.binghamton.edu/157en.htm
16. Ibid.
17. Matthieu Bussière and Arnaud Mehl, "China's and India's Roles in Global Trade and Finance: Twin Titans for the New Millenium?," *ECB Occasional Papers*, no. 80, January, European Central Bank, 2008, http://www.ecb.int/pub/pdf/scpops/ecbocp80.pdf. Accessed on 17 December 2009.
18. "Full text of Kevin Rudd's Speech to the Asia Society Australasia," *The Australian* 05 June 2008, http://www.theaustralian.com.au/politics/full-text-of-kevin-rudds-speech/story-e6frgczf-1111116541962
19. Christophe Jaffrelot, "India's Look East Policy: an Asianist Strategy in Perspective," *India Review*, vol. 2, no. 2, (April 2003), pp. 35-68, 46; Prakash Nanda, *Rediscovering Asia: Evolution of India's Look East Policy* (New Delhi: Lancer Publishers & Distributors, 2003).
20. Pranab Mukherjee, "Asian Economic Integration: Towards an Asian Economic Community," Speech at the High-Level Conference in New Delhi, Ministry of External Affairs, Government of India, 12 November 2007. [Online, cited 15 March 2010]. Available at <http://meaindia.nic.in/speech/2007/11/12ss02.htm>.

1

Two Decades of India's Look East Policy

Vibhanshu Shekhar

Once an inward-looking player operating within the confines of the hostile geopolitics of South Asia, India, after approximately twenty years of its eastward engagement, plays an important role in deliberations over multiple cooperative enterprises, economic integration and the prevailing security discourses in the eastern Asian hemisphere. India is connecting with the Asia-Pacific more than ever in many avenues including inter-governmental engagement, volume of trade and investment, range of defence and security cooperation, and people-to-people interaction. A protectionist and closed economy until the 1990s, India is now engaged with the East Asian countries in developing an East Asian economic community. Similar outward expansion can be seen in the arena of security, as evident from bilateral and multilateral naval exercises, security agreements and overall strategic partnerships with several countries of the Asia-Pacific. The range of India's engagement in the eastern Asian hemisphere has gone beyond traditionally important political, economic and strategic issues, extending to areas such as information and technology, human resources development, disaster management, science and technology, multimedia, and tourism. India's growing strategic presence in the Asia-Pacific finds its explanation in the multi-faceted Look East Policy (LEP) that has steered India's diplomatic overtures towards the East since 1992.

The LEP has evolved as a response to (a) stagnating South Asian regionalism, (b) domestic economic challenges and (c) altered strategic alignment in the aftermath of the Cold War. India's initial exercises towards regional cooperation within South Asia under the South Asian Association for Regional Cooperation (SAARC) framework remained hostage to intra-mural conflicts (primarily India's bilateral conflicts with Pakistan, Bangladesh and Sri Lanka), postponed summits, and a lack of regional consensus.[1] The dismal performance of the SAARC and the denial of membership by the Asia Pacific Economic Cooperation (APEC) drew India's attention to the fast-growing East Asian economies, which were not only registering collective prosperity, but also willing to engage India strategically. The economic crisis of the late 1980s and subsequent shift in India's economic outlook towards globalisation and economic liberalisation offered a conducive atmosphere for large-scale politico-economic cooperation with the liberalized and export-oriented ASEAN (Association of Southeast Asian Nations) economies. Moreover, the end of the Cold War dismantled ideological polarization between the India-Vietnam-USSR and ASEAN-USA combinations, facilitating the revival of India's multi-dimensional relationships with ASEAN.

India became a sectoral dialogue partner of ASEAN in 1994, full dialogue partner in 1996, member of the ASEAN Regional Forum (ARF) in 1996, and has shared Summit-level engagement with ASEAN since 2002. Though vaguely conceived in 1992 as an initiative catering to the geo-politics of Asia-Pacific, the LEP, in contrast, is a multi-faceted foreign policy initiative today, operating through various channels of multilateral institutions and bilateral strategic partnerships.

THE FIRST PHASE (1992-2001): INSTITUTION-BUILDING AND CAUTIOUS ENGAGEMENT

Though the Look East Policy received a definitive regional outlook in 2001 when ASEAN decided to hold the annual summit-level meeting with India, the policy had already set in motion processes of cooperation during the first ten years after the LEP's inception (1992-2001), which can be termed as the phase of 'confidence-building and cautious engagement.' Preliminary institutional mechanisms emerged and a tentative agenda of cooperation was drawn during the early 1990s.

Spurred by reciprocal overtures, an alignment of the economic and geo-strategic considerations of India and ASEAN began taking shape during the mid-1990s, enabling the LEP to position India on a stronger footing within ASEAN. In response to the LEP, then Prime Minister of Singapore, Goh Chok Tong kicked off an 'India fever' with his 1994 speech to draw attention to the rise of India. In a similar fashion, Thailand also floated the Look West Policy in 1997 in an effort to look for markets and investment, of which India formed the primary target. Welcoming India's first participation in the ASEAN Post Ministerial Conference in 1996, S. Jayakumar, noted, "India can provide ASEAN with vital links to the Indian Ocean and ASEAN, on the other hand, can be India's springboard into the Asia-Pacific. It would be hard to imagine an Asia-Pacific without India's participation."[2]

The logic of mutually beneficial economic cooperation formed the most powerful driving force of the LEP. While ASEAN offered India a model for economic growth and a platform for engagement with the market economies of East Asia, the latter provided the former a vast opening market. As a result, India's economic relations with ASEAN witnessed annual expansion during the early years of the LEP. Between 1991 and 1995, India's annual exports to ASEAN grew by approximately 40 per cent and its annual imports from ASEAN grew by 23 per cent.[3] ASEAN countries (including Vietnam) accounted for twelve per cent of FDI in India and eight per cent of India's total trade.[4] Moreover, by 1996, Thailand had become the third largest, Singapore the sixth largest, and Malaysia the seventh largest investor in India.[5]

The alignment of economic interests seemed more rewarding for ASEAN when India escaped the crisis and continued the growth story. The emergence of India as a big market and the lack of domestic demand within ASEAN economies offered an important economic incentive to the export-dependent ASEAN economies for further strengthening India-ASEAN cooperation. To quote I K Gujral, India's representative during its first participation in the ASEAN-PMC, "the minds of foreign ministers participating in the ASEAN-PMC meetings were riveted on the 250-300 million-strong Indian consumers and the attainment of seven per cent growth in 1995-96."[6]

Sub-regional Prop for Bilateral Engagement: BIMSTEC and MGC

The sub-regional path of the LEP, which began taking shape during the late 1990s, is an outcome of (a) India's desire to further strengthen its relationship with the mainland Southeast Asian countries, (b) India's growing frustration with the moribund SAARC (South Asian Association for Regional Cooperation), and (c) the perceived necessity of counter-balancing China's growing strategic influence in Myanmar and the Bay of Bengal.[7] However, it is Thailand's Look West Policy, enunciated in 1997, that augmented India's sub-regional engagement with mainland Southeast Asia.

The first important step was taken in June 1997 when, at Thailand's suggestion, a new sub-regional initiative, the Bangladesh-India-Sri Lanka-Thailand Economic Cooperation (BIST-EC) was launched in Bangkok. Later in December 1997, Myanmar was included and BIST-EC became BIMST-EC. Nepal and Bhutan became members in 2003, and the name was again changed to the BIMSTEC (Bay of Bengal Initiative for Multi-sectoral, Technical and Economic Cooperation) at the first summit, held in Bangkok in July 2004. Concretising the notion of a Bay of Bengal community, the BIMSTEC offered India an avenue to wriggle out of stagnating SAARC framework and diversify engagement with mainland Southeast Asia.

Two issues have drawn attention – the BIMSTEC FTA and physical connectivity. The BIMSTEC is working towards creating an integrated economy, using the economic dynamism of India and Thailand as two important pivots. The member countries signed a Framework Agreement for a BIMSTEC Free Trade Area during the 6th Ministerial Meeting, held in February 2004. The Asian Development Bank conducted the BIMSTEC Transport Infrastructure and Logistics Study (BTILS) in August 2006 to identify the bottlenecks and suggest remedial measures.[8]

Though the BIMSTEC engaged India with Myanmar and Thailand, the communist Indochina (Cambodia, Laos and Vietnam) still remained outside the purview of the LEP, reminding India of a gaping hole in its strategic positioning in Southeast Asia. In spite of the strong political and strategic equations that India shared with Vietnam during the Cold War years, and the mutually shared 'China-threat theory,' their relations had begun to stagnate during the 1990s due to 'India's static mindset.'[9] A much-needed opportunity came in 2000 when the then Foreign Minister of Thailand, Surin Pitsuwan, suggested that India set up an institution, which could enhance its relationship with the Indochina countries.[10] The suggestion led to the formation of the Mekong-Ganga Cooperation Initiative, involving India and five Mekong basin countries – Cambodia, Laos, Myanmar, Thailand, and Vietnam. The MGC aimed at accomplishing three-fold objectives – (a) enhancing ties with the Indochina countries, (b) developing appropriate counter-balancing response to China's strategic overtures in the Bay of Bengal and (c) extending the LEP to the Indochina. In contrast to the strategic underpinnings of the MGC, the content of cooperation covered primarily what the Indian Ministry for External Affairs called 'soft areas' like tourism, culture and education.[11]

Though the two sub-regional initiatives fared marginally both in terms of agenda-setting as well as their implementation, their significance rather lies in India's growing engagement with two principal players of mainland Southeast Asia – Myanmar and Vietnam. In fact, India's bilateral relations with these two countries have seen significant advancement in terms of cooperation in the areas of vital strategic importance, such as defence and security cooperation, energy cooperation, economic cooperation and the issue of greater connectivity. An important example of enhanced India-Myanmar relations is the Kaladan multi-modal transit-cum-transport project, signed in April 2008. The project envisages an upgradation of the Myanmarese port at Sittwe, maritime access to the landlocked north-eastern states and development of the inland water transport network in the region. With the total bilateral trade of US$1.19 billion, India has emerged as the fourth largest trading partner of Myanmar after Thailand, China and Singapore. Similarly, India's bilateral trade with Vietnam went up from

US$642.46 million in 2004-05 to US$2.14 billion in 2008-09. India and Vietnam has signed a strategic partnership agreement in 2007. Since then, the relationship has reached a new strategic high.

Entry into the ARF: Balancing Pan-Asia-Pacific Security Dialogue

The mutually perceived 'China threat theory' formed a key component of India-ASEAN strategic alignment during the early years of the Post-Cold War era. In the wake of limited strategic withdrawal of the US from Southeast Asia and the lurking fear of China as an aggressive and destabilizing force in the region, some ASEAN players (primarily Singapore and Indonesia) viewed India as a potential balance against China. The fear of perilous conflict was further exacerbated by the conflicting territorial claims and infrequent military altercations during the early 1990s over the South China Sea involving China, Taiwan, Vietnam, the Philippines, Malaysia and Brunei. China's growing inroads in Myanmar and the Indian Ocean had alarmed both India and ASEAN members alike, leading to India's membership in the ARF, that was formed with the objectives of engaging regional powers – China, Japan and India, in order to maintain strategic power parity in Southeast Asia.[12] Moreover, the ARF remained the only multilateral framework facilitating India's pan-Asia-Pacific engagement that, in turn, remained security-centric, lived upon the 'China-threat theory' and followed a 'balance of power' strategy.

During the first eight years (1996-2004) the LEP focused primarily on two processes of confidence building and common agenda-formation in the ARF. These processes were facilitated by the two-track methods of the ARF deliberations – track-I (Ministerial Meetings) and track-II (Council for Security Cooperation in the Asia-Pacific). An important contribution of the ARF came in the form of its milder criticism of India's nuclear tests in May 1998.[13]

Nevertheless, India's participation in the ARF has remained limited for various reasons. First, the ARF's annual deliberations remained disrupted and divided over the issues of the South China Sea and Myanmar.[14] Second, ASEAN's control over the ARF deliberations and its 'comfort' or evasive way of conducting the affairs undermined the importance of the ARF, characterized as a 'talk-shop.'[15] Finally, India remained inactive and non-committal in the ARF due to its own years of strategic insularity and its long-standing nervousness while dealing with security issues multilaterally. It took India nine annual meetings before it could finally offer in July 2004 'any help in principle' in securing the Straits of Malacca.[16]

SECOND PHASE (2002 ONWARDS): ASEAN-CENTRALITY BUT PAN-ASIA-PACIFIC CANVAS

Situations began to change during the late 1990s. The years of economic growth, enhanced bilateral trade, a stable democracy, and improved strategic cooperation with key players in ASEAN enabled India to project itself as an emerging economic powerhouse and an important strategic player in the Asia-Pacific. The new perspective on India along with ever-growing security and economic engagement prompted ASEAN leaders in November 2001 to engage India at the highest political level, introducing parity in ASEAN's engagement with India in relation to the former's engagement with the Northeast Asian countries.

The new status of summit level multilateral engagement with ASEAN, characterized as the second phase of the Look East Policy, elevated India's status from an outsider dialogue partner to a stakeholder in the ASEAN-driven cooperative deliberations.[17] The annual summit meeting significantly expanded the agenda of cooperation by enabling India to outline strategic priorities and policy choices under a single overarching framework. Moreover, the second phase of the policy has seen enormous expansion in terms of the geographical canvas of the policy.

Greater Economic Integration and Community-building

The second phase of the LEP has augmented a new integrative discourse in the LEP – India as an important part of any community-building process in the eastern Asian hemisphere. While speaking at the ASEAN-India summit held in Bali in 2003, the then Indian Prime Minister called upon the ASEAN leaders to work together towards an Asian Economic Community and stated, "if the 14 of us combine into a broader Asian Economic Community, it can promote our overall economic competitiveness and create a new engine of growth for the entire region."[18]

To push the integrative agenda, India signed the Framework Agreement for the Comprehensive Economic Cooperation (CECA) and announced a unilateral Open Sky offer to the ASEAN economies to boost connectivity during the 2nd India-ASEAN Summit in Bali in October 2003. The Open Sky offer aimed at facilitating easy movement of tourists and businesses by removing restrictions on the number of flights operated by the airlines from the ASEAN countries to or from any city in India. India has also embarked on the process of signing bilateral FTAs with select Asian countries, resulting in a CECA with Singapore in 2005 and the Early Harvest Programme (EHP) with Thailand in 2003. India signed a Comprehensive Economic Partnership Agreement (CEPA) with South Korea in August 2009. India and Malaysia have already conducted five rounds of negotiations over the bilateral FTA, with the sixth round scheduled to be held in

July 2010 in New Delhi. India and Japan are negotiating on the modalities of a framework agreement for a bilateral FTA. Moreover, India is conducting feasibility studies on bilateral FTAs with Australia, China, Indonesia, and New Zealand.

The integrative discourse received a major thrust when India and ASEAN signed an 18-point agreement titled "India-ASEAN Partnership for Peace, Progress and Shared Prosperity" during the 3rd Summit in November 2004 in Vientiane, Laos. The Partnership agreement adopted a Plan of Action that laid down a comprehensive agenda for India's long-term and full-scale engagement with ASEAN in almost every area of international significance. Moreover, the wide-ranging agendas of cooperation in the Plan of Action have offered India and the ASEAN countries an opportunity to go beyond the government-led mechanisms and initiate people-centric and civil-society-led cooperation.

It took more than twenty meetings, five years and regular political interventions for India and ASEAN to agree to a roadmap for the FTA in goods in August 2009, and the agreement entered into force in January 2010. While India's overall trade with the ASEAN countries increased from US$2.4 billion in 1990 to US$45.34 billion in 2008-09, East Asia has emerged as India's largest trading partner since 2007-08. Similarly, the two sides have adopted an ASEAN-India Aviation Cooperation Framework in November 2008, though the agreement has to go through tough negotiations before it reaches the stage of implementation. There are several similar bilateral air services agreements India has signed with Thailand, Malaysia and Singapore.[19] As a result of these agreements, more than two million Indians visited Southeast Asia in 2007, reflecting growing people-to-people interaction between India and ASEAN.[20]

India's campaign for its inclusion in the East Asian community-building process received an important stimulus in December 2005 when it became a member of the East Asia Summit (EAS). The EAS has launched a feasibility study to examine the potential and possibility of a Comprehensive Economic Partnership in East Asia (CEPEA), an initiative proposed by Japan. The CEPEA represents half of the global population and two-thirds of the global GDP, prompting Surin Pitsuwan, the Secretary General of ASEAN, to call it 'the world's largest business space in a vibrant and more integrated East Asia.'[21] However, the Japanese initiative of CEPEA is essentially an outcome of great power rivalries involving India, Japan and China. In furtherance of the process of economic integration, the EAS has formed the Economic Research Institute for ASEAN and East Asia (ERIA) in June 2008. However, the CEPEA is still in infancy and faces contestation from among the members favouring APT (ASEAN Plus Three or ASEAN Plus China, Japan and South Korea) Framework.

Connecting India's Northeast with Southeast Asia

In order to develop physical connectivity with Southeast Asia, the LEP has turned towards its bordering areas of the Northeast that share historical and cultural linkages with mainland ASEAN countries. India's north-eastern states have emerged as the starting point of any initiative towards greater physical connectivity and sub-regional economic integration with Southeast Asia given their strategic location and historical-cultural linkages. The MGC member countries have launched two ambitious infrastructural projects of connecting Delhi and Hanoi with the rail network and building an India-Myanmar-Thailand Trilateral Highway, connecting Moreh in Manipur to Mae Sot in Thailand. The Thai government has proposed to link the transport initiatives under the MGC with similar initiatives taken under other multilateral initiatives of the Greater Mekong Sub-region (GMS), BIMSTEC, and the ACMECS (Ayeyawady-Chao Phraya-Mekong Economic Cooperation Strategy).[22] The India-ASEAN Car Rally from Guwahati, India to Batam Island, Indonesia in Nov-Dec 2004 highlighted the significance of the Northeast as an important connecting link between India and Southeast Asia. While speaking in Guwahati in November 2004 the Secretary General of ASEAN characterised the Car Rally as reflective of "the existence of land route connectivity that could facilitate and be a catalyst to free flow of trade, investment and tourism between ASEAN and India."[23]

The Indian government has made a two-fold concerted effort of enhancing the border trade between the Northeast and Myanmar and showcasing the trade and investment potential of the north-eastern states in Southeast Asian countries. It convened the 'Northeast Trade, Investment, and Opportunity Week' in Thailand in October 2007 and in Vietnam in February 2009. Thailand also has shown keen interest in developing economic and cultural interaction with the Northeast. Several big business delegations from Thailand have already visited the north-eastern states of Assam, Mizoram, and Tripura since 2007-08.

Towards Energy Security

In consonance with India's ever-growing demand for energy supplies and the emergence of energy as an important priority of India's overall foreign policy, the energy security has emerged as an important component of the LEP as well. The LEP has pursued energy diplomacy both at the multilateral and bilateral levels. While the multilateral cooperation has remained subject to the dynamics of multilateral forums, the bilateral cooperation has paced up significantly during the last five years. In fact, energy has emerged as one of the most significant components of India's relations with three principal strategic players of Southeast Asia – Myanmar, Indonesia, and Vietnam. While India's energy diplomacy, in the cases of Myanmar and Vietnam, has focused primarily on natural gas and crude petroleum, it has focused on both natural gas as well as thermal energy in the case of Indonesia.

India, since 2005, has engaged with Myanmar in energy cooperation, a process which the Indian government has pursued more aggressively after its failure in 2007 in securing the supply of natural gas from two offshore blocks (A1 and A3) in the Shwe Gas reserves in the Bay of Bengal in Myanmar. The military regime in Myanmar had awarded the supplies of natural gas to China in an apparent trade-off for the Chinese support to the regime at the United Nations Security Council.[24] The then Indian Minister for Oil and Natural Gas, Murli Deora, visited Myanmar in September 2007 and signed an agreement with the Myanmar Oil and Gas Enterprise for a 100 per cent stake in the exploration of three blocs (AD-1, AD-3 and AD-9 deep-sea blocks), off the Rakhine coast of Myanmar.[25] India and Myanmar are also working out the modalities for setting up the hydel power project along the Chindwin river in Myanmar.[26] Out of its total contracted investment of US$189 million as of March 2010, India spent US$137 million in the oil and gas sector in September 2007. Besides Myanmar, India is also bilaterally developing energy cooperation with Vietnam. The Indian oil exploration company, the ONGC (Oil and Natural Gas Corporation) Videsh Limited, has been involved in a major joint venture offshore exploration in southern Vietnam. The ONGC-VL has also signed a Production Sharing Contract (PSC) with Petro-Vietnam, which made India the sixth largest investor in the country in 2007.[27]

India is studying the possibility of procuring natural gas from Indonesia through an under-sea pipeline from Aceh to the Nicobar Islands. Addressing a joint meeting sponsored by the New-Delhi based business forums – the FICCI (Federation of Indian Chambers of Commerce and Industry) and CII (Confederation of Indian Industry) – the then Indonesian President Ms. Megawati Sukarnoputri, during her visit to India in 2002, had expressed her country's willingness to supply oil and gas to India. In contrast to Myanmar and Vietnam, where only the public sectors are involved, Indonesia has seen large-scale involvement of the Indian private sector in energy procurement. Spice Energy, an Indian company, entered into an agreement with the Indonesian Pertamina for the annual supply of Liquified Natural Gas (LNG) for its proposed Haldia Import and Regassification Facility to be set up by 2011.

Tata Power has entered into an agreement with a Singapore-based Company – Mercator Lines, which will transship 3.2 million tonnes of coal from Indonesia in the next four years to India. Surana Industries of Chennai has acquired a 49 percent stake in PT Agate Resources Indonesia (PTARI), and Star Emmsons Resource has bought Bara Energy Makmur (BEM) of Indonesia, which owns two coal blocks in the country.[28] The Reliance Power Ltd., has acquired three coalmines in the South Sumatra province in Indonesia, investing approximately US$1 billion.[29]

At the multilateral level, India has participated in EAS meetings over issues of energy efficiency and developing a common energy grid in the region. During its second summit at Cebu, the Philippines, in January 2007, the EAS adopted a declaration on energy security with the objectives of increasing energy efficiency, mitigating greenhouse gas, reducing dependence on fossil fuels, and guaranteeing a stable energy supply. The EAS has constituted three "Work Streams," addressing different aspects of multilateral cooperation on energy security.[30]

India as an Asia-Pacific Power

While delivering the Singapore Lecture in April 2002, the then Indian Prime Minister, Atal Behari Vajpayee declared India as 'a principal player in Asia-Pacific,' and stated, "India's belonging to the Asia-Pacific community is a geographical fact and a political reality. It does not require formal membership of any regional organisation for its recognition or sustenance."[31] The pan-Asia-Pacific posturing of the LEP augments India's growing desire to (a) shape the maritime strategic discourses prevailing between the South China Sea and the Arabian Sea, (b) participate in the cooperative dialogue carried out by the ASEAN-driven multilateralisms, and (c) project itself as an important player within the geo-politics of Asia-Pacific. Two issues need special attention – India's naval engagement in the Asia-Pacific and India's strategic overtures in the ASEAN-driven cooperative frameworks.

First, India's maritime security engagement began acquiring a pan-Asia-Pacific character during the early years of the twenty-first century, spurred by two important developments. The *Alondra Rainbow* episode brought forth the growing importance of maritime coordination among the countries, strategic outreach of the Indian navy and India's own projection as a benign maritime power.[32] Second, the rising spectre of maritime piracy and terrorism and the growing vulnerability of the Straits of Malacca as a soft target alarmed the littoral states regarding the safety and security of their main trading passage. Maritime governance has, over the years, emerged as an important agenda of the LEP with the dual projection of India's major power ambitions and its benign image. The Partnership Agreement of 2004 brought about qualitative change in the nature and content of India-ASEAN security cooperation. Improvising the focus and modalities under the Joint Declaration of 2003 that refers only to counter terrorist cooperation, the Partnership Agreement brings within its ambit the whole gamut of non-traditional security issues such as terrorism, trafficking in drugs, arms smuggling, and maritime piracy. For the first time, maritime security emerged as an agenda of multilateral cooperation during the 4th ASEAN-India Summit, held in December 2005 in Kuala Lumpur, further emphasized at the 6th ASEAN-India Summit in Singapore in November 2007.[33]

India has entered into different sets of maritime security cooperation – capacity-building, coordinated patrolling, training of security personnel, and wide ranging naval exercises with countries in the Asia-Pacific, such as Australia, China, Indonesia, Malaysia, Singapore, Thailand, the USA, and Japan. India conducted the Malabar series of exercises in April 2007 with the Japanese and US navies (off the Japanese coast) and in September 2007 with the navies of Australia, Japan, Singapore, and the USA in the Andaman Sea. Remarkably, these initiatives have taken place outside the purview of the ARF. In an another step towards multilateral maritime governance, India and other countries of the Asia-Pacific signed a Regional Cooperation Agreement on Combating Piracy and Armed Robbery against Ships in Asia (ReCAAP) in November 2004, and the agreement became operational in October 2006. The ReCAAP is the first ever governmental initiative to counter armed robbery and sea-piracy against ships involving countries of South, Southeast and Northeast Asia. India along with other member countries of the newly constituted ASEAN plus Defence Ministerial Meeting (ADMM) called for coordinated approach to tackle maritime security threats during its inaugural meeting in October 2010.

Second, the year of 2005 marks an important shift in India's strategic importance in the Asia-Pacific. While India and Japan signed the Global Partnership in April, India and the USA signed the civil nuclear energy cooperation in July 2005. The Indian entry into the EAS during the same year is an outcome of its growing strategic ties with select ASEAN players, its changing geo-strategic profile in the Asia-Pacific, and increasing proximity with two important global players in Asia – Japan and the USA.

As the twenty-first century unfolds, the discourse of an 'Asian Century' is exhibiting two parallel trends: (a) the rise of Asian powers – China, India and Japan, and (b) the shrinking geo-political space of these powers, bringing them in turn to each other's doorsteps. Each of these powers is engaged in strategic manoeuvrings to ensure that the emerging regional architecture maximizes its interests and facilitates its great power ambitions. Nevertheless, a concrete picture remains elusive and academic contestations continue in search of a definitive answer to the emerging challenges in the region. Such a scenario remains inherently unstable, carrying the spectre of big-power rivalries in the region, a proposition that has elevated the LEP to a new strategic level by augmenting new strategic partnerships in Asia as well as granting the membership of new-emerging multilateral initiatives in East Asia.

India continues to strengthen its strategic engagement with the region by expanding the scope of bilateral relations, developing strategic partnerships with select Asian players, and enhancing its participation in the multilateral cooperative frameworks in the region. Two important trends are visible in India's response to the rapidly changing strategic scenario in East Asia. First, India has signed strategic partnerships and strong defence engagement with select Asian powers – Australia, Indonesia, Japan, South Korea and Vietnam. A second important strategy seems to be integrating its economy with the East Asian economies (bilaterally as well as multilaterally) and pushing for India's greater role in the regional institutions.

The LEP multilateralism under the newly formed EAS, viewed in this perspective, works through its bilateral equations, continued China-threat theory, and the balance of power strategy. India's entry into the EAS reflects the emergence of India as an important power centre in the evolving security architecture of the Asia-Pacific and one of the most powerful drivers of economic growth in the region. The 2009 Summit of the EAS has dwelt in length on issues that concern not the member states alone, but rather the entire continental and global politics – climate change, global economic crisis, combating economic crisis through the G-20. However, it is yet to see if the EAS is trying to develop as a background forum of Asian players before they take part in the actual G-20 meetings. The EAS also offers India an opportunity to revive cultural and historical links with countries in the East, leveraging its own heritage. The EAS member states have already agreed to revive the old Buddhist Nalanda University in the province of Bihar in India.

While taking part in the inaugural meeting of the ASEAN Plus Defence Ministerial Meeting (ADMM+), New Delhi claimed to be a genuine player of the Asia-Pacific, relied on normative calls for building peace and stability in the region, and identified the already-recognised threat of terrorism and piracy. The contribution India seems to have made at the forum was its call for developing 'cooperative approaches' towards regional security dialogue.

Both the Indian establishment and academia need to devote more resources and expertise in debating the country's long-term strategy in the world's most dynamic and challenging region of the Asia-Pacific in the context of its changing international outlook as a rising great power. New Delhi cannot afford to continue the policy of 'gauging the waters' that it practiced at the ASEAN Regional Forum during 1990s. India as an emerging power is expected to play a much bigger role in steering these ASEAN-driven multilateral processes, which form one of the central pillars of India's strategic positioning in the Asia-Pacific.

Conclusion

The LEP has lent a structured outlook to India's eastward engagement by spelling out the agendas and strategies, institutionalizing inter-governmental and non-governmental interactions, and ensuring periodic articulation at the highest political level. The regular inter-governmental interactions, India's relative freedom in setting the agenda of discussion under the ASEAN+1 summit meetings, and a growing convergence of interests have facilitated a steady pursuit of the policy.

The Look East trajectory has seen gradual inclusion of sensitive matters for multilateral deliberations, such as opening India to the outside world, utilising the Northeast link to physically connect to Southeast Asia, and shedding its shell mindset while participating in the multilateral forums. Some of the apparent examples are the signing of the India-ASEAN CECA, the framework agreement towards the India-ASEAN Open Sky Regime, transport linkages, maritime security and terrorism. However, if the tense negotiations for years over the India-ASEAN FTA are any pointer, India faces the need of greater political will to take risks and implement the agenda, as the country embarks on complex bilateral and multilateral FTA negotiations with the East Asian economies.

A big question stares both the LEP as well as India's overall eastward engagement –where should the policy go from here? The prevailing Asian atmosphere of historical rivalries, growing assertion of state sovereignty, emergence of destabilising non-state actors and non-traditional threats, and the global economic crisis require innovation and activism on the part of the Indian policy-makers. The LEP connects India not to the eastern Asian hemisphere alone but also to the players outside Asia, for example with Europe through the Asia Europe Meeting (ASEM). The ever-widening geo-political canvas of the LEP and the multitude of engagements necessitate a long-term foreign policy vision based on a nuanced approach to the evolving complexities in Asian as well as global politics. A long-term and pan-Asian positioning of the LEP depends on how New Delhi continues building domestic and regional consensus over sensitive issues, utilises its strong relations with select Asian players, and efficiently steers the LEP involving great powers, major powers, middle powers, small powers and even island states.

ENDNOTES

1. Ananya Mukharjee Reed, "Regionalization in South Asia: Theory and Praxis," *Pacific Affairs*, vol. 70, no. 2, (Summer 1997), p. 235.
2. S. Jayakumar, "ASEAN and India: A New Partnership," ASEAN Secretariat. [Online, cited 12 February 2010]. Available at <http://www.aseansec.org/4752.htm>.
3. Ibid.
4. Jaishree Sengupta, "A Partnership in the Offing," *The Observer*, 02 September 1996.
5. K.P. Nayyar, "India Hopes its Reforms will attract ASEAN Interest," *Indian Express*, 19 August 1996.
6. I.K. Gujaral, "Lands of the Asian Miracle," *The Hindu*, 10 August 1996.
7. Man Mohini Kaul, "Regional Groupings: An Overview of BIMSTEC and MGC," *South Asian Survey*, vol. 13, no. 2, (2006), p. 314.
8. Joint Declaration, Second BIMSTEC Summit, New Delhi, 13 November 2008. [Online, cited 21 February 2010]. Available at <http://www.bimstec.org/2ndBimstecSummit_pdf/2nd_BIMSTEC_Summit_Declaration%5B1%5D.pdf>.

9. J.N. Dixit, "Cultivating Myanmar and Vietnam: A Broader Look-East Vision," *The Indian Express*, 12 November 1997.
10. Swaran Singh, "Mekong-Ganga Cooperation Initiative: Analysis and Assessment of India's Engagement with Greater Mekong Sub-region," *IRASEC Occasional Papers*, no. 2 (2007), p. 24.
11. Press Briefing by Secretary (East), "The forthcoming visit of Prime Minister to Cebu to attend 5th India-ASEAN Summit and 2nd East-Asia Summit," Ministry of External Affairs, Government of India, no. 12263, 10 January 2007. [Online, cited 24 February 2010]. Available at <http://meaindia.nic.in/pressbriefing/2007/01/10pb01.htm>.
12. Barry Buzan and Ole Waever, *Regions and Powers: The Structure of International Security* (Cambridge: Cambridge University Press, 2003), p. 161; Amitav Acharya, "A New Regional Order in Southeast Asia: ASEAN in the Post Cold War Era," *Adelphi Paper*, no. 279, (1992), p. 13.
13. S.T. Devare, *India and Southeast Asia: Towards Security Convergence* (Singapore: ISEAS, 2006), p. 76.
14. David Martin Jones and Michael L.R. Smith, "Making Process, Not Progress: ASEAN and the Evolving East Asian Regional Order," *International Security*, vol. 32, no. 1, (Summer 2007), pp. 177-178.
15. David Martin Jones and Michael L.R. Smith, "Making Process, Not Progress." p. 155.
16. 'Natwar Meets Megawati, Talks Terror with EU Team', *Indian Express*, 02 July 2004.
17. C. Raja Mohan, *Crossing the Rubicon: The Shaping of India's New Foreign Policy* (New Delhi: Penguin, 2003), pp. 212-213
18. Quoted in Tan Tai Yong and See Chak Mun, "The Evolution of India-ASEAN Relations," *India Review*, vol. 8, no. 1 (January–March 2009), pp. 34-35.
19. Yogendra Singh, 'Even Skies are not a Limit: India-ASEAN Cooperation in Aviation Sector', IPCS Special Report, no. 58, September 2008. [Online, cited 07 January 2010]. Available at <http://ipcs.org/pdf_file/issue/807440892SR58-Yogi-Aviation.pdf>.
20. Chairman's Statement of the 6th ASEAN-India Summit, Singapore, 21 November 2007, ASEAN Secretariat. [Online, cited 31 December 2009]. Available at <http://www.aseansec.org/21133.htm>.
21. "ASEAN and its East Asia Summit Partners Establish Own OECD-like Think Tank," *ASEAN Secretariat*, 04 June 2008. [Online, cited 26 May 2010]. Available at <http://www.aseansec.org/21608.htm>.
22. 'Report of the Fifth Ministerial Meeting of the Mekong-Ganga Cooperation', Ministry of External Affairs, Government of India, 2 August 2007, 13020. [Online, cited 24 February 2010]. Available at <http://mea.gov.in/event/2007/08/02ev01.htm>.
23. Ong Keng Yong, 'First India-ASEAN Car Rally 2004', *ASEAN Secretariat*. [Online, cited 18 May 2010]. Available, at <http://www.aseansec.org/16594.htm>.
24. Gideon Lundholm, "Pipeline Politics: India and Myanmar," Power and Internet News Report, 10 September 2007. [Online, cited 2 March 2010]. Available at <http://www.pinr.com/report.php?ac=view_report&report_id=679&language_id=1>.
25. "India Pledges 150 mln dlr Investment in Myanmar as Protests Swell," Agence France Presse, 24 September 2007. [Online, cited 2 March 2010]. Available at <http://afp.google.com/article/ALeqM5g7vegac7tzzHhkO9QHTGJt9Lal2g>.
26. "India Signs Four Economic Agreements with Myanmar," Press Release, 24 June 2008, Department of Commerce, Ministry of Industry and Commerce, Government of India.

[Online, cited 2 March 2010]. Available at <http://commerce.nic.in/PressRelease/pressrelease_detail.asp?id=2278>.

27. "Indian investment Wave Flows into Vietnam," VietNamNet Bridge, 02 May 2008. [Online, cited 1 March 2010]. Available at <http://english.vietnamnet.vn/biz/2008/05/781116/>.
28. "Surana buys 49% in Indonesian coal mine," *The Hindu Business Line*, 10 January 2008.
29. "Reliance Power buys 3 coal mines in Indonesia," *The Financial Express*, 03 May 2008.
30. P.S. Suryanarayana, "East Asia Summit Explores Free Trade Area Prospects," *The Hindu*, 23 July 2008.
31. "Visit of Prime Minister Shri Atal Bihari Vajpayee to the Republic of Singapore and the Kingdom of Cambodia," 7-13 April 2002, Ministry of External Affairs, Government of India, New Delhi 2003, p. 40.
32. The Indian navy, tipped by the Piracy Reporting Centre in Kuala Lumpur, rescued in 1999, after a successful chase in the high seas, a Japanese ship, *Alondra Rainbow*, which was hijacked in the Indonesian waters.
33. 'Chairman's Statement of the Fourth ASEAN-India Summit Kuala Lumpur', *ASEAN Secretariat*, no. 18079, 13 December 2005 [Online, cited 18 June 2010]. Available at <http://www.aseansec.org/18079.htm>.

PART I

EMERGING STRATEGIC LANDSCAPE IN THE ASIA-PACIFIC

2

Emerging Strategic Architecture in Asia-Pacific: Challenges and Responses

A.N. Ram

I

Arguably, the post-Cold War globalized Asia-Pacific remains somewhat fluid and in search of a tenable medium-term equilibrium. The geo-strategic and economic architecture of the region is still evolving and a new equilibrium is taking shape. The pieces of the jigsaw still remain to fit into a settled slot. While the region is unique, diverse and fraught with disparities, its evolving paradigm, arguably, is characterized and being shaped, among others, by the following emerging imperatives:

- Some would argue that in recent years, the US, which had dominated the region during the Cold War years and more recently as the sole super power, has redefined and possibly even downscaled her regional priorities, resulting in what some would call a strategic vacuum in Asia-Pacific. The current US focus, though not exclusive, appears to be on China and Northeast Asia. The US, apparently, is not unduly concerned about her non-inclusion in the East Asia Summit (EAS); nor does she appear to be overly keen to purposefully reactivate the somewhat moribund Asia-Pacific Economic Community (APEC) or participate proactively in other Asia-Pacific arrangements. She does not appear to give priority to taking on new regional commitments. The global war on terror and the danger of proliferation of weapons of mass destruction (WMDs), materials, and expertise, no doubt, are US priorities, but these appear to be selective and in consonance with her larger global view and policy. If this argument were to be advanced further, then it would be logical to assume that the US would prefer her regional partners to play a more pro-active and substantive supporting role in the regional context. Japan, Australia, South Korea and, perhaps, India would, in US calculations, be expected to assume greater regional politico-strategic responsibilities. This, indeed, could be the rationale behind the idea of promoting a regional response to the emerging challenges, involving Australia, Japan, South Korea and India, now actively being propagated specifically by Australia and Japan, no doubt, at US behest.

- China, unquestionably, is the rising global power with a strong regional and global agenda. Evidently, China is slowly but surely occupying the strategic space being vacated by the US and is taking advantage of the short-term regional opportunities whether strategic, political or economic. China's strategy also appears to be to work in partnership with regional countries rather than to go it alone, albeit on her own terms. In any case, China would like to work towards blunting any scope for causing her discomfiture. Her evolving strategic ties with ASEAN, her now pre-eminent position in North and East Asia and her leadership and pro-active role in the Asia-Pacific institutions viz, EAS, 3+1 dialogue with ASEAN, Asean Regional Forum (ARF), APEC, North-East Asia Six Party Talks, Shanghai Cooperation Organization (SCO), ASEAN Cooperation for Development (ACD), track II Council for Security Cooperation in Asia-Pacific (CSCAP) etc. are all integral parts of the evolving Chinese strategy in the region. At the bilateral political level, China has developed special strategic relations with countries like Myanmar, the Indo-China countries and neighbouring countries surrounding her, apart from forging deeper political and economic links with the other regional countries purely on political considerations and not always insisting on arithmetical reciprocity. In furthering this policy, she has taken tactical steps to downplay – not abandon – her territorial and other differences with the countries of the region [e.g. on the Spartly Islands issue and her still persisting border and political differences with some neighbours], has signed and ratified regional agreements like ASEAN's Treaty of Peace and Amity and a path-breaking Free Trade Agreement with ASEAN. She has also shown pro-active interest in the ASEAN Free Trade Area (AFTA), ASEAN Economic Community (AEC), ASEAN Security Community (ASC), the Chiang Mai Initiative, etc. Briefly, China's growing presence and goals in the region have raised a number of issues resulting in new challenges and forging of new equations in the Asia-Pacific. In the 1960s, China was a feared political force aiding and abetting in subversion and insurgencies in some countries; today, even as the Chinese embrace tightens, China is not feared and, in fact, held in awe and respect. The imperative of China's dominance is manifest and compelling. The ASEAN countries, in the 1960s and 1970s, had used economic integration and enmeshing as an instrument of policy to blunt Chinese propensities to cause them discomfiture; today China is using the same strategy to further her own regional politico-strategic and economic interests.

- As stated above, it is argued by some that countries like India, Japan, South Korea and Australia should play a more proactive and high profile role in the Asia-Pacific to counter the Chinese. This was apparently a purpose at that time of Prime Minister Abe's visit to India in August 2007 and the many calculated overtures made by him to India. The Americans would surely welcome a greater role by these countries in cooperation with some other countries, under, of course, US leadership and direction. The Japanese, it appears, may have lately lost some edge in the Asia-Pacific and may be in search of strategic partners. The Japanese Prime Minister Abe's cogently articulated proposal during his visit to India in August 2007 for an "axis of democracy" comprising India, Japan, Australia and South Korea is, no doubt, in pursuance of that policy. Japan, it appears, would prefer to proceed collectively rather than traverse the path alone. The Japanese proposal is in consonance with US strategic aims and purposes in this region. Our Prime Minister's earlier call for an "Arc of Advantage" was made mostly in the context of India's evolving economic relations with the Asia-Pacific and may not have had any strategic implication. It, therefore, should not be confused with the Japanese proposal. The joint naval exercise, Malabar, involving Japan, the US, Australia, Singapore and India, held in September 2007 and the earlier exercises, may however, have a larger strategic message from the point of view of these countries, possibly inspired by the US. In recent times, the Japanese and others have shown interest in consolidating and deepening their strategic relations with India. Their often troubled relations with China, manifested recently following the Yasikuni shrine visit by their former Prime Minister and the continuing tense situation on the Korean Peninsula, apart from the domestic political and economic uncertainty, have more or less bogged Japan down to her own immediate neighbourhood and preoccupations. It would appear that Japan, passing through an unsettled phase and constrained by her present preoccupations, may take time to play her legitimate optimal role in regional and global affairs. Australia and South Korea, by themselves, may not be able to play a significant leadership role. Australia has been keen to improve the quality and content of her relations with India and must be concerned over the fallout of the continuing racial attacks on Indians in that country. Her on-again and off-again suggestion to consider selling natural uranium to India, if India signs the Non-Proliferation Treaty (NPT) and accepts safeguards, has to be seen in this larger context of keeping options open with regard to India. ASEAN, some believe, is not even convinced of Australia's credentials in the region. In any case, some analysts would argue that Australia's focus has been the South-Pacific, the adjoining region and her strong links with the West rather than East and Southeast Asia. Also, Australia has carefully and deftly calibrated her relations with China, which she considers highly important. Therefore, to what extent this apparently misplaced hope of nascent convergence of regional interests of countries like Australia, Japan, South Korea and India, along with those of ASEAN, is aimed at containing the growing influence of China is a matter of conjecture not based on facts, but that at one time, perhaps, could have been a driving force of US calculations and the calculations of her allies in the Asia-Pacific. India, on her part, may not have any such strategic purpose as she would, independently, like to develop and maintain good and mutually beneficial relations with China and not get involved in the ascribed US led strategy of containing China. China's position in the International Atomic Energy Agency (IAEA) and in the Nuclear Supplier's Group (NSG), guarded and reluctant, on the question of granting waiver to India and Chinese insensitivity to India's other concerns will in the future no doubt demonstrate her real intentions towards India. China will not test India beyond a point on contentious issue, even though she will demand a price for her restraint. She realizes that the India of the 2010s is not the same as the India of the 1960s. There is nothing free that the Chinese offer but they seem to have a pragmatic strategic view of the evolving situation.

- India's Lookeast Policy, initially, was premised more on economic rather than on strategic considerations. More recently, however, India has expanded her low level links with the Asia-Pacific to include political, defense, maritime, strategic and hitherto unexplored areas of economic cooperation. The Lookeast Policy, in other words, has now acquired a strategic dimension. The Southeast Asian countries too are beginning to see strategic convergences evolving with India. To them, India provides an additional option and an enhanced comfort level. Their own Lookwest Policy takes into account India's potential political and military strengths, apart from her enormous economic and other attractions. The growing non-economic convergences include areas such as the war against global and regional terrorism and extremism, trans-national crime, cross border subversion and insurgencies, natural disasters and pandemics, climate change and maritime cooperation, including safety of sea lanes, ports, economic zones, etc. The economic convergences also go beyond traditional trade and commerce and now include areas such as energy security, HRD, environment, S&T and the new emerging areas of the knowledge economy. India is appearing to look attractive and a new imperative is beginning to become evident.

- On her part, India is now looking at her growing relations with her eastern neighbours from the prism of her domestic compulsions, particularly in the Northeast and in the Andaman Sea. Some of these problems, it is now recognized, have transnational dimensions and implications. Peace and normalcy in the Northeast, for example, cannot be fully restored and ensured without the cooperation of Bangladesh, Nepal, Myanmar and Thailand. This region is unique and historically has always had transnational connectivity. Subversion and terrorism, drugs and its nexus with crime and trans-border trade and economic links, for example, have to be seen in a historical and traditional context. Over 95 per cent of the borders of the Northeast are with neighbouring countries, a reality we can ill afford to ignore. While there is no precise estimate of trans-border informal trade, it is widely believed that it is larger than formal trade. There are other trans-border links too based on cultural affinities, tradition, connectivity and ethnicity that have governed relations between the Northeast of India and the neighbouring countries. Likewise, the security of the Andaman Sea, the sea-lanes and our economic zone will need sub-regional cooperation with countries like Thailand, Myanmar, Indonesia and Bangladesh. Cooperation in preserving the ecology, environment and the unique fragile bio-diversity of this region is also an imperative, which we cannot ignore. This region has emerged as a hub of piracy, poaching and maritime crimes. Even intelligence-gathering by foreign powers in this space is said to have increased. If China's growing influence and presence (China has military bases in Myanmar close to India and plans to augment her military presence in this strategic space) in this region is to be contained and managed, strategic links with our eastern neighbours are indispensable. That is a rationale of our renewed Look East policy in the contemporary context. The Asia-Pacific now again is our strategic partner.
- While all this makes for closer and mutually supportive relations between India and Southeast Asia, it would be too simplistic to look at the evolving India-ASEAN relations from the prism of countering China or her growing influence alone. While India does wish to expand and deepen her growing all-round relations with ASEAN and the Asia–Pacific, she does not see herself as a counter – weight to China. On the other hand, Sino-Indian relations, in spite of continuing tensions, are by and large

satisfactory and are growing to our mutual advantage; our two-way trade is nearing the US$ 60 billion mark and growing at about 20 per cent per annum; China has emerged as India's number one trading partner ahead of the EU and the US; Indian investments in China and vice versa are growing; India and China are both present in the Asia-Pacific, Central Asia and the Gulf and are endeavoring to evolve a triangular partnership involving Russia; they, as major consumers, have an overriding interest in energy security and in shaping a new world economic order in which they have a voice commensurate with – and even beyond – their stake and interests. There are evident convergences. All three countries now sit on the G-8 high table and have overarching global responsibilities.

- There are other complementarities in shaping a new economic architecture, managing climate change, in the Doha Round of trade talks and there is enough space for India and China to work alongside in all these areas. In strategic terms, India still has, and will have in the future, problems with China, but she need not look at China as an adversary or a rival. We hope that China too will be sensitive to India's concerns and understand the value of good neighbourly relations. There will be areas of tension and friction but there is no reason why the two countries should not develop a modus vivandi. The Asia-Pacific certainly should be an area of cooperation rather than confrontation. While concern is legitimate, India should not overreact to China's present policy of support for Pakistan as this is bound to change with improved relations between China and India and hopefully between India and Pakistan. China's overt and covert support for Pakistan's nuclear and missile programmes is a matter of concern to India and to the international community. China's somewhat guarded and negative comment on the recently concluded Indo-US nuclear energy cooperation agreement is symptomatic of China's unease over India's emergence as a major regional and global power with deepening relations with the US, which she fears could potentially challenge her pre-eminence. India and the other countries will have to engage China in dialogue rather than leave China alone. It is in our interest to see China act as a responsible global player subject to international discipline. Indian diplomacy's greatest challenge in the coming years will be to balance her relations with China, even as it seeks to protect India's long term national interests, an exercise that is not going to be easy but which is not beyond our ingenuity. Bill Gates was right in believing that the choice for the world is not between India and China but rather the reality may be that the world will have to engage and deal with India plus China as partners in the future. "Chindia" is the need of our times.

- The EU, historically, has had very close relations with some parts of the Asia-Pacific. However, following the emergence of a uni-polar world order, the EU it would appear, has put on the back burner its once close ties with the Asia-Pacific. EU's current priorities, it appears, are more Europe and trans-Atlantic centered rather than genuinely global. Perhaps China, and to some extent now India, are exceptions. While the EU is a participant in Asia-Pacific fora like ARF, APEC, Asia-Europe Meeting (ASEM), CSCAP etc., its participation and profile appear to some to be low key, if not proforma, rather than substantive. Unfortunately, India-EU and EU-ASEAN Summit level dialogues have so far been used to focus mainly on bilateral issues, mostly economic, in which the two have strong interest. A strategic partnership should involve a comprehensive exchange of views, action and engagement on global issues covering all subjects and regions. India and the EU – and ASEAN and EU – should, therefore, cover in their dialogue other possible areas of cooperation in the Asia-Pacific region including, for example, on issues like combating terrorism, trans-national crime, energy, environment, economic cooperation, maritime issues and on harmonizing views on global economic and strategic issues. Likewise, India and ASEAN and ASEAN and EU should also cover extra-bilateral issues such as the above in their dialogues at all levels. The same is true of Russia. India and Russia and EU and Russia must also expand the scope and canvas of their interaction beyond bilateral or national agenda issues.

II

Even as the strategic architecture in the Asia-Pacific is undergoing a qualitative transformation, the underlying factors shaping and influencing such transformation and realignment could also include, among others, the very nature of new security challenges facing the region. Not many believe that a conventional conflict or war is imminent in Southeast Asia; rather the current discourse is increasingly focusing attention on existing and emerging non-traditional threats (NTSs) to security. No country or society is immune or insulated from such threats which are transnational and often involve non-state actors. These threats have been described above and recent literature on this subject is increasingly focusing and analyzing their implications on security and stability and their potential to destabilize polities, particularly democratic and pluralistic ones.

III

How has ASEAN responded to this emerging scenario? The "ASEAN way" which is the hallmark of its policy response provides the answers. Even as ASEAN engages in pragmatic and non-confrontational diplomacy, its responses are almost invariably well-considered, subtle and nuanced to meet the requirements of particular situations and to protect and further ASEAN interests. What, then, are the salient ingredients of this ASEAN policy response?

- ASEAN, historically, has used the instrument of economic policy to respond to emerging challenges. Indeed, the very creation of ASEAN, in some measure, was to meet the challenge of communist subversion through what many believed to have been Chinese sponsored insurgency in several parts of Southeast Asia. ASEAN's successful response then was to create an economic web of interdependence and linkages which would act as a benign force to blunt this vulnerability. Economic interdependence and linkages were seen as a policy response, among others, to counter the spread of insurgency.
- As this policy evolved, a vested interest seemed to have been created in sustaining peace; the temptation to disturb the status quo gradually yielded ground to a shared interest in peace and prosperity through economic linkages. Today, for example, China-ASEAN relations have acquired such strategic content and value that China is not only not feared but respected as a friend and a desired partner. China today is unquestionably the single most important factor in Southeast Asia with overarching mutually beneficial relations with all Southeast Asian countries, including strategic and political relations. Even on the vexed issue of the disputed Spartly Islands, the Chinese are not willing to assert themselves beyond a point and seem to have tactically placed the military option on the back burner. This is in sharp contrast to China's policy in regard to other territorial disputes. The ASEAN+3, Free Trade Agreement (FTA), East Asia Summit (EAS), the endorsement of the ASEAN Treaty of Peace and Amity, ASEAN Regional Forum (ARF) and other arrangements between China and ASEAN – more than with any other non-regional dialogue partner – are all instruments for creating and sustaining equilibrium in ASEAN's relations with China.
- However, the tightening Chinese embrace in Southeast Asia is also a matter of some concern; hence, ASEAN's lookwest policy, its growing and deepening strategic links with India, its strong economic relations with Japan, South Korea and Australia and its continuing close and mutually supportive relations with the United States and, to a lesser extent, with EU and Russia. Diversified foreign policy options are an integral part of ASEAN strategy.
- Within this framework, even as ASEAN has chosen to meet the apparently receding traditional threats to security through diplomacy and

economic instrumentalities, its response to meeting the new non-traditional challenges outlined above appears to be guided by pragmatism and is, therefore, nuanced. The recent ARF discourse on security has clearly focused on building peace and maintaining stability by going beyond confidence building measures (CBMs) to preventive diplomacy (PD) and conflict prevention and resolution. The ARF Vision Statement and numerous ARF documents/statements speak about this as the best option to promote, notwithstanding the difficulties and differing views among ASEAN members. PD and conflict prevention and resolution appear to be the preferred current ASEAN/ARF response.

- In so far as non-traditional threats to security are concerned (viz, terrorism, transnational crime, maritime security, natural and manmade disasters, disease and pandemics, proliferation of weapons of mass destruction, materials and technology etc), ARF appears to be still debating the threats and its possible responses. But here again, regional cooperation and creating an institutional regional framework appears to be the preferred response. Here too PD is advocated.
- ASEAN institutions are also being reshaped and new ones created to meet the emerging challenges. Apart from the growing role and importance of ARF as the overarching regional security dialogue forum, a possible ASEAN Security Community (ASC) is also being discussed, although there are differences on the need and workability of such an institutionalized forum. Instead, broader military to military exchanges with both regional and non-regional powers is being actively promoted, especially with countries like India, China and Australia. ARF is being strengthened and it is proposed to give it a prominent role in maintaining peace, conflict resolution and preventive diplomacy. The ARF Chair, the Friends of the Chair, the ARF Experts and Eminent Persons Group (EEPs), the track II Council for Security Cooperation in Asia-Pacific (CSCAP) and the ASEAN Secretary-General are all being co-opted in this process. Regional and global "best practices" are being studied for replication; and capacity building and enhancement recommended through training, sharing of information, attachment of experts etc. ARF is also proposing to provide good offices and share best practices on PD with governments and civil society. Inputs from think tanks and defense institutions (e.g. institutes of strategic studies (ISISs) are being sought. The Annual Security Outlook (ASO) reports are being refined as inputs for CBMs and PDs. Regional and extra-regional cooperation arrangements are being given shape and engagement upgraded and intensified. In brief, new mechanisms to meet both traditional and non-traditional threats to security are being worked out and put in place. On

the economic front, the idea of an ASEAN Economic Community (AEC) and a single ASEAN market, apart from AFTA and other regional arrangements, are being pursued with some success. ASEAN is now increasingly moving in the direction of becoming one unit with common policies, approaches and instrumentalities.

IV

China, India, ASEAN, Japan, South Korea and Australia are pillars of the emerging Asia-Pacific architecture. In a globalized world order, a modus vivandi among all these powers, if not active cooperation, is necessary to maintain peace and stability. The US, EU and Russia could, from outside, play a very important supportive role to ensure regional equilibrium and stability. three-fourth of the world's population inhabits in this region, which also accounts for about two-third of the global GDP. It is also the fastest growing region of the world and, as demonstrated recently, can act as the engine for global growth and stability. In that sense, this century could be driven by the Asia-Pacific. No part of the world can remain unaffected by the fortunes of this region. The coming decades will clearly determine whether the Asia-Pacific will find long term equilibrium or continue to remain in a fluid situation. India has a deep and abiding interest in the peace and prosperity of this region as also of her western flank. In that sense, India and China, along with ASEAN, could be the fulcrum of the emerging geo-strategic and economic order in Asia-Pacific on which the edifice of global and regional peace and prosperity could be built and sustained.

3

Managing Great Power Rivalry in East Asia: Towards an Asian Security Order

Varun Sahni

Drivers of Change in Asia

This chapter presents six broad points and together they give some sense of an emerging Asian order. This is a region in which there are multiple stories of growth, emergence and rise. First, it is very important to keep in mind that there is not just one story of growth, but rather multiple stories of growth. Since, in many cases, it refers to continent-sized states, those stories of growth translate in some cases to the emergence of the middle power that is taking on the attributes, over time, of great powers. On the other hand, the rise of a state suggests the state soon taking on system-shaping capabilities.

There is a need to understand the distinction between the emergence and rise. Emergence is a good way to describe India and rise is a rather good way to describe China. In this scenario, relative growth rates become increasingly important because they have a direct impact on power differentials. The question therefore then is not only whether a state or an economy is growing, but also the rate at which it is growing, and the rate that it is growing relative to other significant states.

The third point relates to the military establishments in the Asia Pacific. They are all, with a few exceptions such as Japan and Singapore, moving from labor-intensive ways of guaranteeing security to more capital-intensive ways of doing so. Methods differ from country to country; in some cases it is the national service system that is now being replaced with voluntary service. In other cases it is reducing the size of the forces, but in any case, military modernization in some form can be seen across this broad region.

A fourth factor is the revolution of rising expectations. Though expectations are rising, there are different levels of global engagement in terms of various social groups, geographical regions, and economic sectors that make up this part of the world. Obviously there are those who are benefitting and those who are losing out. Fifth, multiple democratic revolutions, irrespective in some ways of state structure or regime type of these individual countries, are taking place across this region. They are occurring even though the political system itself in any particular country is authoritarian or non-democratic, primarily because of a knowledge revolution. Just the very fact that individual men and women or citizens have greater access to knowledge and information, transforms their societal and indeed their individual and group realities.

Finally, a very obvious point is that there is a competition over resources. That wherever you look in this region one can see that there is a sense in which there are resource countries across the horizon and around the corner.

Towards an Asian Order

There are a lot of things that we do not know, and the more actually we look into what can be termed as 'the mist of the future,' the more the uncertainties exist. Let us just look at some of the major powers in Asia. China is rising, but can China's rise be sustained over the next two decades? In the face of many internal contradictions, India is emerging, but can this emergence really sustain itself, or is India going to be shackled by its unique blend of incapacity and indecision when it comes to its own neighborhood. Japan is normalizing, but will that process of normalization be able to withstand Japan's perhaps irretrievable demographic decline? Russia is resurgent, but will Russian resurgence continue to be determined largely or entirely by the level of global hydrocarbon prices? The US we consider to be a permanent presence in Asia, but the time has come when we've got to begin to start asking, is it? Does the permanence that we have assumed about the United States in this part of the world continue to exist? We know the US is preponderant globally, but for how long can this preponderance persist? We have to ask these questions about the United States because there is clear domestic mismanagement in the country and some of that mismanagement relates to state structures and government. A lot of them have to do with the way the economy has been organized and is running. And also there are rising rivals. There are rising rivals to the United States across Asia. We need to consider this carefully because a lot of those rivals are also partners in prosperity with the United States. Therefore a very complex dynamic emerges.

What can we say about the emergent shape of Asia? The map of Asia is changing. For the first time perhaps in Asian history, certainly for the first time in the post-colonial history of Asia, we can see a continent-wide security interdependence emerging in Asia. Asia was always a continent, but Asia was never a region. A region is a zone in which there is, among many other attributes, security interdependence, i.e. what one state does inevitably has an impact on the security of another state for good or for ill. In that sense, there is now a continent-wide security architecture linked quite clearly to the rise of China that is rising across the Asia-Pacific. In geopolitical and geostrategic terms, there cannot really be an Asia without China. China geographically links Asian countries. Otherwise Asia would just be a conglomeration of regions. In the past, there was an East Asian dynamic that was different from a Central Asian dynamic, which was different from a South Asian dynamic, which was different from a Southeast Asian dynamic, and so on and so forth. It is the rise of China that is now, in effect, linking these various security dynamics into one continent-wide dynamic. In concrete terms it means that a security analyst in India can no longer ignore developments in the Korean peninsula. The rise of China is, in fact, changing that forever, because what happens in the Korean peninsula is going to have an impact upon China that is going to influence the positions China takes in security terms, and that in fact is going to have an impact upon South Asia, an effect on India or an individual in Indonesia.

Asia the continent is becoming Asia the region. These various regional dynamics, one suspects, over time will diminish and there will be a broad continent-wide security dynamic that is going to in some ways define all of us. China is working very hard to signal to all of its neighbors that its rise is peaceful. In fact, it has gone beyond peaceful rise now. It is now talking about harmonious development. It is very important for China to signal this. And those who rule in Beijing now understand the importance of soft power, the signals they send. So the signal China is sending is that, this is the odyssey of a large country on the road to development. But the other way in which one can view this obviously is the onward march of a rising power. Ultimately that question remains. Is this the onward march of a rising power, or is this ultimately a large, underdeveloped, developing continent-sized country that is now developing very rapidly? How the rest of Asia, India in particular, will respond to the rise of China becomes one of those core questions about the emerging Asian order.

Some Southeast Asian scholars, primarily Kishore Mehbubani, argue that we should not see China's rise in the way, for instance, we saw the impact of the rise of Germany in the late 19th and early 20th century. We should not see China as the 21st century version of Wilhelmine Germany. What these scholars argue is that the rise of China, in some ways, merely indicates, in historical terms, a reversion to certain pre-modern and pre-European/Asian orders that were based on notions of hierarchy and tributary relationship with China. Mehbubani says that, in a way, China's centrality or a tributary relationship with China is something all Asians recognize and understand. In other words, there is a deep historical memory of Chinese ascendance, and that deep historical memory will reassert itself as China rises. The rest of Asia, in other words, would consider China's rise in some ways to be natural.

Now, it is difficult for an Indian analyst to agree with what Mehbubani says since India did not share that historical memory about the Chinese ascendance. Even if there is a deep historical memory about Chinese ascendance across much of Asia, that memory does not exist in India, the only other large continent-sized country (Indonesia is a very large maritime country, not a continental country). The Himalayas stood in the way of that memory ever having been created in the case of India. So it really doesn't matter if that memory exists in the rest of Asia. The only other large continental sized country that ultimately matters when it comes to these core questions of power balances does not share that memory of Chinese ascendance. India and China, in fact, met for the first time when Zhou En Lai and Jawaharlal Nehru met. Before that, it was a different type of interaction. It was a civilizational interaction perhaps. It was an interaction of plant species, tea coming there and being planted in the foothills of the Himalayas. But if we are talking about it as an interaction of political import, India and China meet for the first time when Zhou En Lai and Jawaharlal Nehru meet as two sovereign, territorial, post-colonial states. So when India and China encounter each other they encounter each other as sovereign territorial states, post-colonial, large, developing, but, sovereign and territorial. Any analyst who somehow assumes that India-China relations can escape the logic of sovereign territoriality, is missing something very critical.

This links to the fourth broad point, which is about political modernity itself. This is not just a peculiarity of India and China, but rather much of Asia firmly remains under the throes of what we may call Westphalian modernity. It is epitomized by the sovereign territorial state. It makes sense for Europeans to talk about the post-modern perhaps, but it doesn't make sense for those located in Asia because we are still firmly living in the era of political modernity. It means that the core political dynamic across Asia is of the sovereign territorial state perfecting its sovereign territoriality. That explains China's obsession with Taiwan, India's obsession with Kashmir, the normalization of Japan. One will not be able to understand why territorial disputes persist in ASEAN despite these countries' evolving more and more to almost a security community. Why are they not a security community? The reason there are not security communities is because they are Asian, and in Asia we are still living in a different historical moment. We're living in a moment of political modernity. Though we may try to pretend that we can create European dynamics on the Asian land mass and its surrounding oceans but that is fundamentally an exercise in futility. One cannot be post-modern before you are modern, and most of the societies in Asia are still struggling to become modern. It is critical for us when we consider the emerging Asian order.

This means that the logic of political realism with its power balances and its security dilemmas continue to drive the inter-state politics in large parts of Asia. The balance of power politics lies at the heart of all the regions of Asia, possibly with an exception of Southeast Asia. However, some questions remain about the nature of the balance of power, which leads to an earlier point made about the continental security interdependence. One is, over time, going to see the balance of power politics moving out of these regional arenas in which it had been located for the last 50-odd years to the continental arena as a whole. For instance, if India is concerned about China setting up very close links with its regional neighbors, how is India going to play the game? It is going to play the game at two levels. First, it is going to try to build strategic links with Bangladesh or with Myanmar or with Nepal or with Sri Lanka. Second, it is going to build links with Indonesia, Vietnam, Australia, Korea, and/or Japan. In other words, the balance of power politics is no longer going to be located within these regional spaces that were so familiar to us. Some of the ways in which we have viewed regions and areas are going to have to change fundamentally.

The fifth broad point that looks at the future Asian order in terms of the balance of power politics is to see it as if it were a directory of the great powers of the region. It is a notion whereby a group of Asian great powers would provide guarantees of security, stability and order to all the states of Asia, a notion that a few great powers in Asia could in fact become the security guarantors for all of Asia. Now, it is not such a fanciful idea because the Europeans tried it themselves at a time in which Europe began to become a continent-wide security zone. The Eurasians tried it as well. That was precisely the way they ended the Napoleonic Wars. They ended the Napoleonic Wars, and they came up with a Europe where they in fact tried to do exactly the same thing, have a concert of Europe. Lenin, for instance, the former Russian prime minister, has talked about the Big Three – China, Russia, and India. Other scholars have talked about Japan, China, and India. Lenin stated in one of his writings in 1923, "in the last analysis, the outcome of the struggle will be determined by the fact that Russia, India, China account for the overwhelming majority of the population of the globe." The idea is an interesting one, because the idea really is that because of their sheer mass, if China, India and Russia were ever to work together, were ever to act in concert, they would play a world historical role. The Pentagon, during the Clinton years when it was trying to make sense of the world, came up with the idea of the three large Eurasian transition states and these three large Eurasian transition states were again the same three – Russia, China, and India.

Conclusion

Therefore, the question is – can there be a directoire? One of the factors that will likely work for or against this idea of Asian great powers working together to guarantee security and order in Asia, is the question of economic growth rates, competitiveness and cooperation. Three questions remain. Is China going to remain the only rising power? Will Russian decline be eventually reversed? Will India start catching up? One can give a series of questions but in some ways the answers to these questions supply some clues about whether we will actually see the emergence of a concert of the great powers of Asia. Another question would be – would greater economic interaction and the inevitable competition that would follow lead to instability, or would it lead to the discovery of a larger set of neutral interests? However, just as important as economic factors are the social-political dimensions. Here we are looking at such factors as social cohesion, national unity, and territorial integrity. In terms of ethno-politics, for instance, one needs to look at some of the troubled regions and their implications – Tibet, Xinxiang, Mongolia, Siberia, the Indian Northeast. These are regions in which the policies of these three states will inevitably impact one another, often in negative ways. So if we think about Siberia, for example, can there ever be a concert between Russia and China if large parts of Russian Siberia are now Chinese-speaking? If there is significant Chinese population now living in Siberia, can we really imagine Russia and China working in concert? Similarly, any Indian policy has an impact on Tibet, and thereby has an impact upon China. Other such cases can be Mongolia and the Indian Northeast.

Besides, there are geopolitical issues. We have unresolved borders, differential economic and demographic growth rates, and unregulated population movements. All of these complicate in a phenomenal way the formation of a Big Three Alliance that otherwise may make a lot of sense to us. There is also a fundamental question – can these states remain or survive as cohesive and united sovereign entities? We also have questions, which are not just economic or socio-political, but questions of ideology, politics and stability. China's political system throws up all sorts of questions. What is the direction in which Chinese politics will evolve? Over what time frame will this evolution take place? What will be the nature of political participation in China in the future? What will be the impact of this political participation on the stability of the Chinese system? What about India? Will India have a new majoritarian form of government? Or are we going to see Indian politics being a politics of coalition-building into the foreseeable future? Similarly in the case of Russia, will the Russian state fully manage to recapture the commanding heights of state power?

There are developments taking place outside of these three countries. What about the Atlantic Alliance? What about European Union? If the European Union emerges as an autonomous locus of decision-making, would it not make Russia even more Euro-centric? It is one thing if Europe remains tied to the North Atlantic Alliance, but what if Europe over time evolves autonomously? That would increase the pull of Europe for Russia and would therefore, to that extent, move Russia away from whatever its Asian imaginings may be. Just as important as this is the future role of Japan. We can all see that a strategically autonomous Japan would easily upset any applecart of Asian security.

Finally, the only route to an Asian order that is going to work for all the states of Asia is not a balance of power system, or even a directoire of great powers. It is some form of cooperative security. It is creating a regional security arrangement across Asia as an alternate road to contain Chinese power, to maintain stability in Asia, and also to minimize the role of the United States on the Asian continent. It's going to be a long and torturous process. We know that from the European experience. The Helsinki process in Europe took forever to get created, and it has certain elements that will never be acceptable in Asia, such as the internal dimension. But, having said all of that, we need to begin the diplomatic task and the political task of creating a cooperative security architecture in Asia. It will be well worth the effort. It would reduce the size of arsenals in Asia. It would enmesh Chinese and American capabilities in Asia within a larger cooperative process. It would lead, over time, to the evolution of a new and authentic Asian identity. It would build habits of cooperative behavior on the Asian continent. And it may even, if it works out well, play a positive role in the democratization of China, which of course, for the long-term stability of Asia is critical. It's not only important for China and Chinese people, it's important for all of Asia, and this sort of a cooperative process could make that possible.

To sum up, there are a few tasks more challenging and worthwhile than to begin this groundwork for the construction of a cooperative security mechanism in the Asian land mass and the surrounding oceans. And as a start, the major powers in the Asia-Pacific need to meet at least once a year regularly to discuss their security concerns and share information that is mutually reassuring.

4

Geo-economic Imperatives vis-à-vis Geopolitical Rumblings in the Asia-Pacific Region

Y. Yagama Reddy

Geopolitical theories, generated at the end of 19th century and labeled as classical geopolitics, were initially concerned with the realm of interstate conflicts. Rudolf Kjellan (1864-1922), who is credited to have coined the term 'geopolitics' as 'the science of the state in the realm of space,' developed Ratzel's (1844-1904) 'Lebensraum' (living space) theory into an organic view of the state, espousing that the 'superior' cultures deserved more territory. Alfred Thayer Mahan advocated an Anglo-American alliance to counterbalance Eurasian land powers. At the dawn of the 20th century, Halford Mackinder (1861-1947) focused on maintaining Great Britain's global preeminence in the face of challenges from the ambitious land power of Germany. Though Mackinder's geopolitical postulations did not engage Britain, which was in the euphoria of its naval supremacy, his three-line geopolitical equation became quite appealing to Nazi Germany, which craving was territorial expansion. Though Japan's 'Greater East Asia Co-prosperity Sphere' had kindled the Asian consciousness, it later proved to be of Japan's imperialistic designs in latent form, as vindicated by the Berlin-Rome-Tokyo axis formed during the Second World War. Though classical geopolitics was vilified along with the collapse of Nazism, the US embarked on its geostrategic vision with an aim to emerge as a post-War world power. As Mackinder's Heartland theory was the intellectual basis for the Cold War strategists and the proponents of NATO, Nicholas Spykman's (1893-1943) Rimland theory called for an active and non-isolationist US policy to maintain balance of power in the 'Old World' in order to prevent any challenge to the US.

The imperialist geopolitics paved the way for Cold War geopolitics that revolved around the US-Soviet antagonism. George Kennan's (1904-2005) call for containment was subsequently supported by the 'domino' theory, evolved as a corollary of the US National Security Council's Policy document (NSC-68).[1] Thus, geopolitics as the struggle over the control of spaces and places focused on the conflict between the two superpowers in pursuit of maintaining their spheres of influence. This antagonistic competition turned into a historically unprecedented global-scale confrontation. The regional conflicts over the spheres of interest in the Asia-Pacific region had also attained the form of Cold War, manifested as Korean War, Sino-American tie over Taiwan and Second Indochina War, as well as defense treaties such as the US-Philippines mutual treaty, the ANZUS trilateral treaty and multilateral defense alliances like SEATO. Thus, the Third World of poor and developing countries became zones of fierce competition, rather a theatre of superpower politics. Sadly, this global geopolitical power game completely ignored the realities of human geography.

Even as the Cold War-related geopolitical nuances were being debated, the collapse of the Soviet Union pulled the curtains down over the Cold War and heralded in an era of globalization, which is all about a reconfiguration of relations of economic and political power. Globalization, though popularly known as a global market-driven process with focus on liberalization for foreign capital and investment flows, is a multi-dimensional phenomenon of growing connectedness and interdependence encompassing economic, political, cultural, security and environmental relations across the borders. The post-Cold War era has witnessed geo-economic visions stressing the relative decline of states and the importance of the transnational flow of goods and services, capital and labour, and technology and ideas – a phenomenon popularly known as transnational liberalism or neo-liberalism. Trans-nationalism of the new global order subscribes to regionalization efforts towards cooperation to gain access to the goods (both manufactured and natural), institutions (for capital investment) and human resources (both technical expertise and human labour). Contrary to the transnational liberalism are the viewpoints stressing the power of transnational geo-cultural blocs over neo-liberalism, as advocated by Huntington in his *Clash of Civilizations.*[2] It is fondly hoped that the multitude of regional cooperative mechanisms would be a prelude to the emergence of multi-polarity, which is expected to foster global level stability. It is in this backdrop of ambitions and anxieties of the states in the Asia-Pacific region that this paper attempts to examine the impact factor of globalization in pursuit of regionalization and assess the conditions conducive to the survival of geopolitical formulations.

Asia-Pacific in Regional Perspective

It is somewhat perplexing to offer well-defined boundaries for a vast region like the Asia-Pacific region, as to be identified as an entity. In several instances, authors have either contextually or conveniently used the term, Asia-Pacific, with scant regard to the region forming factors and processes. Some have included the entire Asian continent abutting the Pacific Ocean. Should it then exclude the Indian sub-continent, for it does not have a Pacific Ocean frontage? Should India, if not the entire South Asia, as well as Australia and its adjunct South Pacific island realm find place in the mosaic of Asia-Pacific region? Just because of littoral status, should North and South Americas in the eastern rim of Pacific Ocean be included as part of this region?

Diversity manifesting in complexity almost in every aspect has had a decisive impact on the historical and political evolution of this region. To make matters worse, colonial masters sufficiently undermined the regional character. The European-coined toponyms testify to their indifference to the intrinsic realities of the region. Just as the international borders were ill-drawn by the colonial masters, the boundaries of sub-regions in the Asia-Pacific realm defy the intrinsic realities. The whims of Allies predominated in naming the theatres of the Second World War in the Asia-Pacific region. Cold War tensions hardly offered any scope for evolving regional cooperation mechanisms. In many instances, regional groupings such as SEATO were so hastily and loosely knitted as to meet the fate of becoming defunct and eventually extinct. In several other cases, regional bodies hardly addressed the regional peculiarities that could inhibit the much expected regional integration. Mention may be made of BIMSTEC, APEC, MGC, EAS and Kunming Initiative, which transcend the frontiers of the conventional regional bodies. Apart from these trans-regional organizations, there are regional economic initiatives like AFTA and RTIA, besides regional security dialogue forums as, for instance, ANZUS, FPDA and ARF as well as the Summit meetings, like ASEAN+3 and ASEAN+l.

A maze of proposals, which have been advanced all over the world for carving out regional groupings, reminds us of the factors of mathematical equations or the compounds produced out of chemical reactions. A raft of regional arrangements is a testimony to *laissez-faire* approach, what is to be known as hybridization of regions. Just as the higher yields are expected of hybrid varieties of plant and animal species, these regional bodies tend to enliven the spirit of regional cooperation in the matters concerning trade, investment and tourism. The post-Cold War globalization has caused a spurt in forming regions, but with scant regard to the scientific rationale being imminently adopted in any regionalization dialectics. Suffice it to say, the region forming factors and processes hardly address the infirmities of regional frameworks mushrooming all over the world in the wake of globalization. Thus there has arisen a need for focusing on the *modus operandi* of the regional groupings originated on account of compulsions and compromises testifying to *modus vivendi.*

Bruce Russett is reported to have listed five characteristics of a region: geographical proximity, social and cultural homogeneity, shared political attitudes and behaviour, political interdependence in the form of shared institutional membership, and economic interdependence.[3] These characteristics need to be analyzed in the context of seeking appropriate boundaries to the Asia-Pacific region. The Asia-Pacific's being geographically too expansive, as can be visualized from the politico-physical map, defies the attempts at defining it as a single region. If geometry defies the regionalization process, so does the physical make-up betray the expected regional character. River catchment area offers no solution to this daunting question. Just as it lacks a discernible geographical identity, Asia-Pacific has not acquired commonality in either socio-cultural milieu or political mileage, in the absence of shared history, ethnicity, language, religion and culture. In the midst of great deal of ambiguity persisted over the geographical extent of 'Asia-Pacific,' it has emerged as a region of global significance to meet 'transnational aspirations' on a 'win-win' situation.[4] Surprisingly, the post-Cold War new economic order, enunciating the interdependence among the nation-states, has driven them to look far beyond their territorial limits. The political and economic interdependence, as Bruce Russeett has observed, has made the nations in a region like the Asia-Pacific so closely linked as to accrue the benefits for mutual advantage.[5] With the centre of gravity of the world economy gradually shifting to Asia in the 21st century, the concept of 'One Asia' and several such other expressions as 'Asian Century,' 'Asian Community,' 'Asian Identity' and 'Asian-ness' have underscored the need for regional integration. While giving credence to this 'Asian Solidarity,' the geographical contiguity and functional rationale seem to justifiably offer a regional framework for the 'Asia-Pacific' embracing the entire Asian landmass as well as the Pacific island realm abutting the Asian continent. This is reckoned as a logical proposition, as vindicated by the East Asia Summit of December 2005.

Geo-economic Imperatives

Most pertinent to this theme is a glimpse of the policies of the European colonial powers in the wake of industrial revolution in the 18th and 19th centuries. The scramble among the European powers for markets in Asia and Africa had set in motion a chain of reactions. The European trading stations in the coastal fringes of Asia and Africa were replaced by the protectorates, which were subsequently transformed into colonies. European powers' virtual control over their overseas possessions became *sine qua non* in order to ensure the uninterrupted supply of raw materials from the colonies to the European industries and marketing for the industrial goods in the colonies. As a consequence, the European Companies that had for long enjoyed *laissez-faire* policy of their mother countries were required to follow the tenets of mercantilism. With scant regard for the trading regulations, European powers were committed to the capitalist gains out of their Colonial enterprises. This had prompted Marx and Engels to level a criticism that "the logic of capitalism was the formation of a single world market."[6] On the contrary, emergence of communist states led to the existence of two schools of economic philosophy – Capitalism or the free democratic world and the socialist doctrine or the totalitarian world. Obviously, the states in each of these two blocs were entitled to enjoy the most favored nation (MFN) treatment rather most preferred nation (MPN) in their respective blocs.

In yet another form, some other countries are not totally relieved of the syndrome of post-colonialism, as a vestige of colonial past, which is dubbed as "a synthesis of what was imposed and what survived."[7] Though countries like India embarked on the import substitution-manufacturing policy so as to lessen their dependency on other nations, many a newly independent state had their erstwhile colonial masters as their trading partners. Thus, the post-war period had witnessed the world getting divided into trading blocs. The Cold War had further divided the world on ideological lines that invariably resulted in the emergence of security paradigms – NATO, CENTO, SEATO and ANZUS of the US-led Western bloc and Warsaw Pact and related security instruments of the Soviet-led communist bloc. For all the tall claims of technological advancement, the transfer of scientific and technical expertise as well as the flow of economic assistance was strictly confined to the respective ideological domains. The net outcome of this Cold War compartmentalization was the deprivation of nation states of their right of access to the fruits of expertise and knowledge. In many a case, smaller states were handicapped by lack of accessories to the equipment, initially procured from a particular bloc. In the absence of universal standards in instrumentation, several other countries failed to import accessories imminently required for making the equipment operational. Thus, one way or other, nation-states became victims of the tyranny of ideological-divide. Evidently, all the activities of human geography became subordinate to the nuances of geopolitics of Cold War era.

The breakup of the Soviet Union marked the beginning of a doctrine that is popularly known as the new economic order of globalization. Significantly, the Cold War geopolitical views or discourses are renewed, but invariably re-specified in the wake of continuous involvement of the states/territorial entities in competition along the fault lines of geo-economics. Yet, the states are conscious of the impact of interdependence on their domestic and foreign policies in the form of losing their autonomy and mutual suspicion. Unlike the subordinated modality of mercantilism, which relied on the methods of war, geo-economics is identified with the weapons of commerce. Economic interdependence, besides being compatible with trade liberalization, is conducive to peace and stability; thus the spirit of commerce, as argued by the German philosopher, Immanuel Kant, defies the war, inasmuch as the nation-states rely more on the pacific means of conflict-resolution than on the lines of warfare.

Undisputedly, globalization's becoming an important aspect of international life underscores the principles of interdependence of nations that forms the basis for regional cooperation. Regionalism in the Asia-Pacific, once existed in its weakest and contested level, gained prominence in order to overcome chronic insecurity and rivalry among the states.[8] Amitav Acharya, in a comprehensive analysis of the relationships between globalization and interdependence vis-à-vis national security and development, considered "globalization and interdependence as tools of national security and regional order."[9] He further elaborated that the increased economic interdependence thwarts the attempts to settle conflicts by war and instead subscribes to pacific means of conflict resolution. This global political economic order, though reflects economic insecurity of the states, points to the emerging multi-polar system that is expected to create greater peace and stability.

Apparently, the relationship between globalization and regionalization represents the distinction between *de facto* economic integration and *de jure* political institutionalization.[10] Unlike the European Union, identified with a 'closed' regionalism, reinforced by a centralized hierarchy of power, and managed by a strong institutional framework, the Asia-Pacific regionalism pursuits are typified by 'open' regionalism, responding to the tenets of geo-economy. Even as the Asia Pacific region moves onto the stage of pursuing trading relations without discrimination against outsiders, regionalization is supported by such track-II organizations as, for instance, Pacific Economic Cooperation Council and Council for Security Cooperation in the Asia-Pacific. While globalization has given impetus to regionalization, globalization in the Asia-Pacific tends to promote regionalism in the context of policies being adopted by the states to enhance the credibility of regional members vis-à-vis external actors having potentials of FDI.[11] It is gratifying to note that interdependence dampened strategic rivalry among the states in the Asia-Pacific, whose shared commitment to economic globalization serves as a stabilizing factor in the Asia-Pacific regional balance of power.[12]

All-pervasive Geopolitics

Interestingly, while the debate on the dialectics of globalization and regionalism is proliferating, complex and multidimensional problems of security in the Asia-Pacific region are also being paid due attention. Though the region would not face a possible threat of external interference in the wake of *detente* among the regional powers, there is competition among the regional and external states for the economic and trade benefits access to natural resources and markets of export goods and services as well as contest over political, cultural and other forms of influence. The potential sea bed resources, which are considered essential for the economic development in view of the precarious agriculture-based economy, have strengthened the claims of the littorals on the extent of Exclusive Economic Zones (EEZs). Weak states, even in the matters concerning their territorial sovereignty, are very much worried of their due share in the marine resources. It is obvious that all the littoral states would attach much importance to exploration of sea bed resources, inviting foreign investment especially in oil and natural gas. In the absence of well-defined and well-demarcated maritime boundaries, as in the case of South China Sea, every littoral state would stake overlapping claims. Economic competition among the states that involve productive resource exploitation would aggravate political tensions so much as to incur huge expenditure on military preparedness. Furthermore, states would have an excuse for military confrontation under the pretext of a threat to national security objectives such as the sovereignty and territorial integrity.

Curiously enough, it is not the question of EEZs; it is all about the sovereignty over the open seas between the islands of the South Pacific realm. Unlike in the past when geopolitics was the exclusive preserve of states, contemporary geopolitics involves individuals, NGOs, private companies and even the protest movements having their stakes in the control of territory and the extraction of resources.[13] Arguably, geo-economic activity shall carry all along with it the risk of competition among transnational actors that would become a source of conflict, much to the chagrin of the states concerned.[14] The transnational and non-state actors, which have become significant determinants of foreign policy orientation and behaviour of nation-states, have evolved into an important stage of contributing to the process of globalization.[15] The greedy MNCs involved in regional economic pursuits would definitely make the maritime realm a flashpoint. The region, through which important sea lanes and air routes are passing, is a habitation of democratic, communist and authoritarian regimes, besides a home of eight of world's ten military forces and five (Russia, China, India, Pakistan, and North Korea) of nine nuclear armed power states.[16] The presence of about one lakh (96,900) American troops in the Asia-Pacific region still points to "the never ending" US's period of leadership.[17] The US remains as the major player in the Asia-Pacific region[18] through a host of bilateral alliances, as for instance, with Japan, South Korea, Thailand and the Philippines.[19]

Though the end of Cold war created a relatively peaceful climate conducive to the regional developmental efforts, this region always contains the seeds of potential conflict at various levels, whose origins go beyond the Cold War.[20]

Included in this list are the confrontation between North Korea and South Korea, tensions across the Taiwan Strait, disputes over the ownership of Kurile islands between Japan and Russia, maritime disputes among the littoral states of the South China Sea over the juvenile archipelagic islands, the Sino-Indian border dispute, illegal cross-border migration from Bangladesh into India, China's tacit back-up for Pakistan's military overtures against India, and the US bases in the Indian Ocean. There are some regional conflicts, as in the case of Cambodia and Myanmar, as well as inter-state conflicts as, for example, the territorial disputes over Sabah (between Malaysia and the Philippines), overlapping claims over Batu Puteh (Malaysia and Singapore), and dispute over the islands of Sigitan and Lipadan (Malaysia and Indonesia).

The Asia Pacific region is also confronting a challenge in the wake of building up defense capabilities by way of modernization and upgradation of the armed forces and weapons in the name of greater military preparedness. Though the Asian financial crisis led to the reduction in defense spending, the Asia-Pacific states later on have hiked their defense budgets under the pretext of defending the territories with long coastlines, [21] owing to insularity. This has resulted in intra-regional military disparities causing mutual suspicions. These include the US-Philippines agreement on Visiting Forces, New Guidelines for the US-Japan alliance, the US plans to introduce the Theatre Missile Defense system to Taiwan, and the US new policy that could enmesh the Korean peninsula, besides the threatened economic security by globalization. All these issues have for long reminded the nation-states of their collective responsibility to settle the disputes by peaceful means. Thus, the security dialogues of various forms at different levels have also become imperative in the wake of security challenges by transnational crimes, sea piracy, drug and human trafficking, arms smuggling, environmental damage, and proliferation of weapons of mass destruction.

Though regional security cooperation is a response to the common external threats, about the same time, the security cooperation in this region is elusive in the context of its being still conducted outside the regional framework. The more the engagement of external powers, the more the perception of threat to the regional stability. More often than not, the objectives of security dialogue forums would get overlapped to the extent of confusing the spirit of regionalization and thereby undermining the very purpose of regional-cooperation mechanisms. External threats or disturbances would thus warrant the participation of the concerned nations in a regional security framework; and regionalization of this kind, as is largely feared, would only escalate tensions that would undermine the spirit of interdependence. Thus, there is limited scope of security cooperation, as long as the territorial disputes remain unresolved, the external great powers are involved in military security cooperation mechanisms, the external threat perception remains unchanged and the bilateral approaches to the inter-state border problems remain at the low-ebb.

Evidently, the Asia-Pacific region is in dire need of an effective security cooperation mechanism for enhancing mutual understanding and trust and of seeking consensus through (1) bilateral military alliance, (2) mutual trust and confidence, and (3) regional security dialogues. This approach speaks of the relevance of confidence-building measures as the most appropriate vehicle in an era of unresolved disputes, and ill-defined security concerns fueling threat perceptions and mutual suspicion. Of much relevance to this context is the proliferation of terrorist activities in the region stretching from the Pamir Knot in the Western Himalayas through Northeastern India as far east as eastern Indonesia, which is termed as an 'arc of instability' undermining the spirit of the much professed 'arc of advantages'. Though the geo-economic priorities/ modalities are becoming the dominant themes of a state, the trade-related quarrels may likely land them in military alliances.[22] Geo-economic equations, which constitute a paradigm of globalization, are likely to ignite the geopolitical conflagrations. The experts of new global order find that the geo-economics would neither become a substitute to geopolitics nor would it totally obliterate the latter. In essence, globalization articulates a reconfiguration of relations of economic and political power at the global level, what could be termed as geopolitics of globalization. Thus, the prophecy that globalization would manifest in a geopolitical "end game" is a mere rhetoric. In conclusion, geo-economic considerations, though gained prominence in the entire Asia-Pacific region, would not obliterate geopolitical anomalies in their entirety.

ENDNOTES

1. Flint, Colin, "A Framework for Understanding Geopolitics" (chap.1: pp.1-31), *Introduction to Geopolitics*, (Routledge, New York: 2006), p.22.
2. Huntington, Samuel P., *The Clash of Civilizations and the Remaking of the World Order*, (Simon and Schuster, New York: 1996).
3. Quoted in Palmer, Norman D., *The New Regionalism in Asia and the Pacific*, (chap.1), (D.C. Heath & Co., Pennsylvania: 1991), p.7.
4. Wilson. R., "Imagining 'Asia-Pacific': Forgetting Politics and Colonialism in the Magical Waters of the Pacific," An Americanist Critique, *Cultural Studies*, 14, 2000, pp. 562-92.
5. Palmer, Norman D., *op.cit.*
6. Jessop, Bob, "Reflections on Globalization and its (il)logic(s)," in Olds, Kris, Dicken, P., Kelly, Philip F., Kong, Lily and Yeung, Henry Wai-chung (eds.), *Globalization and the Asia-Pacific*, (Routledge, London: 1999), p.28.
7. Thompson, C., *The Weekend Australian*, 7-8 June 1997, quoted in Olds, Kris, et. al., *op. cit.*, p. 239.
8. Wesley, Michael, "Mediating the Global Order: the Past and Future of Asia-Pacific Regional

Organizations," (pp.154-165), in Lovell, David W. (ed.), *Asia-Pacific Security Challenges,* (Institute of Southeast Asian Studies, Singapore: 2003), pp. 154-55.

9. Acharya, Amitav, "Globalization, Interdependence, and Regional Stability in the Asia-Pacific," (chap. III: pp. 41-66), in Dewitt, David B. and Hernandez, Carolina G. (eds.), *Development and Security in Southeast Asia,* (vol. III: Globalization), Ashgate, Hampshire; 2003), pp. 42-46.
10. Higgottt, Richard, "The Political Economy of globalization in East Asia: The Salience of 'region building' in Olds," Kris, et. al., *op. cit.*, p. 91.
11. Higgott, Richard, in Olds, Kris, et. al., *op. cit.*, pp. 93-94.
12. Acharya, Amitav, in Dewitt, David B. and Hernandez, Carolina G. (eds.), *op. cit.*, p. 47.
13. Flint, Colin, *op.cit.*, pp. 16 and 25.
14. Luttwak, Edward N., "From Geopolitics to Geo-economics: Logic of Conflict, Grammar of Commerce," in O' Tuathail, G., Dalby, S. and Routledge, P. (eds.), *The Geopolitics Reader,* (Routledge, London: 1998), p.129.
15. Higgott, R., Underhill, G. and Bieler, A. (eds.), *Non-State Actors and Authority in the Global System,* (Routledge, London: 2000).
16. Davison, Remy, "Introduction to the New Global Politics of the Asia-Pacific," in Connors, Michael K., Davison, Remy and Dosch, Jorn (eds.), *The Global Politics of the Asia-Pacific,* (Routledge Curzon, New York: 2004), p.1.
17. Flint, Colin, "Setting the Geopolitical Context" (chap.2: pp.33-54), *Introduction to Geopolitics,* (Routledge, New York: 2006), pp. 44 and 47.
18. Desker, Barry, "New Security Dimensions in the Asia-Pacific," *Asia-Pacific Review*, 15(1), 2008, pp. 56-75.
19. Hara, Kimie, "Rethinking the 'Cold War" in the Asia-Pacific," *The Pacific Review*, 12 (4), 1999, pp. 515-36.
20. Djiwandono, J.S., "The strategic Dynamics of Post Cold War Southeast Asia," (chap. 11: pp. 170-180), in Roy, Denny (ed.), The *New Security Agenda in the Asia-Pacific Region,* (Macmillan Press, London: 1997), p. 171.
21. Tow, William T., *Asia-Pacific Strategic Relations: Seeking Convergent Security,* (Cambridge University Press, Cambridge: 2001), p.127.
22. Luttwak, Edward N., *op.cit.*, p. 127.

5

Rise of China and Its Impact on ASEAN

G. Venkat Raman

While some scholars have been very suspicious of the growing might of China. Others have said that as long as China is comfortable and acknowledges the fact that its growing rise in the international stature has been more as a result of the way it has benefitted from its cooption in the international system there is no major worry on the China front.

The Chinese leadership has always gone to great lengths to pacify the 'China threat' alarmists and has left no stone unturned to characterize the growing might of China as one of 'peaceful development' rather than 'peaceful rise'. Moreover, the Chinese have time to time spoken about the Chinese economy as a developing economy with many imbalances in their economic rise to allay fears. Unfortunately the Chinese have not succeeded in making their neighbouring countries and regions perceive China as a friendly country. One can go on to add that the US financial crisis and its aftermath has given new impetus to the 'China threat' syndrome. On the one hand it has boosted China's international image with many of the world leaders commending China's role and increasing expectations from China in terms of the leadership it is capable of providing. It has also influenced China's own perception of itself in the international system and the way other countries in the world perceive China. Whereas other countries, especially the ASEAN countries and countries at the Asian level, have become increasingly suspicious of the growing stature of China, the fact that the Chinese themselves are apparently not confident enough to take the mantle of a superpower. Unsure of its own position in the international system, it has tended to oscillate between flexing its muscles and espousing the cause of a 'responsible' and friendly country. This has complicated things for the analysts, sinologists and others as to what would be the impact of the latest turnaround in the various debates concerning the 'rise of China'.

This chapter is divided into two parts. The first part looks at various debates revolving arould the 'rise of China'. The second half of the article examines the impact of the 'rise of China' on ASEAN.

The Rise of China Debate and Its Increasing Relevance

'When China wakes, it will shake the world' said Napoleon. The world is now, if not shaken, very suspect and insecure about China. Untill the 1990s China was seen as a 'candidate' great power, but ever since the subprime crisis in the US, there has been no doubting the fact that China is now an indisputable power. As scholars like Avery Goldstein[1] have pointed out, since the early 1990s much of the debate about the rise of China has addressed two questions: how fast are China's economic and military capabilities increasing, and how should the world respond to this emerging great power?[2]

One of the issues facing China watchers is that given China's current position in the international system, how does one actually get to measure China's 'power', and what are its main determinants? William Wohlforth has looked at indicators that many believe are the building blocks of international influence and has given these parameters the label of 'estimated power'. In the case of China the 'estimated power' can be measured in terms of its economic and military might.

China's extraordinary economic growth and its more than modest military might has led realists to portray China as a growing superpower in an era that has been characterized as witnessing 'the descent of the west' and a 'reorientation of the world' toward the east. China will try to use its growing influence to introduce changes in the international structure by espousing the cause of reshaping the rules and institutions of the international system to better serve its interests. On this basis alone, other states in the international system will perceive China as a growing security threat. This kind of an international structure is bound to have frequent frictions, but fortunately in today's world, which is characterized by states glued to certain extent with the adhesive of globalization and intertwined with forces of economics, trade and commerce, and politics, one will witness states having friction in terms of favoring or opposing the status quo of the present international system on terms different from the earlier eras in history.

To add to this fact, we have ample reasons to argue that one has an international structure from which China has benefitted for a long time. But what have given new lease of life to the 'china threat' theory is the apprehensions stemming from 'transitional anxieties' on the part of actors having high stakes in the rise of China. It is common knowledge that in international poltics a certain international system is shaped by few powerful states along with their likeminded allies to pursue their own objectives. But as the wheel of history revolves there is an emergence of new aspiring states seeking to change the international structure and thereby reframe and rewrite the rules of the international regime. Emerging states want to add to their new found status, and declining states are very apprehensive and suspicious of the power shift and the consequent implications on their weakened positions. It is such moments that generate possibilities of mutual misperceptions on the part of the established powers and the aspiring powers.[3] 'China rise' theorists, who can be called 'China Rise Alarmists', argue that in a world that has become extremely regime oriented and institutionalized in terms of international rules and regimes, China has no option but to adhere to the existing system.

'China Rise Alarmists'

Realist scholars like John Meisherheimer have been very unsparing in portraying a China whose rise won't be so peaceful. In his article 'Why China's Rise Will not be Peaceful' he argues that China is likely to dominate and maximize the power gap between itself and its neighbors. He further argues that China will want to make sure that it is so powerful that no state in Asia has the wherewithal to threaten it. He has however conceded that a powerful China need not flex its military muscle, but is likely to 'dictate the boundaries of acceptable behavior' to its neighbours. An increasingly powerful China would be determined to push the US out of Asia.[4]

A section of scholars opine that as per the power transition theory the rise of a new power like China inevitably disorders the relative power balance of the international system. China is a threat, according to this school of thought, because it challenges the existing balance of power.[5]

A strong school of thought in the US has been very apprehensive about the rise of China and its impact on the US in terms of a long term threat and therefore a very defining impact on the international system. In Asia also there have been grumblings with regards to the growing economic might of China and its likely spillover effects in military terms. It has led to reasoning on the lines that one saw during the rise of Japan at the end of the 19th century.

Anti-China Threat Alarmists

A section of scholars like David Lake and others have questioned the realist conclusions about the rise of China and have described the realist interpretations as one based on an inadequate paradigm. David Lake forcefully argues that today's international system is characterized by hierarchy and therefore is characterized by a shift from 'power-balancing to bandwagoning'.[6] He further argues that this characteristic of the international system has led to rethinking on whether the earlier realist fixation with power and power-balancing alone can adequately anticipate the behavior of a rising power such as China.[7] Richard Rosecrance has argued that in an age of 'vulnerability interdependence', not even the US can boast of having attained unipolarity of economics despite its military might. Hence, it is highly unlikely that China will be seeking to take a revisionist path and would seek to destroy the present system.

Scholars like John Ikenberry and David Shaumbaugh have viewed China as a benign rising power. John Ikenberry, for instance, has argued that given the current international order predominantly shaped by a US led western coalition of states it is difficult to visualize China upping the ante to pursue an anti status quoist agenda. First, the current international order is based on a regime, which creates conducive conditions for rising states like China and India to advance their economic and political goals. China has already discovered massive economic returns that are possible by operating this pen market system. Second aspect is the coalition nature of leadership. The current stakeholders of the current order include a coalition of powers arrayed around the US – an important distinction. These leading states, most of them advanced liberal democracies, do not always agree, but they are engaged in a continuous process of give and take over economics, politics, and security. Third, the post-World War II western order has been relatively more democratic and all encompassing than ever before and, therefore, more open and institutionalized.[8] This has paved the way for an international system which has laid adequate foundations for co-operative behavior on the part of the state actors despite the odd occurrence of anarchic situation.[9] The incentives these features create for China to integrate into such an international order are reinforced by the mileage it seems to derive. The Chinese leadership understands that China's integration in today's globalized world is an irreversible process and its interests have got so much enmeshed that China won't benefit much from rocking the boat. For instance, China not only needs continued access to the international economic system, it also wants the protections that the system's rules and institutions. In fact, one can even argue that China seems to be benefitting from the system to such an extent that it is their western counterparts who are feeling the heat and seeking to espouse their causes by seeking certain changes in their favor. To cite an example in this regard, Beijing has increasingly accepted global trade rules thereby leading to increase in FDI in China and growing volume of its international trade. Seen in the above light the rise of China need not lead to a major rift between established powers and the rising and aspiring power like China.

The above account brings us to the question as to what is the impact of the 'rise of China' on its South East Asian neighbors. Before one goes on to examine the relations between China and the ASEAN in the light of the 'rise of China' debates it is pertinent that one gets a precise picture of the historical evolution of China-ASEAN relations.

Historical Evolution of China-ASEAN ties

Ever since the 1960s the Chinese leadership has been seen by the South East Asian countries as one which has been sympathetic to the communist groups and communist backed insurgents in the ASEAN region. This kind of perception on the part of the South East Asian nations had often led to a threat perception anticipating aggressive expansionism by military means in the foreseeable future. China ASEAN relations can be divided to four distinct phases as follows: (1) Phase I (1967-78): Domestic Preoccupations, (2) Phase II (1978-89): 'De Facto Alignment against Vietnam', (3) Phase III (1989-97) Sino-ASEAN Relations after Vietnam's Pullout from Cambodia, and (4) Phase IV (1997-present)[10]

Phase I (1967-78): Domestic Preoccupations

During the first phase China as well the South East Asian nations were very much preoccupied with various developments in their respective domestic arenas. However in whatever semblance of relationship they have had, it was basically based on distrust of China on the part of the ASEAN countries. However the Sino-US rapprochement prompted a rethink on the part of the ASEAN countries to do a rethink as regards their relationship with China.

Phase II (1978-79): 'De Facto Alignment against Vietnam'

During this phase there was lack of unanimity as regard the ASEAN's policies towards China. This phase was also a very important period in the sense that the Sino-US rapprochement was nearing its complete normalization. With US and China both opposing Vietnam's occupation of Cambodia. Malaysia and Indonesia were the two standout countries which were wary about China's role in the ASEAN region. This phase soon evolved into another phase with Vietnam's intervention in Cambodia coming to an end. With this development there was bound to be redefining of Sino-ASEAN ties because the end of Vietnam's Cambodia occupation led to a certain kind of void in the ties. The end of cold war and the unpredictable nature of US role in the ASEAN region facilitated Sino-ASEAN ties which led to simultaneous operation of competitive and co-operative dynamics.

Phase III (1989-97) Sino-ASEAN Relations after Vietnam's Pullout from Cambodia

This phase was historically unprecedented for Sino-ASEAN relations because important ASEAN member states like Indonesia, Singapore and Brunei expressed their desire to establish normal relations with China. These developments took place at a time when the US was reassessing its role in the ASEAN region and seeking to review its security arrangements in the ASEAN region. ASEAN countries were wary of the fact that the US review would lead to Chinese usurpation of the resultant void in the security environment. This paved the way for ASEAN to have a relook at their ties with China.

Another issue which concerned and worried the ASEAN member states in the nineties was the South China issue. The Chinese actions in the South China Sea spurred the signing of the Declaration on the South China Sea in the year 1992. Yet another significant development during this phase saw the Philippines alleging that China had occupied the Mischief Reef in 1995 with China vehemently denying the allegation. These developments once again brought the issue of the Spratlys Island dispute into limelight.

Although his phase marked some frictions between China and ASEAN countries in the security arena there were also positive developments. This period marked the beginning of an era which laid the foundations of improved economic relations and co-operation in Sino-ASEAN relations. The ASEAN started appreciating the significance of closer trade relations with China. Simultaneously, the ASEAN countries started exploring possibilities of the growing Chinese economic might by seeking new ties at the bilateral and multilateral level. On the multilateral front, this period saw the emergence of 'ASEAN plus three,' South China Sea workshops, Asia Pacific Economic Co-operation. Each of these involved China.

The expansion of the regional arrangements under the multilateral framework was basically inspired by the realization on the part of the ASEAN member states that they were too small and their voices too low to be vociferous enough to contain the growing Chinese influence.

Phase IV (1997-present)

The Asian financial crisis marked a new phase in the Sino-ASEAN relations because this era saw China playing a decisive role in providing succor to the ASEAN member states by not devaluating its currency despite lot of pressure and thereby demonstrated its regional leadership. This phase also marked the signing of the landmark free trade agreement between china and ASEAN. However, this period saw the return of the US in South East Asia in the aftermath of the 9/11 attacks on WTC, New York. As part of its global war on terror the US wanted to play a more pro-active role in the region. This development was bound to have its own share of pros and cons. On the positive side the ASEAN countries had the advantage of not being overwhelmed by either of the two, namely, the US and China. On the flip side this development meant that the ASEAN countries also had to be content with certain exigencies when they would be sandwiched between the Chinese and the American interests in the ASEAN region and taking sides would be definitely not worth the effort.

The financial crisis strengthened the Sino-ASEAN relations. China was able to capitalize on the disappointments ASEAN had to experience when the member states found IMF conditionalities to be highly intrusive, inappropriate, and insensitive' to their specific economic and political conditions. What helped the cause of the Chinese further was the disappointment expressed by the way the US opposed the Japanese suggestion of establishing an Asian Monetary Fund. Some ASEAN countries like Malaysia were openly critical of the Japanese role in the financial crisis of 1997. The Chinese sensed that the time was ripe to make a decisive move and win the hearts of the ASEAN member states by issuing a joint statement on China-ASEN co-operation during an unprecedented China ASEAN summit in 1997.

In the above account of the historical evolution one can see that the China-ASEAN relations have been on an upswing with every phase evolving to a higher plane of relationship between the two countries. So does this indicate that all is well with the China-ASEAN relations and they have not been unaffected by the 'rise of China'? The next section would by and large deal with this question. This question becomes all the more relevant especially when one considers the Chinese threat to ASEAN countries in the economic arena, especially after its WTO accession and thereby adversely affecting the FDI inflows and the volume of trade (between ASEAN and world in terms of the export competitiveness of the former) in ASEAN region. When one considers the growing stature of China after the financial crisis in 2008 then one can sympathize with the ASEAN states that they have to invest adequate diplomatic efforts to have a matured understanding and relationship with China.

ASEAN's Threat Perceptions and the Rise of China

A very useful tool to analyse the likely impact of growing rise of China and its impact on ASEAN would be to anticipate ASEAN's threat perceptions of Chinese 'intentions' in the region and how china seeks to address these concerns. Jeffrey W Legro, a reputed International Relations scholar once pointed out that, "the debate over China is not about what China wants today, but what it might want tomorrow."According to power theorists, the rise of China could lead to a fundamental change in the way Chinese think and approach and may be even challenge the world order. As Robert Gilpin had stated about China, "as its (in this case China's) relative power increases, a rising state attempts to change the rules governing the system." This view of China has two likely scenarios with China being the 'patient hegemon' or the 'innocent giant'.[11] The 'patient hegemon' portrayal of China would be one where China would patiently bide time and wait for the right opportunity to flex its muscles once it is confident of dictating terms to other countries and seek to address what it perceives as historical injustices meted out to it at one point of time or other. The 'innocent giant' picture would lead to a China which would temporarily like to tread the path of integration with the current world order but over a period of time might change course and seek to revise the existing order. Thus one of the telling impact of growing 'rise of China' from ASEAN's standpoint would be to grapple with the challenge of identifying the threat perceptions and after sound speculation decide which China would it be dealing with as China grows in power, a China which is going to be an 'innocent giant' or a China which is going to be a 'patient hegemon'. ASEAN has to grapple with various complexities of anticipating Chinese foreign policy goals and its diplomatic efforts in the region and protect their national interests. Adopting the right kind of 'hedging strategy' and carefully devise co-operative and competitive mechanisms to deal with an unpredictable challenge would definitely be one of the most challenging assignments for foreign policy makers and diplomats in the ASEAN region.

Nicholas Khoo and Michael Smith have pointed out that one of the crucial oversights in the literature on China's relations with ASEAN member states is the lack of a comparative focus.[12] These two scholars argued that China's relations with ASEAN in the current period are compared with relations during the cold war. They proposed a change in this analysis by suggesting that a more useful approach would be to contrast China's relationship with Southeast Asia with the US' relations with this region. To support their arguments, these two scholars point out that the US has extensive defence ties with Indonesia, Malaysia and Singapore. Moreover the Southeast Asian nations have joint military exercises with the US but China has no comparable military ties with the South East Asian states. This indicates that the ASEAN states are wary of growing might of China and to meet any aggrandizing tendencies and actions from China the ASEAN states would like to cover themselves under the US security umbrella which can also prove to be deterrent for any nefarious designs on the part of China. As a Southeast Asian diplomat went on record to state, "...Basically our choice is between a hegemony in Washington or a hegemony in Beijing. We are still choosing the United States."[13]

Last but not the least like other countries in the world in general and Asian states and more importantly China's neighboring countries and ASEAN states in particular have to contend with a Chinese foreign policy which is a product of its own 'collective ideas'.[14] Chinese leaders' depiction of their country as one that has been victim to aggrandizing behavior in a world infested with aggressors also contributes to the caution and suspicion that China displays.[15] Michael Yahuda, an eminent Sinologist has termed this kind of behavior of the Chinese as leading to a "diplomatic culture of entitlement."[16] Possessing such a sense of victimhood makes it hard for the country to be sensitive either to the sense of entitlement that other countries might have, or to its bigness, or to the fears that its geopolitical dominance can evoke in its neighbors.[17] The influence of this feature of Chinese foreign policy making and more importantly other national actors in the international arena perceiving the Chinese on these lines makes them suspicious about the growing rise of China. The post US financial crisis era has compounded worries on this front for China seems to have been suddenly catapulted to an exalted position for which it may not be ready at the hindsight to occupy. A hesitant aspiring power which has been provided the mantle of leadership and more responsibilities at a global level can sometimes lead to a 'split personality' kind of behavior on part of China. It can become more unpredictable with the Chinese foreign policy blowing hot and cold vibes and sending confusing signals to its Asian neighbors. Contending with such a growing power can be another major challenge facing the Asian neighbours.

Conclusion

To conclude, one would like to state that as long as China's foreign policy is oriented towards the world order in terms of integration, aberrations apart, ASEAN can expect more or less an issue based approach. In the economic arena mutual ties would definitely be on an upswing though the growing economic might of China will cause ripples and insecurity of sorts among ASEAN nations. However, the China thret theory is not going to be of such proportions that it will lead to a major shift or changes in the ASEAN region. The reason being that in the aftermath of the financial crisis China has new set of problems to grapple. Its exports which have been increasing at a highly impressive rate is going to decline in the medium to long run because the western and European markets will not have the same buying power in the years ahead. Moreover the FDI in mainland China is also not going to be of the same levels seen till now because there will be gradual dearth of capital for FDI in China as a result of the impact of the US financial crisis. When one considers the fact that the Chinese have some major issues to address in terms of regional balances in the mainland and the recent change in its development strategy from an export driven to a more inward looking strategy of boosting domestic consumption to improve its economic might then can conclude to a reasonable extent that the ASEAN region as will not have face the prospects of facing a china which will seek to antagonize its South East Asian neighbours.

ENDNOTES

1. See Avery Glodstein, 'The Diplomatic Face of China's Grand Strategy: A Rising Power's Emerging Choice', *The China Quarterly*, 2001, pp. 836-64.
2. Ibid, p. 835. Though Goldstein in his article had mentioned about the significance of response of the world in general and US in particular to the growing rise of China, one would like to point out that at least at the Asian level, it is pertinent that one gives ample

attention to how the ASEAN countries and countries like India respond to the growing rise of China for there are compelling reasons for these nations to be wary of a rising China.

3. For different types of power transitions and their likely impact on existing international order see John G Ikenberry, "The Rise of China and the Future of the West," *Foreign Affairs*, January/February 2008, Vol. 87, Issue 1.
4. For John Mearsheimer's views on China please refer to his article "The Future of the American Pacifier," *Foreign Affairs*, September-October 2001, pp 46-61. Also relevant to see the same author's updated article on the subject in the April 2006 issue of *Current History*.
5. William A Callahan, "How to Understand China: The Dangers and Opportunities of Being a Rising Power," *Review of International Studies*, Vol. 31, No.4 (October 2005), pp.701-714.
6. David Lake, "The New Hierarachy and the Future of East-West Relations," *International Studies Perspective*, Vol. 7, No.1, February 2006, pp. 23-30.
7. See James C Hsiung, "China's Second Ascent and International Relations Theory,"
8. See Ibid.
9. The Six party talks regarding the Issue of North Korea's Nuclear Programme can be cited as an important example where countries with diverse national interests like Japan, US, South Korea, North Korea, Russia and China have made efforts to peacefully resolve the issue of denuclearizing the nuclear peninsula.
10. The section on historical background of the Sino-ASEAN relations has been influenced by Alice D Ba, "China and ASEAN: Renavigating Relations for a 21st Century Asia," *Asian Survey*, Vol. 43, No.4 (July/August 2003), pp. 622-47.
11. See Jeffrey W Legro, "What China will Want: The Future Intentions of a Rising Power," *Perspectives on Politics*, Vol. 5, No. 3 (September 2007), pp. 515-534.
12. See Nicholas Khoo, Michael L R Smith, David Shambaugh, "China Engages Asia? Caveat Lector," *International Security*, Vol. 30, No.1 (Summer 2005), pp 196-211
13. As quoted in *op cit*, p. 202.
14. Jeffrey Legro has defined 'collective ideas' as collective beliefs of societies and organizations about how to act. According to Legro, there is adequate literature to establish link between 'collective ideas' and its role in determination of foreign policy'.
15. See Rosemary Foot, "China in the ASEAN Regional Forum: Organizational Processes and Domestic Modes of thought," *Asian Survey*, Vol. 38, No. 5 (May, 1998), pp. 425-440.
16. Ibid, p. 436.
17. Ibid.

6

US-ASEAN Re-engagement: Balancing China in the Asia-Pacific

Vibhanshu Shekhar

Introduction

Three important developments that took place in Southeast Asia in 2010 have come to re-define the nature and dynamics of the region's engagement with the United States – the most powerful player in today's international politics. First, in response to the Chinese designation of the South China Sea as an area of 'core national interest,' the American Secretary of State, Hillary Rodham Clinton claimed free passage in the disputed area as America's 'national interest.'[1] Second, the US, in order to influence the trajectories of ASEAN-driven cooperative processes, became a member of the East Asia Summit in October 2010 and also participated in the ADMM (ASEAN Defence Ministerial Meetings) Plus. Finally, the US President visited Indonesia along with three other important Asian players – India, Japan and South Korea in November 2010, integrating Southeast Asia into its larger strategic discourse on Asia. The visit witnessed a Joint Declaration of comprehensive partnership between USA and Indonesia that highlighted Indonesia's call for greater role in Southeast Asia and Obama's appreciation of Indonesia's democratic outlook.[2]

In fact, Southeast Asia seems to have regained its Cold War position of being one of the pivots for the US in the latter's grand strategy towards the Asia-Pacific. While participating in the second US-ASEAN summit, held in New York in September 2010, the President of the United States, Barrack Obama, identified re-engagement with ASEAN as a central component of its overall strategy of playing a leading role in Asia. These developments outline the emerging contours of the relationship, which, in the coming years, are going to considerably shape the regional structure of power.

US-ASEAN Relations during the Cold War Era: ASEAN as a Pivot

The US-ASEAN strategic alignment during the Cold War era evolved in the backdrop of (a) the prevailing structure of international politics, marked by a great power rivalry between the USA and the USSR and consequent bloc politics, and (b) the emergence of Southeast Asia as an important theatre of the USA-USSR rivalry. The American policy of containment of communism and its advocacy of domino theory brought it in direct military confrontation with the Ho Chi Minh-led communist Vietnam. With the rise of communist regimes in the Indochina, the regional structure of power came to be polarised into two definitive blocs of the USSR-supported communist versus USA-led capitalist regimes. In other words, the regional relationships began developing on the basis of existing global bloc politics. ASEAN countries gradually began coming closer to the US and were soon identified as important pivots in America's overall strategic positioning in the region.

The US-ASEAN strategic engagement had three important components – developing military bases and alliance partners in the region, building strong defence and security relations with important players like Indonesia, and facilitating the creation of an effective regional grouping to bring together non-communist countries of the region. Thailand and the Philippines were members of SEATO (Southeast Asian Treaty Organisation), set up in 1954 to counter the rise of communism in Southeast Asia and develop a security alliance mechanism in the region. The US set up a military base in Singapore and overhauled its military bases in the Philippines (Subic and Clark bases) and they were used extensively during the Vietnam War for logistics, operations, reconnaissance and medical services. As a support base for America's Seventh fleet, the Subic base provided a major thrust to America's forward deployment strategy in the Pacific.[3]

The USA also developed a wide-ranging defence, security and economic cooperation with the Suharto-led military regime of Indonesia, which had emerged as an important 'bulwark' in the US effort towards containment of communism in the region.[4] The US assistance to Indonesia included training for Indonesian military personnel in the US, sales and supplies of defence weaponry, and large-scale economic assistance to the country. The US also played an important role in the Dutch withdrawal and transfer of control over West Papua to Indonesia and supported the Indonesian annexation of East Timor in 1975 in the name of containing communism. The US not only provided unilateral economic assistance to Indonesia, but also mobilised support for financial assistance from individual countries as well as multilateral institutions, such as the World Bank and International Monetary Fund. The Inter-Governmental Group on Indonesia

(IGGI), comprising of developed western nations and Japan, proved to be the main coordinating agency for assistance to Indonesia. For example, the US not only pledged to give financial assistance in 1968 but also convinced Japan to give assistance to Indonesia.[5]

An important aspect of America's engagement with the ASEAN regional grouping during the Cold War era was to develop and sustain an 'anti-communist' front that could work as a countervailing force against a communist Indochina.[6] In pursuit of these objectives, the US played an important role in reducing intra-mural tensions among members and facilitating economic and political cooperation in the region. While the ASEAN countries were learning to live together (notwithstanding their bitter rivalries), the US support proved to be the building block for ASEAN, allowing the regional grouping to facilitate cooperation and dialogue among the member states. Highlighting America's contribution towards ASEAN, the former Prime Minister of Singapore, Goh Chok Tong stated,

> "The US involvement in Vietnam bought precious time for the ASEAN countries to put their house in order and to lay the foundation for the grouping to develop into a cohesive organisation. ASEAN economies began to take off, spurred by US investments and a friendly American market...The US presence has been a determining reason for the peace and stability Asia enjoys today. It has helped turn an unstable region of tension and strife into a booming and dynamic Southeast Asia."[7]

The US-ASEAN dialogue mechanism, initiated in 1977, was a step in that direction. As a part of the dialogue mechanism, USA and ASEAN "focused on issues such as economic development, the extension of US preferential trade arrangements to ASEAN members, and the promotion of direct investment from the United States to Southeast Asia."[8] This system of engagement continued untill the end of the Cold War when new sets of issues brought about structural transformation in the politico-strategic landscape of the region and consequently in the US-ASEAN engagement.

Retreat of the US during the Post Cold War Era

The onset of the post-Cold War era witnessed gradual strategic withdrawal of the US from the region, and this retreat was seen and felt in the arena of military presence, economic cooperation, support to the regional grouping and in terms of America's engagement with the individual ASEAN countries. The US military resources from the bases in the Philippines were transferred to Saudi Arabia during the Gulf War of 1990-91 before these bases were closed by 1992.[9] The US-ASEAN economic cooperation experienced similar downscaling. The financial assistance coming from the West declined and US economic support remained minimal when the region was facing its worst economic crisis during the late 1990s. The minimal assistance coming from the US in time of the region's worst crisis was viewed as the country's deliberate neglect toward ASEAN, which it once supported vehemently. A similar sense of US withdrawal was perceptible in terms of its participation in the ASEAN cooperative processes. The ASEAN Regional Forum could not move beyond confidence building and the US participation could not go beyond cosmetic presence in the annual meetings of the forum. Later, even annual presence was downgraded.

There were three fundamental reasons for the US retreat in the aftermath of the end of the Cold War era. First, the threat of communism on a global scale was no longer felt and therefore the state of constant preparedness was no longer required. In other words, the end of the Cold War era removed the raison-d'être of the US-ASEAN strategic engagement and, therefore, diminished the importance of ASEAN temporarily as a pivot in America's Asia strategy. Moreover, the US had begun shifting its strategic focus towards the Gulf region.

Second, as the ASEAN member-states began emerging as tiger economies and moving towards extending the membership of the grouping to other countries of Southeast Asia, they found opposition coming from the US. The US opposition was viewed by the ASEAN countries as unwarranted and out of place, prompting the ASEAN countries to come up with their own Asian way in opposition to the growing demand for democratisation and political and human rights in the region. Mahathir Mohammad of Malaysia, Lee Kuan View of Singapore, and Suharto of Indonesia emerged as ardent advocates of the Asian Way and questioned the legitimacy and feasibility of adopting Western democracy in the Oriental societies. They characterised the call for democratisation as Western effort of bullying. Myanmar and Indonesia had emerged as primary targets of the Western criticism against large-scale violations of human rights. In the face of growing international outcry against human rights violations by the Indonesian military in East Timor, the US curtailed its economic assistance to Jakarta and suspended military cooperation with the Indonesian Special Forces.

Finally, the inclusion of Myanmar in ASEAN received constant opposition from the US and European Union. As the efforts for the inclusion of Myanmar were underway, the US imposed further economic sanctions on Myanmar, exerting greater pressure on ASEAN not to admit Myanmar within its fold. ASEAN rejected the US pressure and went ahead to include Myanmar in its fold. Donald E. Weatherbee argued that the stand taken by ASEAN vis-a-vis Myanmar's membership, in opposition to the American approach, needed to be understood in the broader context of the ASEAN countries' growing frustration at American lecturing on human and political rights in the region.[10] While the then US Secretary of State, Madeleine Albright, condemned Myanmar in the annual meeting of the ARF in July 1997, ASEAN focused on building consensus on the policy of constructive engagement towards Myanmar.[11]

Besides, there were several other points of discord, such as growing perception among the people of a few ASEAN countries about the US being anti-Muslim, the George Soros phenomenon, also widened the gap between ASEAN and USA.

Southeast Asia in the Twenty-first Century

Two major developments that occurred during the first decade of twenty-first century have brought Southeast Asia back into the strategic focus of America – the global war on terror, and the rise of Asian great powers. These two developments have transformed the politico-strategic landscape, not only of Southeast Asia alone, but also of the entire Asia-Pacific. In fact, the US-ASEAN re-engagement is essentially, a response to these two-fold challenges facing the region in the twenty-first century.

9/11 Attacks and Bali Bomb Blasts bring ASEAN and the US closer

The rise of radical Islam in Southeast Asia, with Indonesia being the epicentre of such a phenomenon, brought the US back to the region with the issue of counter-terrorism emerging as an important component of America's global strategy. While the September 11, 2001 terrorist attack prompted the US to launch a war on terror, the Bali Bomb Blast of October 2002 highlighted the global outreach of terrorist network. Southeast Asia began to be viewed not only as a victim of Islamic terrorism but also a safe haven for the terrorists to devise strategies for regional operations. The Indonesia-based *Jemaah Islamiyah*[12] with a pan-Southeast Asia operational network, began to be viewed as a regional arm of Al-Qaida's global network of terror and, therefore, provided the US an important reason to develop greater engagement with the Muslim regimes of Southeast Asia as well as coordinate its counter-terrorism globally. Moreover, the scale, planning and strategies of the 9/11 attack highlighted the growing strength and reach of non-state actors, creating the fear of nuclear or biological terrorism. The rise in sea-piracy in and around the Strait of Malacca made the choke-point and sensitive installations of Singapore along the coast vulnerable to maritime terrorism.

The enormity of the impact of these potential dangers prompted ASEAN and the US to sign a Joint Declaration in August 2002 calling upon both the sides to share intelligence and information on terrorist networks, possible operations and their financing.[13] Moreover, the two sides also agreed to develop coordination among law-enforcement agencies and comply with various UN Security Council resolutions against terrorism. Several new initiatives, such as Proliferation Security Initiative (PSI) and Container Security Initiative (CSI) were launched and the ASEAN countries were expected to be active pariticipants in these initiatives. The then US Secretary of State, Colin Powell announced "$31 million to train police, $16 million to build a counterterrorism unit, and $4 million for army counter-terrorism training for Indonesia over several years."[14]

The 9/11 Commission Report, besides eliminating the terrorist sanctuaries and networks, stressed America's greater engagement with the Muslim societies and foreign governments in developing a comprehensive strategy against terrorism.[15] The recommendations of the report were incorporated in the Intelligence Reform and Terrorism Prevention Act of 2004 of the US. In its pursuit of greater engagement with the Muslim world, the US resumed its economic assistance to Indonesia, Thailand and the Philippines in 2002. The then US President George Bush visited Indonesia in 2003 and declared the US's intention to assist Indonesia in its fight against terrorism through capacity building and sharing of information. The two countries conducted a joint counter-terror exercise in May 2005 and the US declared in February 2006 that it would help the Indonesian military in developing technical skills.[16] While the US assistance to Indonesia in the fight against terrorism has come in the form of indirect assistance, the US assistance to the Philippines' counter-terrorism measures has been much more direct with the US military also being involved in the operations.[17]

Great Power Politics and Pressure of Performance on ASEAN

As the global discourse on terrorism began to subside, a completely new challenge – the rise of Asian Powers – has brought the US and ASEAN together. As the Asia-Pacific inches towards the gravity of global politics, the regional strategic discourses are being dominated by the spectre of great power politics riding on the rise of two major powers – China and India. These players are experiencing robust growth in their internal and international capacities, as evident from continued economic growth, military modernisation, and the development of more nuanced approaches to their foreign relations. As a result, they are able to exert power and influence in a much wider geographical canvas and in a much more definitive manner than they could twenty years ago.

In contrast to its welcome posture towards the rising India, the region of Asia-Pacific has exhibited a sense of insecurity and uncertainty about the rise of China, primarily among the neighbours along the latter's southern and eastern rim. Much of this insecurity arises out of an opaque nature of the rise of China, its long-standing territorial or boundary disputes with its neighbours, and a somewhat the aggressive nature of China's approach to contentious issues, such as the South China Sea dispute. ASEAN's response to the challenge of great power politics has come primarily in the form of (a) institutionalising great power relations by bringing them together in a dialogic framework, (b) regulating the agenda of cooperation and raising the stakes in regional cooperation, and (c) engaging multiple powers that could constrain the behaviour of a single great power.

If the developments during the last five years are any indicator, ASEAN seems to be losing its tactical grip over the regional strategic discourses. The evolving structure of great power politics has drawn the attention away from multilateral strategic dialogue and regional cooperation towards great power rivalries and evolving unstable regional geopolitics. In fact, the regional and global attention has focused on what the rise of these powers mean for the world, whether China's rise can be a stabilising or destabilising process, whether India can balance China in the future or whether the US is joining hands with India and other Asian powers to counterbalance China. It is rarely being asked whether and how ASEAN will continue facilitating regional cooperation and neutralise the negative implications of the evolving great power politics in the region. In fact, the ascent of great power politics has posed one of the most formidable challenges to the ASEAN-driven cooperative processes in three specific ways.

First, the ASEAN-driven cooperative processes are gradually emerging as a theatre of great power rivalry. As a regional cooperative interlocutor, ASEAN has embarked on creating cooperative space to facilitate dialogue among regional players. It finds its agencies – ASEAN+1 initiatives, ASEAN Regional Forum (ARF), East Asia Summit (EAS), and now ASEAN Plus Defence Ministerial Meeting (ADMM+) – emerging as avenues for great power projection. Apparently, there appear to be fissures within ASEAN on a variety of issues, including the ASEAN Charter, principle of non-intervention, greater economic integration, and responses to the rise of major powers in Asia that are becoming evident and may weaken the ASEAN cooperative efforts. China had also proposed to hold the EAS in Beijing in 2006, an idea summarily rejected by ASEAN.

Second, the ASEAN-driven regional architecture is coming under enormous pressure from the hostile nature of relations among the major powers, nearly hijacking the agenda of these regional initiatives and giving them a somewhat partisan outlook. In the face of growing opposition to China's dominant role and the latter's perception of growing anti-China lobby within the EAS, Beijing has begun to focus its energy and resources on ASEAN+3 cooperative framework. As a result, ASEAN+3 and EAS are emerging as parallel processes of cooperation, causing diversion of resources, inhibiting greater scope for regional cooperation and leading to further polarisation even in meeting common regional challenges. Such a competitive scenario brings out the possibility of these forums losing comprehensive regional support and emerging as partisan initiatives. While China may stop contributing to the growth of the EAS and focus its energy on developing ASEAN+3 initiative, Japan may have become more involved in the ASEAN+6 initiative (now ASEAN+8 with the entry of USA and Russia).

Finally, can ASEAN continue to work as a regional conflict management agency in the face of growing domination by great powers? The events in the South China Sea in 2010 suggest that it has not been able to perform this role in the region. The notion of peaceful resolution of the South China Sea dispute, as once formulated and mutually agreed by both China and ASEAN during the late 1990s, seems to have been undermined with the Chinese designation of the South China

Sea as an area of 'Core National Interest,' an epithet kept reserved only for what China considered more sensitive conflict zones such as Taiwan or Tibet. This stance indicates China's growing aggression towards ASEAN and the US diplomatic intervention points towards ASEAN's depleting strategic capital in what has come to characterised as 'Socialising China.' For example, the US presence in the South China Sea seems to have received much more attention than the country's membership of East Asia Summit, even though they somewhat reflect similar strategic objective – reducing China's growing influence in the region.

The near-absence of ASEAN from the global focus on the regional strategic debate hints at the possibility of gradual de-emphasis on the leadership of ASEAN in setting the agenda of cooperation in the region. Such a process can further diminish the dialogic and collaborative significance of these institutions, and paving the way for greater adherence to unstable great power rivalries than cooperative politics. It is this context of great power rivalry, growing Chinese influence in Southeast Asia and gradual emasculation of ASEAN leadership that explains America's return to the region. The USA augmented its re-entry into the Asia-Pacific by deciding to become a member of East Asia Summit, signing a comprehensive partnership with Indonesia and sending its naval fleet for interaction with the Vietnamese navy in the South China Sea.

Key Objectives of the Re-engagement: Balancing China and Strengthening ASEAN

The growing US-ASEAN strategic engagement aims at re-asserting not only America's long-standing security cooperation with the ASEAN countries but also the former's position of strategic pre-eminence in the region. The most important driving force for the re-engagement has come in the form of an uncertain nature of China's growing diplomatic and strategic influence and the latter's perceived aggression in the region. To quote Kishore Mehbubani, Singapore's former diplomat, "The US realizes that if they are to retain American influence in this region, they must be able to match what China is doing. If China is improving its ties by leaps and bounds with ASEAN, it is not in America's interest to be left behind."[18]

The strategic engagement with the US offers ASEAN a much needed support mechanism against the prevailing uncertainty in the politico-strategic landscape of the Asia-Pacific. Moreover, the US can play the role of a balancer in case the regional politics begins shifting towards a volatile structure, marked by rivalries among the Asian powers, primarily China, India and Japan. While the engagement remains a threat-induced and insecurity-driven process for ASEAN, it forms an important pillar for the United States' great game in Asia.

Methods and Strategies of the Re-Engagement

The US Secretary of State, Hillary Clinton, while attending the fifth EAS meeting in October 2010, unfolded its two-fold strategy of tapping on both bilateral as well as multilateral resources to further its strategic interests in the region. The bilateral engagement can be further sub-divided into two categories of (a) alliance partners, and (b) new-found strategic/natural partners. While Thailand, Singapore and the Philippines fall into the first category, Vietnam and Indonesia can be understood as part of the second category. There are three fundamental components of the evolving nature of the US-ASEAN re-engagement.

Strengthening Bilateral Security Engagement

First, the US has made a concerted effort to revive defence and security cooperation with Indonesia, initiate strategic engagement with Vietnam and express its willingness to engage the Myanmarese junta. Obama's Indonesia visit in November 2010 witnessed a Joint Declaration of a comprehensive partnership between the USA and Indonesia that highlighted the latter's call for a greater role in Southeast Asia and Obama's appreciation of Indonesia's democratic outlook. The Joint Declaration characterised the bilateral partnership "critical not only to the bilateral relationship, but to addressing key regional and global challenges." The declaration called for joint efforts in building the agenda in the East Asia Summit, Asia-Pacific Economic Cooperation and G-20 forums. The US offered to provide the Indonesian Air Force with two squadrons of retrofitted used F-16A/Bs at one-third the price of a new aircraft and the offer is being viewed as an effort to strengthen its ties with Indonesia.[19] Indonesian Foreign Minister and the US Secretary of State Hilary Clinton participated in the first bilateral joint commission in September 2010 under the Comprehensive Partnership that released an action plan to implement it. The US agreed in July 2010 to resume defence and security ties with the Indonesian Special Forces that were suspended in 1998 after the reports of their involvement in the large-scale human rights violations in East Timor and other parts of Indonesia. The US government had offered immediate assistance to Indonesia in the aftermath of the Tsunami natural disaster in 2005.

Another important country that has figured prominently in the USA re-engagement with Southeast Asia is Vietnam. Signalling a new era in the US-Vietnam relations, the Vietnamese Prime Minister Prime Minister Nguyen Tan Dung and the US President Bush singed several bilateral agreements in June 2008 in the field of foreign military sales, visit of Peace Corps, bilateral education task force etc.[20] The two countries have launched an annual security dialogue to discuss a host of non-traditional security issues, primarily maritime security, nuclear non-proliferation, climate change, disaster management and peace-keeping. So far three such dialogues have taken place. Vietnam has signed an MoU on civilian nuclear energy cooperation with the US and participated in the Global Initiative to

Combat Nuclear Terrorism and the Megaports Initiative, which aim at nuclear non-proliferation.

The US has changed its policy even towards Myanmar, away from sanctions and international isolation towards pragmatic engagement, sending its senior-level diplomat for dialogue in November 2009. Senator Jim Webb of Virginia became in August 2010 the first member of the US Congress to visit Myanmar in ten years.[21]

Growing Naval Presence

An important aspect of enhanced strategic engagement has occurred in the form of America's growing naval engagement in Southeast Asia and the ASEAN countries, shedding previous reservations, have welcomed the US presence.

The anti-submarine exercise has emerged as an important part of the US strategy of increasing its naval presence and manoeuvrability. The main reason for this set of exercises has come from China's growing inventory of nuclear submarines and its efficient application in securing the maritime corridors in Southeast and Northeast Asia. It was reported in June 2009 that one of the US destroyers was hit by sonar, fired by the Chinese submarine off the coast of the Philippines.

The latter half of the year of 2010 saw a somewhat sudden and an unprecedented presence of US warships in Vietnamese waters. These warships – the USS George Washington a nuclear powered carrier, and the USS John S. McCain destroyer – were visiting Da Nang port, the Vietnamese coast off the South China Sea. The visit of the US warships took place in September 2010 in the backdrop of the Chinese declaration of the South China Sea as an area of its 'core national interest.' The US and Vietnamese navies participated in trainings, exercises, and search and rescue operations. The two navies, for the first time in the history of independent and unified Vietnam, were engaged in a friendly duel.

The US navy has also enhanced the level of its engagement with the Indonesian navy (*Tentara Nasional Indonesia-Angkatan Laut*). Several US ships visited Indonesia in May 2010 during the 16th annual Naval Engagement Activity (NEA) exercise that forms an important bilateral component of Cooperation Afloat Readiness and Training (CARAT).[22] The US delegation characterised the naval engagement with Indonesia as an important part of America's maritime strategy of building global partnerships.[23] The CARAT involves different sets of naval exercises between the navies of the US and six ASEAN countries (Brunei, Indonesia, Malaysia, Singapore, Thailand and the Philippines) and the US. The 2010 CARAT also included Cambodia and Bangladesh. The US navy has also been engaged in the joint exercise with six ASEAN countries (Brunei, Indonesia, Malaysia, Singapore, Thailand and the Philippines) since 2002. The annual exercise is known as Southeast Asia Cooperation Against Terrorism (SEACAT) and it focuses on information sharing and coordinated responses.[24] Moreover, the United

States, while participating in the first ADMM Plus meeting in October 2010, stressed on the need for cooperation in the area of maritime security and even proposed to develop an agenda on the theme for the next meeting.

Participation in the ASEAN-driven Cooperative Processes

The United States, during the last two years, has made a calibrated effort to enhance its presence and play an important role in the ASEAN-driven regional cooperative processes. The US signed the Treaty of Amity and Cooperation in 2009, hosted the US-ASEAN summit in New York in 2009, became a member of the East Asia Summit in 2010 and participated in the first ADMM Plus meeting in October 2010. Notwithstanding its long-standing reservations, the US finally acceded to the Treaty of Amity and Cooperation in February 2009, opening the possibility of its membership in the East Asia Summit. As per the admission criteria of the EAS, a member country must be a signatory of the TAC (apart from other criteria of being a dialogue partner and substantial economic engagement) in order to become a member of the EAS. Welcoming the first visit of any US Secretary of State to the ASEAN Secretariat in Jakarta in February 2009, the ASEAN Secretary General, Surin Pitsuwan, identified her visits as a serious effort on the part of the US 'to end its diplomatic absenteeism in the region,' and the growing 'importance of ASEAN in the regional architecture.'[25] Responding to the Secretary General's remarks, the US Secretary of State, Hillary Clinton characterised the US-ASEAN re-engagement as "an important part of our new approach to development and diplomacy, what we call 'smart power'."[26]

The two sides held their first annual summit meeting in November 2009 in Singapore. The US President, Barrack Obama identified ASEAN as 'a key partner in the promotion of peace, stability and prosperity in the Asia-Pacific region,' named an Ambassador for ASEAN affairs, and opened up of a US Mission to ASEAN in Jakarta.[27] The Second US-ASEAN summit, held in New York in September 2010, was the first ever summit that ASEAN held with any of its dialogue partners outside Southeast Asia. Participating in its first EAS meeting in Hanoi in October 2010, the US Secretary of State, Hillary Clinton called upon the leaders to adopt an 'active agenda to settle maritime disputes.' While taking part in the inaugural meeting of the ADMM+ in October 2010, the US identified maritime security and piracy as two important security challenges confronting the region.

Nothing explains the US intent of its engagement with ASEAN more than the changing nature of its participation in the ARF. The ARF as a regional security initiative had begun losing its charm during the late 1990s and the member states had begun losing their interests in making the annual meetings more result-oriented. As a result, the ARF had emerged more as a talk-shop. On the contrary, the US Secretary of State, Hillary Clinton, used the forum in July 2010 to announce its important policy statement on South China Sea.

Conclusion

A mutually beneficial relationship is evolving which, in the coming years, is going to considerably influence the regional structure of power. Southeast Asia has certainly become a part of the USA's larger Asia discourse. An apparent advantage of such a policy is greater strategic space for the regional powers including ASEAN to focus on regional cooperation, engaging other powers while the US balances China in the region. Such a policy can force China to commit to the ASEAN process and allow its greater socialisation by ASEAN. With Obama's recently concluded Asia visit, the US took an important step towards exploring the fast-growing and industrialising Asian markets for the American goods and consolidating its strategic engagement with a coalition of countries which share one common concern – how to effectively moderate an enormous swell in the strategic and economic power of China. However, the US-ASEAN re-engagement can further militarise the strategic discourses in the Asia-Pacific with a greater thrust on military modernisation, scramble for energy and other strategic resources and coalition-building process. While the re-engagement can put a check on China's aggressive ambitions in the region in the near future, the policy might trigger greater militarisation and modernisation of China's military since it faces direct confrontation with the much more advanced military of the US.

It is yet to be seen whether the US involvement in the ASEAN process is going to strengthen ASEAN process or further enhance the latter's dependency on great powers for regional security.

ENDNOTES

1. Christopher Bodeen, "China Attacks US-Asean Interference in South China Sea Dispute," *The Irrawaddy,* 22 September 2010, http://www.irrawaddy.org/article.php?art_id=19523
2. "U.S.-Indonesia Joint Declaration on Comprehensive Partnership," *The White House*, 9 November 2010, http://www.america.gov/st/texttrans-english/2010/November/20101109102136su0.2631146.html
3. Michael F. Kimlick, "U.S. Bases In The Philippines," *Global Security*, 1990, http://www.globalsecurity.org/military/library/report/1990/KMF.htm
4. Mustaqim Adamrah and Abdul Khalik, "From Cold War Bulwark to Equal Partner?", *The Jakarta Post*, 9 November 2010, http://www.thejakartapost.com/news/2010/11/09/from-cold-war-bulwark-equal-partner.html
5. Dewi Fortuna Anwar, *Indonesia in ASEAN: Foreign Policy and Regionalism,* (Singapore: ISEAS, 1994), p. 200.
6. K.S. Nathan, "US-ASEAN Relations in the Context of ASEAN's Institutional Development: Challenges and Prospects," http://library.fes.de/pdf-files/bueros/singapur/04601/2007-3/nathan.pdf
7. Goh Chok Tong, "ASEAN-US Relations: Challenges," *ASEAN Secretariat,* Keynote speech at the ASEAN-United States Partnership Conference New York, 07 September 2000, http://www.aseansec.org/2806.htm

8. K.S. Nathan, "US-ASEAN Relations in the Context of ASEAN's Institutional Development: Challenges and Prospects," *op.cit.*
9. Sheldon W. Simon, "U.S. Interests in Southeast Asia: the Future Military Presence," *Asian Survey*, vol. 31, no. 7, (Jul., 1991), p. 662.
10. Donald E. Weatherbee, "Growing Pains: ASEAN's Economic and Political Challenges," *Asia Society Working Pappers*, December 1997.
11. Ibid.
12. For details on *Jemaah Islamiyah* see *White Paper: The Jemaah Islamiyah Arrests and the Threat of Terrorism*, Ministry of Home Affairs, Government of Singapore, 7 January 2003, http://www.mha.gov.sg/publication_details.aspx?pageid=35&cid= 354; *Indonesia Backgrounder: How the Jemaah Islamiyah Terrorist Network Operates,* International Crisis Group (ICG) Asia Report, no. 43, 11 December 2002; Sidney Jones, "The changing nature of Jemaah Islamiyah," Australian Journal of International Affairs, vol. 59, no. 2, June 2005, pp. 169-178; Zachary Abuza, "Tentacles of Terror: Al Qaeda's Southeast Asian Network," *Contemporary Southeast Asia,* vol. 24, no. 3, (December 2002), pp. 427-65; Vibhanshu Shekhar, *Politics of Islam, Nation-building and Development: Ethnic Violence and Terrorism in Indonesia,* (New Delhi: Anamika Publications, 2011), pp. 211-14.
13. "ASEAN-USA Joint Declaration for Co-operation to Combat International Terrorism (2002)," *Privacy International,* 1 August 2002, https://www.privacyinternational.org/article/asean-usa-joint-declaration-co-operation-combat-international-terrorism-2002
14. Bruce Vaughn, "Indonesia: Domestic Politics, Strategic Dynamics, and American Interests," *Congressional Research Service Report*, The Library of Congress, 3 April 2006, p. 22.
15. "Terrorism in Southeast Asia," *Congressional Research Service Report*, The Library of Congress, 7 February 2005, http://www.fas.org/sgp/crs/terror/RL31672.pdf
16. Bruce Vaughn, "Indonesia: Domestic Politics, Strategic Dynamics, and American Interests," *op.cit.*
17. Michael Vatikiotis, "Rights and wrongs of Asia's 'war on terro'," *Asia Times Online,* 6 April 2007, http://www.atimes.com/atimes/Southeast_Asia/ID06Ae01.html
18. Edwin Chen and Julianna Goldman, "Obama Meets Leaders of Asean, Myanmar, to Counter Chinese Clout," *Bloomberg,* 15 November 2009, http://www.bloomberg.com/apps/news?pid=newsarchive&sid=aa_Vb6QPBiBg
19. Sheldon W. Simon, "US-Southeast Asia Relations: Full Court Press," *Comparative Connections,* vol. 12, no. 4, (October-December 2010), p. 55.
20. "Timeline: US-Vietnam Relations," *Contemporary Southeast Asia,* vol. 32, no. 3 (2010), p. 353.
21. Ibid, p. 436.
22. "Indonesia Welcomes Task Group for Naval Engagement Activity," *Comderson Three One,* Pacific Fleet, United States Navy, 26 May 2010, http://www.public.navy.mil/surfor/cds31/Pages/IndonesiaWelcomesTaskGroup.aspx
23. Ibid.
24. "Southeast Asian nations conduct anti-terror naval exercise," *People's Daily Online,* 19 August 2008, http://english.people.com.cn/90001/90777/90851/6480275.html
25. "Remarks With ASEAN Secretary General Pitsuwan: Beginning a New Era of Diplomacy in Asia," *US Department of State,* 18 February 2009, http://www.state.gov/secretary/rm/2009a/02/119422.htm
26. Ibid.
27. "Joint Statement – 1st ASEAN-U.S. Leaders' Meeting," *ASEAN Secretariat,* 15 November 2009, http://www.aseansec.org/24020.htm

PART II

MULTILATERAL INSTITUTIONS IN THE ASIA-PACIFIC: A ROAD AHEAD

7

Multilateralism and Regional Security in the Asia-Pacific

Ganganath Jha

The Asia-Pacific region, encompassing a vast territory from East Asia to the South Pacific, is full of cultural diversity, ethnicity and socio-economic problems.[1] China is the most populous, resourceful, and ambitious. On the other hand, Japan, South Korea, Hong Kong, Singapore and Australia are affluent. North Korea has proliferated nuclear bombs and threatened regional security environment. In the meanwhile, there are problems of poverty and underdevelopment in some countries like Tuvalu, Kiribati, Papua New Guinea, East Timor and Cambodia. Some South Pacific states are always afraid of natural disasters such as tsunami, landslides, earthquakes and haze. They are also afraid of demographic changes as witnessed in the case of New Caledonia, Fiji and Australia. Given the situation as existing in the Asia-Pacific, the western world has evolved its own strategies to create a situation so that nations in the Asia-Pacific transform their behaviour to suit them, but Asians are willing to guard their interests. They are talking of Asian resurgence and dreaming of an "Asian Century." How the interests of the East and West can be synchronized, how the institutions of regional security should function, and how the scope of power politics can be minimized are important issues for peace and prosperity of the Asia-Pacific. It requires cooperation and understanding to address complexities of regional security. The United Nations, which was expected to protect the interests of all nations, is faced with structural issues at the institutional level. It failed to safeguard security interests of Afghanistan, Iraq, Pakistan, New Caledonia and a number of other members of the organization. Hence the dialogue for multilateralism at the regional level assumes importance.

What is multilateralism? Jonathan Crystal (2008) says that "multilateralism is an agreement or alliance among three or more members. Yet multilateralism also has a qualitative dimension. In this sense, it refers to rule-governed behaviour in which states refrain from their pursuit of immediate goals, presumably in order to achieve long-run interests through cooperation.[2] Another scholar, John Ruggie, has noted that multilateralism is an institutional form that coordinates relations among three or more states on the basis of generalized principles of conduct without regard to the particular interests of the parties or the strategic exigencies that may exist in any specific occurrence.[3] Yet another expert Amitav Acharya has stated that in the economic arena, the key principle of multilateralism is non-discrimination. In the security field, multilateralism involves the creation of a non-exclusionary setting for order maintenance, conflict regulation and peace. Both in the economic and security arenas, the primary objective of interactions is to discourage participating actors from discriminating against each other, promote transparency and mutual reassurance, and resolve contentious issues peacefully and constructively.[4]

In particular three normative principles constitute the institution of multilateralism. First, indivisibility refers to the notion that all actors are equal participants in the cooperative endeavour. It is illustrated by the concept of collective security, where an attack on any state is seen as an attack on everyone. Second, nondiscrimination implies that any benefit received by one state must be available to all, as exemplified in the most-favoured-nation principle of the World Trade Organization. Third, diffuse reciprocity refers to the idea that concessions and rewards balance out over the long run and states do not need to insist upon a strict tit-for-tat exchange.[5]

There have been multilateral efforts for regional security alliances in the Asia-Pacific that did not achieve the desired results. The Southeast Asia Treaty Organization (SEATO) for example, was established with much fanfare in 1954 with the membership of Thailand, Pakistan, Australia, New Zealand, Britain, France, the Philippines and the United States. The signatories had resolved to support each other in security matters. An attack on one member was to be considered an attack on all, but certain developments after 1962 caused withering away of the very spirit of collective security idea.

Thailand under Field Marshal Sarit Thanarat wanted SEATO intervention in the Laotion civil war. But there was no consensus amongst the partners for such an action. As the Ho Chi Minh Trail, the supply lane of the NLF forces, passed through Laos along the Vietnamese border under the protection of Pathet Lao in the area, Thailand projected it as a serious threat to the security of the region. Thailand and the United States wanted to reverse the tide of communist advances in the Indo-China region in tune with the containment drive. However, there were some SEATO members who opposed intervention and argued their support for neutrality towards Laos. In March 1961, Thailand requested SEATO to dispatch troops to Laos to strengthen anti-communist forces, and the proposal was placed before the SEATO Ministerial Council, but member nations could not find a consensus except to send a warning to Pathet Lao of the grave consequences if they disregarded the spirit of neutrality as per the Geneva Agreements of 1954.

Thailand was unhappy with the outcome. The Thai Foreign Minister, Thanat Khoman demanded that SEATO should be reorganized and the rule requiring unanimity be revised. He declared that Thailand's faith in the alliance had been shaken. Thailand was not ready to stay long in a state of insecurity in the midst of hostile neighbours. Prime Minister Sarit was more critical of SEATO, saying that Thailand might leave the SEATO if it did not take a strong and immediate step to halt communist advances in Southeast Asia. On the other hand, the US was so much concerned about developments in Thailand that it began to give assurances through ministerial visits and subsequently invited Thai Foreign Minister Thanat Khoman to the US in March 1962. Thus a Thai-US joint statement was issued on 6 March 1962, reiterating US assurances to Thailand of full support in the event of any communist aggression.[6] It solemnly promised Thailand that in rushing its help it could not wait for the unanimous approval of cooperation of other member nations of the SEATO, so that the action taken might not be too slow or too late. The joint statement clearly stated that "In the event of communist armed attack against Thailand, the US intends to give full effect to its obligations under the treaty to act to meet the common danger in accordance with its constitutional processes. This obligation of the US does not depend on the prior agreement of all other parties to the treaty, since this treaty obligation is individual as well as collective."[7]

Thailand was very satisfied to receive the guarantees of security from the US, but the signing of the joint statement suggested that there was something wrong with the functioning of SEATO, that it had no consensus on vital issues of collective security and also that a partner had to look for bilateral arrangements to protect its national security. France was unhappy at the unilateralism of the US in SEATO and Pakistan felt so frustrated that it had to come out of SEATO. It was unhappy because SEATO did not intervene on its behalf in the war against India in 1965 and 1971. When the US lost its war in Vietnam in 1975, SEATO became defunct. In retrospect, we find that SEATO failed because the partners did not respect the norms of multilateralism. The US wanted containment of communism and so it was supporting SEATO. Pakistan was hostile against India and had nothing to act against communist China or Vietnam. Thailand was sensitive against the resurrection of Laos and wanted to keep it subservient. Thus the US, Pakistan and Thailand wanted to use SEATO to fulfil their own strategic interests. Britain, France, Australia, New Zealand and the Philippines were not to gain from the regional agenda of Pakistan or Thailand. It was difficult to keep the partners together, but when the US started acting unilaterally, other partners left every burden on the United States to resolve.

The qualitative dimension of multilateralism, as Jonathan Crystal says, "demands a behaviour in which states restrain their pursuit of immediate goals, presumably in order to achieve long-run interests through cooperation. It refers to the notion that all actors are equal participants in the cooperative endeavours."[8] Some efforts towards regional security have flopped because the well established norms of multilateralism have not been respected. The Five-Power-Defence agreement amongst Malaysia, Singapore, Australia, New Zealand and Britain and the ANZUS pact amongst Australia, New Zealand and the United States were benevolent in nature. Britain dominated the proceedings of FPDA and the US dominated the proceedings of ANZUS.[9] All the participants were never considered equal and those alliances were merely used for military training, recoinnassance and strategic exchanges. However, ARF (ASEAN Regional Forum), which was established in 1994 to cooperate in security matters has taken some important initiatives in tune with the spirit of multilateralism and it will be appropriate to discuss them here.

In fact, it was in the backdrop of Chinese threat that the idea of the ARF had been mooted. People's China had already declared sovereignty rights over the South China Sea. It had declared the Paracels and the Spratlys as its own territories. It had attacked Vietnamese possessions at Truong-Sa and occupied Louisa Reef and Fiery cross Reef and later on attacked the Philippine possessions at Kalayan and occupied Mischief Reef. Malaysia, Vietnam, the Philippines, Brunei and others who had territories in the Spratly region were feeling concerned and threatened. They wanted to diffuse belligerence of the adversaries through Musjawarah and negotiation.

Barry Buzan (2003) has noted that "one way of understanding the setting up of the ARF is to see it as a response to ASEAN's inability to construct itself as a counterweight to China, and the need therefore to try to socialize China into being a good citizen. In addition to concerns about China's interventions in Cambodia, its disputes with Vietnam and its expansion in the South China Sea, there was also concern about its growing influence in Burma. Chinese support for the military junta in Burma not only strengthened the junta against its domestic rebels and the civil opposition, but also allowed China to deploy intelligence facilities in the Indian Ocean."[10] All these were disturbing and hence the proposal to establish the ARF was accepted in the Bangkok meeting of ASEAN in 1994. All the members of ASEAN and its full dialogue partners became members of ARF. Hence China, Japan, the US, Russia, India and Australia and others joined together for a multilateral security dialogue for the most crucial part of the Asia-Pacific.

The ARF meeting in Brunei discussed the ARF concept paper in 1995 and came out with a road map of future development and institutional structures. The concept paper proposed development of the forum in three stages, namely (a) Promotion of Confidence building measures, (b) Preventive diplomacy mechanisms, and (c) conflict resolution mechanisms. There was broad consensus over the concept paper, but the Chinese representative argued that since the ARF is only a dialogue forum, it should not be designed as a formal institution aimed at resolving conflicts. The Chinese opinion was given weight and thus conflict resolution mechanism was modified as "the elaboration of approaches to conflict."[11]

The concept paper also suggested measures as exchanging annual defence postures on a voluntary basis, increasing dialogues on security issues on a bilateral, sub regional and regional basis, maintaining senior-level contacts and exchanges among military institutions, and encouraging participation of the ARF members in the UN conventional Arms Register. The concept was an exploration of regional arms register, prior notification of major military deployments, a regional peace keeping training centre, dispatch of fact finding missions and cooperation to enhance maritime surveillance and security.[12]

The ARF has evolved a preventive diplomacy mechanism at track I and track II levels and thereby promoted security dialogues to neutralize regional hawks. Thus several workshops on the South China Sea were held in Indonesia, in which all the claimants of the Spratlys had taken part. In fact, ever since the incident of Chinese encroachments at Mischief Reef in 1992, ASEAN leaders had agreed that there should be a greater cooperation on security matters within the grouping. The ASEAN Ministerial Meeting in July 1992 had already issued a statement calling for a peaceful resolution of the dispute concerning the Spratlys in the South China Sea, but substantial progress in that direction were not visible. However, when Vietnam became the member of ASEAN and ARF's concept paper became ready, multilateral dialogues started. In 1999, ASEAN established a special committee to formulate a code of conduct for the South China Sea to be observed by all claimants to the Spratly Islands.

A draft code of conduct was approved in November 1999. China was hesitant to give its consent to the code of conduct and argued that it would accept the proposed code only as a set of guidelines and not as a legally-binding document.[13]

Nevertheless, China began to participate in discussions subsequently with ASEAN officials on the proposed code of conduct. The opinion making institutions like the Chinese Academy of Social Sciences (CASS) and Institute of

Asia-Pacific Studies reported that the emergence of multilateral security cooperation in Asia-Pacific is an unstoppable trend. Thus it is imperative for China to involve itself in the multilateral process in a pragmatic way. It recommended that China proactively shape the development of mechanisms from within, in order to ensure a favourable position in a fluid and complex security environment. It had a positive impact on top Chinese leadership.[14] In November 2002 foreign Ministers of China and ASEAN adopted a declaration on the conduct of parties in the South China Sea, agreeing to promote a peaceful environment and durable solutions for the area, to resolve territorial disputes by peaceful means, to refrain from undertaking activities that would aggravate existing tensions (such as settling unpopulated islands and reefs), and to initiate a regular dialogue of defence officials.

China has been one of the most active participants in ARF dialogues. According to Cheng Chwee, two factors have helped this development. First is the institutional features of the ARF. The forum, an extended model of ASEAN, has been operationalized on the basis of the "ASEAN way" which is featured in the forms of informal, wide consultative, consensus and an incremental approach.[15] The second factor that assuages China's suspicion of multilateral institutions is ASEAN's unique role in maintaining an equal relationship with major powers. For China, the fact that the ARF is led by ASEAN and not other big powers such as the US and Japan is politically acceptable and in fact preferable. These two factors together convinced China that the ARF would not develop into an anti-China alliance. Although China is actively involved in the ARF, its bottom line is to ensure that the forum will retain its diplomatic and political nature and not involve an intensive security mechanism that could undermine its strategic interests.[16]

Involving China in ARF multilateralism has proved a success for the ASEAN states. A safety valve have been created where the adversaries can channel their perception and grievances. However, this arrangement is not to the satisfaction of all the forum members. The United States, which had been the dominant actor in the politics of Asia-Pacific for decades, is not satisfied. It has been arguing for democracy, human rights and free trade. It has been expressing its concerns about human rights violations in Myanmar. It has been reminding about assassination, displacement and persecution of Rohingyas, Karens, Shans and NLD leaders, yet substantial steps are not taken. The principles of non-interference and constructive engagement are cited as ailibis to allow military dictatorship to continue in Myanmar. It is understood that the Chinese factor in Myanmar is the major deterrent and the ASEAN advertently is not willing to do anything that could offend Chinese rulers. Again the production of opium, narcotics and related drugs in the golden triangle area of Myanmar remains unchecked. The ARF as a security forum was expected to take initiatives, but its preventive diplomacy in that direction is ineffective.

There are other issues of regional security threats that need utmost attention. The ASEAN region is the home of the terror organization Jemaah Islamiah, linked with al-Qaida, aimed at destabilizing several regional governments and establishing a pan-Islamic caliphate, encompassing the Indonesian archipelago, southern Philippines, Southern Thailand, Malaysia, Singapore and Brunei. As there is large population of Muslims in the area, the apprehension has been that they may provide shelter to them.[17] The feeling of Muslim Umma (community) generating brotherly ties are difficult to be suppressed. The terrorist organizations are active in Malaysia, Indonesia, Singapore, Thailand and the Philippines. An organization Known as Maunah (Brotherhood of Inner Power) raided a military armoury in the village of Sauk (Malaysia). However they were overpowered by army commandos after a bloodshed. Again another organization KMM (Kumpulan Militan Malaysia) under Abu Jibril tried to bomb a shopping mall but failed. KMM members have received training at Mujahidin training camps in Afghanistan, who wanted an Islamic fundamentalist regime in Malaysia.

Indonesia has also witnessed Islamic extremism in recent years. Jemaah Islamiah, under the leadership of Abu Bakar Bashir and Abdullah Sungkar, has promoted terrorism and bloodshed. The bombing of Kuta Beach of Bali in 2002 killed 202 people, mostly foreigners. Again there was a suicide bombing of the Marriott Hotel in Jakarta in 2003, which killed 12 people. Another bomb attack on the Australian Embassy in 2004 Killed 11 people. In 2005 a bomb attack in Bali killed 23 people. Thus Jemaah Islamiah has unleashed fear and tension for the general people with bombing, beheading and shooting. Although the government of Indonesia have outlawed Jemaah Islamiah and arrested its members, they are unable to stop them from sneaking in the Sulu and Mindanao areas of the Philippines. The Moro Islamic Liberation Front (MILF) askar Jundullah and Abu Sayyaf group extend support to Indonesia's terrorists with materials and moral support. Founded in 1991 by Abu Sayyaf, this terror group has had strong connections with al Qaida and thus it has got the lethal training and funding of the latter. It knows the use of explosives and has indulged in serious crimes, including ferry bombing in Manila Bay, which killed more than 100 people.[18]

Again there are terrorists from across the national frontiers who trespass into the alien territories in order to commit an orgy of violence and terror. They are completely indoctrinated and well-trained to devastate select targets. The terrorists involved in 9/11 or 26/11 had come from outside. They had been facilitated to operate with the support of the local people. They had been working so astutely and secretly, that they remained unnoticed till they blew the Trade Center towers in New York or the Taj Hotel in Mumbai. Armed with sophisticated weapons and suicide bombers, they prove lethal and deadly. Such people have no place to remain in the civil society, but there are some who attach them importance. The political leaders in certain parts of the world enlist their cooperation in order to fulfil their ambitions, and hence there is a deal with the terror groups. Such a deal is secret and it is impossible to catch the politicians for the deal. Similarly there are countries, which are committed to respect the principles of non-interference, but clandestinely provide shelter, support and training to terrorists. They nurture the growth of fanatic elements with men and materials. For instance, Pakistan has been assisting the terrorists in Afghanistan and India and vitiated the environment for regional cooperation, yet it is difficult to sue Pakistan in the International Court of Justice. South Asia remains the poorest region because of the lack of political and security cooperation.

There is growing concern about the security of Southeast Asian Waterways, especially the Straits of Malacca. This narrow waterway, which is of vital strategic importance, has been threatened by high levels of piracy. More than half of the world's trade and oil traverses through this strategic waterway. However the cases of piracy around Indonesian waters are disturbing. The US, Japan and Australia are alarmed at the incidents of piracy and the region is gradually responding to US led initiatives designed to improve port and container security as part of preventive measures against piracy, i.e. the Container Security Initiative and International Port Security Programme.[19]

Again there are cases of ethnic separatists in Myanmar, China, Indonesia and the Philippines, who are constantly working for subversion of their states. There are some failed or rogue states such as Pakistan, Myanmar and North Korea, whose actions are provocative. There are Islamic terrorists calling for Jehad (Holy war) to establish Islamic states and in retaliation there are counter organizations.[20] The scope of capacity building to counter terrorism is limited and therefore the security situation is faced with serious complexities.

The nations of the Asia-Pacific felt extremely concerned when Islamic fanatics led an attack on the US trade towers on 11 September 2001. On 12 September, ASEAN condemned the attacks and urged greater international cooperation to counter terrorism. The ASEAN Summit meeting in November issued a Declaration on a Joint Action to combat terrorism. The summit encouraged member countries to sign or ratify the international convention to sign or ratify the international convention for the suppression of financing of terrorisms to strengthen national mechanisms against terrorism, and to work to deepen cooperation, particularly in the area of intelligence exchange, international conventions to combat terrorism and the possibility of developing a regional anti-terrorism convention. The summit at the same time rejected any attempt to link terrorism with religion, race or country. In 2002, resolve to combat terrorism was reiterated, and in the 2003 ASEAN summit, ASEAN Police Chiefs proposed the establishment of a network of national anti-terrorism task forces, to work in close coordination with one another. The ARF workshop in 2002 proposed financial measures against prevention of terrorism. Thus the ARF meeting in Brunei in 2002 issued a statement of individual and collective intent to prevent any financing of terrorism. The statement included commitments by participants to freeze the assets of suspected individuals or groups, to implement international financial standards and to enhance cooperation and the exchange of information.

India, which became a member of the ARF in 1996, treats the latter as an important forum to understand regional security perspectives. India is not satisfied with the performance of the SAARC. As the largest country, its intensions are questioned if it tries to take any initiative to contain security threats, and on the other hand keeping a low profile does not help the cooperation to grow. However India's role in the ARF has been appreciated. It has been hosting multi-nation naval exercises and conclaves at the strategic Andaman and Nicobar Islands in the name of "Milan", in which Australia, New Zealand, Bangladesh, Brunei, the Philippines, Myanmar, Thailand, Indonesia, Sri Lanka, Singapore, Vietnam and Malaysia are taking part. "Milan" basically is a biennial conglomeration of Asia-Pacific maritime navies, to foster bounds of friendship across the seas and share views on common maritime issues.[21] From four navies in 1995, it has grown to include a dozen now. Apart from humanitarian and search and rescue operations, the focus of "Milan" exercise is cooperation against maritime terrorism, piracy and poaching. India is also conducting Malabar exercise with the United States in the region. In 2007, Malabar exercises had also included Australia, Japan and Singapore navies, which has been held in the Bay of Bengal. This exercise had annoyed China which projected it as 'axis of democracy' emerging in the Asia-Pacific. China was sensitive that the exercise had been held in the vicinity of Myanmar, which is under their strategic influence. Although Malabar exercises are held between India and the United States, they would like it to be a multilateral engagement. India on its part is trying to display that its engagement in maritime affairs in the region is to work for securing the Western flank of the ASEAN. However, this endeavour will be successful in the long run if its security concerns are properly addressed.

The ARF includes all the great powers and provides regional states with an opportunity to build social and political connections and, hopefully diffuse conflict situations before they become dangerous. But as Shaun Narine observes, "there are many significant problems with the ARF, and many reasons to believe that it cannot work as ASEAN envisions".[22] First, historical and political circumstances that shaped ASEAN and allowed it to functions effectively simply do not apply to ARF. ASEAN faced common external threats and so they cooperated effectively to prosper. On the other hand, the powerful states of Asia-Pacific are not similarly threatened. Second, in keeping with the "ASEAN way", the ARF is meant to seek consensus and avoid issues of conflict. It is unlikely that all of the ARF's participating states will be willing to postpone discussing controversial international issues while waiting for social and political ties to develop. Third, ASEAN claims a proprietary right to determine the ARF's agenda. However, it lacks the standing to enforce this claim.[23]

Asia-Pacific multilateral institutions cannot be modeled on the pattern of, for example the European Union. As Shaun Narine of St. Thomas University has observed the Asia-Pacific region is not capable of creating equivalent structures. The most important factor in binding the EU together has been its pre-existing economic ties. In Asia, the economic structures are evolving and there are competing nations like China, Japan, Australia, Canada, India, Malaysia and South Korea, whose complex security, political and social relationships are difficult to elaborate.[24] ARF is not a grouping of like minded nations. It includes nations whose interests and perspectives regarding regional security differ. For instance, David Martin Jones and Michael Smith do not believe that there is remarkable achievement in China-ASEAN relations, as ARF multilateralism has been manipulated to China's favour. On the other hand, Hiro Katsumata has argued that ASEAN and China have collaborated on developing a win-win approach by establishing a set of common interests to enhance peace in the region. ASEAN has guided the latter to pursue cooperative security within ARF framework by demonstrating the value of its approach to regional cooperation. Thus instead of being maniputed by China, ASEAN has been engaged in socializing Beijing into its cooperative security norm.[25]

While summing up, it can be stated that multilateralism in the Asia-Pacific is in an evolutionary stage. Presently it is faced with certain problems. As most of them have experienced colonial rule and have different historical, cultural and political systems, their perceptions differ. Some of them are concerned to maintain their separate identity. They very often talk about 'Asian Values' and do not want to do anything radical to transform their traditional system. However, the notions of an 'Asian century' inspire them to work together. If the actors of multilateralism will consider them equal, if the gains will assist the uplifting of socio-economic life, and if the cooperation would promote peace and prosperity, multilateralism will be successful. Any effort to project the US as a threat to sovereignty of third world for advocating democracy and human rights, are retrogressive. At the same time, any effort to malign China for its role in Asia-Pacific are faulty. Again the projection of Islamic world as supporters of terrorism are counterproductive. Common welfare and collective prosperity are the uniting factors. If the effort is made to provide intellectual output for resurgence of Asia, universal brotherhood, and peaceful coexistence, consensus for support to multilateralism in Asia-Pacific will certainly grow.

ENDNOTES

1. According to Far East and Australasia yearbook, "Australia, Brunei, Cambodia, China, Cook Islands, East Timor, Fiji, Hong Kong, Indonesia, Japan, Kiribati, Laos, Malaysia, Marshal Islands, Myanmar, Micronesia, Nauru, New Zealand, Nieue, New Caledonia, Northern Mariana, North Korea, Palau, Papua New Guinea, Philippines, Singapore, South Korea, Tuvalu, Tonga, Thailand, Vietnam, Vanuatu and Western Samoa" are referred as an integral part of Asia-Pacific. South Asian states of Afghanistan, Bangladesh, Bhutan, India, Maldives, Nepal, Pakistan and Sri Lanka, are not yet included.
2. Jonathan Crystal (2008), "Multilateralism", International Encyclopedia of Social Sciences, 2nd Edition, Vol. 5, Thomson Gale, p. 320.
3. John Gerard Ruggie (1992), "Multilateralism: The Anatomy of an Institution", International Organization, Vol.46, no.3, p.571.
4. Amitav Acharya (1997), "Ideas, Identity and Institution Building: From the 'ASEAN Way' to the 'Asia-Pacific way',", The Pacific Review, http.www.informarworld.com/smpp/title-content=t713,207111,p.325.
5. Crystal, no.2, p. 320.
6. Rusk-Thanat Joint Statement, 6 March 1962, para=3.
7. Ibid.
8. Crystal, no.2, p. 320.
9. The ANZUS, which was signed in 1951, was to coordinate their efforts for collective defence for the preservation of peace and security pending the development of a more comprehensive system of regional security in the Pacific area, and the opening sentence of the pact indicated that the essence of the treaty would be to treat Australia and New Zealand at par with the Philippines and Japan, which had agreed to station the US armed forces to assist preservation of peace and security in the area (for further details see "ANZUS Treaty" http:astralianpolitics.com/foreign/Anzus/anzustreaty.shtml.)
10. Barry Buzan (2003), "Security Architecture in Asia: the interplay of regional and global levels", *The Pacific Review*, Vol. 16, no. 2, p. 155.
11. Kuik Cheng Chwee (2005), "Multilateralism in China's ASEAN policy. Its evolution, characteristics and Aspiration", *Contemporary Southeast Asia*, Vol. 27, no.1, p.107.
12. Amitav Acharya, np.4, p. 327.
13. Kuik Cheng-Chwee, no.11, p. 106.
14. Ibid.
15. Ibdi, pp.107-108.
16. Ibid, pp.112-13.
17. Andrew T.H. Tan, (2008) "The Security Challenges of East and Southeast Asia", The Far East and Australasia, Routledge, p.10.
18. For an understanding of this aspect, see Zachary Abuza (2003), Militant Islam in Southeast Asia: Crucible of Terror, Lynne Rienner Publishers pp. 2-12.
19. Tan, n.17, p.10.
20. Abuza, n.18, pp.1-20.
21. "Multi-nation navy exercise at Andaman", The Times of India, 2 February 2010.
22. Shaun Narine (1998), "ASEAN and the Management of Regional Security", Pacific Affairs, Vol.71, no.2, Summer, pp.209-10,
23. ibid.
24. Shaun Narine, "Some General Thoughts on ASEAN's Role in Asia-Pacific Multilateralism", 10 November 2009.
25. Hiro Katsumata, David Martin Jones and Michael L.R. Smith, (2008), "ASEAN, Regional Integration and State Sovereignty", *International Security*, Vol.33, no.2, Fall, pp.182-83.

8

India and East Asia Summit: A New Opportunity in Engaging East Asia

A Lakshmana Chetty

The 21st Century is widely believed as the Century of Asia. At a time when economics emerged as the dominant factor in the domain of international relations, the breathtaking economic growth of Asia helped it to emerge as a centre of "global geostrategic and geoeconomic activity". The international business community has caught "Asia fever" and is sharpening its focus on this radically progressing Continent. Asia's spectacular economic performance in the 21st century reminds one of 16th C. AD when China and India together accounted for 50 per cent of world GDP, with each sharing roughly 25 per cent. If the startling forecasts by American investment bank Goldman Sachs economist, Jim O' Neil, are to be believed, history will turn full circle as Asia is all set to retake its prime place in the global economy. O' Neil predicted 'India's economy could be larger than all but the US and China in 30 years' and China's economy would be 25 times larger than the US by 2050. Japan would be one of the six largest economies in 2050.[1]

Asia has come to be recognised as an economic powerhouse as well as a technological powerhouse. Asia has two demographic titans, India and China, and three of the world's five largest militaries. The world's largest holders of foreign reserves are found in Asia. When such rapid changes indicating the dramatic rise of Asia are taking place, the absence of a pan-Asian regional organisation, unlike in other continents, such as Africa, Europe and America, is obvious. In order to fill the void, Prime Minister Manmohan Singh proposed an Asian Economic Community (AEC) at the Third India-ASEAN Business Summit in Bali on October 21, 2004. The AEC, envisioned by Premier Singh, while focusing on

Pan-Asian economic cooperation and integration, "would constitute an 'arc of advantage', across which there would be large-scale movement of people, capital, and creativity". The AEC concept was appreciated and approved by a number of Asian nations including Singapore and Japan.

Even though the AEC initiative could not take concrete shape, ASEAN, which had already evolved the ASEAN+3 (ASEAN + China, Japan and South Korea, the three economic giants) and ASEAN+1 (ASEAN + India) processes, succeeded in launching the East Asia Summit (EAS), with members drawn from the Asian continent and the adjacent Pacific region: ASEAN+3 and India, Australia and New Zealand. Far from being an exclusive forum, the EAS kept its door open to inviting extraregional powers who mattered much to the region. While the AEC's dominant feature was economic cooperation and integration, the EAS has politico-security and socio-economic dimensions. As a "rising regional and global" power and as one of the three major powers in Asia, India became a founder-member of the EAS despite the efforts of certain countries to exclude New Delhi. In this paper, an attempt is made to trace the events leading to the establishment of the EAS as an inclusive organization, and to describe India's benign role in strengthening the EAS so as to make it evolve into an East Asian Community before it culminates in the establishment of an Asian Community.

Origin and Growth of EAS Concept

The geopolitical consequences of the Asian financial crisis of 1997-98 accelerated the trend towards multilateral grouping, while strengthening the ASEAN which represents "the interdependent nature of its economic and political system." When the US did not respond appreciably to the crisis-affected ASEAN countries, China offered $ 4 billion in aid and also agreed to desist from devaluing its yuan in order to keep the ASEAN economies afloat. Japan too went to the rescue of the ASEAN countries by extending considerable financial assistance despite the fact that Japan's economy too was suffering from the shock of the financial crisis. The Asian financial crisis gave fillip to Malaysia's initiative of the East Asian Economic Group (EAEG) which was subsequently rechristened the East Asian Economic Caucus (EAEC), in the early 1990s. The formation of ASEAN+3 in 1997 and the holding of its first summit two years later, giving a call for regional integration, were the direct results of the financial crisis.[2] Formation of the EAS could also be attributed to the East Asian countries' perceived US domination of the Asia Pacific Economic cooperation (APEC). China and Malaysia even contemplated the forming of a pressure group within the APEC, to protect their interests.[3]

Following the recommendation of the East Asia Vision Group, comprising eminent intellectuals from ASEAN+3 countries, to set up an East Asia grouping, which would develop into an East Asia community wedded to the promotion of peace, stability and cooperation, the EAS concept began to take a concrete shape.[4] In 2004, ASEAN leaders at their Vientiane summit, decided to hold the East Asian Summit in Kuala Lumpur in 2005 with 16 members – ASEAN+3, India, Australia and New Zealand. Accordingly, the first East Asia Summit was held in Kuala Lumpur on December 14, 2005, being "a forum for dialogue on broad strategic, political and economic issues of common interest and concern with the aim of promoting peace, stability and economic prosperity in East Asia." The EAS would focus on "promoting development, financial stability, energy security, economic integration and growth, eradicating poverty and narrowing the development gap in East Asia through technology transfer and infrastructure development, capacity building, good governance and humanitarian assistance and promoting financial links, trade and investment expansion and liberalization."[5]

Debate on Membership and Organizational aspects of EAS

Once the decision to launch the EAS was taken, and before its inauguration, two issues relating to the composition and organizational matters of the EAS had to be sorted out. On the issue of membership, there arose certain differences among the ASEAN states and also among the +3 countries. The former Malaysian Prime Minister and the author of EAEC concept, Mahathir, going by geographical definition, insisted on excluding the peripheral nations like India.[6] Mahathir's successor Badawi held fast to his mentor's view, which was shared by China. The Chinese Premier Wen Jiabao's comments that "the East Asia Summit should respect the desires of the East Asian countries and should be led only by East Asian countries," indicated China's inordinate ambition to play a dominant role in shaping the regional dynamics.[7] On the contrary, Japan advocated India's inclusion in the EAS because Japan firmly believed that India was "the only regional power that has potential to play the role of balancer, especially as China becomes dominant."[8]

In order to counter effectively China in the East Asian forum, Tokyo also wanted Australia and New Zealand to be included, and Japan's stand was shared by the ASEAN countries such as Singapore, Vietnam and Indonesia. When its plans to prevent the entry of India, Australia and New Zealand went awry, Beijing proposed the creation of a core group with ASEAN+3 within the EAS, which would "pilot the larger multilateral moves to create an East Asian Community for economic cooperation and strategic/security coordination."[9] But the consensus was that the East Asia Summit should not give rise to the so-called class differences between "ASEAN+3" AND "ASEAN+1". Malaysian Premier and the host of the Summit wisely declared that "the East Asian Summit together with the ASEAN+3 and the ASEAN+1 process could play a significant role in the process of community building in the region." Summit Declaration therefore, rightly emphasized the "principles of equality, partnership, consultation and consensus."[10]

China also sought to keep the US out of the EAS and succeeded initially in doing so the US did not figure among the founding fathers of the EAS. As Mohan Malik, a strategic analyst, pointed out, China's original idea was to establish an East Asian version of the SCO,[11] which was founded under the leadership of China in Shanghai 2001 to constrain the role of the US, which traditionally has been playing a key role in setting the agenda and shaping the goals for multilateral cooperation in the region. This being so, China's aggressive postures in the South China Sea, where Southeast Asian littoral states such as Malaysia, Brunei, Vietnam and the Philippines have been claiming certain islands, as well as in the East China Sea, where Japan laid claims on a cluster of small islands, and Beijing's sustained pressure on India regarding Kashmir and Arunachal Pradesh, have rattled the countries of the region. Southeast Asian countries accused China of being a bully.[12] The US intervened by declaring that it had a national interest in seeking territorial disputes in the South China Sea resolved, ensuring vital shipping lanes that remain open for everyone. China's highhanded behaviour, therefore, convinced the East Asian states that they should bring in the US to counter China. It may be noted that the Kuala Lumpur Declaration on the 1st East Asia Summit stated that the EAS "will be an open, inclusive, transparent and outward–looking forum". Accordingly, the fifth EAS held in Hanoi on October 30, 2010, invited the US, a long-standing "resident power" of the region, as well as Russia, an intimate neighbour of China, to join the EAS in 2011.

From India's point of view, the entry of the US and Russia into the EAS augurs well as New Delhi has been advocating an inclusive EAS so as to enable the stake holders in the region like the US and Russia to strengthen the region by being active. Further, India's relations with the US are on the high and Russia has been India's traditional friend and potential supplier of military hardware. India is also grateful to both the US and Russia for extending open support to India which has been aspiring to become a permanent member of the U.N. Security Council.

There was also a debate on the prospective leader of the EAS process – whether it would be ASEAN, or ASEAN+3 or all the members of the EAS. China came out openly with its preference for ASEAN+3 to drive the organization. Confident of its proposal being accepted by the other members of ASEAN+3, China even volunteered to host the second EAS. The ASEAN leaders, however, emphasised the need for ensuring the Association's "centrality" to an expanded EAS as well.[13] ASEAN wanted to remain the "political nucleus" of the EAS and to retain the control of this "geopolitical forum" because it did not want the East Asian grouping to get embroiled in power politics. In the end, the EAS declaration made no reference to any primary role for the ASEAN+3 in running the new forum.[14] The EAS declaration categorically stated that ASEAN would remain "the driving force" of the EAS. This meant that the EAS would be hosted and graced by the

ASEAN Chair and held back-to-back with the annual ASEAN summit.[15] Prime Minister Manmohan Singh appreciated the ASEAN initiative to convene the EAS, stressing that a "safe and experienced driver would take the forum to the destination".[16]

Even though India was invited to become a member of the EAS where it was considered an "equal member" alongside China, Japan, South Korea, Australia and New Zealand, the regional players, particularly Singapore, Thailand and Malaysia, were unhappy with India. This was largely due to India, having entered into a slew of pacts, agreements and FTAs, failed in matters of their implementation which was obvious in the poor follow up of the India-Thailand FTA and Comprehensive Economic Cooperation Agreement (CECA) with Singapore because of hurdles in the process of liberalization, like the dogmatic political parties and the nonchalant bureaucracy. ASEAN countries made a scathing attack on India for including strategically important items like oil and gas and trifles such as lavatory seats, dolls, and chewing gums in the 1414 "negative items list."[17]

Even though they were disappointed by India's slow pace of integration with the East Asian region, countries like Singapore and Indonesia had endorsed India's claim to the membership of the EAS so as to neutralise the growing Chinese influence. A perceptive Indian analyst remarked, "India must be aware that it has not been invited to EAS because of its rising economic potential alone but more as a balancing force to offset the China factor."[18] Similar sentiments were expressed by Indonesian diplomat Wiryono Sastrohandoyo: "We see the central problem as China. China is growing so fast and people are not sure of its intensions. It needs a balancer. That could be India, Australia and New Zealand at least economically."[19] Seen in this perspective, there was need for India's faster integration with the region and India's admission into the EAS has heightened this need, and hence the need for an analysis of India's role in realizing the EAS's goal of building a community in East Asia.

India's Contribution to building East Asian Architecture

India perceived the EAS as a platform for building regional architecture to widen and to deepen the regional cooperation and integration. Therefore, time and again India expressed its commitment to strengthen the EAS process. The stated objective of the EAS is to explore and to expand cooperation in a wide range of areas including political security, transport and communication, economy and investment, health, education and training, science and technology, and tourism and culture. Given the fact that India has made tremendous strides in all these areas and India's engagement of ASEAN and its multifaceted relationships with the ASEAN members states were yielding encouraging results, India was ideally placed to fortify EAS. Reflecting on India's engagement with the EAS, External Affairs Minister (EAM) Pranab Mukherjee told a gathering in Jakarta on June 18, 2007:

> India remains committed to further intensifying its relations with this region. The pursuit of regional economic integration, emphasis on South-South cooperation, promotion of societal links through cultural cooperation and educational exchanges, as well as an increased focus on security cooperation and countering threats to national security, will remain important pillars of our engagement with East Asia.[20]

Economic Cooperation

In India's engagement with East Asia, which is the home for three of the world's largest economies, economic cooperation is obviously a priority area. Quite appropriately, India, as a major economic power, seeks to impart greater impetus to its economic interaction with the region through trade and investment flows. India also encourages regional states to invest in India's various sectors, including infrastructure, steel, shipbuilding, hydrocarbon, energy resources, biotech and pharmaceuticals, to mention a few.

India's growing economic integration with East Asia is reflected in its trade with the region, which has registered an impressive growth. During 2005-2009, India's imports from East Asia rose by 215 per cent while exports increased by 117 per cent.[21] India's two-way trade with East Asian countries had crossed $ 80 billion in 2007, making the region India's largest trading partner ahead of the EU and the US. East Asia has also emerged as an important region for investment flows.[22] Of all the member countries of the EAS, it is with China that India's trade grew phenomenally despite their border row. During 2005-09, India's exports to China rose from $ 5 billon to $ 9 billon, whereas imports from China registered five fold rise from $ 7 billion to $ 32 billion.[23] Thus, the balance of trade is heavily in favour of China. During his talks with Premier Manmohan Singh in Hanoi on October 29, 2010, China's Prime Minister Wen Jiabao said, China was "very conscious" of the trade imbalance with India and listed some of the steps being taken by Beijing to address this issue.[24]

Even though India is the largest recipient of Japanese ODA, India-Japan bilateral trade is far short of potential. India-Japan bilateral trade is expected to touch $ 20 billion mark in 2010 while India-Korea bilateral trade goal of $ 30 billion is set to be realised well before the target date of 2014.[25]

In order to give big boost to India's trade relations with the East Asian countries, India has begun to enter into Comprehensive Economic Partnership Agreements (CEPA), CECAs and FTAs. India's FTA with ASEAN (limited to goods) became operational from January 1, 2010. Singapore enjoys the distinction of being the first country with which India concluded CECA. India-South Korea concluded a CECA, which became operationalised on January 1, 2010. The CECA negotiated by India and Malaysia in the shortest time possible, will come into force from July 2011. New Delhi is confident that similar agreements with Thailand and Indonesia are in the pipeline. Japan and India finalized a CEPA coinciding with Premier Manmohan Singh's visit to Japan in October 2010. Significantly, it is Tokyo's first-ever pact with a big economy. So far, Japan has not signed an economic pact with either the US, its long-standing ally, or with China, an immediate neighbour in the ascendant. It is an all embracing model agreement between a developed and a developing economy, which places both sides on "an equal footing."[26] Foreign Secretary Nirupama Rao termed the economic pact an alliance between Japanese technology and capital and a young Indian labour force.[27] As the former Premier of Singapore, Goh Chok Tong, has pointed out, the conclusion of a CECA with various East Asian countries would give mutually-beneficial partnerships "a strong boost". It would send a powerful signal to the international business community about India's commitment to economic liberalization. It would lay the foundation for enhanced links between India and East Asia.[28]

Yet another component of India's economic integration with the region is investments. Since the poor state of infrastructure acted as a disincentive to foreign investors in India, the Government of India (GOI), besides spending hundreds of billions of dollars to upgrade its infrastructure in terms of roads and highways, ports and airports, railways and shipping, has been inviting the East Asian nations such as Malaysia, Japan and South Korea, to invest in a big way in infrastructure projects. Seizing the opportunity, Japan, as a Japanese diplomat said, "decided to shift our aid programme to infrastructure rather than poverty alleviation."[29] The first action that the present Democratic party of Japan has taken soon after coming to power, was to kick off the $ 90 billion Delhi-Mumbai Industrial Corridor, which, when completed, would give India a state-of-the-art manufacturing and exporting base. Japanese firms, whose investments in India did not exceed Rs. 2000 crore a year, invested a hefty Rs. 9000 crore in 2007. Opinion polls indicated that 70 per cent of the Japanese firms said that India was their preferred investment destination.[30] Unlike Japan, which is chiefly interested in investing in India, Malaysia feels "the expansion of mutual investment will contribute to the reciprocal growth of both countries". During Prime Minister Manmohan Singh's visit to Malaysia in October 2010, both countries agreed to "further strengthen existing bilateral collaboration in infrastructure development and involvement in infrastructure projects."[31] Singapore encourages its nationals to invest in India, also expecting Indian companies to do so in Singapore. In 2007, there were well over 2500 Indian companies in Singapore forming the fourth largest foreign presence in that country.[32] South Korea's investments in the infrastructure and manufacturing sectors are expanding. The India-South Korea Joint Committee on Investment Promotion is designed to give a boost to South Korean investments in India and Indian investments in South Korea. South Korea's Steel major Posco has committed to invest $12 billion in an integrated plant in Orissa.

Several companies of the East Asian countries including South Korea, Indonesia and Singapore, expressed keenness in investing in Andhra Pradesh and also agreed to form a consortium comprising the state government and the public/private sector trade associations of these countries to facilitate the investment in infrastructure, manufacturing and food-processing sectors.[33]

Political Interaction

Sound political ties with the countries of the region go a long way in building the future architecture of the region. India, therefore, sought to develop friendly ties with all the nations of East Asia. India has been paying particular attention to promote its relations with Indonesia – a large pluralistic democracy like India in Asia-which have been crucial for India in developing ties with the other ASEAN countries. A new chapter in the bilateral relations of these two countries started in November 2005 when President Susilo Bambang Yudhoyono and Prime Minister Manmohan established a New Strategic Partnership and identified a range of areas of cooperation for mutual benefit. Demonstrating India's excellent relations with Indonesia, New Delhi invited President Yudhoyono to be the 'Chief Guest' of India's Republic Day Celebrations in January 2011.

India has assigned "a Special Position" to Singapore, which is among the earlier countries to acknowledge and appreciate India's reform. Singapore remains a "strong partner" and an "enthusiastic advocate" of India. Meeting on the occasion of the 17th ASEAN Summit in Hanoi in October 2010, Singapore Prime Minister Lee Hsien Loong and Prime Minister Manmohan Singh reaffirmed 'the excellent state of relations between their countries'. Prime Minister Lee congratulated his Indian counterpart on India's successful hosting of the 2010 Commonwealth Games.[34] Exchange of high level visits is the defining feature of expanding India-Malaysia bilateral relations. While Malaysian Premier Abdul Razak paid an official visit to India in January 2010, Premier Singh returned the visit in October 2010 when both leaders issued a 'Joint Statement on the Framework for the Malaysia-India Strategic Partnership'. On this occasion, Premier Razak described himself as a great admirer of Manmohan Singh for "transforming India into an economic powerhouse."[35]

India's political ties with South Korea and Japan, which are on the fast track, deserve special mention. India-South Korea bilateral ties based on the "long-term Cooperative Partnership for peace and prosperity", established in 2004, are witnessing healthy development. There is "steady growth" in high level exchanges and contacts between the two countries. Suffice it to mention that the President of South Korea, Lee Myung-bak, was the "Chief Guest" at the celebrations to mark the Republic Day of India on January 26, 2010. The India-Japan strategic and global partnership, launched in 2006, symbolised the transformation of relations between the second and the third largest economies of Asia. Prime Minister Manmohan Singh's high profile visit to Japan in October 2010 greatly boosted the bilateral ties. Dung this visit, India made a fine gesture by offering to supply rare earth minerals which were denied by Japan's traditional supplier, China. In the joint statement 'Vision for India-Japan Strategic and Global Partnership in the Next Decade' issued in Tokyo on October 25, 2010, the two Prime Ministers expressed confidence that their bilateral cooperation would contribute to "sustained peace and prosperity in a changing and dynamic Asia and the world".[36]

Even though India's relations with China are not trouble free, India has established "Strategic and Cooperative Partnership for Peace and Prosperity" with China. The President of India paid an official visit to China in May 2010. New Delhi has been striving to have good working relations with its largest neighbour. Beijing too reverted from its new found 'frown' diplomacy to the 'smile' diplomacy. Meeting on the sidelines of EAS in Hanoi on October 30, 2010, Chinese Premier Wen was all praise for Prime Minister Manmohan Singh's "sagacity and wisdom."[37] Premier Wen also recalled an earlier statement by the Indian Prime Minister that there was enough space in the world for both countries to realise their development aspirations, and added that there was enough scope also for China and India to have cooperation in all areas. The meeting between the two leaders was also viewed by the strategic analysts as a positive development which "set the stage for the two countries to work at addressing a trust gap that has developed in recent months".[38]

India's summit level dialogues and a web of economic pacts with the regional powers underscore New Delhi's comfort level in the East Asian region.

Defence and Military Cooperation

India, which has been associating itself with security promotion initiatives in various parts of the world, believes that it has a vital role to play in building the security architecture in the East Asian region. At a time when the region's economic and political clout is rapidly growing, the regional states are confronted with the security problem of ensuring power equilibrium. In this situation, the East Asian countries are driven to make security arrangements with the powers within the region and outside. Thus, India and Japan concluded a security agreement in October 2009, which was described "as a significant milestone in building Asian power stability."[39] The expanding defence cooperation between India and Japan is reflected in the growing number of bilateral visits by top defence and military officials.[40] During Indian Premier's visit to Japan in October 2010, further discussions were held on expanding defence and security cooperation under a defence framework agreement signed earlier.[41] Significantly, there is political unanimity in Japan in developing closer security ties with India. Pointers to that are the two rounds of talks and increasing frequency of joint military exercises, and the first round of 2+2 talks (involving the Defence and Foreign Secretaries).[42]

India maintains dialogue and exchanges with South Korea in the area of defence through regular high level military exchanges. Both are also exploring the possibilities of joint venture cooperation in R&D, and manufacture of military equipment including transfer of technology and co-production. Both countries feel the necessity of greater cooperation between the navies and coast guards in areas pertaining to the safety and security of international maritime traffic. In a joint statement issued during the visit of the President of South Korea to India in January 2010, both the countries shared the view that "developing long-term cooperation relations in the realm of security and defence will contribute to peace and stability in the Asia-Pacific region."[43]

India's defence ties with Malaysia, Singapore and Indonesia are steadily growing. India is participating in the comprehensive mechanism on the Straits of Malacca and Singapore for enhancing navigational safety and environmental protection.[44] In 2010, three Indian Navy ships visited Malaysia and one ship touched ports in Indonesia, Singapore and Brunei as part of India's maritime diplomacy. Along with other Southeast Asian countries, Malaysia has been participating in the Indian Navy-hosted "Milan" exercises off Andaman and Nicobar Islands.[45]

Even with China, whose aggressive postures have alarmed India and the other nations of East Asia, India has been cultivating defence cooperation. Flag meetings and border interactions are going on. However, high level defence exchanges have been put on "pause" after a senior Indian officer was offered a stapled visa by China. Nonetheless, China has been repeatedly requesting India to resume the full range of defence exchanges.[46]

Developmental Programmes

Prompted by a firm belief in sharing its developmental experiences with its fellow developing countries in the East Asian region, India participated in development cooperation programmes. India's active association with the "Initiative for ASEAN Integration" programme, specially designed to speed up the economic development of the less developed countries such as CLMV countries (Cambodia, Laos, Myanmar and Vietnam), deserve particular mention. India sharpened its focus on human resource development through training, scholarships, and establishment of entrepreneurship development centres.[47] It is heartening to note that India's ITEC (Indian Technical and Economic Cooperation) programme and IT Centres particularly in the CLMV countries, are highly popular. The East Asian states are fully utilizing ITEC slots offered by India every year for training experts. All these initiatives are directly contributing to the realisation of the cherished ambition of the EAS leaders. Chairman's Statement of the First East Asia Summit read thus. "We agreed to deepen integration and cooperation in order to promote the creation of a harmonious and prosperous community of nations."[48]

Climate Change

As a responsible member of the global community, India is willing to make a contribution to mitigate the impact of climate change. India and Japan are jointly working on the project of clean coal technologies. At the 2009 Copenhagen negotiations on climate change, India and China were together. They are once again working together on their strategy for 2010 Cancun negotiations, "despite all the bad blood over China's aggression over visa issue and Indian ire over the border."[49] India has offered its expertise (in increasing the share of clean and renewable energy in its energy mix) with the East Asian nations.[50]

Combating Terrorism

As a country that is the worst victim of international terrorism, India is keen to extend all possible assistance to the countries of the East Asian region to curb terrorism. India and ASEAN issued a "Joint Declaration for Cooperation to Combat International Terrorism" in Bali on October 8, 2003.[51] India and Japan agreed "to enhance greater cooperation in combating terrorism through information sharing and counter terrorism training."[52] India and Myanmar are working in close cooperation in tackling the "pernicious problem" of terrorism. They resolved not to allow their respective territory to be used for "training, sanctuary and other operations by terrorist and insurgent organizations and their operatives."[53]

Disaster Management

Disaster Management is yet another area which allows much scope for India to work with the East Asian countries. In view of India's rich experience in remote sensing satellites, the Chinese hoped to benefit from cooperation on disaster monitoring satellite constellation. China also expressed keen interest in jointly working with India on developing a constellation of Chinese radar satellites specially for disaster warning, monitoring and management.[54] The high tech 24/7 Tsunami Warning Centre was set up in the Indian National Centre for Ocean Information Services (INCOIS) in Hyderabad in 2008 to share "timely and accurate" tsunami-related data with 22 Asian countries.[55] India was among the first countries to rush emergency relief assistance to Myanmar in the aftermath of cyclone Nargis in 2008. India's timely help to mitigate the sufferings of the Myanmarese affected by cyclone Nargis and the tsunami-affected Southeast Asian countries, in particular Indonesia, in 2004, was universally acclaimed.

Energy Security

Energy is the prime mover of economic growth. Sadly, India's domestic supply of energy is not keeping pace with the ever growing demand for the energy of India's galloping economy. India is the third largest consumer of energy in the region, the other two being China and Japan. Therefore, there is enough room for cooperation and coordination in addressing the problem of energy security effectively. In this regard, certain interesting proposals were put forward by India for the consideration of the East Asian countries, as part of Asian energy cooperation: building an Asian strategic petroleum reserve (ASPR); the creation of an Asian energy response system; joint exploration or oil equity sharing by the oil companies of China, Japan, India and South Korea in third countries, joint patrolling of the sea-lanes, especially Malacca Straits through which the bulk of the oil and gas supplies pass for the region; building an Asian gas/oil pipeline connecting the JACIK countries.[56] These proposals could not take shape in an atmosphere charged with trust deficit.

Meanwhile, regional states have been making their own bilateral and multilateral arrangements to meet the challenge of energy security. India, for its part, is seeking to gradually switch over to cheap, clean and eco-friendly renewable sources of energy, such as solar energy and wind energy from non-renewable and depleting sources of energy. In order to deploy 20,000 mw of solar power by 2022, India launched an ambitious solar mission in January 2010.[57] Demonstrating its passion for renewable energy, India organised a three-day Delhi International Renewable Energy Conference (DIREC) in October 2010 in which, among others, China took active part.[58] In tapping renewable energy sources, India, while offering its expertise to the East Asian nations, wants to benefit by their expertise. In fact, the Chairman's statement of the first EAS had underlined the need for "cooperation in the energy field including development of fuel efficient technologies and alternative energy sources." India could benefit by the expertise of China, which leads the world in manufacturing capacity of solar, wind and biogas renewable energy, investing about $ 35 billion in renewable energy in 2009, a figure that puts it ahead of the US.[59] EAS countries such as India, Japan, China, the Philippines and Indonesia evinced keen interest in 'gasohol', which Thailand has been making efforts to provide for long time.[60] Addressing the challenge of energy security, the EAS had set up "work streams". While Japan, Malaysia, and Thailand were jointly making studies on energy efficiency and conservation, the Philippines and India were piloting the evaluation of the bio-fuel sector, and

Singapore and Australia were consolidating a study on energy market integration within the EAS region.[61] Quest for sources of energy has the potential to threaten peace and security in the region. In view of the rich oil and gas reserves in the South China Sea and the East China Sea, there are conflicting claims over the islands between China on the one hand and countries like Malaysia, Brunei, Vietnam, the Philippines and Japan on the other. Unless the countries concerned settled the issue in a friendly and cooperative spirit, the realisation of an East Asia Community will be nothing but a mirage.

Civil Nuclear Energy

In order to narrow the gap between demand and supply of energy within the country, India pins hopes on civil nuclear energy. For effective implementation of its ambitious nuclear energy programme, India needs to share technology and know-how with the East Asian countries such as Japan and South Korea. Japan, which refused earlier to cooperate with India in this area on the ground that India has not signed NPT, has of late agreed to have a dialogue in this regard. The joint declaration released at the end of Premier Singh's visit to Japan in October 2010 read thus: "The two Prime Ministers reaffirmed that cooperation in this (civil nuclear) sector will open opportunities for developing the India – Japan strategic and global partnership. They encouraged their negotiators to arrive at a mutually satisfactory agreement for civil nuclear cooperation at an early date". A top Japanese official said that Tokyo's decision to begin civil nuclear talks with New Delhi was largely influenced by Japan's recognition of India's "importance".[62] While India and Japan are still in the stage of holding dialogue on nuclear cooperation deal, India and South Korea have clinched a deal on civil nuclear cooperation. South Korea becomes the ninth country to sign the nuclear agreement after New Delhi got the waiver form the NSG in 2008. The other eight are the US, Russia, France, Canada, Mongolia, Kazakhstan, Argentina and Namibia.

Cultural Cooperation

Given India's long standing historical and cultural ties with the region, cultural cooperation is another area of promise for promoting regional integration. Prime Minister P. V. Narasimha Rao, the architect of India's 'Look East Policy', in his famous Singapore lecture on September 8, 1994 stated:

> While India has been observing the Asia-Pacific drama objectively, we cannot ignore the fact that our civilizations are organically linked to those which have founded so many of the nation states of East and Southeast Asia. The evidence lies in the temples of Java, Indochina and Thailand, in the manifestations of the great religions of Buddhism and Hinduism that spread across this vast continent, and more aptly today, in the physical origin of ASEAN and other countries of the Asia-Pacific region. In these communities living here in peace with other, we have a true example of the Asian symbiosis.[63]

Therefore, if a new relationship is to be forged in the region it needs to be created on the solid foundation of cultural bonds that already exist in East Asia. India's interaction with the East Asian nations, therefore, has cultural dimension among others.

On October 25, 2010, Sri Sri Ravishankar, an Indian spiritual leader, opened a retreat for yoga and meditation courses in the suburbs of Beijing to "provide people a path to have clearer, calmer and happier lives". Presenting Chinese perception of the retreat, Chen Haosu, President of the Chinese People's Association for Friendship with Foreign Countries (CPACF), which invited Sri Sri to China, said: "We hope this will bring happiness to people. Chinese people have an enthusiasm and passion for Indian culture. In the past 30 years, we have seen fast development of the Chinese economy. Now people will also require more spiritual activities".[64]

As part of its temple diplomacy, India is offering its services for renovation/ conservation of ancient magnificent temples in East Asia built by dynasties that had links with India. An Archaeological Survey of India (ASI) team was involved in conserving the Ta Phrom temple in Cambodia's world renowned Angkor Wat Complex and another Cambodia's 11th century temple, Preah Vihar.[65] Myanmar's Military dictator, Than Shwe, during his visit to India in July 2010, acknowledged officially the marvellous job of restoration of Myanmar's historic Ananda Temple by India. Recognizing the need for further strengthening cultural exchanges and people-to-people contacts, South Korea and India designated the year 2011as 'Year of Korea' in India and 'Year of India' in South Korea.[66]

The crowning glory of the EAS is its decision to revive Nalanda University, "the ancient seat of learning," The former President of India, Abdul Kalam, put forward the Nalanda proposal and it gained concrete shape when the government of Bihar and the GOI gave legislative sanction providing "a legal basis for going ahead with the implementation of the project."[67] However, credit goes to the EAS for initiating the Nalanda project. At the fourth EAS held in Hua Hin in Thailand in October 2009, the leaders "endorsed and extended their support" for setting up Nalanda University as "an international institution of excellence in education with a continental focus."[68] In fact, the EAS leaders issued a separate Joint Statement in this regard. Private donors and the governments of the East Asia region are expected to offer necessary funds to meet the estimated cost of Rs. 1005 crores of the Nalanda project. While the GOI made available Rs. 50 crores to set in motion the Nalanda project, the Bihar government offered 500 acres of land.

The chief objective of the Nalanda project, as the Minister of Information and Broadcasting Ambika Soni said, is "to facilitate the revival of Nalanda as a centre of excellence in East Asia and South Asia reflecting the role played by the

University in ancient times".[69] It is hoped that the University would contribute to the promotion of regional peace and vision by bringing the future leaders of East Asia together and by relating them to their past which could enhance their understanding of the perspectives of each other and enable them to share that understanding globally.[70] The University would promote study and research in disciplines such as philosophy, language, history and other areas of higher learning. True to its international character, the University would draw faculty as well as students from the global pool. While welcoming India's initiative to revive Nalanda University, Japanese Premier Kan expressed "Japan's continued support to this initiative which will strengthen the cultural and civilisational bands between the countries of Asia".[71]

Gratified by the East Asian countries' "strong desire to substantially strengthen their links with India in all areas," Premier Manmohan Singh proposed that India and the East Asian countries could jointly organize a commemorative expedition in 2011-12 on the sea routes, developed during the 10th to 12th centuries to link India with East Asia.[72] Elaborating on this proposed event former Foreign Secretary (East) Ravi Said:

> In the 10th to 12th centuries India did trade with Southeast Asian countries, and some of the Indian traders guilds were established even in East Asia. So, an effort would be made to commemorate that during the 2012 event by which ships can touch these ports, which were trading ports in the olden days, and also the modern ports that must be near those old ports wherever these ports exist. Historical records exit as to where the old ports were and the new ports are at places where we know they exist. So, a kind of voyage is being planned.[73]

Singapore, which was considered by India as a "window" to the countries in East Asia, has not missed any opportunity to highlight India's accomplishments in its glorious past in East Asia as part of its cultural diplomacy. Singapore played a benign role in promoting Nalanda project, basically "a part of an East Asia Summit initiative". Singapore Foreign Ministry said in a statement that the ancient Nalanda University was preeminent for several centuries and, at its peak, hosted 10,000 students from all over the world.[74] In fact, it was Singapore which came up, as far back as in 2006, with the "Nalanda Proposal" according to which Nalanda would be the "ideal site" for establishing a 21st century learning institution linking South and East Asia. Singapore Foreign Minister George Yeo has been serving as a member of 'Nalanda Mentor Group' (NMG) which, headed by Nobel Laureate Amartya Sen, has successfully completed its mission of designing the institutional framework of the proposed Nalanda University. Singapore is also the home for 'Nalanda Sriwijaya Centre' set up at the Institute of Southeast Asian Studies in 2009. The Chief objectives of the Centre are:

1. "To develop the 'Nalanda idea' of fostering Asian connectivities" and

cross-cultural influences as well as the 'Sriwijaya idea' of Southeast Asia as a place of mediation and linkages among the great civilizations.

2. To promote and develop research skills needed to understand the civilizations of Asia and their interrelationships.
3. To build regional research capabilities and infrastructure for the study of the historical interactions among the civilizations and societies of Asia."[75]

As part of its programme of publication of research results, the Centre has brought out *Nagapattinam to Suvarnadwipa: Reflections on the Chola Naval Expeditions to Southeast Asia.* Singapore's close association with the Nalanda Project and the establishment of research bodies to unravel the dynamics of India's intimate association with East Asia in the past and the joint press statement of the 4th East Asia Summit on the revival of Nalanda University, reinforce the view that India is culturally an inalienable partner of East Asia.

Infrastructure Development

India has also been playing a commendable role in areas like infrastructure development, tourism, and health. Besides inviting the East Asian countries to invest in India's infrastructure development, New Delhi has been making its own contribution for improving transport and communications in the region by which India also would benefit along with the regional states. Kaladan Multi-Modal Transit Transport Project, which was formally launched in 2008 and will be completed in 2013 as per schedule, "envisages connectivity between Indian ports on the eastern seaboard and Sittwe Port in Myanmar and then through riverine transport and by road to Mizoram." GOI is also extending assistance to infrastructure projects such as Tamu-Kalewa-Kalemyo and Rhi-Tidim road projects, Trilateral Highway between India Myanmar and Thailand, besides supplying locomotives and constructing transmission lines.[76] As Prime Minister Manmohan Singh has pointed out, these initiatives and the India – ASEAN Car Rally in 2004, which covered ten countries before being terminated in Indonesia, would bring India and the East Asian countries "closer – physically and virtually – and create the necessary linkages" which would "further bind our countries together."[77]

Tourism

Tourism, besides promoting understanding and cultural bonds among the peoples of the countries of the region, serves as a money spinner. On October 27, 2010, India and Malaysia concluded an MOU for cooperation in tourism which would encourage the growing flow of visitors to both countries. Interestingly, India is the sixth largest source country for inbound tourism to Malaysia, while Malaysia is the tenth largest source country to India.[78] Tourism traffic between India and Singapore has been "growing steadily". EAM Krishna, during his visit to Singapore in March 2010, expressed the hope that 'visa on arrival' scheme for Singapore nationals coming to India "will prove popular."[79] Following the signing of an MOU by India and Japan, Tokyo is expecting a spurt in the number of Indian visitors.[80]

Health

India, which has made rapid strides in combating HIV/AIDS, malaria and other diseases, has a lot to offer to the East Asian countries in the health sector. In October 2010, India and Malaysia concluded an MOU on cooperation in the traditional systems of medicine which made India the second country with which Malaysia has inked such a pact.

Conclusion

India, an acknowledged regional and global power, was invited to join the EAS as a founder member and to strengthen the process of the EAS by promoting the principles, objectives and priorities of the East Asian forum. In fact, India's engagement of East Asia in a serious way could be traced to the beginnings of Indian association with the ASEAN process in 1992 as a Sectoral Dialogue Partner from which New Delhi subsequently graduated as a Full Dialogue Partner in 1995 and Summit Dialogue Partner in 2002. Therefore, India's association with the EAS, by all means, represented a new opportunity for New Delhi to engage East Asia. India more than lived up to the expectations of the East Asian nations by taking its interaction with the region to new heights thanks to its emergence as a major economic power. The Indian Prime Minister's frequent high profile visits to the countries of East Asia, which were returned by the leaders of these countries, speak of growing cordiality and warmth in India's relations with the region. Comprehensive Economic Partnership Agreement with Japan, Comprehensive Economic Cooperation Agreement with Malaysia and similar arrangements with Thailand and Indonesia in the pipeline, security cooperation and cooperation in a host of other realms symbolise new dynamism India has imparted to the process of its engagement of East Asia on a win-win basis.

Even though it was heard in many a quarter that India's entry into EAS was designed to counter China, India did not subscribe to such a view because New Delhi, which believes that the need of the hour is to shun rivalries, is committed to promote peace, prosperity and stability in the East Asian region as a prelude to developing a continent-wide regional architecture. This is particularly so at a time of mounting tensions among the major players of this region such as China, Japan and South Korea and the region-wide concern as to how to manage with China's "rapid rise." During his visit to India in early November 2010, President Obama told India not merely to "Look East," but to "Engage East" so as to promote security and prosperity in the region. India has been very much engrossed in the task of promoting regional development, prosperity and security for a long time. India perceives its strategic partnership with East Asia – a region emerging as "the next big theatre in global affairs"[81] – as one of the defining relationships of the 21st century.

ENDNOTES

1. Jim O' Neil, "Dreaming with BRICs: The path to 2050," Global Economics Paper No. 99, https:// www.gs.com.
2. For an excellent account of the origin and growth of the concept of EAS, see S.D. Muni, "East Asia Summit and India," *ISASS Working Paper* (Singapore), October 3, 2006.
3. *Ibid.*
4. Jusuf Wanandi, "The need and the challenge for an East Asian Multilateral Regional Institution", *Asian Affairs* (Hong Kong), No. 26, 2005.
5. "Kuala Lumpur Declaration on the 1st East Asia Summit" Kuala Lumpur, December 14, 2005, www.mea.gov.in/declarestatement/2005/12/14jd02.htm.
6. Jehangir S. Pocha, "A Continent Divided," *Business World* (New Delhi) January 2, 2006.
7. Mohan Malik, "East Asia summit," *Australian Journal of International Affairs,* June 2006, p. 208.
8. Pranay Sharma, "Eastward Ho", *Outlook*, October 25, 2010 p. 32.
9. P.S. Suryanarayana, "For an East Asian Umbrella," *Frontline*, August 26, 2005, p. 60.
10. D.S. Rajan and Raakhee Suryaprakash, "East Asian Summit-An Appraisal," ISAS *Insights* (Singapore), No. 10, December 30, 2005.
11. Malik n. p. 7, p. 210.
12. Tini Tran, "ASEAN to bring in US to counter China", *Deccan Chronicle*, October 30, 2010. Also see Philip Bowring, "Postcard from Hanoi : G-2 is a terrible idea," *Ibid*, November 3, 2010.
13. *The Hindu*, October 28, 2010.
14. *Ibid*, December 16, 2005.
15. *Ibid*, December 15, 2005.
16. *Ibid.*
17. Pocha, n. 6.
18. C.S. Kuppuswamy, "India's Look East Policy: More aggressive Better Dividends," http://www.saag.org/0/05Cpapers17%5Cpaper. 1663.html).
19. *Ibid.*
20. http://meaindia.nic.in/pressrelease/2007/06/18/pr.03.htm.
21. Department of Commerce, Ministry of Commerce and Industries, Government of India, http://commerce.nic.in/edib/default.asp.
22. *The Hindu* November 13, 2007.
23. *Ibid.*
24. *Ibid*, October 30, 2010.
25. *Strategic Digest*, July 2010, p. 757.
26. P.S. Suryanaryana, "New Economic Idiom in Look East Policy," *The Hindu*, October 26, 2010.
27. *Ibid.*

28. *New Asia Monitor* (RIS, New Delhi), October 2004, p. 3.
29. Pramit Pal Chaudhuri, "Why Japan wants to be friends with India" http://www.hindustantimes.com/why-Japan-tilted-towards-India/Article-617444.aspx
30. *Ibid.*
31. "Joint Statement on the Framework for the Malaysia – India Strategic Partnership," http//www.kin.gov./my/web/guest/home?ppid=101-Instance-yto6xp-p-lifecycle=oesp-p-state=normal&p-p-mode=view&p-p-col-id=c)
32. *Strategic Digest*, July 2007, p. 923.
33. *The Hindu*, November 9, 2010.
34. www.app.mfa.govsg./.../view-press-print.as...
35. www.thaindian.com/.../India-Malaysia-annou...
36. See "Joint statement: Vision for India-Japan Strategic and Global Partnership in the Next Decade, October 25, 2010," http://www.mea.gov.in.
37. Neena Gopal, "India rises in East in China's shadow," *Deccan Chronicle*, October 31, 2010.
38. Editorial, "Looking East, Properly", *The Hindu*, November 5, 2010.
39. Brahma Chellaney, "Powering a dynamic, Multipolar Asia," *Ibid*, December 30, 2009.
40. *Ibid.*
41. India-Japan Joint Statement, n. 36.
42. *The Hindu*, October 25, 2010.
43. "India-Republic of Korea Joint Statement: Towards a Strategic Partnership," *Strategic Digest*, February 2010, pp. 191-195.
44. *The Hindu*, October 27, 2010.
45. *Ibid*, October 28, 2010.
46. *Ibid*, October 25, 2010.
47. *Strategic Digest,* February 2010 p. 173.
48. http://www.aseansec.org/18104.htm.
49. Suhasini Haider, "The great subcontinental green game," *The Hindu*, November 1, 2010.
50. *Strategic Digest*, October2010, p. 927.
51. http://www.aseansec.org/15276.htm
52. India-Japan Joint statement, n. 36.
53. *Strategic Digest*, October 2010, p. 989.
54. *The New Indian Express*, September 25, 2007.
55. *The Hindu*, May 9, 2008.
56. Nagesh Kumar, *To wards a broader Asian community: Agenda for the East Asia summit*, (RIS, New Delhi November 2005, p.13).
57. *Strategic Digest*, September 2010, p. 866.
58. *The Hindu*, October 27, 2010.
59. Suhasini, n.49.
60. Muni, n.2, p. 27.
61. *The Hindu,* July 23, 2008.
62. Suryanarayana, n.26.
63. For text of Premier Rao's speech, see *Strategic Digest*, October 1994, pp.1411-18.
64. *The Hindu*, October 27, 2010.
65. *Deccan Chronicle*, November 20, 2007.
66. *Strategic Digest*, February 2010, p. 193.

67. For a scintillating account of the project of revival of Nalanda University, see N. Ravi, "Look East Policy-Millennium apart," *The Hindu*, October 07, 2010.
68. *Strategic Digest*, November 2009, p. 1225.
69. *The New Indian Express,* July 9, 2010.
70. *Deccan Chronicle* August 13, 2010.
71. India-Japan Joint statement, n. 36.
72. *Strategic Digest*, November 2009, p. 1226.
73. *Ibid*, p. 1233.
74. *The Hindu*, August 01, 2010.
75. http://www.iseas.edu.sg./nic
76. *Strategic Digest*, October 2010, pp. 976 & 989.
77. *New Asia Monitor*, (RIS, New Delhi), October 2004.
78. *The Hindu*, October 28, 2010.
79. *Strategic Digest,* April 2010, p. 434.
80. *The Hindu*, October 26, 2010.
81. P. S. Suryanarayana, "Islands of tension," *Frontline*, December 3, 2010, p.61.

9

Indonesia and the New Regional Dynamics

Hariyadi Wirawan

As most of the Cold War's dust has generally settled down in Asia, a new kind of 'war' seems once again to rage in some parts of East Asia (including Southeast Asia) and in other parts of the region of the continent in a much milder form. This may produce an impression that the situation is very much in control. Underneath that seemingly quiet environment might in fact lurk an outburst of tensions and even conflicts as bigger powers are being bogged down by smaller players of the region in an attempt to enhance their political bargains.

Being one of the most dynamic regions, East Asia really deserves more meticulous observation as the one-time regional politico-military hot spot to become one of the most strategic, economic, as well as significant trading hub of the world. Indonesia, as one of the players in the region, has found itself in the midst of an intriguing and challenging, Southeast Asian regionalism. Association of Southeast Asian Nations (ASEAN), which initially was an attempt to move away from intense and delicate political conflicts in the region during the Vietnam War, has moved on to become a more open and inclusive group embracing multilateralism. It is, therefore, much clearer for Indonesia to start moving forward with so much anticipation about passing the new turbulence at the very point of the crossroads.

Multilateralism in the Asia-Pacific Region

One of the most well-known sub-regional institutions in the Asia–Pacific, which emerged during the height of Cold War, is ASEAN. Starting with only five Southeast Asian countries, namely Indonesia, Malaysia, the Philippines, Singapore, and Thailand, ASEAN was initially meant to dispel any communist threat through a two-pronged approach, one was carried out by military means in Vietnam War, and the other front was economic development.

Apart from several existing internal technical difficulties, ASEAN, however, enjoys a relatively stable unity. By asserting its rejection of any military affiliation, ASEAN has established itself as one of the most durable institutions in one of the most volatile regions in post-Cold War East Asia. And it was clear from the very beginning that the persistence of US economic backing to some of countries, considered as the weakest chain of member states, has enabled ASEAN to pass through one of the most difficult tests, during which conflicting ideologies ragged up the area. China and the Soviet Union had tried to exercise their powers to exert influences over the least developed countries, whilst the US had tried very hard to contain, through military means, any possible intrusion that might reduce its presence and influence in the area.

With the end of Vietnam War, ASEAN adopted some moderation in outlook by pursuing a more peaceful approach. By doing this, ASEAN expects to achieve a wide spectrum of cooperation that may lead to regional stability. In pursuing new security concepts, ASEAN, which has such diversity interests was looking for a new cooperative security that could be accepted by most parties of the region.

The absence of any more conflict in Southeast Asia, especially after the agreement of the Cambodia peace deal, had reaffirmed to ASEAN leadership the importance of *widening*, as well as *deepening* process of the organization. The China-Vietnam proxy war had also convinced leaders of ASEAN to engage an even wider cooperation in order to have a greater base for a solid and yet workable multilateralism. The wind of change in socialist countries in Asia provided the best opportunity for ASEAN to widen its cooperation, notably the shifting of approaches, from putting emphasis on largely economic dimension towards a security multilateralism.

With the rise of several regional powers in East Asia, notably China and South Korea, along with long-standing older players like Japan, ASEAN has asserted itself to climb up the ladder of a security arrangement that would make ASEAN able to take part in any security matter in the region. The increase of self-confidence amongst ASEAN leaders had assured themselves in getting all South-east Asian countries coming in to its fold, with the expansion of all ten sub-regional states on to ASEAN. Then the process of deepening has practically begun.

The acknowledgement of a real challenge of outward threats as well as the existing problems from within had inspired ASEAN to establish the ASEAN Regional Forum (ARF) whose task is to manage any eventuality in the regional security affairs, based on accepted norms of ASEAN, i.e. non-interference in the internal affairs of member states. Although the ARF has a strong legality and direct backing of ASEAN leaders, hence, security matters that evolved during much of its existence were largely being directly dealt with by the leaders of ASEAN (the then Indonesia's Suharto, Malaysia's Mahathir Mohammad, Philippine's Ferdinand

Marcos, and Singapore's Lee Kuan Yew). So, although the ARF may still be playing some role in certain cases, with the advent of a more challenging environment, it is still far from being a powerful body.

Region's Power Politics

The world has witnessed one of the most significant phenomena in Asia with the rising of some of its developing countries, such as India and China. And for many reasons, the rise of China has presented a lot of concerns due to its tremendous economic performance. At the same time, having been successful in reducing its ever-boiled relations with Pakistan, India has also come to the picture of becoming one of the most significant players in Asia, in economic as well as in political fields.

With the US busy tackling terrorism and Europe in economic downturn, it is logical for countries that sustain economic turmoil to come up with a more ambitious agenda. ASEAN, on the other hand, was also experiencing a sense of losing direction, primarily after the absence of previous strong leaders. The new wave of democratization of Southeast Asia has led countries in the region to give more attention to domestic matters, and has found themselves providing more focus to extra regional bilateral relations than the other way around. That has caused an immense pressure for ASEAN countries to take sides. And when the pressures from bigger states become stronger, then division of the institution's priorities was inevitable.

Having no specific common platform for more industrialized three East Asian countries (China, Japan, and South Korea) to interact directly, the Trio came up with the concept of expanded regionalism covering all ASEAN states and the Trio is known as ASEAN+3. This 13 countries would provide a perfect synergy for producer's North and consumer's South, in the sense that the Trio would symbolically become providers of technology and capital, whilst ASEAN would basically the provider of natural resources and labor. Although that symbolical division of labor does not go along a strict line, this would surely invite other players to take part.

The more assertive China and the waning of US presence in the region have prompted other regional powers to counterweight. Japan has always been trying to check China's build up through other measures. The configuration that has been set up for new alignment in East Asia is considered too dear for Japan. With a fragmented ASEAN, Japan would work up bilateral pressure on ASEAN countries in trying to avoid China domination. In 2002, for example, under the direction of China, a proposal of an East Asian free trade agreement was adopted. The 10+3 countries agreed to the proposal was spearheaded by China to prepare a blue print of East Asian Community. And with this, a new multilateralism which covers all eastern flank of Asia seemed set to be operational.

The seed of the regional flashpoint lies in the weakening of ASEAN cohesion and conflicting political interests within the grouping that have led countries like the US, Japan, and India to lose patience. Restless developments in many of ASEAN countries have cast doubts on ASEAN's ability to actually lead multilateral institutions. Japanese and American leaders were almost convinced, therefore, that China has succeeded in putting pressure on ASEAN, and at the same time, managed to play one or another with the US and Japan as is the case of North Korea and Myanmar. Moreover, China has shrewdly convinced ASEAN, that the grouping should be at the driver's seat on East Asian regionalism.

That framework, finally, has to give in. At the 13th ASEAN Summit, it was clear that 10+3 framework will no longer be used as the main vehicle, instead at 3rd East Asian Summit, it was agreed to adopt Japan's proposal to include Australia, New Zealand, and India. With the strong backing of the US, Japan has finally succeeded in breaking up the awkward cohesion of East Asia by taking in extra regional countries to its fold.

Indonesia: Responses and Challenges

It is openly acknowledged, that Indonesia favored the expansion of the ASEAN, but has been ignoring the current process of deepening of East Asian community. No one, however, has clearly come up with a straightforward answer as to why Indonesia has opted to take a U-turn on this issue.

The most plausible answer to this question can actually be traced to several reasons. *Firstly*, though Indonesia, maintains a strong bond with China, there are, however, genuine fears among economic decision makers in Jakarta, that it is being dominated by imports, especially consumer goods, from China. China's leadership in an extended regionalism would be catastrophic to Indonesia's economy which is relying on its oil and gas export to China. *Secondly*, Indonesia has long suspected that Malaysia would come as second in command if the formation of East Asian community should materialize. Malaysia has been endorsing, since the years of Prime Minister Mahathir Mohammad, a limited East Asian regionalism in the Asia-Pacific by excluding the US, which many believed had got strong endorsement from Beijing, something that would make China grateful to Malaysia. Judging from the current strained relations between Jakarta and Kuala Lumpur, people may see the logic behind it. *Thirdly*, with an array of massive support to fight home grown terrorism from western countries, notably the US and Australia, along with the fact of Indonesian leader's closeness to the US, it is not difficult to anticipate the response of Indonesia's decision makers when asked to put priorities of Indonesia-the West on top of the list.

At the state level, it is obvious that the prospect of Indonesia being looked down by even other regional member states within ASEAN, not to mention bigger players, is set to be seen. Efforts by the Indonesian government, for example, to mediate in Thailand-Cambodia border tensions had been coldly responded by both parties, something that would not have happened during Suharto era. From the very beginning of the inception of the 10+3, Indonesia was worrying about losing its strategic importance to its competitors, such as Malaysia and Thailand. Indonesia was so concerned that the 10+3 concept might be reversed into '3+10' if China, Japan, and South Korea could finally find their common platform through other means and ways. That would be disastrous to Indonesia's national interests, since most of economic indicators would prefer Malaysia and Thailand, or even Vietnam to be the main partners of the Trio, and Indonesia would be left as simply secondary.

Under the existing scenario, Indonesia seemingly has to choose from whether to opt for a more balanced East Asia policy or striving for the commitment of deepening the process of East Asian community, in which ASEAN may still have the chance to be at the driver's seat, and at the same time, counterbalance China and Japan through the policy of 'trade one off another'.

It seems that, whatever benefits that Indonesia might be getting, the country has not been able to reduce its dependence on external players. Indonesia is more than willing to include countries like Australia, New Zealand, and India to the 10+6 formula, but the main reason for that was very much political. It is the US that draws the line. Indonesia had no option but to swallow the pill. The main expectation of the already drawn up picture of the existing regionalism is, and has to be, political commitment in delivering welfare and stability in the region. In this regard, that is why Indonesia has been firm in asserting one of ASEAN norms, that is "...pacific settlement of disputes and the 'ASEAN Way' of institution building...". If the formula serves only to shifting of battleground on to ASEAN, and fails to reach the expectations of the many, then, it is the right time for Indonesia to rethink of the position it has taken.

REFERENCES

Acharya, Amitav, "Collective Identity and Conflict Management in Southeast Asia", in Emmanuel Adler and Michael Barnett, eds., *Security Communities* (Cambridge University Press, 1998).

Kassim, Yang Razali, ed., *Strategic Currents: Emerging Trends in Southeast Asia*, S. Rajaratnam School of International Studies (Singapore: ISEAS, 2009).

Khoman, Thanat, "ASEAN: Conception and Evolution" in Kernial S. Sandhu, et al, eds., *The ASEAN Reader* (Singapore: ISEAS, 1992).

Leifer, Michael, "The ASEAN Peace Process: A Category Mistake", *Pacific Review*, vol. 12, no. 1 (1999).

Soesastro, Hadi, "Pacific Economic Cooperation: The History of an Idea", Ross Garnut and Peter Drysdale, eds., *Asia Pacific Regionalism: Readings in International Economic Relations* (Pymble, NSW: Harper Collins, 1994).

PART III

INDIA AND SOUTHEAST ASIA

10

India's Conviviality with Southeast Asia: Traversing the Saga of 'Look East' Achievements-Hindrances Dichotomy

Tridib Chakraborti

In the annals of Indian foreign policy since the end of the Second World War, Southeast Asia, as a region, had time and again been accorded its importance, which was volatile in nature. This volatility of Indian foreign policy towards this region during the Cold War period largely evolved due to the latter's attempt to avoid the East-West power struggle and antagonism. This resulted in that India, since 1947, had commenced an alternative conduit and path of survival for the newly independent countries of the world. Its objective of the pursuit of peace was to be obtained not through joining any military alliance, but by judging an issue on its merit. In a world where alliances and counter-alliances were the order of the day, India indicated clearly that it did not wish to be drawn into any alliance. This initiative later came to be known as non-alignment, which emanated out of strategic compulsions and socio-economic and political requirements of the country at that point of time. New Delhi's response to the bipolar world in the post-Second World War era stood differently than the experiences of the Southeast Asian countries, with most of the latter getting embroiled in Cold War politics. Therefore, India's foreign policy priorities towards these countries during the Cold War years had been determined in terms of super power equations and political turbulence within the region, and thereby failed to re-link the cultural, religious and historical consanguinity of ancient times. During this time, India and some countries of Southeast Asia (mainly the ASEAN members) remained "awkward" strangers and their relationship lacked marrow. However, since the late-1960s,

India, owing to its own strategic computations, day by day, came closer to the former Soviet Union. This proximity between New Delhi and Moscow was further strengthened following the former's recognition of the Vietnam-backed Heng Samrin government of Cambodia in July 1980.[1] This stand of New Delhi brought the Indochina States closer to it, on the one hand, and alienated the ASEAN members, on the other. Thus, the dearth of warm political relations and economic linkages of India with the ASEAN members exacerbated the cleft between the two sides, which in other words meant that New Delhi did not risk surrendering its close ties with Hanoi and Moscow as it valued its warm relations with these countries as much more strategically important than its standing among the ASEAN members.

In the early 1990s, global and regional politics had undergone qualitative transformations. With the crumple of the former Soviet Union and the end of the Cold War, coupled with the onset of globalization, nations were beginning to apprehend that the means to making wealth was by securing international trade and encouragement of foreign investments. Free market rules following the proven philosophy of mass capitalization dominated the international political scene over governing ideology in this period. The new world order thus provided scope for redefining the territorial compass of the groupings of the future. Thus, India, in the new global milieu, inaugurated the New Economic Policy under the leadership of P.V. Narashima Rao in 1991. This novel policy had embarked on a substantive and wide ranging programme of economic reforms, restructuring and liberalization, and thereby bringing the Indian economy in line with the economies of the world and the ASEAN countries at large. India, during this time under the Prime Ministership of P.V. Narasimha Rao, announced its 'Look East' policy, which was very well calculated and thought-out,[2] and bolstered by India's objective attempt to engage with East Asia. He perceived that the end of the Cold War had given India an opportunity to broaden its relations with and to focus on countries which were traditional friends and partners of long-standing and special importance, but with whom relations were compromised due to the imperatives of cold war politics. Therefore, India's 'Look East' Policy is a product of both the vigour of liberalization and the craving to replicate the East Asian growth miracle.

To ASEAN, India's size, population, educated middle class, industrial base, military strength, technical capability, ancient cultural history, and presence of overseas Indians are factors in its favour. Moreover, ASEAN's perception of New Delhi as an emerging regional power and China as a source of security threat, coupled with the grim situation in the South China Sea because of conflicting claims over the Spratly Islands, the stand off in the Taiwan Straits and the Korean Peninsula and the troubled ties among US, Japan and China, had convinced ASEAN of the need for a paradigm shift in India-ASEAN attachments. It was also felt by the ASEAN members that India's image and peaceful rise as a benign power accrued significant strategic benefits for them to play a more effective role in the region to counter China as a source of security threat. Thus, mutual needs affected their convergence. New Delhi's 'Look East' policy coincided with ASEAN's 'Look West' line, and this newfound regionalization drive ultimately led to an overall normalization of relations between India and ASEAN.[3] As a result, the ASEAN countries had taken India in full cognizance, not only from its politico-economic perspective, but also from the strategic consideration. Consequently, within a short span of time, India's status graduated from sectoral dialogue to Summit-level partner within the ASEAN orbit, and it was promoted as a participant of the East Asia Summit in 2005. This promotion of India's status was not at all a one-way story. The Indian foreign policy makers, for the first time in their foreign policy domain, had given a definite priority towards this region, and that process of prioritization, known as 'Look East' policy, started its course with the famous speech delivered by the then Indian Prime Minister, P.V. Narasimha Rao at Singapore in 1994. Besides this, within a short span of time, at New Delhi, the ASEAN-India Joint Cooperation Committee held its first meeting, and the two sides started political dialogue and consultations at the senior official's level in 1998. In addition to ASEAN-India Business Council, the two sides agreed to set up three ASEAN-India working groups dealing with development cooperation, science and technology, and trade and investment, respectively. Thus, with these mutually reciprocal interactions, ASEAN's closer ties with India began to take shape world politics by displaying the decades of relative ignorance of an economically emerging, politically mature and strategically vital, dynamic India in the orbit of the Southeast Asian region. However, India's interaction with the Southeast Asian countries through its 'Look East' policy in the initial years generated some impetus to its economic, political and strategic ties towards the economically developed countries within ASEAN, which it clearly lacked towards the rest of the countries of Southeast Asia that were economically fragile. The purpose of the article is to highlight the major achievements of India's 'Look East' policy since 1994. The paper will also analyze the core achievements and hindrances behind the accomplishment of this policy and will suggest the ways to make this policy more pragmatic without losing focus of the central destiny.

India's 'Look East' Policy: Congregated Momentum

Since the announcement of 'Look East' policy in 1994, India in September 2003, officially declared that its policy had entered Phase II, which implied an expanded definition of 'East' – extending from Australia to China and East Asia, with ASEAN as its core – and marked a shift in focus from exclusively economic issues to economic and security issues, including joint efforts to protect sea-lanes, coordination on counter-terrorism etc. The process of this announcement actually started since 2002, when New Delhi conducted regular annual summits with ASEAN along with China, Japan and the Republic of Korea. These political level interactions were further strengthened through the Senior Officials' meetings, as also those of specialized working groups in functional areas. India-ASEAN functional cooperation includes cooperation in sectors such as Science and Technology, Human Resources Development, Health and Pharmaceuticals, Space Sciences, Agriculture, Information and Communication Technology, Transport and Infrastructure, Tourism and Culture and Small and Medium Enterprises etc. Therefore, the announcement of 'Look East' Phase II, unsurprisingly raised doubt as to why New Delhi proclaimed the latter, without announcing the former period of Phase I of 'Look East' policy earlier. Did this signify that the First Phase of its 'Look East' policy had failed to produce the expected phantom as envisioned by Indian foreign policy makers initially? The truth remains that India's 'Look East' policy in Phase I, mainly concentrated on offering confidence-building measures to some countries of Southeast Asia, as New Delhi concentrated more on the economically developed members of ASEAN (i.e. Singapore, Malaysia, Thailand, Indonesia and the Philippines) rather than on Indochina States (Vietnam, Laos and Cambodia) and Myanmar (VCLM), which were economically weak, politically vulnerable, and lately incorporated within the ASEAN trajectory. Besides this, New Delhi's sluggish pace of reforms of economic liberalization, coupled with the lack of stable governments at the Centre and the 1997 financial crisis faced by ASEAN members, largely stalled the generation of better outcome of India's VCLM policy in 'Look East' Phase I. Further, the impact of globalization and slow adjustment of the Indochina States with reference to the socialist-oriented economy had greatly obstructed the flourishing of ties between India and the VCLM countries.[4]

Furthermore, another important event, which provoked New Delhi to extend its 'Look East' policy more towards East Asia, was the inclusion of Myanmar in the ASEAN orbit. The ingress of Myanmar in the ASEAN Regional Forum (ARF) in July 1996, followed by the status of full membership of ASEAN in July 1997, gave New Delhi the opportunity to share a common land border with an ASEAN member state. India's emphasis on developing its eastward trade access to Myanmar clearly illustrated the Indian Government's resolve to mend and enhance its historic ties with Myanmar,[5] and thereby dilated New Delhi's economic, security and political opportunities with the countries of Southeast Asia. But, in spite of knowing fully well the economic weaknesses of Myanmar, New Delhi's strategy to reshape its historical links and develop its common land border with Myanmar in order to alleviate the poverty and under–development in the region was determined mainly to overcome the reduction of unremitting tensions in the Northeast region. By taking advantage of Myanmar as a gateway to Southeast Asia, New Delhi attempts to convert the Northeast region from a security burden to a region of economic prosperity. Moreover, by improving the road route between India and Myanmar via the Northeast, New Delhi will eventually connect a section of the Asian highway from Singapore to Istanbul. This development of linkage with Myanmar in India's mindset has been not to challenge China's strategic position in Myanmar, but through its 'Look East' policy tacitly to win over the minds of the Myanmar people by supporting the pro–democracy movement and to detach the military junta from Chinese influence strategically.[6] Another signpost event, which took place during this time, was the signing of the Mekong-Ganga Cooperation (MGC) on 10 November 2000 in Vientiane among five neighbouring countries namely Myanmar, Thailand, Cambodia, Laos and Vietnam, which further accelerated the development of bilateral ties between India and the less developed countries of Southeast Asia. This initiative was designed to define regions in the new global economy, while keeping their native identity and character intact. It was mainly aimed at broadening and intensification of joint efforts at economic cooperation between India and ASEAN countries in the Mekong Basin. One major goal of this sub-regional initiative was to enhance the transport links that span India, Myanmar, Thailand, Cambodia and Vietnam and thereby, to intensify the joint efforts at economic cooperation between India and ASEAN and the development of overland transport links between Indian and the countries of the Mekong basin that would facilitative cross-border movements of goods and services in order to strengthen the India-ASEAN Free Trade Area (FTA).[7] A major vision of this programme is to establish a Delhi-Hanoi road and railway link in the near future, and also to develop transportation networks including the East-West Corridor project and the Trans-Asian highway. These important initiatives are entirely looked to as the development of transport and infrastructure links, which would ease the cross-border movement of goods and services across these nations and in the process, facilitate the operation of the ASEAN-India FTA. Further, the linkages between India and these countries of Indochina over land might give New Delhi an opportunity to expedite the economic development of its Northeast region. Therefore, though clogged, India's 'Look East' policy towards the less developed countries of Southeast Asia clearly exhibited an upward mobility of bilateral relations. It is to be noted here that before the formation of MGC, in June 1997 under the aegis of India and Thailand, BISTEC (Bangladesh, India, Sri Lanka, Thailand – Economic Cooperation) was formally launched – later known as BIMSTEC – with the primary goal of acting as a vehicle for promoting trade and tourism in the Bay of Bengal region and offered New Delhi with an opportunity to strengthen its ties with the eastern neighbourhood, much in conformity with the core of its 'Look East' policy diplomacy. It was also felt by the Indian policy makers that in order to foster political partnerships with the countries of Southeast Asia, working out physical connectivity through road and railway links and negotiating free trade arrangements would remain the main guiding principle, since BIMSTEC has logistically placed India closer to Southeast Asia through the Myanmar-Thailand link. In other words, India has gained a natural gateway to the east through the territories of Myanmar and Thailand to reach the heart of Southeast and East Asia. Thailand, as an important ASEAN component, can facilitate the pace of trade liberalization and regional economic cooperation within BIMSTEC. Like India, Thailand also visualizes the linkage between India-Thailand-Myanmar as part of the broader strategy of cooperation between India and Southeast Asia as a whole against the backdrop of its 'Look West' policy, for which, BIMSTEC would act as a bridge between South and Southeast Asia through its initiatives.[8]

India's vigorous mobility of its 'Look East' diplomacy reached its height, when the ASEAN leaders at their Seventh Summit held in Brunei in November 2001, agreed to convene the ASEAN-India Summit. The decision for a separate ASEAN-India Summit clearly demonstrated that New Delhi was not treated at par with the countries of East Asia (i.e. Japan, China and Korea), but it provided an opportunity to India to prove its economic influence and dynamics in the region. This promotion of India as a new actor in the orbit of ASEAN's economic, political and strategic process was a product of more than one decade. The promotion of India's status by ASEAN produced its dividend when the First ASEAN-India Summit took place on 5 November 2002 in Phnom Penh. A Joint statement, issued at the end of the Summit, highlighted both the principles as well as the future road map of ASEAN-India cooperation. In this Summit, the then Prime Minister of India, Atal Behari Vajpayee represented India and had the distinction of being the first leader not only of India but also from the entire South Asia to address the ASEAN Summit. Hun Sen, Prime Minister of Cambodia inaugurated this Summit and launched 'The Phnom Penh Agenda: Promoting Shared Prosperity and Peace Across ASEAN.' This included a Four Point Agenda, comprising of enhanced cooperation in the Greater Mekong Sub-region (GMS); complementary to the implementation of Initiative for ASEAN Integration (IAI); promotion of ASEAN Tourism; special ASEAN focus on fighting terrorism and promoting sustainable environment, including the ratification of the Kyoto Protocol. Apart from participation at the Summit, the Indian Prime Minister proposed to create an ASEAN-India Free Trade Area by the year 2012, which, covering about 1.5 billion consumers with a combined GNP of US$ 1.7 trillion, that would gradually eliminate the trade barriers between the member countries of ASEAN and India. The Indian Prime Minister also agreed to offer greater tariff concessions to less developed members of ASEAN, namely Laos, Cambodia, Vietnam and Myanmar. At the end of ASEAN-India Summit in Phnom Penh, the Prime Minister Vajpayee, in a press conference said that, "our intention is with each of the ASEAN countries to enhance our level of dialogue, our economic interaction and political interaction and to have credible and respectable portfolio of activities that are going on with them."[9]

While highlighting this Summit as a major achievement of India's 'Look East' policy, the Ministry of External Affair's **Annual Report: 2002-03** of India, described this event as "a significant development in our relations with ASEAN countries, as India joined the ranks of a handful of countries with which ASEAN has Summit dialogues, namely, China, Japan and South Korea. This up-gradation is a natural culmination of ten years of progressive engagement with ASEAN.... It is also a vindication of India's 'Look East' policy which seeks to build on our historical and cultural ties with the region to create a mutually beneficial strategic and economic relationship."[10] Therefore, this India-ASEAN Summit was, no doubt, a watershed event in the history of bilateral relations between India and Southeast Asia since the fall of the former Soviet Union.

Meanwhile, India's growing propinquity with the Southeast Asian countries received more vigour, when in October 2003, Prime Minister Atal Behari Vajpayee attended the Second India-ASEAN Summit in Bali and sent a strong message about New Delhi's importance and vows to forge closer links with the region. In this Bali Summit, three important accords were signed on comprehensive economic cooperation, combating terrorism and facilitating India's accession to the Treaty of Amity and Cooperation (TAC) with Southeast Asia respectively. The Indian Prime Minister also went a step further by offering a unilateral "open skies" policy to specified Southeast Asian airlines, which will be allowed to operate daily flights to the four metros in India and unlimited flights to eighteen tourist destinations in India,[11] and also announced New Delhi's decision to extend special and differential treatment to ASEAN countries depending on their levels of development to improve their market access to India. Taken together, these steps clearly assured considerable improvement in economic, political and security cooperation between India and its Southeast Asian neighbours – extending from Myanmar to the Philippines.

The confidence of Southeast Asian countries in India once again received a major boost when in May 2004, the United Progressive Alliance (UPA) under the Prime Ministership of Manmohan Singh, came in power by replacing the NDA government. This new government, like its precursor, renewed India's closer ties with the countries of Southeast Asia, and commenced the foreign policy, which was purposeful, result-oriented and highly pro-active in its entirety. The Minister of External Affairs, K. Natwar Singh, of this new UPA government, on 31 May,

2004, in a meeting with top Indian diplomats from SAARC and ASEAN countries, categorically emphasized the future policy options of New Delhi and strongly reiterated the political, economic and strategic importance of Southeast Asia in India's foreign policy domain. He said: "We will further strengthen bilateral relations with them, as well as our interaction with ASEAN since it constitutes a major dimension of our foreign policy." The same mindset was once again reiterated, when K. Natwar Singh in an interview to *The Jakarta Post* on 2 July, 2004 said: "India's foreign policy attaches primary importance to relations with our immediate neighbours in South Asia Association for Regional Cooperation (SAARC) as well as in ASEAN. We remain committed to strengthening India's 'Look East' policy and to constructing a long-term partnership with ASEAN. Under the Framework Agreement concluded last year, we have just commenced negotiation of a Free Trade Agreement. We are also working on an India-ASEAN Summit in November this year. Politically, we completely share ASEAN's vision and the principles of harmonious and good neighbouring relations established by the ASEAN Treaty of Amity and Cooperation, to which India acceded last year."[12] Thus, India's 'Look East' policy had attained its multi-dimensional and multi-pronged outlook by 2004.

This attention of India's ASEAN policy reached its culmination when New Delhi, under the Prime Ministership of Manmohan Singh, participated in the 3rd India-ASEAN Summit held on 30th November, 2004, in Vientiane. In this Summit, India and the ASEAN members signed a historic partnership pact titled "India-ASEAN Partnership for Peace, Progress and Shared Prosperity." The pact outlines a multi-pronged action plan for boosting trade, investment, tourism, culture, sports and people to people contacts. The four-page partnership accord and nine-page action plan envisaged cooperation in multilateral forums e.g. the WTO and addressed 'common challenges of economic, food, human and energy security.' The pact was signed to realise the full potential of the ASEAN-India Regional Trade and Investment Area (RITA), in accordance with the Framework Agreement on Comprehensive Economic Cooperation signed by India and ASEAN in Bali, at the Second ASEAN-India Summit held in 2003. In an important move to brace the economic ties, India and ASEAN members decided to set up a RITA to facilitate the flow of Foreign Direct Investment (FDI) in the region and enhance regional monetary and financial cooperation, besides promoting an Asian market. The pact covers a long-term plan committed to creating a Free Trade Area by 2011 with five ASEAN members (Brunei, Indonesia, Malaysia, Thailand and Singapore) and by 2016 with the rest of the members. It also laid special emphasis on infrastructure and transport development and cooperation in gas-related projects. As part of cooperation in infrastructure, the plan called for expediting completion of India-Myanmar-Thailand trilateral highway and its extension to Laos and Cambodia apart from strengthening air connectivity, and agreed on investment promotion and double taxation avoidance. It also aims at improving financial stability, regional monetary, and financial cooperation, apart from further developing capital market of the region. Thus, this Third India-ASEAN Summit clearly laid out a short to medium term road map of India and ASEAN cooperation in various sectors, which, according to the Ministry of External Affairs of India, "forms the inner core of countries in ASEAN's political relationship with the rest of the world."[13]

The multi-dimensional approach through India's 'Look East' policy achieved its height when the Indian Prime Minister Manmohan Singh, on 14 December 2005 participated in the First East Asia Summit (EAS) held in Kuala Lumpur, under the auspices of ASEAN. This confidence of ASEAN as well as promotion of India's status was, no doubt, quite an unparalleled event in the history of India's Southeast Asia policy. The formation of the EAS can be termed as the first step for establishing an East Asian Community along the lines of the European Economic Community. Sixteen members participated,[14] and the criteria laid down for new members (mainly India, Australia and New Zealand) includes acceptance of the Treaty of Amity and Cooperation (TAC), a central agreement on inter-state relations among ASEAN states and others that agree to it. Surprisingly, the United States has been excluded altogether from this East Asia Summit, and the understanding among the members was of not allowing any non-regional power to get into this group. The Indian Prime Minister, Manmohan Singh, the only South Asia representative in this First East Asia Summit, clearly said that it was important for India to be in a group that had the "potential to play a major role in global affairs. Its composition, evolving agenda and format give it the potential to play a major role in global affairs. India's presence in this group from its very outset is an opportunity we value."[15] The Indian Prime Minister, at the end of this meeting described this East Asia Summit as "a historic meeting." Thus, India's presence and participation, in the First East Asian Summit, was no doubt a good beginning for the country's ultimate integration with that region. In the East Asian Summit, the economy and trade were the core issues, and a historic decision was taken to work towards the world's largest free trade area, covering some developed and developing economies and agreed among themselves to promote "development, financial stability, energy security, economic integration and growth", besides narrowing the development gap through technology transfer. For New Delhi, the EAS can be seen as the penultimate step in its integration with Northeast Asia and Southwest Pacific, and a stepping-stone to joining the Asia Pacific Economic Cooperation (APEC) forum. Therefore, through its 'Look East' policy mechanism, New Delhi's participation in the East Asian Summit could provide another dimension to the efforts at regionalism in Asia, which were hitherto being restricted to ASEAN. Thus, India's ASEAN policy has clearly exhibited three distinct features so far, and they are:

(i) India has managed to develop a multi-faceted relationship;
(ii) A successful defence diplomacy has been put in place; and
(iii) Unlike in the past, New Delhi is not averse to participation in regional and multilateral security or economic fora.[16]

So far, New Delhi has participated in all the India-ASEAN and East Asia Summit meetings. In the last East Asia Summit meeting held in Hua Hin, Thailand, in October 2009, the Indian Prime Minister, Manmohon Singh said "I am extremely satisfied with the outcome of the India-ASEAN Summit. I found a strong desire among the ASEAN countries to substantially strengthen their links with India in all areas. This includes not only economic cooperation and trade but also science and technology, human resource development, protection of the environment and deeper political and security cooperation.... and therefore the sky is the limit for our engagement with this region."[17] He also called for an Asian Regional Trade Agreement as a pivotal step towards the integration of the region into a broader "Asian Economic Community." This statement has been quite strategically vital for New Delhi in the context of its 'Look East' policy, under the second tenure of the United Progressive Alliance (UPA) government established in 2009 and once again reiterated India's policy of new regionalism towards the countries of Southeast and more East Asia. Therefore, in the context of the changing world order, presently New Delhi is looking more towards the Asia-Pacific region with greater concerns and hopes. However, these outlook and initiatives need to be nursed and sustained patiently over a long period without losing the focus on the core objectives.

Imprints of Achievement of India's Look East Policy

India's 'Look East' policy presently has an experience of nearly two decades. During this time, India has gained many economic, strategic and political advantages in the Asia Pacific region by executing it. However, though India's performance with reference to its 'Look East' vision has remained quite amenable, it has not been significant enough if one compares China's accomplishment with ASEAN during the same time. While taking stock, it is clear that there are certain obstacles, both within the formulation of India's 'Look East' policy and certain major obstructions faced by New Delhi, emanating from regional and extra-regional powers, which essentially remain the main pitfalls to making it more effective in its entirety. India's soft power strategy can play a pertinent role in making this policy more effective in nature.

The **First** major achievement of India's 'Look East' policy involves strategic and security cooperation, and increasing its area of influence in the Southeast Asian region, with a view to becoming a major player in the emerging balance of power in Asia. India's security relations with Southeast Asia improved radically after the end of the Cold War and it involved joint security cooperation mechanisms to protect sea-lanes and pooling resources in the overt war against terrorism. The Indian Navy has been clutching an effective role in combating terrorism and piracy in the Malacca Straits, and has offered to assist the littoral states in the implementation of the 'Eyes in the Sky' programme for patrolling the piracy-infested Straits of Malacca. The terrorism menace, both from within and across borders, as faced by both India and the countries of Southeast Asia, has been embarked upon by both of them through close monitoring, coordination and with joint efforts, since these sea lanes are very critical for India's growing trade with ASEAN and other countries of East Asia.

Indian and ASEAN navies began conducting naval exercises from 1991. The Navies of the Bay of Bengal from Bangladesh, India, Sri Lanka, Indonesia, Malaysia, Singapore and Thailand have been coming together in a joint exercise, aptly called MILAN. The India-Singapore Agreement in 2003 produced the first exercise on Singaporean waters and the two navies have held joint naval exercises for the last few years. They recently concluded an exercise termed SIMBEX in the South China Sea. Likewise, a bilateral agreement with Indonesia resulted in an exercise with it in 2004.[18] Among other areas where India and the ASEAN members are jointly harmonizing their efforts are the problems of insurgency, trafficking of small arms and drugs, illegal migration, environmental pollution, narcotics traffic, and other security-related issues, including the safety of the sea-lanes-of-communication (SLOC), which have been indispensable for the development of economic richness of the region. This changing mindset among India and the countries of Southeast Asia gathered its momentum after the11 September 2001 attacks on the United States, which posed a new threat to global and regional security, in the backdrop of which both ASEAN and India faced grave vulnerabilities and decided to work together to build peace and security in the region.

Another important reason behind ASEAN's closeness towards India has been China's rising power profile and especially its naval incursions into the South China Sea in additon to China's expanding acceptance worldwide. The sudden collapse of the Soviet Union and the withdrawal of US troops from strategic locations in the region gave China a strategic space and thereby altered the balance of power in Asia. The Southeast Asian countries, under such a milieu, deemed it appropriate to guard against Chinese influence by setting up vital sea-lanes of communications such as Taiwan, Malacca, Sunda and the Lombhok Straits and accordingly perceived India, with the largest naval forces in the Indian Ocean and nuclear capabilities, as a strategic partner to balance China's growing power in the region.[19] Conversely, there have also been apprehensions within ASEAN regarding India's Navy and nuclear capabilities as India itself possesses the ability to yield substantial influence and power in the region. "But India's willingness to accede to the Treaty of Amity and Cooperation in Southeast Asia in 2003 and its endorsement of the Southeast Asia Nuclear Weapons Free Zone (SEANWFZ) has gone a long way in assuring the region of India's intent.

ASEAN looks at India's security needs more as a factor emanating from the compulsions of the geopolitical position that India holds, rather than being a derivative of any hegemonic designs on India's part."[20] Better coordination of naval activities between India and ASEAN presently gathered its momentum following the announcement of the Indian Maritime Doctrine of 2004 and New Delhi's sincere role in the wake of the Tsunami disaster. This was no doubt a major gain of India's 'Look East' policy.

Furthermore, within these nearly two decades, India has steadily expanded its ties with the East and Southeast Asian countries in the sphere of defence collaborations. To this effect, New Delhi has trained the Thai pilots for flying Sea Harriers. It also agreed to help Vietnam to upgrade its Mig-21 aircrafts. Likewise, Indian help was sought for training pilots and for securing spare parts for the Malaysian Mig-29s. Singapore's defence relations with India have been special. Singapore held joint Air Force exercises with India. India practiced F-16 combat with Singaporean F-16s before it had the same experience with the US. The Defence Cooperation Agreement between Singapore and India signed in 2003 and with Vietnam in 2007 were also very significant.

Another milestone event was the holding of regular joint military exercises between India and most of the countries of Southeast Asia. Since 2000, the bilateral naval exercises were a manifestation of a more strategic 'Look-East' policy; the Indian Navy has sent warships, tankers and submarines to Japan, South Korea, Thailand, Indonesia and Vietnam for bilateral exercises and as a gesture of goodwill, through regional confidence-building and cooperation mechanisms like the ASEAN Regional Forum (ARF), the Regional Cooperation Agreement on Combating Piracy and Armed Robbery against Ships in Asia (ReCAAP) and the MILAN exercises that India holds every alternate year.

This maritime security diplomacy of India has undoubtedly brought the Southeast Asian countries closer to each other. Therefore, within a short span of time, as a rising power possessing nuclear weapons, India is regarded as having the capability to play a "swing" role in the global and regional balance of power. ASEAN, Japan, and South Korea see closer ties with India as providing a useful balance and a hedge against China's current economic dominance and future uncertainties. Smaller countries in the region, fearing unilateralism by the big powers, also perceive India as a potential security provider and create a genuine higher level of mutual comfort between them. So, all these achievements are the integral components of India's maritime policy towards the East in the context of its 'Look East' diplomacy.[21]

The **Second** major achievement of India's 'Look East' policy engrosses its economic engagement policy with the Southeast Asian countries. During it's nearly two decades long interaction with ASEAN, one might ask whether ASEAN has accepted New Delhi as a major regional player or only as a secondary player in Asia-Pacific's economic and security colonnade. India, through its political, economic and strategic relations with the countries of Southeast Asia, has been able to demonstrate its genuine interests towards the region. Through its 'Look East' policy, New Delhi has clearly put up a realistic performance in its development of relations with some economically advanced countries of Southeast Asia, though this could not be repeated with others who were economically vulnerable and late entrants within the ASEAN orbit. Singapore is now investing more in selected areas in India, and Singaporean companies have been active in information technology, communications, construction and ports. Malaysia's relations with India, which were based for a long time on palm oil exports and counter trade, have now taken on new dimensions with Malaysian companies' involvement in the power and road building sectors in India. In the other direction, Indian companies have also invested in Thailand, Malaysia and Indonesia in pharmaceuticals, textiles, paper and pulp manufacturing and palm oil refining.

Besides this, New Delhi also developed better economic ties with Thailand, Indonesia and the Philippines. But it lacked attention towards Brunei, another developed country within Southeast Asia, the per capita Gross Domestic Product (GDP) of which remains second only to Singapore, due to unknown reasons. Presently economic cooperation and the trade scenario have acquired a prominent place between India and Southeast Asia, owing to their emerging complementary economies. Trade ties between them over the years have clearly exhibited sharp increases in India's exports to this area. ASEAN accounted for 3.6 per cent of India's exports to the world in 1980, which by 1992 increased to nearly 6 per cent. In terms of value, India's export to ASEAN countries had more than quadrupled in 1992. And, in the later years, India's trade in terms of both exports and imports with ASEAN increased very rapidly. In fact, India's exports to ASEAN have increased by over 280 per cent in the last five years, and India's imports from ASEAN countries have increased by around 220 per cent. In 2008-09, total merchandise trade stood at over US$ 45 billion, and this way the exports target to the region by 2010 looks very realistic. India's trade with the Southeast Asian countries, during the year 2007-08 was US $390,88.33 million and which remained 10 times more than the year 1992-93. However, the Balance of Trade, except for the year 1993-94, has always titled in favour of the Southeast Asian countries (see Table 1).

Among the Southeast Asian countries, Malaysia and Singapore have been India's most prominent trading partners, and India's trade with Laos has been the

Table 1: India's Trade with Southeast Asian Countries

(Value in US $ Million)

Year (April-March)	Exports	Imports	Total Trade	Balance of Trade
1990-91	748.00	1474.00	2222.00	-726.00
1991-92	1022.30	1274.60	2296.90	-252.30
1992-93	1508.25	2230.24	3738.49	-721.99
1993-94	1981.71	1950.00	3931.71	+31.71
1994-95	2326.27	3059.50	5385.76	-733.23
1995-96	3177.77	3881.88	7059.65	-704.11
1996-97	3353.46	4492.58	7846.04	-1139.12
1997-98	2987.21	5177.91	8165.12	-2190.70
1998-99	2090.35	5865.13	7955.48	-3774.78
1999-2000	2721.05	6281.73	9002.78	-3560.68
2000-01	3362.20	5210.49	8572.69	-1846.31
2001-02	3945.86	5767.12	9712.98	-1821.26
2002-03	5219.16	6565.61	11784.77	-1346.45
2003-04	6494.35	10058.46	16552.81	-3564.11
2004-05	8,425.89	9,114.66	17540.55	-718.77
2005-06	10,411.30	10,883.68	21294.98	-472.38
2006-07	12,603.86	18,089.64	30693.50	-5485.78
2007-08	16,413.52	22,674.81	390,88.33	-6261.29
2008-09	19,140.63	26,202.96	453,43.59	-7062.33
2009-10 (April-December)	12,818.01	18,086.59	30904.60	-5268.58

Source: Prepared by the author from various tables and pages based on **Ministry of Commerce Annual Reports**, Government of India, New Delhi, April-March 1990-91 to April-December 2009-10.

least in value terms. In 2007-08, when India's trade with the world stood at US$ 413 billion, ASEAN accounted more than 10 per cent of India's global trade. Among Southeast Asian countries, Malaysia, Thailand and Singapore have become the major source of FDI into India. From a negligible amount in 1991, cumulative approved FDI from ASEAN has so far reached more than US$ 5 billion. Compared to other regional groupings, ASEAN is the 5th most important market in the world in terms of Indian exports and 4th in terms of imports. However, compared to other dialogue partners of ASEAN, the volume of trade and investment flows between India and ASEAN remains very low. India, during the period April 2000 – July 2008 totalled US$ 6.0 billion, and ASEAN accounted for 8 per cent of India's total FDI inflows (US$ 74.8 billion). Similarly, Indian investments in the ASEAN region amounted to US$ 9.7 billion during April 1996 to December 2007, and ASEAN's share in India's total FDI outflows accounted for19.6 per cent during the same period, with Singapore as the largest destination for India's global FDI outflows.

To achieve its 'Look East' policy, India is negotiating bilateral free trade agreements (FTAs) with Southeast and East Asian economic powers. India has entered into a number of pacts, agreements and FTAs with Thailand and Singapore; there are also plans to create a free-trade area with Brunei, Indonesia and Malaysia by 2011 and with the remaining ASEAN countries – the Philippines, Cambodia, Laos, Myanmar and Vietnam – by 2016. A major achievement by India during this period has been the setting up of joint working groups with Malaysia, Indonesia, etc., for working towards Comprehensive Economic Cooperation Agreement. However, on 13 August 2009 at Bangkok, after six years of negotiations, the India-ASEAN Free Trade Agreement (FTA), as part of the Comprehensive Economic Cooperation Agreement (CECA), was finally signed. The agreement was only for trade-in-goods and did not include software and information technology. This FTA Agreement in goods will integrate the two globally important economic blocks for mutually beneficial economic gains. Under the ASEAN-India FTA, the ASEAN member countries and India would eliminate tariffs for about 4000 products (which include electronics, chemicals, machinery and textiles) out of which duties for 3200 products will be reduced by December 2013, while duties on the remaining 800 products will be brought down to zero or near zero levels by December 2016. Also, with the signing of the FTA between India and ASEAN countries, Thailand has been targeting to conduct US$ 10 billion bilateral trade in 2010. In 2008-09, trade between the two countries stood at around US$ 6 billion.

On 14 December 2005, India attended the First East Asia Summit (EAS) meeting where, with the world's major trading bloc leaders, New Delhi endorsed an enlarged ASEAN Free Trade Agreement (AFTA) to promote further regional integration for mutual economic and political benefits between ASEAN and the world's other trading blocs (e.g., India, the US, the EU, East Asia, Oceania, and Russia). The endorsement is consistent with India's post-1991 reforms, 'Look East' policy, and economic diplomacy. As a result of this eco-political approach, the world's trading blocs have seen rapid increase and its strong dynamics in trade with India. Since India announced its Move East policy, it has pursued a combined multilateral, regional and bilateral facet of trade policy with the major trade partners of East Asia, which it lacked in the past years. This resulted in that presently, India maintains a relatively active diplomatic effort in East Asia, and the process of singing FTA is on the way. In August 2009, India signed a Comprehensive Economic Partnership Agreement with South Korea. With this participation of India in the East Asian economic process, New Delhi presently has established more extensive and better relations with the region than perhaps it has ever had, and therefore the endorsement of the world's leaders at the First EAS for an enlarged ASEAN-FTA or an EAS-FTA and similar frameworks where space for ASEAN+India, East Asia+India, APEC, China-India or even Australia-India trade agreements have generated their momentum.

In fact, India's overall bilateral trade relations with East Asian countries increased from Look East Phase-I to Move East Phase or Look East Phase II. The Trade figure of India's Look East Phase I in 1997-98 was US $ 2089.81 million, and this figure was US $1901.02 million in 2001-02. These decreases in the trade figures were mainly because of the sudden financial meltdown, which affected these countries and New Delhi's lack of economic attention towards the East Asian region. (See Table 2 for details). However, trade figures during these years were in favour of this region. This poor performance of economic ties with the East Asian countries drastically improved when the Government of India officially extended its 'Look East' policy to Phase II, beyond Southeast Asia to the Pacific region. This extension naturally displayed its economic outfit and consolidation and growth of bilateral relations. Thus, trade figure in the first year of India's Look East Phase II i.e. in 2002-03 was US $ 2027.10 million, and this figure in 2008-09 was US $13542.65 million, thus recording an increase of more than 6 times. (See Table 3 for details) Therefore, India continues to attach due importance to countries of Southeast Asia and the Pacific region as envisioned in our 'Look East' Policy-I and II.[22] Furthermore, India's presence and participation, first in a Summit with the ASEAN and then in the First EAS is no doubt a good beginning for the country's ultimate integration with that region. In fact, rapid integration with East Asia as part of India's 'Look East' Phase II policy has made the region India's largest trade partner, ahead of the EU and the US. India is evolving an FTA with ASEAN, and is presently studying Free Trade Areas (FTAs) with Japan, China and South

Table 2: India's Trade with East Asia before Move East Phase

(Value in US $ Million)

Year (April-March)	Exports	Imports	Total Trade	Balance of Trade
1997-98	515.66	1,574.15	2089.81	-1058.49
1998-99	460.48	1,545.37	2005.85	-1084.89
1999-2000	491.08	1,197.22	1688.30	-706.14
2000-01	493.52	1,182.11	1675.63	-688.59
2001-02	506.76	1,394.26	1901.02	-887.50

Source: Prepared by the author from various tables and pages based on *Ministry of Commerce Annual Reports,* Government of India, New Delhi, April-March 1997-98 to April-December 2001-02.

Korea, trying to integrate itself as a part of the growing larger web of FTAs in the region. Moreover, in the East Asian Summit, economy and trade were the core issues and a historic decision was taken to work towards the world's largest free trade area, covering some developed and developing economies.

Table 3: India's Trade with East Asia since Move East Phase

(Value in US $ Million)

Year (April-March)	Exports	Imports	Total Trade	Balance of Trade
2002-03	604.39	1,422.71	2027.10	818.32
2003-04	703.52	2,751.29	3454.81	2047.77
2004-05	859.82	4,050.17	4909.99	3190.35
2005-06	1,004.49	5,280.74	6285.23	4276.25
2006-07	1,482.24	7,574.57	9056.81	6092.33
2007-08	1,412.52	8,356.41	9768.93	6943.89
2008-09	1,754.22	11,788.43	13542.65	10034.21
2009-10 (April-December)	1,248.87	9,076.90	10325.77	7828.03

Source: Prepared by the author from various tables and pages based on *Ministry of Commerce Annual Reports,* Government of India, New Delhi, April-March 2002-03 to April-December 2009-10.

Therefore, in a nutshell, the beneficial effects of good economic governance or productive and correct policy reforms initiated by India in the post-Cold War years and followed by its 'Look East' policy since mid 1990s seem to have been substantiated empirically through the above data which reveals that India has certainly achieved a major economic benefit through its 'Look East' diplomacy.

The **Third** accomplishment of India's 'Look East' policy has been its enthusiastic engagement with Southeast and East Asia, which I have discussed earlier. The First East Asia Summit (EAS), which was held in December 2005 in Kuala Lumpur, consisting of 16 countries (ASEAN, China, Japan, Korea, India, Australia and New Zealand) remained a historic event in emerging global politics. This new space in the East Asian region has marked a return of India's active dialogue and participation in the politico-economic processes at work in the larger Asia-Pacific region. For New Delhi, the EAS can be seen as the penultimate step in its integration with the East, and a stepping-stone to joining the Asia Pacific Economic Cooperation (APEC) forum, based on solid state of emerging ties with the countries of Southeast Asia. The recent participation of India in the 4th East Asia Summit, held in Hua Hin, Thailand in October 2009, where the EAS leaders endorsed the establishment of Nalanda University as a centre of excellence in education and international understanding, as proposed by India, was a remarkable event.

The **Fourth** achievement of India's 'Look East' policy has been its active participation in the Initiative for ASEAN Integration (IAI) programme – a regional framework for development of integration and cooperation – aimed at narrowing the development gap mainly with the CLMV (Cambodia, Laos, Myanmar and Vietnam) countries within ASEAN and enhancing regional integration. While respecting the Singapore Prime Minister, Goh Chok Tong's proposal of IAI taken in the Fourth Informal Summit in November 2000, at Singapore, India, being a responsible 'Dialogue Partner' of ASEAN, actively played a constructive role in the process. India has successfully completed the "Railway Training Programmes" for 48 trainers from CLMV countries in India. In addition, New Delhi is presently implementing a project, namely "India-Singapore Joint Training Programme for CLMV in English Language Training" and has been involved in an Entrepreneurial Development project in each of the CLMV countries. The objective of this project is for India to provide technical and advisory services to these countries for the establishment of Entrepreneurial Development Institutes in each of these countries, as part of efforts to train entrepreneurs and prepare small enterprises that face the challenges of globalization. So far, New Delhi has already established Entrepreneurship Development Centres in Cambodia, Laos and Vietnam, and in Myanmar it will be set up very soon. ASEAN countries have looked upon this active focus of New Delhi on the IAI programme as a sign of India's commitment to play a positive role in ASEAN's regional initiatives and its processes.[23]

Fifthly, though small in nature, convergence of better understanding between ASEAN and India has been evident clearly with reference to non-traditional security challenges, particularly in the areas of climate change and natural disaster relief. Southeast Asia, with its densely populated coastlines and huge agricultural sectors, is particularly vulnerable to climate change. According to Asian Development Bank (ADB) and World Wildlife Fund (WWF) reports, ASEAN countries, particularly impoverished ones like Cambodia and Laos, could face major risks from energy shortages and declining crop yields in the near future, while low-lying 'mega-cities' such as Manila and Jakarta will be highly vulnerable to rising sea levels, tropical storms, droughts and heat waves.[24] Meanwhile, in India, monsoon seasons are getting more difficult to predict and may become shorter in duration (as evidenced by the prolonged drought that affected two-thirds of the country in the last few years), cyclones could become more frequent and intense, and crop yields could decrease by 30 per cent by 2050.[25] Under such a situation, both India and ASEAN agreed to share a common commitment to assist each other in disaster relief, an avenue for cooperation that was clearly exhibited by the 2004 Indian Ocean earthquake and tsunami that rocked South and Southeast Asia, one of the deadliest natural disasters in recorded history. While ASEAN and India have facilitated cooperation in the area of non-traditional security by, for instance, creating an India-ASEAN Network on Climate Change and the Green Fund, there remains great potential for further collaboration in the future, such as cooperation in the agricultural sector to meet the challenges of food security.[26]

The **last, but not the least** achievement has been that in the last few years, New Delhi participated in a number of ASEAN Regional Forum (ARF) activities relating to confidence-building measures (CBMs), maritime search and rescue, peace-keeping, non-proliferation, preventive diplomacy and disaster management and found them productive and useful for the facilitation of the introduction of appropriate CBMs among participant nations.

Major Encumbrances on India's 'Look East' Policy

India's 'Look East' policy during its nearly two decades of performance has failed to display the expected result, unlike China's attempts during the same period. There are several obstacles responsible for obstructing the smooth and effective trajectory of India's 'Look East' performance and these factors are discussed below:

First, China does not favour a strong Indian presence and influence in Southeast Asia. Knowing fully well that India is the only country that could challenge its ascendancy and potential hegemony in Asia, Beijing tries hard to keep New Delhi under pressure. Generally, China believes that India is a sheer South Asian regional actor. Its continuous promotion of Pakistan and Myanmar remains a major concern for India still today.

However, over the last decade or so, the Chinese have been somewhat bamboozled and intrigued by the steady development rate of India's economy and its political stability. So, it has no option but to consider India more seriously in its regional strategic calculus.

China, through its diversified strategies applied at multilateral and bilateral levels in the Southeast Asian region and by aid and assistance to the ASEAN countries during the East Asian Financial Crisis and the recent global meltdown in 2008, has earned colossal confidence from the ASEAN end, which India missed towards this region. China has also pragmatically resolved the territorial land disputes with most of its neighbours and generated an encouraging environment for enhancing its position and economic development process with most of the countries of Southeast Asia. Furthermore, China's entry in SAARC in 2005, as an Observer member and its growing dominance in Southeast Asia became causes for India's disquiet as well. China's continuous military assistance to most of India's neighbours and mainly to Pakistan, for its nuclear programme, became a serious destabilizing factor for Indian diplomacy in South Asia. Also, unlike China, India cannot rely on FDI as a springboard for achieving a well-developed economy, thriving on service sectors and tertiary industries.

Besides this, in the Post-Cold War years, Beijing has created its image as a power, not aggressive but benign in nature among the countries of Southeast Asia. This image has been exhibited by China through employing its soft power posture. The modalities of its soft power include the 'five principles of peaceful coexistence'; cooperative security; unconditional foreign aid (mainly through Official Development Assistance); limited sanctions; mutual accommodation; international democracy; cultural diversity; privatization and marketzation, but under state guidance; experimentation and gradualism; export-led growth, with restrictions on imports; a consultative, but non-pluralistic, political system etc.[27] In a nutshell, China is actually using traditional trade-craft and diplomacy in a very soft manner to win the minds of the Southeast and South Asian countries.

Secondly, India's weak handling of its 'Look East' policy failed to adopt a sufficient strategic space of its relationship with Myanmar. New Delhi should invest more money in Bangladesh and Myanmar, which China had done so far quite pragmatically. There is a need to cooperate with both these countries in water, energy, transport, drug trafficking, illegal migration, infrastructure, and investment projects. Besides this, procurement of energy from the outside world has remained the core of New Delhi's economic strength. Quest for energy resources prompted by the increasing demand of domestic energy requirements forced both India and China to bid aggressively for overseas oil assets. Unfortunately, Chinese firms, in several deals, have outsmarted India's energy diplomacy. Thus, in recent years, the Chinese companies have vigorously invested in Myanmar. Out of 26 Chinese foreign investments, 16 projects have exclusively concentrated nearly 70 per cent in terms of investment value, invested mostly in the energy and mining sectors.[28] Most embarrassingly, India also lost a deal in Myanmar where no open bidding was held. Subsequently, Myanmar decided to decline gas supply to the Myanmar-Bangladesh-India pipeline. Instead, it signed an agreement with Petrochina, under which Myanmar's ministry of Energy decided to sell 6.5 TCF from A-1 block in the Shwe field off the coast of Rahine State to Yunnan Province, containing 2.88 trillion to 3.56 trillion cubic feet of gas, for 30 years, starting from 2009.[29] Interestingly enough, Myanmar officials have said that the country could still supply gas to the tri-nation gas pipeline from other gas blocks, if Bangladesh and India were successful in ironing out their differences. Therefore, India should play a more pro-active role to develop better ties with Bangladesh if it wants to procure energy from Myanmar. In fact, if India considers its 'Look East' policy as a train, which has a specific destiny, then New Delhi must take its South Asian neighbours, mainly Bangladesh, as its co-passengers to make its policy a cost-effective one.

Thirdly, if India wants to make its 'Look East' policy an effectual one, New Delhi must use its North-eastern region as a connecting point. 98 per cent of the northeast region's borders are shared with Bangladesh, Myanmar, Bhutan, and Tibet. Its only land link with the rest of India is through a narrow sliver of territory in Bangladesh, through which the latter refuses to give transit facilities to India. Not fully integrated – both economically and emotionally – with the rest of India, the north-eastern region lags behind the rest of India in development and suffers from widespread insurgency movements. In order to help the northeast region overcome these inbuilt constraints, India's strategy would be prudent to make the region develop industrially. Otherwise, no policy initiative can make the 'Look East' policy an effective one, insofar as the northeast is concerned.

In recent years, New Delhi has taken few initiatives in this context. The year 2004 was an important watershed in the history of India's northeast for two reasons. **First**, in November 2004, the Indian Prime Minister, Manmohan Singh, for the first time, referred to Assam as the 'Gate to the East' This, in turn, brought the northeast into the ambit of the 'Look East' policy frame as a launching pad for India's political and economic engagement with the ASEAN region. **Secondly**, the India-ASEAN Car Rally, which was flagged off from Guwahati in Assam in 2004, brought home both the viability and urgency of developing physical connectivity between northeast India and Southeast Asia for India's economic integration with ASEAN.[30]

More importantly, on 22 May 2010, Anand Sharma, Union Minister of Commerce and Industry (India), while addressing the North-East Trade and Industry Ministers' Conclave at Guwahati, said that the government was keen to ensure better connectivity with the rest of the ASEAN countries to bring about a dynamic change in the economic development of the region. He said "route connectivity is the key to the development of the region and with this view in mind we are keen to develop the Trans Asia Highway and also look at new and better routes connecting the region with South East Asia". He further emphasized that initiative was taken in order to "build" roads across borders, and linking the region with India's northeast through railway would allow greater movement of Indians in the region, for which two 'border hats' and 14 Integrated Border Customs posts have been set up in the north-eastern region as well.

To develop the region's infrastructure and remove the infrastructural bottlenecks, the Government of India, during the Eleventh Plan period, sanctioned Rs. 31,000 crore, of which, during the year 2010-11, the Centre has sanctioned transport subsidy of Rs. 200 crore, central interest subsidy of Rs. 40 crore and capital investment subsidy of Rs. 31 crore. This action was taken by the Government in order to pursue a holistic approach towards providing subsidy to the region for ensuring "that investors come and opportunities are created."[31] Therefore, in order to make India's 'Look East' policy an effectual one, New Delhi must take into cognizance the Northeast States as a First Class Bogey of its 'Look

East' Train. Interestingly enough, China is presently playing a strategy of developing its backward regions through greater economic ties with South and Southeast Asia and Yunnan's provincial government plays a far more active role in attracting foreign investments to the province than the northeast Indian states.

Fourthly, connectivity provides an opportunity rather than constraints, and it should be realised that by enhancing connectivity, ties with Southeast Asia would be revived, thereby creating a network of interrelationships that can have an important political and economic outreach. At the Second India-ASEAN Summit held Bali in October 2003, the Indian Prime Minister, Atal Behari Vajpayee, offered an 'Open Skies' policy to specific Southeast Asian Airlines, which would be free to operate daily flights to the Indian metropolitan cities linking all 10 ASEAN capitals.[32] This unilateral initiative taken by India was the result of its realization of the need for better connectivity between India and ASEAN. Under the 'Open Skies' policy, the Indian Prime Minister, in his speech at the 6th India-ASEAN Summit, held in Singapore on 21 November 2007, mentioned that, there are over 215, 115 and 50 direct flights operating every week between India and Singapore, Thailand and Malaysia respectively.[33] In spite of this performance, the civil aviation sector of India has been facing a number of challenges. Presently, there are no direct flights to Vietnam, Cambodia, Laos, Brunei and the Philippines. Besides this, in order to make New Delhi's connectivity diplomacy an effective one, India should accelerate its transport link with Vietnam, Cambodia, Laos and Myanmar (VCLM countries), which would stimulate economic activities and spill over the economic benefits into underdeveloped areas of the region. Therefore, the rail link would have two significant contributions – boosting bilateral trade between India and ASEAN, and bringing the Indochina States closer to its fold through connectivity, as they have been traditional friends of India.

Fifthly, as I have discussed earlier, in the thoroughfare of India's 'Look East' policy, certain important events took place in the Southeast Asian region, which had major spill over effects on India's overall Southeast Asian policy. The inclusion of Myanmar within ASEAN provided India a land boundary to go along its long maritime perimeter with the Southeast Asian region. As a result, within a short span of time in June 1997, BIMSTEC was established, based on the linking of the littoral states of the Bay of Bengal, and on 10 November 2000, the Mekong-Ganga Cooperation (MGC), another sub-regional organization was formally launched at Vientiane. With the formation of these sub-regional organizations, India's 'Look East' policy was made more inclusive and inter-linking than what it was in the early 1990s.[34] Unfortunately, the performance of these sub-regional organizations has so far failed to exhibit a concrete outfit, and for that New Delhi must play a more prominent role in order to make the BIMSTEC and MGC effective.

Sixthly, insofar as India's Look East CLMV and Brunei policies are concerned, there is no evidence of a clear vision about what we want and how to get it. There is hardly any visible coordinated posture or approach, with too many wobbly canons around. Often, India seems to be shooting at its own toes instead of at the objective. Thus, there is an urgent need to change the existing mindset in order to become commercially competitive in today's fast-paced international milieu.

Seventhly, Thailand has identified India's northeast as an important destination for investment, a potential sub-regional market centre within the framework of Bangkok's 'Look West' Policy. Cultural similarities, historical ties and geographical contiguity between the two regions have further facilitated the economic rationale. The imperatives for Thailand's investment in the northeast region of India stem from three important considerations, reflecting its long-term strategic objectives of the 'Look West' doctrine. First, India's northeast offers a substantial alternate market and transit for sub-regional economies in the Bay of Bengal for the export-driven economy of Thailand. Secondly, the investment in the northeast would enable the Thai companies to further diversify the sources of raw materials, especially natural resources, such as rubber and bamboo, which constitute Thailand's important international exports. Thirdly, energy remains a strategic component of Thai economic interest in the north-eastern region. Energy, especially natural gas and hydroelectricity, forms one of the most important components of Thai investment strategy, given the huge potential offered by the north-eastern region in these areas.

Thai companies' willingness to invest in the energy sector is backed by two key considerations. First, the energy would be essential for operationalising Thailand's production facilities in the region. Secondly, the energy sector in the northeast offers huge incentive for investment due to its growing demand in India. The development of local transport networks in the region is another important area in which Thai companies are willing to invest.[35]

Furthermore, tourism has figured as one of the major thrust areas in the proposed Thai investment in the northeast. India must avail the mindset of Thailand's Forward Looking Policy in order to make the north-eastern region a centre of economic development and thereby, accelerate its connectivity diplomacy in order to make its 'Look East' policy more effective and concrete in nature. In this context, New Delhi should encourage and promote Thai economic motivations in the northeast, obviously taking prime cognisance of its vital national interests.[36]

Eighthly, India still remains outside the Asia Pacific Economic Cooperation (APEC) forum. India also lags behind China and Japan in almost all spheres of this pan-East Asian cooperation due to its weak and almost inert policy towards this region. It has been felt by many East Asian countries that India has so far appeared less proactive than China with respect to certain critical regional issues.

Finally, India has entered into a number of pacts, agreements and FTAs with countries of Southeast Asia, but its implementation record has been quite dismal, while comparing with China and other countries of East Asia. Either the Indian industry faces doubts about its own competitive efficiency, or it does not want competition at home, or it is scared of cheaper exports to India from these countries. Therefore, a realistic mindset will be essential for the Indian industrialists in this competitive global order.

How to Craft the 'Look East' Policy as More Effectual: Some Suggestions

In order to provide a new momentum to India's 'Look East' policy, New Delhi should be more pro-active rather than re-active in nature. New Delhi, in order to fine-tune its strategy, must rely on the execution of soft power as a tool. The major components of this soft power strategy would be culture, education (human resource development), tourism, civil society, information technology, shared experiences of nation building and democracy, Indian Diaspora, etc. India's soft power should act as 'image branding' and 'likeability factor', unlike the past, when New Delhi received negative media attention. Like China, India must employ a variety of tools, like promotion of diaspora, English language, Indian cultural heritage of yoga, classical music, cuisine, dance, religion, festivals, movies of Bollywood, television serials, painting, and literature etc, to exert influence in Southeast Asia.

Trade initiatives such as the India-ASEAN Free Trade Area could help to improve India's regional image also. In some countries of Southeast Asia, India, like China, must provide more aid, and thereby engage in "lobbying-like" behaviour to win Southeast Asian support for their projects. Here, New Delhi must cultivate its Cold War strategic friends like Vietnam, Cambodia and Laos, which the former is lacking presently. Besides this, New Delhi must also upgrade its official image, improve its public diplomacy, establish more Indian language and cultural institutes in various countries of Southeast Asia, and increase the number of scholarships for students to continue higher education in India in order to make it easier for these countries to explore, discover and preserve the shared history.

India must also promote tourism (in order to explain its secular culture and Buddhism) as a vehicle to develop better linkages with Southeast Asian countries. Moreover, Indian books, television shows and joint University collaborations should be encouraged in order to create a vision of India as a constructive regional actor. Indian soft power can be used to help inculcate underlying democratic values such as equality before the law, gender equity and respect for private property. In terms of education, India has much to offer the poorer countries of Southeast Asia, particularly Laos, Cambodia, Vietnam, Myanmar and perhaps Indonesia. It has crafted a relatively small but impressive base of world-class engineering and management institutes, like the Indian Institutes of Technology and Indian Institutes of Management.[37] Actually, India's present status has essentially followed the soft edge of soft power, and if India does not rise to the occasion, Asia will inevitably drift towards a Sino-centric future.

Besides this soft power mechanism, other short-term measures would be essential to make India's 'Look East' Policy competent enough and they are as follows:

> **First**, the road, rail and air connectivity projects should be completed within stipulated time, linking different states with northeast India and Southeast Asia. Road networks and waterways along the river of Kaladan till the port of Sittwe should be developed on a priority basis. **Secondly**, Guwahati and Imphal airports should be upgraded to international standards. Similarly, Guwahati-Bangkok and Guwahati-Dhaka flights should be resumed. **Thirdly**, the infrastructure facilities at the Land Custom Stations at Moreh (Manipur-Myanmar border) and Petrapole (West Bengal-Bangladesh border) need to be upgraded immediately to provide smooth trading operations. **Fourthly**, trade and investment activities should not be held hostage to bureaucratic rules and regulations or inter-ministerial confrontation, such as between the Ministry of Home Affairs (MHA) and the Ministry of External Affairs (MEA). Similarly the DoNER ministry, the MEA, and the Planning Commission need to work in close coordination to ensure effective policy formulation, fund generation and speedy implementation of the adopted policies. **Fifthly**, institutions, such as Indian Entrepreneurship Centres and technical colleges need to be strengthened so that they can develop local skilled work force and empower small-scale entrepreneurs, who can participate in a beneficial manner in the exploitation of agribusiness and food-processing activities. **Sixthly**, the Government of India should take into serious consideration the idea of developing a North East Common Market under the supervision of the North Eastern Council, as suggested by the Chief Minister of Mizoram in November 2004.[38] **Finally**, all the stakeholders – the central Indian Government, the provincial governments, civil society institutions, and other local bodies – have to ensure that the tribal population in states like Manipur, Mizoram, Nagaland, Tripura, practising subsistence agriculture does not get economically displaced and feel alienated in the face of influx of foreign and mainland Indian companies, many of which are multinational corporations.

Conclusion

Having analysed an overview of India's 'Look East' policy, it has been said by the leaders of nations that the 21st Century is the "Century of Asia". Since Asia becomes the engine of growth of the global economy, India and ASEAN must capitalize on their partnership through enhanced connectivity to reap the benefits. For that, expanding and improving road, rail, maritime and air linkages will be crucial due to economic, strategic and other considerations. It can be said that India must change its Cold War mindset in the post-Cold War years and play a more pragmatic, practical and effective role through its 'Look East' policy in order to establish herself as a stable and strong powerhouse in the Asian region. Its overall 'Look East' policy needs to be nursed more without deviating its focus and objectives. New Delhi must re-prioritise the 'Look East' policy, the rhythm of which was lost due to its deep concentration towards Europe and the United States, and make the decade starting from 2010 a 'Decade of Look East.'

Finally, the Indian Prime Minister, Dr. Manmohan Singh, at the 7th India-ASEAN Summit and the 4th East Asia Summit, held in Hua Hin, Thailand in October 2009, said, "I am extremely satisfied with the outcome of the India-ASEAN Summit. I found a strong desire among the ASEAN countries to substantially strengthen their links with India in all areas. This includes not only economic cooperation and trade but also science and technology, human resource development, protection of the environment and deeper political and security cooperation ... and therefore the sky is the limit for our engagement with this region."[39]

Is the "sky" related to the blood connection, which has been recently revealed in the study made by 90 scientists from 10 countries in over 30 scientific institutions including India,[40] who correlated that the majority of the Southeast Asian populations have ancestors in South India? If it is true in its entirety, then the common blood that runs in our vessels would act as the greatest pull in weaving the people of the region into a damask of shared fraternity and make our Look East policy slowly but steadily reach its destiny.

ENDNOTES

1. For detailed analysis of India's recognition of Heng Samrin Government of Cambodia, see Tridib Chakraborti, *India and Kampuchea: A Phase in their Relations, 1978-81,* Minerva Associates (Publications) Pvt. Ltd., Calcutta, 1985.
2. Tridib Chakraborti, "Disparate Priorities: Explaining the Penumbra of India's Look East Policy", in K. Raja Reddy (ed.), *India and ASEAN: Foreign Policy Dimensions for the 21st Century*, New Century Publications, New Delhi, 2005, p. 53.
3. Ibid., pp. 53-54.
4. Tridib Chakraborti, "India's Southeast Asia Policy in the 21st Century: Perambulating the Horizon", in Y. Yagama Reddy (ed), *Emerging India in Asia-Pacific*, New Century Publications, New Delhi, 2007, p.161.
5. Faizal Yahya, "India and Southeast Asia: Revisited", *Contemporary Southeast Asia*, Vol. 25, No. 1, April 2003, p. 93.

6. Tridib Chakraborti, n.2, pp. 66-67.
7. Ibid., p. 63.
8. Tridib Chakraborti, " BIMSTEC: Origin, Growth and Progress", *World Focus*, (New Delhi), Vol. 29, No.1, January 2008, p.14.
9. Joint Statement of the First ASEAN-India Summit, Phnom Penh, 5 November 2002, see http://www.aseansec.org/13198.htm, pp.1-2.
10. *Annual Report: 2002-2003*, Ministry of External Affairs, Government of India, New Delhi, 2003, p. 24.
11. *Annual Report: 2003-2004*, Ministry of External Affairs, Government of India, New Delhi, 2004, p. 38.
12. *The Jakarta Post*, 2 July 2004.
13. For details of this historic partnership pact, see pib.nic.in/release/release.asp?relid=6154 (accessed on March 22, 2010)
14. The 16 members were all ten ASEAN members, China, Japan, South Korea, India, Australia and New Zealand.
15. For details, see www.literateworld.com/india_lead1.htm (accessed on March 23, 2010).
16. G.V.C. Naidu, "Whither the Look East Policy: India and Southeast Asia", Strategic Analysis, Vol. 28, No.2, April-June 2004, p. 344.
17. http://pmindia.nic.in/speech/content4print.asp?id=835 (accessed on March 24, 2010)
18. Vijay Sakhuja, "Cooperative Security in the Straits of Malacca," *Observer Research Foundation (ORF) Issue Brief 2*, New Delhi: August 2005. p. 3.
19. For details, see Christophe Jaffrelot, "India's Look East Policy: An Asianist Strategy in Perspective," *India Review*, Vol. 2, No. 2, April 2003.
20. Shankari Sundararaman, "India and ASEAN," *The Hindu*, 19 November 2002, http://www.mea.gov.in/opinion/2002/11/19o02.htm, accessed on 22 April 2010.
21. For details, see Rajiv Sikri, "India's 'Look East' Policy", *Asia-Pacific Review*, Vol. 16, Issue 1, May 2009, pp. 131-145.
22. *Annual Report: 2004-2005*, Ministry of External Affairs, Government of India, New Delhi, 2004, p. 23.
23. Tridib Chakraborti, "The Distance-Proximity Paradox: Unravelling India's ASEAN Policy over Three Decades", in Anjali Ghosh, Tridib Chakraborti, Anindyo J. Majumdar, and Shibashis Chatterjee (eds.), *India's Foreign Policy*, Pearson, New Delhi, 2009, p. 294.
24. For details, see "The Economics of Climate Change in Southeast Asia: A Regional Overview", Asian Development Bank, April 2009; "Mega-Stress for Mega-Cities: A Climate Vulnerability Ranking of Major Coastal Cities in Asia", World Wildlife Fund (WWF) Report, 2009 and "Climate Change: Strengthening Adaptation and Mitigation in Asia and the Pacific." Asian Development Bank, December 2009.
25. Ranjit Devraj, "Climate Change: India's Monsoon Predictions More Uncertain", *Inter Press Service*, 27 June 2009.
26. For detailed speech, see Manmohan Singh, "Prime Minister's Statement at the 7th India-ASEAN Summit", Indian Press Information Bureau, 24 October 2009.
27. For details, see Z Ying "Assessing China's Soft Power Diplomacy and its Implications on Asia Cooperation", 2006, www.waseda-giari.jp/sysimg/.../200908_si_st_09zhou_paper_f.pdf –
28. For foreign investment in Myanmar, see 'Foreign investment in Myanmar hits 7.6 billion US Dollars', *People's Daily Online*, 18th November 2005 [http://english.people.com.cn/200511/18/eng20051118_222296.html].

29. For details, see "Myanmar pact with Petro China for sale of gas", The Shwe Gas Movement, 11th January 2006 [http://www.shwe.org/news/2006/01/myanmar-pact-with-petro-china-for-sale.html]; see also Anand Kumar, "India-Myanmar Gas Pipeline: Disentangled at Last", Paper no. 1822, *South Asia Analysis Group,* 30th May 2006 [http://www.saag.org/%5Cpapers19%5Cpaper1822.html].
30. R.S. Mooshahary, "India's Look East Policy Integrating The North Eastern Region", for details, see www.sicassam.in/news/21-feb-08.html -
31. *The Hindu*, 22 May 2010.
32. *The Hindu*, 18 October 2003.
33. For detailed speech, see pmindia.nic.in/visits/content.asp?id=174 –
34. Tridib Chakraborti, n.2, pp. 69-70.
35. For details, see Vibhanshu Shekhar, "Thailand's Investment in India's Northeast: Strategies, Potentials and Risks", Institute of Peace and Conflict Studies (IPCS), Research Papers, New Delhi, India, April 2008.
36. For details, see Tridib Chakraborti, "East Meets West: The Emerging India-Thailand Relations in the Post-Cold War Years", in Lipi Ghosh (ed.), *Connectivity and Beyond: Indo-Thai Relations through Ages*, The Asiatic Society, Kolkata, 2009.
37. Sadanand Dhume, "India's Role in Southeast Asia: The Logic and Limits of Cooperation with the United States and Japan", csis.org/files/media/csis/pubs/090201_bsa_dhume.pdf; see also indiangeopolitics.blogspot.com/.../indias-soft-power-advantage.html
38. For details, see Vibhanshu Shekhar, n.35.
39. For detail speech of Indian Prime Minister, Manmohan Singh see http://www.mea.gov.in/
40. *The Statesman*, 12 December, 2009.

11

India ASEAN FTA: Towards Comprehensive Economic Partnership

Amita Batra

This paper undertakes a critical analysis of India's economic relations with ASEAN over the last two decades. While the relationship formally took off in 1991 with the start of India's Look East policy, the institutional framework acquired shape with the announcement of the framework agreement for the India-ASEAN FTA in 2003. The FTA was finally signed in 2009 and has become effective from January 2010. Against a background analysis of the bilateral trade trends, we examine the FTA for its expected benefits for India and scope for expansion to include services and investment. The likely costs of the FTA for India are also analyzed. The paper then proceeds to assess the India ASEAN economic relationship and the FTA as a possible basis for Asian economic integration.

India-ASEAN Economic Relations

Trends in bilateral trade

In the last two decades, India-ASEAN economic relations have acquired significant momentum. The improvement in India – ASEAN ties is reflected in their increasing bilateral trade. The regional bloc is India's fourth largest trading partner. India's trade with ASEAN, which was US$ 13.2 billion in 2003-04, has increased to almost US$ 40 billion in 2007-08. India's exports to ASEAN that were US$ 5.82 billion in 2003-04 have increased to US$ 16.37 billion in 2007-08 and imports from ASEAN accounting for US$ 7.4 billion in 2003-04 have increased to US$ 22.66 billion in 2007-08.These volumes are indicative of the rapid pace at which trade is expanding between India and ASEAN. However, despite the sustained improvement in India – ASEAN trade, India's trade with ASEAN is less than 10 per cent of its global trade while ASEAN's trade with India makes up only 2 per cent of its global trade, indicating the huge trade potential that is yet to be explored between these two regions. The geographical contiguity, proximity, cultural affinity, and economic dynamism of the two regions is similarly indicative of a high potential of trade between ASEAN and India.[1]

India's Trade with ASEAN (US$ billion)

	Exports	Imports
2003-04	5.82	7.4
2004-05	8.42	9.11
2005-06	10.41	10.88
2006-07	12.6	18.08
2007-08	16.37	22.66
% share in India's total	9.8	9.45

Look East Policy

The intensification of India – ASEAN bilateral economic relations may be seen as an outcome of India's 'Look East Policy' that was officially launched in 1991 when India's vision of the world and the evolving global economy underwent a strategic shift. The initiation of the look east policy was a signal that marked the end of India's pursuit of self reliance based on an inward looking growth strategy and the start of an era when India opened up to the opportunities from globalization, in terms of both international trade and investment. The LEP also sent out strong signals that the East Asian region had come to acquire a significant position in India's foreign policy as in economic terms it was to be regarded as a new source of business opportunity as also an inspiration for the new economic development path that it was to embark upon henceforth. India's economic reform programme, it was assumed, would acquire the necessary push as closer association with East Asia would require lower trade barriers and liberalized investment regimes.

As India's economy continues to grow today, the LEP has acquired an added dimension of regional economic integration. Regional economic integration in Asia as a whole has gathered momentum in response to the emergence of continent – wide trade blocs in the north-significantly the EU and NAFTA and the fact that over sixty five per cent of world trade today is being undertaken on a preferential basis. More recently there have been other factors that have contributed to India and East Asia taking forward the agenda of economic integration. In the post 1997-98 financial crisis period ASEAN has needed to regain its economic momentum and regional space. Economic integration with the dynamic Indian economy contributes to both these objectives. For India the slow progress in the process of integration within South Asia has made it necessary to extend its economic vision beyond the confines of its traditional policy and the South Asian region. The emphasis of the Look East policy has been on the economic aspects of India's relations with East Asia, and in particular, the focus has been on India's engagement with ASEAN.

Institutional Framework

In 1992 India became a sectoral dialogue partner of ASEAN with a focus on cooperation in trade, investment, tourism and science and technology. The relationship was upgraded to full dialogue partnership in December 1995 at the fifth ASEAN summit in Bangkok. India became a member of the ASEAN Regional Forum in 1996. The ASEAN – India relationship was upgraded to summit level in 2002. India is now an ASEAN summit partner along with Japan, China and South Korea.

An important milestone in the ASEAN-India association was the hosting of the first ASEAN – India summit in 2002 in Phnom Penh. The first India-ASEAN Business Summit was also held in 2002 in New Delhi and has now become an annual feature prior to the India-ASEAN Summit as a forum for networking and exchange of business experiences between policy makers and business leaders from ASEAN and India.

A clear institutional framework for operationalizing the economic cooperation between India and ASEAN was laid out when the framework agreement for an India – ASEAN FTA was signed during the second India-ASEAN summit held in Bali in October 2003. As per the original schedule negotiations on the agreement were to conclude by 2005 and an Early Harvest Programme (EHP) was to be implemented. In the final form the FTA became effective on January 2010 after having been signed in August 2009. The EHP was not implemented.

India-ASEAN FTA

The India-ASEAN FTA that became effective from January 2010 has a tariff reduction/ elimination schedule covering about 80 per cent of traded goods between the two regions. The gradual tariff reduction schedule beginning from January 2010 is to be fully implemented by the end of 2013 and 2016 in respect of the two "normal tracks". For special products the applied MFN rates are to be reduced in a phased manner. A negative list with 489 items that are excluded from the list of tariff concessions has also been indicated. Simultaneously safeguard measures are provided in case a country's exports exceed 3 per cent of partner country's imports and cause substantial injury to the domestic producers.

The FTA has several positive attributes that make it relevant for the two regions. The FTA will lead to the creation of a free trade area with a combined GDP of over $2 trillion and population of $1.6 billion. In the context of improving bilateral economic relations, the India-ASEAN FTA is perceived as an effective instrument to help exploit the trade potential between the two regions. This is especially true in the post global financial crisis period when it has become imperative for developing countries to find markets for exports as their erstwhile markets in the developed world have been shrinking on account of the crisis. The FTA gives India and ASEAN a chance for export diversification away from their traditional markets like the US and Europe.

Notwithstanding the gains, the FTA deal is likely to spell some costs for the Indian side. While the 600 million people ASEAN market is a definite addition for our exports, in the face of lower ASEAN tariffs relative to India, the FTA liberalization may not imply any major additional gains for India's exports. Instead, the relatively higher cuts that India will have to make in respect of its tariffs may actually lead to increased ASEAN exports to India. This will lead to a further deterioration of the India's trade deficit with ASEAN. Also, the negative list with 489 items is small. This small size is apparently on account of the consideration accorded to the sensitivities of Indian farmers. This is evident from the inclusion of items of agriculture, textiles and chemicals and the extended schedule for special products like pepper, coffee, tea oil and rubber that would effectively reduce duties only in 2019 for these items.

There is, however, an underlying differential in productivity and competitiveness in the respective sectors between India and ASEAN countries. This is particularly true of the plantation sector which is likely to be the hardest hit given the relatively greater advantage that the ASEAN countries have in commodities like tea, pepper, coffee and palm oil. Productivity of pepper is 380 kilograms per hectare in India while it is 1,000 kilograms per hectare in Vietnam and 3,000 kilograms per hectare in Indonesia. Similarly, Coffee productivity in India stands at 765 kg/ha while Vietnam produces 1.7 tonnes/ha.

Higher wage and input costs in India further aggravate this differential. The productivity differentials need to be reduced and this calls for special policies and action from the government of India. A few schemes for productivity enhancement have already been launched. These include the Rs. 1,400 crore scheme for improving social infrastructure in tea gardens, wherein Tea Gardens of Tripura, Cachar valley and Tamil Nadu have been identified, a Rs. 4,900 crore Special Purpose Tea Fund (SPTF) as a 15 year productivity boosting programme has been established, and the Coffee Board has proposed a Rs. 105 crore scheme to replant 45,000 hectares of coffee plantations. Similar schemes are in the pipeline for pepper as well. Fisheries and marine products is the other sector that is likely to suffer as a consequence of the agreement. Further, the threat from Thailand, the world's largest exporter of farmed shrimp, and Vietnam, which is the world's eighth largest seafood exporter, is imminent. Also in regards to the rules of origin (RoO), India has allowed for a relaxed 35 per cent value addition criterion. This in contradiction of the twin criterion and 40 per cent value addition rules that are operational in case of the India – Singapore, and India – Thailand FTAs both member countries of the ASEAN.

India's gains lie in the next stage of the comprehensive trade pact wherein services and investment, both areas of high potential gains for India, are to be included. India is among the top ten services exporting nations globally while ASEAN is a major importer. At US$ 150 billion, ASEAN's imports in this sector are almost half as large as that of the USA. Negotiations for service sector liberalization are ongoing. The potential for investment is also evident in the existing trends. The India – Singapore Comprehensive Economic Cooperation Agreement (CECA), which came into effect in August 2005, includes a bilateral investment promotion treaty, a double taxation avoidance agreement and an air services agreement in addition to an FTA. Singapore is one of the top five investors in India.

In addition to the India-ASEAN FTA, a striking outcome of India's LEP and its deepening association with the region has been its inclusion in the 2005 East Asia Summit (EAS) held in Kuala Lumpur and the options that this forum presents for India and the region to foster economic prosperity and multilateral liberalization. It has opened up ideas about the value of more comprehensive economic cooperation possibilities with East Asia and could be a new and exciting beginning of a process that could evolve into an Asian Economic Community. At the EAS, 16 nations comprising the ASEAN+3 (China, Japan, Korea) +3 (India, Australia, New Zealand) proposed the idea of regional economic integration in Asia on the lines of the European Union. The emerging trends in Asian integration indicate the process is likely to be ASEAN-centric. For India, taking this process forward through strengthening links with ASEAN and the East Asian economies may very well be the future direction of the LEP. This is already evident in India's engagement with the region that is reflected in the form of formal arrangements that extend beyond the ASEAN-India FTA and also the ASEAN region.

India's Broader Engagement with the Region

Besides the India ASEAN FTA, India's increased economic engagement with the region is reflected in the many formal arrangements that it has established with the ASEAN member countries through bilateral, regional and sub regional pacts. Many of these extend to the East Asian economies that in turn strengthens India's bond with the region as a whole. The 'Look East Policy' that was primarily directed towards improving relations with ASEAN in the initial years has quite obviously now progressed to encompass other nations of the region such as China, Japan and Korea.

A Comprehensive Economic Cooperation Agreement (CECA) between India and Singapore was signed in June 2005. The agreement, which came into effect in August 2005, includes a bilateral investment promotion treaty, a double taxation avoidance agreement and an air services agreement in addition to an FTA. Trade in goods, services and investment Singapore is one of the top five investors in India. Future areas of cooperation include infrastructure development, particularly port development, IT park (Knowledge economy), telecom, automobiles, SME, pharmaceuticals and energy. Services liberalization in sectors like Banking, Dentistry, medicine, nursing, Architecture, Accounting and Science and technology, Education and Tourism are also expected to be a part of the agreement. India signed an FTA with Thailand in 2003 and as part of this an EHP for 82 sectors is already under implementation. India is also considering entering into FTAs with Malaysia and Indonesia.

India has entered into a number of bilateral treaties and agreements for cooperation in the fields of trade, finance, science & technology, agriculture, tourism & culture, air services and visa exemption with Laos, Cambodia and Vietnam. India has some major projects in Cambodia in the areas of education, entrepreneurship development and information technology. Myanmar is the only ASEAN country with which India shares both land and maritime boundaries. Myanmar is India's gateway to ASEAN. As part of its 'Look East Policy', India has strengthened cooperation with Myanmar in a number of sectors by extending a number of general and project-specific credit lines to Myanmar in the last few years.

India's membership in sub-regional organizations like BIMSTEC, the Bangkok Agreement[2] and MGC also reflects its association with the ASEAN countries. BIMSTEC comprises Bangladesh, India, Myanmar, Sri Lanka, Thailand, Bhutan and Nepal. This initiative, which is inclusive of countries from both SAARC and ASEAN, is envisioned as a bridge between the two sub regions of Asia. The first ever summit – level meeting for BIMSTEC was held in July 2004 when it acquired its new incarnation as the Bay of Bengal Initiative for Multi-sectoral Technical and Economic Cooperation. The second summit was held in New Delhi in 2008. The BIMSTEC after 18 rounds of negotiations initiated since 2004 has finalized the FTA agreement and now aims to achieve its own FTA by 2017. This is an important element in India's development policy as the Bay of Bengal initiative is dynamic and as a bridge between the more inward oriented South Asia, and the more outward oriented South East and East Asia offers the prospect of widening the network for outward oriented growth in this part of Asia. In fact, through this route India followed by SAARC can reach out to the South East Asian region and beyond to the Asia-Pacific community. India is also a member of another sub regional agreement, the Bangkok Agreement, which was signed in 1975. Its other members are Bangladesh, China, Republic of Korea, Laos and Sri Lanka. The Agreement is at present limited in scope, as it covers only tariff concessions on goods. The Agreement was revitalized in 2001 with the entry of China. China, India and Republic of Korea as members of this agreement indicate the huge market potential inherent in the agreement.

India has recently signed a CECA with South Korea. This is the first comprehensive trade agreement that India has signed with an OECD country. The agreement is expected to have a beneficial impact through trade, investment and services liberalization. The small and medium enterprise sector in particular is likely to benefit by this alliance with Korea. Work on the India-Japan comprehensive economic partnership agreement (CEPA) has been put on the fast-track and the CEPA is well on its way to being finalized. The comprehensive agreement would include facilitation of trade and investment. Trade between India and Japan was 13 billion in 2008-09 and is targeted at 20 billion in 2010. Significant potential is seen in both trade and FDI. In fact, the signing of India-Korea economic partnership pact may have also influenced Japan to accelerate preparations for the India-Japan agreement.

India-China relations have also entered a phase where economics has taken precedence over other issues. China has now emerged as India's largest single country trading partner. In 2007-08 India's exports to China were US $11 billion and imports accounted for US $29 billion. In 2008-09 total bilateral trade was US $50 billion. A Joint Study Group was set up in 2004 to explore opportunities for economic cooperation in trade and investment. Feasibility studies for an FTA have been undertaken. The two economies are already members of the Bangkok Agreement.

India and China have both signed an FTA agreement with ASEAN. The ASEAN–China Free Trade Area (ACFTA) has became effective on January, 2010. India and China are also both members of the East Asia Summit and are hence co-participants in the formation of the Asian Economic Community. In the context it is worthwhile to view the India's engagement vis a vis China with ASEAN – the hub of the Asian integration process. This aspect is discussed in the paragraphs that follow.

India and China: The FTA with ASEAN

India and China are two of the most dynamic economies of the world having registered sustained high growth rates over the last few years. India's average real growth rate between 1995-2004 was 6.1 per cent, while that for China was 9.1

per cent. While the oft quoted context for India's participation or rather, inclusion in the forum is stated to be as a counterweight to China, the economic rationale may prove otherwise. While India and China have both undertaken economic reforms and liberalized their economies, the pace of integration is different in each case. For both exports and imports of goods India's share in the growth of world economy total exports and imports over 1995-2004 is less than 2 per cent in contrast with that for China in which case it is about 8-9 per cent. Overall, India's share in world trade – exports and imports – is only about 1 per cent while China's share is around 5-6 per cent.

As for financial integration India has attained the status of an attractive investment destination and has made large strides in capital account liberalization. Despite this progress India absorbs less than one percent of the global FDI flows while China corners almost 8 per cent. The figures for portfolio investment and foreign exchange reserve accumulation may be more encouraging but it is clear that even though India's participation in the world economy is increasing it is yet not close to the levels attained by China. It may not be fair then to really posit India and China as competing economies in the world. This fact is further reinforced when we undertake a detailed analysis of the comparative advantage of these two economies. When the global comparative advantage of the two economies is analyzed, the picture appears to be very similar as both India and China have maximum comparative advantage in unskilled labor intensive goods followed by technology and human capital intensive goods.

Seemingly, the two economies may appear as competitors. However, when a commodity level analysis of the possible competitive threat that India and China may pose to each other in the global or regional market (ASEAN) is undertaken, it is observed that there are very few commodities for which either India or China pose a direct threat to each other. In fact, there are very few commodities, among their top ten best performing sectors, where the two countries share their comparative advantage regionally or globally. If we trace the trend development in the manufacturing sector of the two economies, it is easy to discern that both India and China are moving along divergent paths. There is a complete lack of correlation and in fact increasing divergence between the Indian and Chinese structure of comparative advantage.[3] (Batra, 2007). India and China have been specializing in different product lines within each product category. India is not a major force in international manufacturing, except in textile and clothing, pearls, precious stones, etc, glass and glassware, miscellaneous manufactures and other unskilled labor-intensive commodity categories given abundance of low-cost labor which makes it acquired specialization and comparative advantage. In contrast, China has experienced dynamism in its manufacturing skills, specialization pattern and consequently export structure. From specializing in unskilled labor-intensive sectors like toys, footwear, apparel and light manufactures in the last decade it has in this decade advanced to office machinery, electrical and electronic equipment and appliances.

China today is the manufacturing hub of the world. Thus, India and China need not be viewed as competing nations, they may in fact complement each other, and it is the latter force that may be worth exploring rather than the 'counterweight' argument positioning of India in the context of Asian economic integration.

ASEAN Led Asian Economic Integration

In the context of the ASEAN – India FTA and the intensification of India's association with the region, it is useful to examine the feasibility of the Asian integration process that appears to be proceeding with ASEAN as the centre. In assigning ASEAN with the task of integrating Asia, it is imperative to recognize that the ASEAN integration process has itself received a push forward only recently at the ASEAN 2007 summit when the ASEAN charter issued a declaration for the implementation of the ASEAN Economic Community by 2015. The Charter is a blueprint for the ASEAN Economic Community aimed at transforming ASEAN into a single market and production base, a highly competitive economic region, a region of equitable economic development, and a region fully integrated into the global economy. Prior to this the ASEAN integration experience has been slow and the ASEAN FTA that was implemented in 1992 with the constituent elements of the common effective preferential tariff (CEPT), Agreement on the ASEAN Investment Area (AIA) for investment liberalization (1998), and the ASEAN Framework Agreement on Services (AFAS) for services liberalization have not been fully utilized or implemented. Some studies estimate that only 3 per cent of the intra-ASEAN trade has availed of the CEPT rates.[4] (Baldwin, 2006). The rather limited ASEAN integration therefore provides weak benchmarks for regional integration in Asia.

To take the process of ASEAN integration forward and for ASEAN to fulfil its role as a strategic hub in Asian integration, strong political will and leadership are the foremost requirements in bringing the economies under a common institutional arrangement. This is particularly important given the development gap among the member nations and their sensitivity to the issue of national sovereignty. In the context the 'ASEAN way' of consensus based decision making needs to change. While it has been able to accomplish peace and regional stability, very little has been achieved in terms of regional integration. Competing export interests of the member economies present another challenge so as to make the ten members identify common interests under a collective singular identity. For the purpose it would do well to enhance the capacity of the present small secretariat of the ASEAN. It has to acquire the status of a regional organization with staff that is capable in terms of number and expertise to handle the delicate national issues as well administrative tasks in the process of regional economic integration. To make regional economic integration in Asia a success this would indeed be a prior requirement.

Given ASEAN's present scope of operation and the magnitude of the task ahead, it may be wise to consider as an alternative mechanism a convergence of the ASEAN+1 FTAs other six economies of the EAS may also be considered. Again though for this to be a successful alternative route to Asian integration some prior requirements would need to be satisfied. First, the ASEAN+1 FTAs need to be compatible. Only if the ASEAN+1 agreements of the plus six economies are compatible with each other would there be hope of linking these agreements to constitute a regional economic entity in Asia in future. At this stage compatibility of the elements of the +1 agreements is difficult to visualize as most of these have already been negotiated. It may be appropriate now that as the individual agreements with ASEAN are pursued the aim of a Pan Asian FTA remains paramount throughout the exercise for all involved. This is required as even though bilateral arrangements provide necessary strategic access to markets they are ultimately and inherently protectionist in nature. Unlike unilateral and multilateral trade liberalization they allow protectionism through a process of liberalization that is conditional upon reciprocity and restrictive rules of origin. As East Asian integration has been largely 'market driven', this should continue to be so and the commercial logic of the market should continue to guide the process. For this the prime responsibility of all governments is to create domestic conditions that will facilitate the market flows. So that as unilateral economic reform and trade liberalization remain the priority focus areas for Asian economies and specifically for India, the bilaterals should be undertaken in a manner that they can promote multilateral trade liberalization limiting the discriminatory effects.

Global Financial Crisis – The New Imperative for Asian Economic Integration

Even while the ASEAN centric EAS and the convergence of plus ones is discussed as an alternative mechanism for Asian integration, a new imperative seems to have emerged on the horizon. The Asian integration that has appeared as an onerous and difficult task in the past has acquired the necessary push from recent global developments. In the face of the consequences of the global financial crisis, in particular, the western tendencies towards protectionism, an integrated region with a coordinated defence mechanism particularly in the area of finance is likely to yield regional stability, a much desired collective goal at this point in time. The 14th ASEAN Summit Meeting in fact made an appeal for coordinated action and bold and urgent reform of the international financial system. The collective entity also emphasized on a more equitable, comprehensive and inclusive world order where the interests and voices of the emerging market economies are better represented. Economic integration of ASEAN is thus imperative for Asian integration and India has both a role and interest in pursuing this agenda. Some options have already been worked upon successfully like the multilateralization of the Chiang Mai Initiative (CMI) and some others are in the pipeline. Significant among the latter are deepening and expanding the Asian Bond Market Initiative and Asian Bond Fund and creation of a regional reserve pool. Simultaneously it is also time for some bold initiatives that include the setting up of an Asian Financial Stability Dialogue to strengthen supervision, surveillance, and dialogue on financial markets and the Asian Infrastructure Finance Corporation given the significance of cross border infrastructure. The extension of these initiatives to India is a likely option in the near future. India's large foreign exchange reserve pool acts as a definite advantage in this context. Coordinated financial action therefore may just be the most feasible option for the region's integration.

Conclusion

The trends in India ASEAN economic relations show clear evidence of a deepening association and an emerging comprehensive partnership between the two regions. The India ASEAN FTA has formalized the relationship. The association that extends to countries beyond ASEAN owing to India's pursuit of its Look East policy can also be reasonably perceived as contributing to the process of Asian economic integration. A further phillip to this process is provided by India's emergence as a strong economic power that has been minimally impacted by the global financial crisis of 2008. There is now ample scope to extend to India many of the financial initiatives established in the region in the wake of the global financial crisis. In the coming years India's association with ASEAN and the east Asian countries is therefore likely to emerge as the basis of economically integrated Asia.

ENDNOTES

1. Amita Batra, "India's Global Trade Potential: The Gravity Model Approach", *Global Economic Review* (Routledge), Vol. 35, No.3, September 2006.
2. Now called the Asia Pacific Trade Agreement, APTA.
3. Amita Batra, "The Structure of Comparative Advantage of China and India: Global and Regional Dynamics", *China &World Economy* (Blackwell) Vol.15. No. 6, 15 November 2007.
4. R. Baldwin, "Managing the Noodle Bowl: The Fragility of East Asian Regionalism," Discussion Paper Series, No. 5561, (Center for Economic Policy Research, UK, 2006).

12

India's Diaspora Policy: A Malaysian Experience

Amit Singh

The political culture of Malaysia has undergone significant change in the last four decades, which has had a major bearing on the minority communities. This aspect is dealt in the paper by examining the constitutional and structural opportunities and constraints facing the minority groups. An attempt is made to study it critically in the background of contemporary Diaspora discourses. The study of Malaysia is of particular relevance; here, though Indians remain socially and culturally separate, it has a political status as a community in the Malaysian model of Multiculturalism. Political contestation, political parties and voting behavior still largely follow ethnic divisions in the country's plural society. However, Malaysia's 'Vision 2020' (under the former Prime Minister Mahathir) perhaps provides answers about the path, the ruling elite wants to take in the future. The document exhorts the Malaysians to make every effort to develop a mature democratic society where there is equitable distribution of the nation's wealth and no racial identification with wealth and economic function.

Introduction

In the contemporary globalised world, the diasporas have been used as a catalyst in developing relations between the nation-states. Etymologically, 'Diaspora', first used in the classical world, has acquired renewed importance in the late twentieth century and has been redefined by the technological revolution of the twenty first century. Diaspora is a term principally applied to Jews and less commonly to Greeks, Armenians, Chinese, Africans and the Indians. In the present world scenario, there are at least thirty ethnic groups that claim to constitute a Diaspora.[1]

The Indian Diaspora across the world ranks second only after the Chinese. People of Indian Origin (PIOs) and Non-Resident Indians (NRIs) are present in all parts of the globe. It has been estimated that the overseas Indian community, numbering over 25 million, is spread over 189 countries. While the history of the Indian Diaspora dates back to the pre-Christian era, large-scale emigration of Indians took place mainly in the 19th and 20th centuries, which can be divided into four phases. The colonial period witnessed unprecedented emigration of indentured and other laborers, traders, professionals and employees of the British Government to the European (British, French and Dutch) colonies in Asia, Africa, Latin America and the Caribbean. However, it was only post-World War II that the most far-reaching emigration of Indians took place, mainly of professionals, to the developed countries namely, England, the U.S.A., Canada, Australia and New Zealand. The oil boom in the 1970s and 1980s saw millions of Indians migrating to the Gulf and West Asian countries. In today's globalised world, Indians in various sectors like IT, medicine, and trade are finding opportunities abroad, which also include a large number of students seeking admission in developed countries, thereby adding to the numbers of the Diaspora. The Indian Diaspora constitutes more than 40 per cent of the population in Fiji, Mauritius, Trinidad, Guyana and Surinam.

Every Southeast Asian country has either PIOs or NRIs. An estimated 6.7 million Indians reside overseas in Southeast Asia, with one-third living in Malaysia and Singapore, 85,000 in Indonesia, 150,000 in Thailand and 50,000 in the Philippines.[2] Myanmar has a sizeable number estimated around 2 million. The rest are scattered over the remaining Southeast Asian countries. The numbers are not sufficiently large for leveraging the Diaspora in these countries, but they are considered important.[3] In Malaysia, around 80 per cent of the Indians are engaged in manual work as either unskilled or semi-skilled labourers; only 6 per cent are in the administrative, professional or managerial positions. According to the Indian Diaspora Report 2001, the Indian population in Malaysia owns only 1.5 per cent of the country's wealth. Divided along racial lines, and reinforced by religion, culture, language, and occupation, Malaysian society faces a constant threat of ethnic hostility. Therefore, the Indian community suffers continuously in Malaysia.

The study will recount the brief history of the Indian Diaspora and also trace the evolution of India's Diaspora policy. It examines the pre-modern period, colonial and pre-independence policies concerning Indian Diaspora. In order to understand contemporary India's policy towards the Diaspora, a survey of the developments of the Nehruvian Diaspora policy is undertaken. The aim is to analyse and explore Nehru's effect on India's Diaspora policy, keeping in mind that India in the 21st century has undergone tumultuous change. In the past six decades since independence, the Indian population has more than trebled, and fresh energies and innovation have been unleashed into what is acknowledged as India's success as a fast growing economy.

The paper focuses on following broad themes; pre-modern period, colonial/British period, India after Independence and the proactive period of cultivating the Diaspora, which began in the 1990s and continues. This study critically analyses the impact of India's Diaspora policy on ethnic Indians in Malaysia. Hence, this paper seeks to answer the following questions: What bearing has India's contemporary Diaspora policy had on the Indian Diaspora in Southeast Asia in general and on Malaysian Indians in particular? What is the fallout of "India's Look-East Policy" on the Indian Diaspora? and Does India differentiate between the 'old' and the 'new' Diaspora in the sharp societal cleavages in countries like Malaysia?

Historical Background

The politico-economic and socio-cultural ties between India and Southeast Asia go back to the pre-Christian era. That era, dominated by the mercantile links also brought Hinduism and Buddhism to the region. Commercial relations had a longer history than cultural contacts. According to Brian Harrison "from at least the sixth century BC onwards Indian traders were sailing to those lands, and down through those islands, in search of gold and tin".[4] Java was colonised by the Hindus between the 1st and 7th century. In the 7th century, the Javanese converted to Hinduism and an elaborate Hindu culture developed by the 10th century. The Hindu kingdom (8th-13th centuries) covered much of Indonesia.[5] The Chola king Rajaraja the Great (AD 985-1018) conquered South India and extended his hold over Ceylon. Under his son, Rajendra (AD 1018-35) the Chola power reached out to threaten the empire of Sri Vijaya in Java and Sumatra. (Sri Vijaya kingdom was founded in Sumatra before the fourth century AD it rose to prominence towards the close of the seventh century AD). The Cholas were expelled from Ceylon in 1070.[6] In the fifth century AD Hindu kingdoms were formed in Java.[7] The people of Java came to share with the Indians their religions, languages, art and architecture, cultural mores, and legal and political ethos and forms.[8] This area was exposed to "the heaviest Indianisation."[9]

Majority of the people of Bali Island still practice Hinduism. The Indian influence is quite visible even in today's Southeast Asia, especially in its languages, customs and the rituals of the royalty. Hindu concepts of kingship and Hindu administrative institutions and ceremonies became so deeply embedded in the royal culture of Southeast Asian Nations that, even after the Islamization of some states, these practices remain till date. The Indian migration during this period was relatively small in scale and limited in geographic scope.[10]

India did not show any political ambitions or expansionism in neighbouring Southeast Asia and other part of the world. Hence, the Indian culture, religion and philosophy were welcome. Mostly because of this reason, after the extensive emigration during the pre-modern period, India did not have any policy or tenets related to their emigrants. One of the most important reasons is that during the pre-modern period, India was divided into small kingdoms, and each of them followed their own individual goals. Therefore, no one denies the fact that there were high possibilities of assimilation of the Indian emigrants in the countries of their adoption.

India constantly derived considerable economic benefits from its contacts with Southeast Asia. The export of gold and spices from the region to India characterized the trade relations of pre-modern periods, whereas in recent times, remittances were sent back home by migrant Indians. The only difference was that in the former period, India supplied goods, while in the latter period, it primarily supplied labour. During the colonial period, the interaction between Southeast Asia and India was limited due to colonization, and whatever interaction they had at that time was dependent on the colonial masters. The bulk of Indians migrated during the colonial era as plantation workers.[11]

No other country in the world is characterised by such diversity as India in terms of culture, language, region and other forms of social stratification. Emigration from India too has been widely varied in social characteristics, such as in levels of education, caste and class, place of origin, religious and linguistic affiliations. The Indian Diaspora is highly differentiated, especially in the case of the "old" and the "new" emigrants. Indian policy towards the Indian Diaspora has also varied from the colonial times to the early years of independence and on to the present times. While it could be discernable that during the colonial period, the British were only interested in replacing 'slavery' by recruiting 'indenture labour' from India, the policies it pursued were essentially to facilitate labour emigration rather than to mitigate their plight in the plantation barracks. Not only were they 'encouraged' to renew the period of their contract under the indenture system, but also the colonial rulers actively discouraged the labour from returning by charging heavy amounts of money for their return passage. This essentially served the interests of the British colonial masters rather than that of the exploited Indian plantation worker.[12] Following the ban on indenture system, the British encouraged the indenture labour to settle down in their island colonies. The British position was that the Indians were simply citizens of whichever colony they lived in. The British left most of their colonies with the legacy of conflict between the indentured labourers and the ethnic population of the host country.

India's Nationalist Leadership first turned its attention to the issue of Indians overseas as early as the 1890s. Several founding figures of the Indian National Congress (INC) travelled abroad to study or work and many of them experienced first-hand the disadvantages that overseas Indians faced. Racial discrimination and restrictive immigration policies in the colonies aided the forging of an emotional bond between Indians overseas and the emerging nationalist leadership. Both groups came together as they were engaged in opposing colonial regimes.[13] Indian nationalism played an integrating role in mobilising the Indian Diaspora around the world to gain India's independence. They were exhorted to identify with India's cause as 'only a free India could hope to protect and safeguard their interests'. Since most of them were taken under a coercive colonial rule, they were visualised by Mahatma Gandhi as a segment of emerging Indian independence where they would share the socio-cultural space within India. Therefore, it was a policy of identification and association, but these trends were limited to the colonial period only.

Evolution and Impact of Nehru's Diaspora Policy

While discussing India's Diaspora policy, one observes that after independence, India followed the policy of disassociation with regard to its Diaspora. The basic principles of India's foreign policy were laid during the independence under Prime Minister Jawaharlal Nehru. In 1957, Nehru stated:

> "Indians abroad should always give primary consideration to the interest of the people of those countries; they should never allow themselves to be placed in a position of exploiting the people of those countries; in fact, we have gone thus far and said, if you cannot be, and if you are not, friendly to the people of that country, come back to India and do not spoil the fair name of India".[14]

The quote reflects the importance that he attached to the positive role Indians could play overseas by assimilating themselves in the host countries. Nehru did not want the presence of Indians to have a negative impact on India's relations with the host countries. Subsequently, there was noticeable continuity and change in India's Diaspora policy, but most of the successive governments followed Nehru's path blindly. Therefore, the conditions of the overseas Indian community deteriorated in most of the host nations, especially Myanmar, Malaysia, Fiji and some of the African and Caribbean countries.

Post-colonial India's policy towards the Diaspora was deeply informed by Nehru as the country's Prime Minister and Foreign Minister. Convinced that it was in the best interest of overseas Indians to integrate into their host societies, he repeatedly argued for them to 'identify themselves with and integrate in the mainstream of social and political life of the country of their domicile.' There were many reasons for India's policy of disengagement and distancing. In the Cold War era, India's foreign policy was based on ideas of neutrality from the 'great power blocs' and solidarity with the 'Third World', in which friendship with newly liberated Africa and Asia was highly valued. Nehru's aspiration to propel India onto the world stage through its leadership of the Non-Aligned Movement depended on the goodwill of Afro-Asian countries, which hosted many Indian communities. Accordingly, India cultivated good relations with Asian and African states, though it meant neglecting the Diasporas interests. It did not adopt an interventionist policy on behalf of overseas Indians, lest India be seen as interfering in the domestic affairs of other states.[15]

It culminated in the Panchsheel, a declaration of world peace and cooperation. This was to unite the Asian and African Nations under a common foreign policy, which was described by Nehru as the recognition of sovereignty and integrity of a country, non-aggression, and non-interference in other countries either for political or ideological reasons, mutual respect and peaceful coexistence.[16] In the long run this was to consolidate Nehru's aim of an Afro-Asian voice and voting bloc in the UN. In fact, had Nehru's government pressed on expatriate Asian rights and privileges, it would have disrupted possible future cooperation between India and the relevant host countries.[17]

In 1977, when a non-Congress government led by the Janata Party assumed power, the first signs of an official rethink vis-à-vis the Diaspora appeared. That official policies strike a balance between safeguarding India's foreign policy interests and show legitimate concern about Indians overseas. Although the Janata government did not remain in power for very long, the debate on expatriate Asians had restarted within the Indian government.

India's Policy towards the Indian Diaspora in Southeast Asia

Southeast Asia did not play a major part in India's Foreign Policy calculations during the 1960s, a period when India was facing major security threats from Pakistan and China. The exigencies of the Cold War, as well as political and economic considerations at home, had a hand in the shaping of India's policy towards the region. This preoccupation with its immediate neighbourhood held back India from formulating a policy towards ethnic Indians. The Indians in Southeast Asia do not evoke the suspicion and hatred of the indigenous peoples. They are small in number, most of them belong to the weaker economical stratum of the society of the host nations, and politically they do not have much influence.

Prof. V. Suryanarayan briefly illustrates two examples that are given below to examine India's policy towards Overseas Indians in Southeast Asia. The first relates to the status of Indians in Myanmar, where unfortunately, New Delhi attached greater importance to the improvement of state-to-state relations rather than protecting the legitimate interests of the Indian community. Soon after independence, the Burmese Government initiated radical land reforms, which hit the interests of the Indian Chettiar community. A total of 27 lakh acres of land, 14 percent of the total cultivable land in Burma, was nationalized. The market value of the land was estimated at Rs. 70 crores. Despite the excellent equations between New Delhi and Rangoon, India could not persuade Burma to pay adequate compensation to the landlords. According to informed estimates, by the

Population of Indian Diaspora in Southeast Asia

Country	Population	NRIs	PIOs	Stateless	% of the population
Brunei	331,000	7,000	500	100	2.3%
Cambodia	11,340,000	150	150	Nil	Negligible
Indonesia	200,000,000	500	50,000	Nil	Negligible
Laos	5,100,000	107	18	NA	Negligible
Malaysia	22,890,000	15,000	1,600,000	50,000	7.3%
Myanmar	46,500,000	2,000	2,500,000	400,000	5%
Philippines	76,000,000	2,000	24,000	12,000	Negligible
Singapore	3,160,000	90,000	217,000	Negligible	9.71%
Thailand	62,000,000	15,000	70,000	Nil	.07%
Vietnam	78,000,000	320	Nil	10	Negligible

Source: *Report of The High Level Committee On the Indian Diaspora* (2001), Indian Council of World Affairs: New Delhi, p. 253.

end of 1961, only Rs. 1.75 crores had been paid as compensation. During the second wave of nationalization in the 1960's under General Ne Win, in furtherance of the Burmese Way to socialism, Rangoon nationalized the petty retail shops owned by the Indians – 12,000 shops with assets worth Rs. 15 crores were taken over by the government. An even greater setback was that the Indians were not even allowed to repatriate their savings. The repatriates complained of demonetization of currency notes, expropriation of properties, confiscation of valuables and other unimaginable humiliations. According to a Policy Note issued by the Government of Tamil Nadu, since June 1963, 144,353 repatriates from Burma have returned to India. Even after a lapse of forty years, the compensation due to these people has not been settled. New Delhi's official stance had been that nationalization was strictly a matter of domestic jurisdiction.[18]

The PIOs who had to flee Burma were very disappointed with the government's policy. The hard reality was that India was hardly in a position to provide any relief to them in the wake of the 1962 conflict with China. India also needed Burma's help to tackle the Naga insurgency. Military intervention was not an option and the isolationist General Ne Win was not concerned about international opinion.[19]

A. Mani argues in his book, "Rising India and Indian Communities in East Asia" (2008), that in Thailand and the Philippines, the Indian migration was mostly from Punjab and Sindh. As non-Muslims from these areas were extremely conscious of their ethnicity vis-a-vis Islam, and they preserved their religious identity as Hindus and Sikhs after migration by maintaining close kinship ties. But Tamils in Thailand have been assimilated into Thai society through inter-ethnic marriage as they were small in number and felt no compulsion to zealously protect their Indian or Hindu identity.

A crisis in Malaysia on the issue of work permits was averted by New Delhi, due to behind-the-scenes diplomacy by the Indian Government. In order to solve the acute problem of unemployment, the Malaysian Government in 1968 introduced the system of work permits for non-citizens in specialized categories. In 1969, Kuala Lumpur announced that the work permits would not be renewed, which, for all practical purposes was a warning to non-citizens to quit their jobs. If the Government had strictly enforced the rules, 55,000 Indian labourers would have lost their jobs. The Government of India and the representatives of the Malaysian Indians were able to persuade the Government to modify the regulations. Kuala Lumpur agreed to speedily dispose-off the applications for citizenship; those who applied for citizenship would be given employment passes. Those who were eligible for citizenship could also apply for it during the work permit period. If the citizens were not forthcoming, non-citizens could continue in their jobs. The last concession was a boon for the Indians, because Malays at that time were unwilling to work in the plantations. A few months later, the Malaysian Government extended the work permits of all those who had applied for citizenship. However, the communal violence, which took place in Malaysia in May 1969, had a traumatic impact on the minority groups. Nearly 60,000 Indians voluntarily returned to India during this period.[20] Therefore, India's Diaspora policy during the Cold War period or after the few decades of the Indian independence can easily be identified as a policy of disassociation with regard to their Diaspora residing not only in Southeast Asia but any part of the world.

Diaspora in India's Look East Policy and Malaysian Indians

The presence of the "new Indian Diaspora", which consists of highly skilled people, has enhanced India's image in Southeast Asia, especially in the fields of IT and medicine. The Government of India is taking great interest in the Indian Diaspora, which is evident from the Report of the High Level Committee and establishment of the Ministry of Overseas Indian Affairs. Increased growth in trade and investment between India and ASEAN has had a positive effect with a surge of skilled workers, professionals and business people to almost all the countries of ASEAN. There is a great demand and respect for these Indian professionals who are so different from the Indian immigrants who went to Southeast Asia in the nineteenth century, especially under the indenture system. The Indians who came as indentured labourers were no better than slaves. There was no question of their having political rights – they were used as tools for the advancement of British commercial interests. They were loyal and industrious and gave no trouble as long as they were allowed to live as separate entities, maintaining their links with "Mother India".

As previously discussed, after independence, India followed the policy of disassociation with regard to its Diaspora. The proactive Diaspora Policy or from 'active-disassociation' to 'active-association' started especially after 1991, when the Indian economy faced a severe crisis arising from the bankruptcy of its foreign exchange reserves. The crisis triggered a process of economic reforms as India prepared itself to exploit the opportunities to counter the threats arising from globalization and liberalization. There was a deep realization that India needed to restructure itself economically and needed investment for infrastructure restructuring, and neither the Indian state nor private sector had the capacity to counter the drastic situation. If India intended to develop economically and remain competitive in a swiftly globalizing world, it had to aggressively pull Foreign Direct Investments (FDI) and the infusion of new technologies. In this context, the larger policy shifts appears in the re-engagement of India with its Diaspora in the 1990s because only affluent section of the overseas Indians, i.e. Non-Residential Indians (NRIs) could have become safeguards for the Indian economy in the 1990s.[21]

This was the same time when India also initiated its 'Look East Policy' under Prime Minister P.V. Narasimha Rao's Congress Government. The Prime Minister's proposal had instant and successful results, with India becoming a sectoral dialogue partner of ASEAN (Association of Southeast Asian Nation) in January 1992 and full dialogue partner in December 1995. In July 1996, India became a member of ASEAN Regional Forum (ARF). As a result, it interacts with ASEAN in various bodies and meetings, which now includes ten countries of Southeast Asia.[22]

When India initiated its Look East Policy towards the Southeast Asian Countries, the large presence of the ethnic Indians in the region was unquestionably in the minds of the foreign policy makers, but unfortunately India could not explore this aspect in strengthening the bilateral as well as multilateral relations with the ASEAN countries despite having historical linkages and geographical proximity. India also missed the opportunity to constructively engage its Diaspora and gratify the aspirations of the Diasporic community.

The Congress government of India was cautious and slow towards addressing the concern of the Indian expatriate. Because of its historical position, it was over-cautious in including PIOs under an overt policy framework. When the Bhartiya Janata Party (BJP) came to power, Indian policy changed very fast for this segment. Historically, Rashtriya Swayamsewak Sangh (RSS), Vishwa Hindu Parishad (VHP), and Antar Rashtriya Sahayog Parishad (ARSP), a support base for BJP, had maintained very close people-to-people contact through its branches among Hindu overseas settlers. In contrast to Nehru's policy of active dissociation of PIOs from Indian foreign policy objectives, the BJP stood for active and overt association of PIOs for foreign policy objectives of India.[23]

In 1998, the government led by the Bharatiya Janata Party, with Atal Bihari Vajpayee at its helm, announced the introduction of a 'PIO Card' for Indians settled in specified countries, promising visa-free travel and privileges in matters of investment and education. In 2000, the government set up a High Level Committee on the Indian Diaspora chaired by L.M. Singhvi, a parliamentarian, jurist and former diplomat-responsible for assessing the issues concerning Indians overseas, suggesting new policy and organisational frameworks, and recommending a country-specific agenda to intensify India's engagement with its Diaspora. On 19 December 2001, the Committee submitted its detailed Report, running into 576 pages, with its recommendations. In 2001, the Indian Prime Minister formally inaugurated the 6th Convention of the Global Organisation of People of Indian Origin (GOPIO) in New Delhi. On the recommendation of the Singhvi committee, the government implemented numerous novel policy initiatives, including the decision to celebrate the Pravasi Bharatiya Divas and institute the Pravasi Bharatiya Samman. Perhaps the most significant initiative was the Indian government's announcement, at the inaugural Pravasi Bharatiya Divas held in January 2003, of sweeping changes to the country's 48-year-old Citizenship Act, granting Indians living in Britain, Canada, Australia, Finland, Ireland, Italy, the Netherlands and the US the privilege of claiming dual citizenship. The restriction of dual citizenship to only one constituency of the Diaspora, the NRIs settled in affluent Western countries, led to widespread criticism from other NRI segments, especially from the West Indies and countries such as Fiji, South Africa, Malaysia and Mauritius, where Indian communities are not well-endowed. In 2004, when a Congress-led coalition spearheaded by Manmohan Singh assumed power, it adopted two significant measures: it established a separate Ministry of Overseas Indian Affairs; and at the Pravasi Bharatiya Divas held in January 2005, it declared that dual citizenship would be extended to all Indians overseas who migrated after the inauguration of the Indian Union on 26 January 1950, subject to the laws prevailing in their home countries, thus eliminating the basis of criticism of the earlier policy. However, at that time the dual citizenship would be granted without voting rights.[24]

In the Eighth Pravasi Bharatiya Divas, which was held at New Delhi in 2010, the Indian Government announced the "Voting-Right" to the overseas Indians community. In such changed scenario, the proactive interest of India in the 90s does not have any element of imperialist design or racist preference as was likely to be construed during Nehru period.

Though Diasporas have emerged as a powerful factor in developing relations between nation-states, it seems to have worked in the reverse in the case of India-Malaysia relations, and several unfortunate incidents have taken place in Malaysia involving the Indian community. Divided along racial lines, reinforced by religion, culture, language, and occupation, Malaysian society faces a constant threat of ethnic violence. The crux of the problem lies in the social and economic conditions of the PIOs in Malaysia. Among Malaysians, those of Indian origin lag behind in many socio-economic indicators and remain marginalized. Forty percent of the serious crimes in Malaysia are committed by Indians; there are 38 Indian-based gangs with 1,500 active members; Indians also form the highest number of those detained under Emergency Regulations. Further, Indians have the highest suicide rate, and account for 20 per cent of child and wife abuse and 14 per cent of juvenile delinquents. In Kuala Lumpur they comprise 15 per cent of the squatters. Malay-Indians are represented through the Malaysian Indian Congress (MIC), which is an important constituent of the United Malay National Organization (UMNO).[25]

After the 1969 racial riots, the Malaysian government's initiation of the Bumiputera policy to embrace indigenous people was a major source of marginalization of the Malaysian Indians. Ethnic Indians are not alone in expressing their grievances against Malaysia's Bumiputera policy; even many Malays are tired with this policy and feel that is has been of benefit only to the rich and powerful, especially the Chinese. Because of the majoritarian politics of Malaysia, there have emerged dispossessed, impoverished, illiterate and politically marginalized Indians, somewhat sandwiched between politically powerful Malays and economically powerful Chinese.

Apart from the continuing socio-economic and politico-cultural discrimination of the ethnic Indians in Malaysia, the growing Islamization of Malaysian society is also one of the major factors for the peculiar condition of the Malaysian Indians. Najib declared on August 2007 that Malaysia has "never been secular because being secular by Western definition means separation of the Islamic principles in the way we govern the country".[26] The above statement of Najib, now the Prime Minister of Malaysia, clearly shows the attitude of the Malay political elites towards other religions and minorities of Malaysia. Over the past years Wahabbis form of Islam has also risen in Malaysia. Therefore, the non-Muslims, especially Hindus, feel that they are completely marginal to the dominant cultural ethos, norms and tradition.

The resentment among the ethnic Indians regarding their marginalization in Malaysian society culminated in a historic protest rally in Malaysia on 25 November 2007, which internationalized the pitiable conditions of ethnic Indians in the country. The HINDRAF, an apex body of 30 organizations, led this protest. Under the banner of HINDRAF, thousands of people joined the peaceful protest against the marginalization, namely in the denial of jobs, fair wages, educational facilities, electoral reforms and equal opportunities and rights. The intentions of Malaysian Government to demolish 79 Hindu temples in the name of "development" and some forceful conversion of the Hindus added fuel to the protest. The rally was meant to support a $4 trillion lawsuit filed in London in August 2007 by the HINDRAF demanding that Britain should compensate Malaysian Indians for bringing their forefathers as indentured laborers and exploiting them; it also sought to amend Article 153 of the Malaysian Constitution which provides Malay supremacy. Malaysian authorities brutally crushed the protest.[27] The government also attempted to link the peaceful HINDRAF rally with terrorists groups such as the Liberation Tigers of Tamil Eelam (LTTE).

The 8 March 2008 general election of Malaysia was held one year ahead of its time as Abdullah Badawi was only in his fourth year as the Prime Minister and the final date of the election was not due until March 2009. It was thus widely speculated that this early call for a renewed mandate was to prevent former deputy Prime Minister Anwar Ibrahim from contesting. During the election campaign, HINDRAF was the major force that vocally used unconventional methods of campaigning. Using the internet, HINDRAF highlighted the wretched condition of the Malaysian Indians, and put forward their demands and agendas. This resulted in the unification and awakening of the Malaysian Indian society and consequently Barisan Nasional was denied two-third majority in the parliament and Malaysian Indian Congress (MIC) was reduced to only three seats from nine seats in 2004; even Samy Vellu lost the election. Later on Samy Vellu resigned from the post of party president.

The Indian leadership totally ignored the Indian Diaspora, except when it occasionally addressed certain issues based on its own convenience. These trends also manifest themselves in the racial attacks on Indians, especially towards Indian students in Australia, when the government of India watched the whole episode as mute spectators and engaged only in lip-service to pressurise the Australian authority. Another example of government apathy to the Indian Diaspora is during Malaysia's recent unrest, in November 2007, when Hindu Rights Action Force (HINDRAF) internationalised the wretched condition of the ethnic Indians in Malaysia; the Government of India's initial response was tight-lipped.

In the March 9, 2003 incident, when nearly 300 Indian citizens, mostly IT professionals in Kuala Lumpur, were 'maltreated' and 'interrogated' by the Malaysian authorities, the Indian government reacted sharply and warned that any repetition of such incidents would affect bilateral ties. The Government of India indicated that it would re-examine bilateral agreements and other trade related concessions given to Malaysia. Foreign Regional Registration Offices (FRROs), including the one in Bangalore, were ordered to verify the credentials of Malaysian nationals registered here. India also expressed its inability to host the Malaysian Health Minister towards the end of March 2003. Earlier in the month, during the visit of the Malaysian Entrepreneur Development Minister, his talks with Indian ministers were confined to the harassment of Indian IT professionals instead of the proposed agenda. Similarly, the Ministry of Sports, in consultation with the External Affairs Ministry, ordered a last minute pull-out of the Indian hockey team from the prestigious Azlan Shah Cup hockey tournament that year.[28]

As history shows, the Indian leadership addressed only a few of the diaspora issues according to its own convenience. During the November 2007 unrest, the Government of India was initially tight-lipped, but after opposition leaders like L.K. Advani and Rajnath Singh of the Bharatiya Janata Party (BJP) expressed concern over the plight of ethnic Indians, Prime Minister Manmohan Singh said "New Delhi was disturbed by reports about the use of force against the protesters in the multicultural Islamic country." An ally of the UPA, the DMK has expressed its concern over the plight of the Tamil Malaysians and demanded the centre's vocal intervention in the matter. In fact, the exodus of Tamils from Malaysia has united the parties across the spectrum in Tamil Nadu as the AIADMK leader J. Jayalalitha and MDMK leader Vaiko also raised their voice against the atrocities of the Tamils in Malaysia (as appears in the various Indian newspaper in the month of November-December 2007).

If both the incidents of March 2003 and November 2007 are compared, in the later, the Indian government acted as a mute spectator or merely indulged in lip-service. Thus once again this bias or the policy of 'dissociation' towards the PIOs was witnessed. The same issue haunted the Indian Government in the 2008 Pravasi Bharatiya Divas.

Indian Prime Minster Manmohan Singh, while inaugurating "Little-India" at the Brickfields, Kuala Lumpur in October 2010 said, "*the Malaysian Government's decision to dedicate the area of Brickfields, which is one of the oldest Indian settlements in the country, as "Little India" is a tribute to the contribution to nation building of all Malaysians of Indian origin.*" He also mentioned that the *"Indian community is well placed to be the bridge of friendship and understanding between India and Malaysia."*[29]

Conclusion

India's Diaspora Policy is not static. It has evolved during various political phases India's political history – the sensitivities of the nationalist struggle, the winning of independence, and the trauma of partition and the creation of the Republican constitution of the Indian Union, engendered important changes in India's relations with the Diaspora. A concern for the treatment of Indian migrant labourers during the nationalist phase was replaced by post-colonial disavowal after independence of any lingering responsibility for those who were now part of a separate nation 'overseas', and later, a tendency to view the skilled migrants who left India as a brain drain. However, by the last decade of the century, during the period of rapid economic liberalisation, the value of the Diaspora was rediscovered, and India adopted a constructive approach towards the Indian Diaspora.

From January 2003 onwards, India hosted one ninth Pravasi Bharatiya Divas (PBD), but it seems to be merely a yearly ritual and annual jamboree of Diaspora. During the initial age of PDB there were a plenty of expectation from the Indian Government especially towards the plight of People of Indian Origin in the host countries, which the Indian Government did not address. Rather Indian Government was more investment centric. Therefore, lesser participation of the overseas Indians occured in recent years. Consequently the Indian media also has lost its interest and there is poor media coverage of the PBD. Now the Overseas Indian Community has realised that the event is more about 'Bharat' rather than 'Pravasi' and the essential is to look forward for something for the 'Pravasis' in the Pravasi Bharatiya Divas. The report of the Singhvi Committee is also an imperfect document on Indian Diaspora. The Indian Government action and reaction related to the concerns of PIOs in the host countries is a great need of the hour. The time has changed; hence, a more pro-active Diaspora policy is required. India should address the concerns of the ethnic Indians anywhere in the world, without jeopardising the relations with the host countries. Only then, the condition of PIOs as well as India will improve globally, as PIOs constitutes more than 75 percent of the Indian Diaspora.

It has been also witnessed that India's Look East Policy does not explore the potential of the Indian Diaspora and therefore, may be summarized as a missed opportunity. If Indian policy makers concentrated on the Diaspora in the Look East policy, then the results of the policy may be more fruitful. Notwithstanding certain inaction and apathy by the Indian Government, the Diaspora emerged as a powerful factor in developing relations between nation-states. The Indian Diaspora has notably acted as a catalyst in strengthening bilateral relations between India and the host nations. The India-US Civil Nuclear Deal is a case in point, as ethnic Indians in the United States successfully lobbied for clinching of the N-deal. However, the recent incidents of maltreatment of the ethnic Indians in Australia and Malaysia seem to have gone against the general trend of strengthening relations between India and the host countries. Now, Singapore is using the Indian Diaspora as an asset by wooing the cash-rich Indian Diaspora in the US for investments, technology and other expertise. This could be an eye-opener for India as well as the host countries having sizable number of Indian Diaspora.

The Indian government has failed to develop a strong economic constituency in Malaysia which could strengthen and expand the bilateral political and economic ties between the two countries. It is also incumbent upon the Malaysian government to develop strong political and economic relations with India, a growing market, a developing economy and a credible political friend. The Malaysian government should cut the red-tape imposed on ethnic Indian business ventures. It should also ensure that Indians are entitled to rights proportional to their share in the population. If the Malaysian government showed greater understanding of the problems of the Indian community, especially in the estate sector and among urban squatters, the conditions of ethnic Indians would improve. These changes would also increase the scope for improving bilateral relations between Malaysia and India. The Government of India, for its part, should promote cultural linkages between Indians and Malaysia and curb illegal Indian immigration to Malaysia.

The second phase of the India's Look East policy is nearly over and now the time has come for India to lay the ground work for the third phase in which they have to concentrate on the strategic aspects of the bilateral relations with the entire Southeast and East Asian region. The Indian diaspora can become the focal point of India-Malaysia relations in the future. Therefore, both the countries should use it as an asset and not treat it as a liability.

ENDNOTES

1. Rondolph Quirk, The American Heritage Dictionary of the English Language: (Boston, US, 2000).
2. http://moia.gov.in/writereaddata/pdf/NRISPIOS-Data.pdf (Assessed on October 1, 2010)
3. Kripa Sridharan, "India and Southeast Asia in the context of India's Rise", in Kesavapany, Mani and P. Ramasamy ed. *Rising India and Indian Communities in East Asia*, (Singapore: ISEAS, 2008), pp. 79-80.
4. Brian Harrison, *South-East Asia: A Short History*, (London: 1966), p.10.
5. *New Webster's Dictionary and Thesaurus* (Danbury: Lexicon Publications, 1992).
6. Hugh Tinker, "Indians in South East Asia: Imperial Auxiliaries" in Colin Clarke et al. eds., *South Asians Overseas Migration and Ethnicity,* (Cambridge: Cambridge University Press, 1990), p.12.
7. R.C. Majumdar, *The History and Culture of Indian People: The Classical Age,* Bombay: Bharatiya Vidya Bhavan, 1988).
8. B.D. Arora, (1982), Indians in Indonesia, in I. J. Bahadur Singh ed., *Indians in South Asia,* (New Delhi: Sterling Publishers, 1982), p.119.
9. Wales, Quaritch H.G. (1951), *The Making of Greater India: A Study in South-East Asian Cultural Change*, (London, 1951), p.195.
10. Nicholas Tarling, (ed.), The Cambridge History of Southeast Asia, from Early Times to C.1800, vol. 1 (New York: Cambridge University Press, 1992).
11. *Report of The High Level Committee on the Indian Diaspora* (New Delhi: Indian Council of World Affairs, 2001), pp. 243-271.
12. *Annual Report of the Agent of the Government of India in British Malaya* (1923-1924), Madras.
13. Brij V. Lal, (ed.) (2006), *The Encyclopaedia of the Indian Diaspora,* (Singapore: National University of Singapore, 2006), p.82.

14. *Selected Works of Jawaharlal Nehru,* (New Delhi 1972), pp.353-68.
15. Brij V. Lal, n.13, p.86.
16. Grover, V. (ed.) (1992), *International Relations and Foreign policy of India,* (New Delhi: Deep and Deep publications, 1992), p.43.
17. C. Heimsath and S. Mansingh, (1971), *A Diplomatic History of Modern India*, (Bombay: Allied Publishers, 1971), p.289.
18. V. Suryanarayan, "Indian and Chinese Communities in Southeast Asia: A Comparative Perspective", in Ajay Dubey ed., *Indian Diaspora: Global Identity*, (New Delhi: Kalinga Publications, 2003), pp. 80-81.
19. J.C. Sharma, Poised to Play Important Role, *Indian Foreign Affairs Journal*, 2008, 3(2): 1-12.
20. V. Suryanarayan, n.18, pp. 80-81.
21. Ajay Dubey, ed. *Indian Diaspora: Global Identity*, (New Delhi: Kalinga Publications, 2003), p.141.
22. Manmohini Kaul, (2001), "ASEAN-India Relations during the Cold War", in Grare and Mattoo eds., *India and ASEAN: The Politics of India's Look East Policy,* (New Delhi: Manohar, 2001) pp. 41-66.
23. Ajay Dubey, n.21, p.141.
24. Brij V. Lal, n.13, pp. 82-89.
25. V. Suryanarayan, "Indian Communities in Malaysia: Challenges ahead", *Journal of Indian Ocean Studies*, 10(1): 2002, 64-80.
26. http://www.catallaxyfiles.com/blog/?p=5556 (assessed on August 10, 2010).
27. Dilip Lahiri, *"Malaysian Indian Community: Victim of 'Bumiputera' Policy",* ORF Issue Brief, 2008, 12: 1-8.
28. Amit Singh, *The Indian Diaspora as a Factor in India-Malaysia Relations*, Article no. 2349, 2007, IPCS: August 7, 2007, (http://www.ipcs.org/article_details.php?articleNo=2349). (assessed on July 23, 2010).
29. PM's remarks during the inauguration of little India at Brickfields, Kuala Lumpur, October 27, 2010, http://www.mea.gov.in/mystart.php?id=519916606&flg=1 (assessed on November 11, 2010)

PART IV

INDIA AND EAST ASIA

13

Building Bridges to East Asia

G V C Naidu

It has been about two decades since India's engagement with East Asia began in earnest through what has come to be known as the Look East policy. By most estimates it is a successful initiative that has made India not merely a factor in the regional security equilibrium but also a major economic player. Although not comparable either to Japan or China at present, its growing role will be a key determinant of the region's economic development as well in regional security architecture. A variety of developments within East Asia have contributed to this as much as India's own concerted forays. In order for the consolidation and strengthening of India-East relations, a number of linkages have come about in diverse forms related to political, strategic, economic, and cultural aspects. In the following, an assessment of the genesis of these linkages, their evolution, and their contribution to the process of India's involvement in East Asia are briefly discussed. It must however be clarified that this analysis is limited to the post-cold war period.

Backdrop

India's involvement in East Asian affairs had been active but failed to last beyond the 1955 Bandung Conference, which India co-sponsored, in part due to the intensification of the cold war. The linkages India developed then were primarily politically guided by its principal goals of anti-colonialism and anti-imperialism, on the one hand, and the creation of a substantial body of neutral nations that are positively inclined to take an active role in global affairs, on the other. A majority of the newly liberated countries were looked upon as potential clientele of this ideology, which subsequently evolved into the non-aligned movement. That the liberation struggles across East Asia were instrumental in shaping India's foreign policy early on is no doubt. India even wanted Japan to be part of the non-aligned group even though it was too obvious that there was no way it could have done so in those circumstances when it was under American occupation.[1] Rather than the narrow motive of advancing its own interests, a kind of idealism drove New Delhi's policy towards East Asia. The wars that India had to fight subsequently put paid to this idealistic notion even as it had to confront the serious prospect of its own unity and integrity coming under grave threat. As a result, it was only starting from the mid-1980s that India was once again appeared to be ready to engage with East Asia, but this time around it had become militarily more confident. Contrary to the previous policy of advancing non-aligned ideology, it was beginning to pursuing its strategic goals.

However, by then so much had happened that while several East Asian countries had moved closer to the US, India had developed close strategic links with the Soviet Union. No doubt India did have diplomatic relations with these countries, but they were neither deep nor strong, with the possible exception of Vietnam after its estrangement from China in the late 1970s. As the only non-communist country that extended diplomatic recognition to the Vietnam-installed Heng Samrin regime in Phom Penh, which ousted the dreaded pro-China Pol Pot and his clique, it had to face the ire of then ASEAN, however justifiable its action was. The gulf was simply too wide to be bridged between India and much of East Asia. Thanks to the end of the cold war this underwent a major transformation.

A serious effort to develop strong and enduring linkages was made once the cold war ended, which also ushered in many fundamental shifts within India – the most important being market-oriented economic reforms that were launched. The changed circumstances certainly provided New Delhi with a golden opportunity to reorient its foreign policy and refurbish its image. A re-assessment of India's thinking in particular towards Southeast Asia began a little before the cold war came to an abrupt end when strong concerns and apprehensions started emanating even as the Indian Navy began undergoing a major expansion and modernisation in the 1980s. In response, the Indian Navy took the initial steps to build confidence by embarking on a series of measures such as regular interaction at senior officers' level, arranging visits to the Andaman base facilities which had been the cynosure of much of the disquiet because of its proximity to the Malacca Strait, holding of bilateral exercises, etc., coinciding with unprecedented changes at the global level. These were the first linkages – though still tentative and nothing of great military significance – that were established in the maritime sphere.

Perhaps economic exigencies of the liberalisation programme that India had begun in the early 1990s, which required attracting huge direct investments and increases in share of global trade, played a key role in compelling New Delhi to pay a lot of attention to East Asia, a region that by then was already grabbing headlines for its economic vibrancy. In order for India to increase its economic interaction with East Asia, betterment of political relations with this region became a prerequisite while showcasing its economic potential and opportunities it could offer. It consequently warranted Indian policymakers to put in place a new initiative specifically aimed at East Asia. The consummation of this came about in the form of the so-called Look East policy. While India was keen and overly optimistic of its forays into East Asia over-estimating its own overall importance, the response from the region was somewhat lukewarm. Frantic and forceful attempts to join the Asia-Pacific Economic Cooperation forum failed to materialise (till today) and similarly India hardly figured, let alone getting involved in the deliberations, when the ASEAN Regional Forum (ARF) was being discussed to deal with regional security. It was obviously felt that both economically and in terms of regional security, India was of little consequence.

A sea change occurred due to certain vital developments between 1992 and 1994 in East Asia. The foremost was the super power military withdrawal from Southeast Asia – the Soviets from Vietnam and the US from the Philippines, which for the first time ensued in a power vacuum in Southeast Asia. This alone would not have been a major worry but for other developments that followed the above. Firstly, the Chinese military publication of a map that included the entire island chain in South China Sea (the Spratly and Paracel Islands) as well as the Natunas (under Indonesian control) as part of China and the PLA's assertion that it would not compromise on issues of territorial sovereignty. Secondly, tensions started mounting in the South China Sea as Beijing staked its claims for those islands under Vietnamese control, resulting in a bloody naval skirmish. Thirdly, shortly later China and the Philippines were embroiled in a dispute over the Mischief Reef in the South China Sea. Finally, ASEAN too had to come to terms with new realities in the changed circumstances wherein its security role had all of a sudden come into sharp focus. ASEAN hence had to embark on measures in regard to regional security. This explains why ASEAN, which was initially unenthusiastic to support the Japanese idea of a regional security platform to replicate the European example, came around as a major benefactor of the ARF in 1993.

Coincidentally, India too had undertaken a fundamental reassessment of its policy and approach towards Southeast Asia firstly and the rest of East Asia later on. The foremost objective was to dispel Southeast Asian concerns about its navy, and then strengthen political contacts at various levels. Establishment of institutional linkages with ASEAN and other ASEAN-led multilateral frameworks became an imperative. Besides, economic reforms were showcased as a major attraction to engage India. Even while New Delhi undertook concerted initiatives to get closer to the dynamic East Asian region, it found to its dismay that it was not that easy in part because its economic reforms were seen to be tentative and teetering, politically it was too detached, and its strategic relevance was still marginal.

Almost around the same time, there was a major spurt in non-traditional security concerns coming to the fore especially on the maritime front. Southeast Asia had become the largest source of piracy attacks and critical shipping routes in the region had become highly vulnerable. Large caches of arms supplied to the Khmer and other rebels to fight the Vietnamese in Cambodia started finding their way into other parts of Southeast Asia as well as India. There was no way these threats could be addressed but through collective efforts. One particular incident involved a Japanese freighter, *Alondra Rainbow*, that was hijacked by the pirates in 1992, but the Indian Coast Guard swiftly swung into action and perpetrators of the crime were chased and apprehended. This event had a tremendous impact on East Asian perceptions about Indian naval capabilities. That incident brought into the limelight the enormous sea power at India's disposal and usefulness of enlisting its support to deal with security issues. Apart from being the largest and most balanced navy in the Indian Ocean littoral, it had a fairly formidable coast guard force. India's geostrategic location was an added advantage to secure the sea lines of Southeast Asia.

The other issue that emerged as a major concern around this time for both ASEAN as well as India was Myanmar, which had been witnessing a major anti-military and pro-democracy movement, on one hand, and Yangon becoming too close to Beijing for others' comfort, on the other. It appeared that not only reducing Myanmar's excessive dependence on China but even to engage it in a more meaningful way than perpetration of its isolation was the best possible political approach. While India fundamentally changed its Myanmar policy, ASEAN for the first time seriously thought of bringing Yangon under its fold.

Against the above backdrop, the Southeast Asian nations took cognizance of India's military might and its ability to contribute to regional peace and security, especially as a potential countervailing power to China. Little wonder that ASEAN simultaneously started efforts to extend its membership to Vietnam, a country that has a rare distinction of defeating some of the world's mightiest powers. This would not only considerably raise ASEAN's political and diplomatic weight but also could potentially help it emerge as an autonomous power centre.

An equally important consideration for ASEAN and to a lesser extent Japan was India's economic potential after the opening up of its market. By then China's blistering growth had had enormous impact on the rest of East Asia. A similar excitement of another mega market emerging in India was a major factor in the new thinking on many quarters. However, it must be pointed out that the initial phase of economic interaction between India and East Asia was far less than previous expectations. New Delhi was hoping to attract huge Japanese investments firstly because of the absence of historical baggage that dogged Japan's relations with the rest of the region, and secondly, because of no clash of interests and complementarity of their economies. Unfortunately for India, its economic liberalisation coincided with the bursting of the Japanese economic bubble, which, in turn, drastically slowed down its earlier investment spree. India certainly was no match either to the ASEAN nations or China in terms of economic attractiveness because of its poor infrastructure, red tape and rampant corruption. Similarly, countries like Singapore and Malaysia were also disappointed, in addition to the above shortcomings, with an excruciatingly slow pace of reforms. For instance, the then prime minister of Singapore, Goh Chok Tong, who announced in his Independence Day address to the nation in 1993 that he wanted to generate a mild India fever, confessed a few years later that fever was effectively inoculated.

With respect to Northeast Asia, then Prime Minister Rajiv Gandhi's successful visit to China laid the foundation for resumption of comprehensive relations between the two. Whereas South Korea was the first country to take a plunge into the Indian market by taking several bold decisions on investments, Japan, aside from coming to terms with the effects of bursting of the economic bubble in 1990, did not find India that attractive. However, the Alondra Rainbow incident had considerable impact in changing Japanese perception about India. While reticent on the economic front, they were keen to engage India strategically, partly because of concerns about security of trading routes in the Indian Ocean and partly due to rapid rise of China. Although the 1998 nuclear tests dealt a setback to India-Japan relations, they were quickly brought back on track after Yoshiro Mori's famous 2000 visit. Thus, by the mid-1990s India was coming into the regional reckoning.

India and East Asia: Development of Multi-faceted Linkages

The relative resilience of the Indian economy came into light when the 1997-98 financial crisis (which snowballed into economic, political and social crises) exposed the vulnerabilities of many of these countries. The rise of China as an economic and military behemoth that was beginning to emerge as the most important country undermining other traditional powers such as Japan and the US, coincided with the above developments. This in more than one way underpinned India's politico-strategic salience, and simultaneously was beginning to provide as an alternative for those worried about excessive dependence on China's market. The linkages as a result have gradually developed at the political, defence and strategic, and economic levels, which are briefly reviewed below.

Political

India's political relations with most East Asian countries, with the possible exception of Vietnam, were at the most lukewarm. After the initial disappointment of failing to elicit strong positive response for Indian overtures assuming that the end of the cold war had removed all the misgivings, New Delhi realised that since ASEAN was beginning to assume a central role in the rapidly changing political and economic environment, now the focus was building institutional linkages with the Association and a number of other regional multilateral mechanisms that were sprouting. A breakthrough came by way of India becoming a Sectoral Dialogue Partner in 1992, and after a three-year probation, it was upgraded to full Dialogue Partnership in late 1995 during the Fifth ASEAN Summit Meeting "reflecting the growing ties between the two sides that have developed in recent years."[2] Meant ostensibly to promote greater economic cooperation, the political import of the dialogue partnership meetings should not be understated.

Simultaneously, it became incumbent for India to target certain countries for deeper engagement. Singapore soon emerged the most important bilateral partner of India, which had been instrumental in strongly supporting India's case for dialogue partnership and membership in the ARF. Indonesia, Malaysia and Thailand were the other countries with which India's relations began to improve significantly. After Vietnam was admitted into ASEAN, given that India and Vietnam had always enjoyed a special relationship sharing a number of common political and security concerns, India's political clout started mounting within ASEAN. The financial crisis, the rapid ascendance of China, growing worries about American long-term involvement in and commitment to the East Asian region, and a variety of non-traditional security challenges, in particular in the maritime security and terrorism brought the focus on India's potential to play an important role. These resulted in India becoming a summit partner of ASEAN in 2002 and a member of the East Asia Summit (EAS) in 2005. Unprecedented progress in India-Japan relations leading to the forging of a strategic partnership also played a vital role in the new equation. Thus, by mid-2000s India had become an important cog in the East Asian political wheel.

Strategic

For all practical purposes, India had been a marginal player for nearly four decades in the East Asian security calculus. But, that began to undergo a transformation – once a security concern, New Delhi was now seen as a potential contributor to not only regional peace and stability, and even provided a kind of balance to regional security order in the wake of China's ascendance. This aspect came to the forefront remarkably lucidly during events in 1992 when the Americans vacated their military bases in the Philippines. This was preceded by a similar withdrawal by the Soviets from Vietnam. This heralded a spectacular and fundamental shift in the East Asian security.

As noted, the Indian Navy took the initiative to re-establish communication links which became the stepping stones to build an elaborate web of strategic interactions with the entire East Asian region. What began as routine confidence building measures have since undergone such phenomenal expansion that now they encompass a wide array of programmes and activities, so much so that they probably now constitute the most successful dimension of India's look east policy. India has entered into one or another kind of defence cooperation agreement with every country of East Asia.

The defence and strategic links include both multilateral and bilateral. The *Milan* is a kind of get-together of naval forces of select East Asian countries hosted by the Indian Navy at the Andaman base held biennially. It began as an attempt to allay concerns about the base by inviting some Southeast Asian countries in the Bay of Bengal rim region, but has since expanded in a big way. A new and militarily significant dimension is India's participation in multilateral exercises with 'friendly' countries. In this context, for the first time in April 2007, Indian naval ships joined Japan and the US forces for joint exercises in the Pacific near Japan. These were followed by a bigger round of exercises towards the end of the year joined, in addition to the US and Japan, by Australia and Singapore. These in a way heralded India's arrival on the East Asian security scene and its role in regional balance of power.

Taken as a whole, India's strategic and defence interactions could be broadly categorised into three types. The first one comprises joint exercises, port visits, joint patrol and other confidence building measures. The simple, passage exercises starting with Indonesia, Australia and Malaysia in 1991 have steadily expanded now to encompass virtually the entire East Asian region, although the intensity varies from country to country. For instance, with Japan, they began as coastguard to coastguard and now they have expanded into cooperation between the two navies. In a unique initiative, India has also undertaken joint patrols with Indonesia and Thailand along their respective maritime boundaries.

The second dimension is in the form of security dialogues and strategic partnerships. It is noteworthy that India has signed the largest number of strategic partnership agreements in East Asia: five out of eight – with Japan, Vietnam, China, Indonesia, and South Korea (in chronological order). Alongside, India has also initiated a variety of security dialogues with several countries of the region. For instance, the steady expansion of strategic and defence cooperation between India and Japan has resulted in three types of dialogues: the Comprehensive Security Dialogue, Defence Policy Dialogue, and Military-to-Military Talks. India has also entered into two security cooperation agreements with Japan, which include a wide variety of issues of mutual concern and interest. The 1993 India-Malaysia MoU, among others, also provided for a Malaysia-India Defence Cooperation Meeting (MIDCOM) to be co-chaired by the defence secretaries.

The 2006 MoU with Australia stated "cooperation in military training, defence industries and defence research and development."[3] Consequent to an agreement signed after Susilo Bambang Yodhoyono's November 2005 visit to India, India-Indonesia Strategic Dialogue at the senior official level started in mid-2006. India and Singapore do not formally hold a strategic dialogue, but have decided to set up a Track II mechanism in the form of a Joint Panel as well as a Joint Ministerial Committee to monitor bilateral relations, including defence.[4] As part of the March 2000 agreement, India and Vietnam also hold period is security dialogues. The first India-Vietnam Security Dialogue took place in 2003. With Seoul, a mechanism called the India-Republic of Korea Joint Commission has been created to enhance defence cooperation. In accordance with the MoU signed with China in 2006, an annual defence dialogue has also been institutionalised. It was agreed during the Indian army chief's visit to China to hold the first such meeting in 2007.[5] The MoU with Australia also envisages setting up of India-Australia Joint Working Group on defence for guiding and monitoring the on-going defence cooperation between the two countries.[6]

The third aspect is the training programme that India has evolved over the years by gradually opening its military establishments to East Asians. Prior to the 1990s much of the training that the Indian military imparted to other countries was to provide places in the national training centres such as National Defence College and Defence Services Staff College, National Defence Academy, and Indian Military Academy. However, in addition to the above, India has opened facilities which were precluded for foreigners. Even Myanmarese troops have begun to undergo training in jungle warfare and counter-insurgency operations in India. There is a regular exchange of military personnel between India and Vietnam for training. Noteworthy is the training Indian soldiers get in Vietnam in jungle warfare. It is likely that the training component of defence diplomacy will acquire greater attention as several countries have shown interest. For many, India is an attractive option because of vast training facilities that its military has built. India also offers virtually every possible terrain to train, from one of the coldest places in the highest altitudes to thick tropical jungles, to an extremely hot desert. India is also a cost effective option.

Economic

Strengthening economic links with dynamic East Asia has been the cornerstone of the Look East policy. It took more than a decade since India opened its economy to appreciate its immense long-term potential. As the tables below clearly indicate,

India-East Asia two-way trade has grown nearly eight times in the last decade or so from just US$ 16.75 billion in 1997-98 to 127.58 billion by 2008-09. India's trade thus has been growing the fastest with East Asia than any other region. Even as the Indian economy expands rapidly, economic links with East Asia are expected to grow correspondingly and its stakes as well. The recently finalised Trade in Goods Agreement between India and ASEAN as part of the Framework Agreement (including services and investments) is expected to contribute to a nearly 25 percent rise in bilateral trade by 2011.

A sign of India's seriousness in constantly strengthening its economic ties with East Asia is the large number of comprehensive economic cooperation agreements/ partnerships (CECA/CEPAs) that it has entered into. Whereas agreements with Singapore and South Korea are already operational (with Thailand it is partially operational), those with Japan, Malaysia and Indonesia are in an advanced stage of conclusion. Similar initiatives have also started with most other countries, including China and New Zealand. That India can no longer be ignored can be gauged by the fact that its GDP is nearly twice that of the whole of Southeast Asian GDP in PPP terms. Thus, India in the near future would have signed the largest number of such agreements with the countries of East Asia so that it would be in a good position to be firmly a part of the economic cooperation and integration attempts currently underway in the region.

Indian Exports to East Asia

(bn US $)

Country	1997-98	1998-99	1999-2000	2000-01	2001-02	2002-03	2003-04	2004-05	2005-06	2006-07	2007-08	2008-09
Taiwan	0.42	0.40	0.31	0.32	0.39	0.36	0.53	0.62	0.63	0.92	1.73	1.50
China PRP	0.61	0.72	0.43	0.54	0.83	0.95	1.98	2.96	6.76	8.32	10.87	9.35
Hong Kong	1.86	1.93	1.88	2.51	2.64	2.36	2.61	3.26	4.45	4.69	6.31	6.66
Japan	2.00	1.89	1.65	1.69	1.75	1.51	1.86	1.70	2.48	2.89	3.89	3.02
South Korea	0.52	0.47	0.31	0.48	0.45	0.47	0.65	0.76	1.83	2,52	2.86	3.95
Indonesia	0.59	0.44	0.33	0.40	0.53	0.83	1.13	1.33	1.38	2.03	2.16	2.50
Malaysia	0.53	0.49	0.45	0.61	0.77	0.75	0.89	1.08	1.16	1.31	2.57	3.42
Myanmar	0.05	0.05	0.03	0.05	0.06	0.07	0.09	0.11	0.11	0.14	0.19	0.22
Philippines	0.18	0.24	0.14	0.20	0.25	0.47	0.32	0.41	0.49	0.58	0.62	0.74
Thailand	0.45	0.34	0.45	0.53	0.22	0.33	0.32	0.41	1.07	1.45	1.81	1.94
Singapore	0.98	0.75	0.67	0.88	0.97	1.42	2.12	4.00	5.42	6.05	7.38	8.44
Vietnam	0.12	0.13	0.15	0.23	0.22	0.34	0.41	0.56	0.69	0.99	1.61	1.74
Total	8.36											43.48

Indian Imports from East Asia

(bn US $)

Country	1997-98	1998-99	1999-2000	2000-01	2001-02	2002-03	2003-04	2004-05	2005-06	2006-07	2007-08	2008-09
Taiwan	0.47	0.37	0.41	0.51	0.56	0.66	0.77	1.09	1.38	1.68	2.40	2.89
China PRP	1.12	1.10	1.28	1.50	2.04	2.80	4.05	7.10	10.87	17.48	27.15	32.50
Hong Kong	0.32	0.45	0.82	0.85	0.73	0.97	1.49	1.73	2.21	2.45	2.70	6.45
Japan	2.14	2.47	2.54	1.84	2.15	1.84	2.67	3.23	4.06	4.60	6.33	7.80
South Korea	0.95	1.40	1.10	.89	1.14	1.52	2.83	3.51	4.56	4.80	6.04	8.68
Indonesia	0.73	0.83	0.95	0.91	1.04	1.38	2.12	2.62	3.01	4.18	4.82	6.67
Malaysia	1.18	1.60	1.95	1.18	1.13	1.47	2.05	2.30	2.42	5.29	6.01	7.18
Myanmar	0.22	0.17	0.17	0.18	0.37	0.34	0.40	0.40	0.53	0.78	0.80	0.93
Philippines	0.02	0.04	0.06	0.06	0.09	0.12	0.12	0.19	0.24	0.17	0.20	0.25
Thailand	0.23	0.27	0.33	0.34	0.42	0. 40	0.61	0.87	1.21	1.75	2.3	2.70
Singapore	1.00	1.39	1.16	1.46	1.30	1.43	2.08	2.65	3.35	5.48	8.12	7.65
Vietnam	0.01	0.01	0.01	0.01	0.02	0.02	0.04	0.09	0.13	0.17	0.17	0.40
Total	8.39											84.10

Source: Ministry of Commerce and Industry, Government of India.

East Asian Multilateralism

Yet another bridge that links India with East Asia is by way of strong bonds that have been forged through a number of regional multilateral frameworks of a diverse kind. From being very sceptical about the role of regional multilateralism, especially security, India has come a long way in emerging as a strong votary of East Asian multilateralism. While India's enthusiasm to join APEC was understandable for economic reasons, its eagerness to partake in the security multilateralism in the form of ASEAN Regional Forum certainly signifies a fundamental shift in its attitude. As part of its commitment to the ARF in terms of providing greater transparency to defence and strategic policies, interestingly, India for the first time produced and submitted a national security paper (equivalent to a defence white paper). The official justification for India's participation in the ARF was as follows:

> We see in the ARF, an experiment for the fashioning of a new pluralistic, cooperative security order in tune with the diversity of the Asia-Pacific region and in consonance with the transition away from a world characterised by poles built around military alliances. We remain ready to contribute to it. Though the ARF covers a broader region, India believes that it is built around the nucleus of ASEAN and is ASEAN driven. Our participation in the ARF demonstrates India's increasing engagement in the Asia-Pacific region, both in the politico-security and economic spheres and underlines our commitment to the objective of sustaining regional peace and stability.[7]

The same eagerness could also be witnessed with regard to other frameworks led by ASEAN. India unleashed a diplomatic offensive to become a Dialogue Partner of ASEAN in 1995 and a Summit Partner from 2002. Unlike the EAEC, by the time the East Asia Summit (EAS) idea was conceived, it was not easy to keep India out despite China's and some ASEAN countries' reservations. It is true that India is yet to become a member of another important mechanism, the ASEAN Plus Three (APT). India has also been an ardent supporter of other inter-regional initiatives such as the Ganga-Mekong Cooperation (GMC) and the Bay of Bengal Initiative for Multi-Sectoral, Technical and Economic Cooperation (BIMSTEC).

Conclusion

There is no question that India's initial foreign policy, in particular the strong commitment to neutrality and non-alignment, to a large extent was shaped by events in East Asia such as liberation movements. It however failed to sustain the momentum in the wake of the intensification of the cold war. The wars it had to fight, which forced New Delhi to concentrate its efforts on strengthening its military, to forsake a grand, pro-active international role, and to get closer to Moscow gradually detached it from East Asia. By the time it was militarily confident in the mid-1980s and ready to engage the region once again, it failed to materialize because of the prevalent political environment. Consequently, a new beginning was made in the aftermath of the cold war and it gradually evolved into a comprehensive engagement in the form of the Look East policy. Events within East Asia aided this process in a big way. The initial lack of a matching response from East Asia to Indian enthusiasm because of its economic insignificance and strategic inconsequence gradually gave way to the development of a multifaceted relationship. An ASEAN-centric political approach led New Delhi to build formidable institutional linkages while bilateral relations with select countries further contributed to greater political understanding. Perhaps on the strategic front the progress has been remarkable with an array of robust defence and security-related linkages emerging. The five out of eight strategic partnership agreements that New Delhi has signed with East Asian countries and a variety of defence and strategic interactions that it has fashioned are testimony to each other's common strategic stakes. The economic dimension came about in the wake of the financial crisis and India's incontrovertible rise in economic power. The fact that India's trade has been growing the fastest with East Asia is a pointer to the region's economic salience. An equally importance facet of India's linkage is its active participation in East Asian economic and security multilateralism by fundamentally shifting its position. A new beginning is also being made to enhance and capitalise on its soft power by consolidating cultural and other dimensions of relations. As a result of these linkages, India has become an inalienable part of the East Asian economic and security discourse.

ENDNOTES

1. In fact, this was one of the main reasons why India-Japan relations failed to take off although they began very well.
2. Communiqué issues at the end of the Fifth ASEAN Summit Meeting, December 1995.
3. *The Hindu*, March 6, 2006.
4. P.S. Suryanarayana, "Singapore, India Set Up Joint Panel," *The Hindu*, June 20, 2007.
5. Palaver Ayer, "India and China to Hold Defense Dialogue Soon," *The Hindu*, May 30, 2007.
6. http://www.rediff.com/news/2006/mar/06mou.htm
7. http://meaindia.nic.in/onmouse/arf1.htm

14

Cultural Diplomacy and India's Look East Policy

Rabindra Sen

Cultural diplomacy has acquired a great deal of relevance, especially in recent years, as a tool of foreign policy. In this paper an attempt is made to relate cultural diplomacy to our 'Look East' policy and to bring out the salience of cultural diplomacy in realizing the objective of an effective 'Look East' policy. After some preliminary remarks about the 'Look East' policy, we look at our relations with ASEAN. The discussion then widens to include brief assessments of our relations with China, Japan, South Korea and Australia as part of our 'Look East' policy. These parts of the paper[1] and the main part dealing with culture and cultural diplomacy are then bridged with a few comments about the importance of India's Northeast in the country's 'Look East' policy.

Initiated during the prime ministership of P.V. Narasimha Rao in the early 1990s, India's 'Look East' policy was an offshoot of two profoundly important developments – one external and the other internal. The external development was the end of the Cold War, and the internal the opening up of the Indian economy.[2] It was against the backdrop of these momentous events that India embarked on its 'Look East' policy, which led to closer interaction with India's long neglected Southeast Asian neighbours. Since it was launched, the 'Look East' policy has been pursued vigorously by successive governments in India.[3] In doing so, India has given paramount importance as much to its economic interests as to its national security and strategic imperatives. India's engagement in East Asia has not gone unnoticed. Emphasizing the need for a reassessment of India's position in light of its ties with the East, for example, Ellen L. Frost observes,

"... for historical, cultural, political as well as for substantial economic reasons India belongs at the East Asian table."[4] "It is time to 're-centre' our notions of Asia so that maps and other geographic concepts reflect India's resurgent links with eastern neighbours. India's political role in the Asian integration movement underscores this need."[5]

Former external affairs minister Jaswant Singh said in 2001 that India's parameters of security "clearly extend beyond the confines of the convenient albeit questionable geographical definition of South Asia."[6] Seen in this light, India's 'Look East' policy represents a shift from South Asia onto the larger geographical space of the Asia Pacific. Slowly but surely, the Asia Pacific region has emerged as the central pivot in the Indian view of Asian stability, and essential to the construction of a security order that will be in India's interest. India would like to fashion a multilateral security order in the Asia Pacific in partnership with the Association of South East Asian Nations (ASEAN).

In an address delivered in 2008 Prime Minister Manmohan Singh said, "...in the world in which science and technology have created a situation where distances have lost their old significance, the concept of neighbourhood is no longer the immediate neighbourhood that we know of. And that is why in the last 15–20 years, we have been trying to look East-ward to South-east Asia, to East Asia. This is where in the last 20 years there has been the most rapid economic and social growth. And that is why we are trying to work very closely to find new avenues of cooperation between India and the ASEAN countries. Also we are trying to expand our cooperation with other countries of East Asia.... The aspiration is ... that we all should work towards a flourishing East Asian Community which will give new meaning to our inter-dependence with countries of South East Asia and East Asia."[7] In January the same year the then External Affairs Minister Pranab Mukherjee had said, "our Look East policy, which was based on ASEAN's economic, political and strategic importance in the Asia-Pacific region and its potential to become a major partner of India in trade and investment, has now evolved to include the Far Eastern and Pacific regions. Our trade with countries of the East Asia Summit, including the ASEAN, has crossed US $ 80 billion. A virtual Asian Economic Community is emerging, which could be the third pole of the world economy, after the EU and the NAFTA."[8] India, as pointed out by Prime Minister Manmohan Singh, is committed to work with ASEAN and other East Asian countries to make the 21st Century truly an "Asian Century".[9] While addressing the Sixth India – ASEAN Summit in Singapore in November 2007, Prime Minister Manmohan Singh said, "India has a stake in ASEAN's stability and prosperity just as we believe ASEAN has a stake in the transformation that India is experiencing."[10] Sharing his vision of an Asian Economic Community consisting of an integrated market linked by efficient road, rail, air and shipping services, he said the creation of this "arc of advantage" would be possible if these countries built a robust international architecture for regional cooperation and action.[11]

Looking Towards ASEAN

South-East Asia is an important region. It is especially so for India because we share maritime boundaries with several ASEAN countries and both a land and maritime boundary with Myanmar. The 'Look East' initiative was intended to realize India's desire and hope of deepening the partnership with the ASEAN countries. Perhaps the most exciting aspect of India's engagement with ASEAN is its importance in establishing a cooperative Asian community.[12] Frequent high level visits, especially in recent years, by Indian leaders have brought into sharper focus India's keen interest in forging ties with the Southeast Asian nations.

Needless to add, this has been reciprocated by the Southeast Asian leaders who have acknowledged India's strategic footprint in the Asia Pacific region and want India to play a larger, meaningful and stabilising role in the region. India is certainly among the countries ASEAN would like to reach out to as it finds it necessary in its own interest to look around and forge closer ties with countries having big stakes in Southeast Asia. Interestingly enough, one ASEAN minister has referred to India as the "western wing of ASEAN" while referring to South Korea and Japan as its 'eastern wing'.[13]

At their 2004 Summit in Vientiane, the Southeast Asian leaders urged their region to look north to China and west to India for new trade links to ensure prosperity.[14] In a speech to business leaders, former Malaysian Prime Minister Abdullah Ahmed Badawi said, "we recognize the emergence of China and India in the global trading environment." Badawi stressed that Southeast Asia needed greater integration with these trading powers – instead of looking at them as rivals – and "cannot remain competitive merely by strengthening intra regional cooperation."[15] Former Philippine President Gloria Macapagal Arroyo also emphasised the importance of including India in accomplishing the task of spreading out the benefits of development through 'expanded' ASEAN integration. "An enlarged East Asian bloc," said Arroyo, "can not only secure the future of ASEAN, but also the future of China, Japan and South Korea."[16] Adding India to that line-up would produce a trade bloc that could compete with the European Union and North America, Arroyo said.[17]

After the initiation of India's 'Look East' policy, the ASEAN-India relationship has grown from sectoral dialogue partnership in 1992 to a full dialogue partnership in 1995 and subsequently even to a summit level interaction. The first ASEAN-India Summit was held in 2002 in Phnom Penh. The progressively closer relationship has led to strengthening of not only economic ties between ASEAN and India, but also political and security linkages, with India joining the ASEAN Regional Forum (ARF) in 1996.[18] According to former foreign secretary Salman Haidar, "acceptance of India as dialogue partner by the ASEAN has remained the most important window for our eastward vision."[19] Over the years, collaborative initiatives have been launched between ASEAN and India in a variety of fields, and strong institutional mechanisms for ASEAN-India cooperation have been put in place.[20] Elevating their relationship to a new height, India and ASEAN (at the tenth ASEAN Summit held in 2004) signed a landmark pact on "peace, progress and shared prosperity" with a call for collective action to fight global terrorism and expand economic ties. Apart from regular high-level dialogue, contacts at the official, business, cultural, academic, media and people-to-people levels have been revived and reinforced.[21]

Strengthening economic linkages between the two sides is a priority for India and ASEAN. Bilateral trade is growing rapidly. The target of $ 30 billion that had been set for the year 2007 was achieved and an ambitious bilateral trade target of $50 billion by 2010 was set. On 13 August 2009, India and ASEAN signed the long awaited Free Trade Agreement in Goods to end duty barriers in the region after more than six years of intense negotiations. The signing of the agreement signals India's firm commitment to its 'Look East' policy of building upon its historical links with the countries of the Southeast Asian region and further deepening and widening the partnership. ASEAN provides a bridge for India to connect with the Asia-Pacific. For India's own neighbourhood peace, security, stability and development, ASEAN and the Indian Ocean Region are strategically important and constitute an integral part of our consciousness.[22] ASEAN countries recognize the role India is capable of playing in their "Initiative for ASEAN Integration" (IAI) aimed at helping the lesser-developed member countries of ASEAN, namely Cambodia, Laos, Myanmar and Vietnam, to catch up with the rest of the grouping.[23] The potential benefits of a closer ASEAN-India relationship go beyond economics. India's accession to the Treaty of Amity and Cooperation (TAC) with Southeast Asia and agreement on combating terrorism marks a shift from just trade and investment to wider economic and security issues, including joint efforts to protect the sea-lanes to ensure energy supply lines and coordination on counter-terrorism activities.[24] Preserving the security and stability of the region is a key goal for ASEAN. India, given its size, strategic location in the Indian Ocean, and military prowess, can play a positive role in this respect.[25]

As part of our 'Look East' policy, reference may also be made to BIMSTEC (Bay of Bengal Initiative for Multi Sectoral Technical and Economic Cooperation), which brings five countries of the Indian Subcontinent (Bangladesh, Bhutan, India, Nepal and Sri Lanka) together with two countries from South East Asia (Myanmar and Thailand) for promoting regional cooperation. The Mekong-Ganga

Cooperation (MGC) is another initiative bringing together India and five ASEAN countries – Cambodia, Laos, Myanmar, Thailand and Vietnam.[26] India has also been made a member of the East Asia Summit. Commencing in Kuala Lumpur in 2005, the East Asia Summit is a meeting of the heads of state/government of regional neighbours – China, Japan, South Korea, India, Australia, New Zealand – and the ten member – states of ASEAN. India's presence in the EAS signals not only a victory for New Delhi's 'Look East' policy but also an implicit 'Look West' policy on the part of India's neighbours to the east.[27]

From the second phase of the 'Look East' policy, there has been a perceptible shift from an exclusive focus on economic issues to a broader agenda involving security cooperation.[28] The military contacts and joint exercises that had been launched with ASEAN states on a low key basis in the early 1990s have now expanded into full-fledged defence cooperation. The establishment of air and land links to East and Southeast Asia has also become integral to our 'Look East' policy.[29]

Looking Beyond ASEAN

It is well known that the geographic scope of the 'Look East' initiative has become enlarged from the initial focus on Southeast Asia to include East Asia and the South Pacific. The now expansive definition of the 'East' covering countries such as China, Japan, South Korea and Australia, invites a brief look at our relationships with these important players.

There has been a dramatic growth in Sino-Indian linkages in the last few years. India considers China as a 'foreign policy priority' and views the partnership as crucial for Asia's emergence as the political and economic centre of the new international order. "As India's largest neighbour and a key emerging player in the international arena, China remains an important priority of our foreign policy and a key component of our 'Look East' policy," said Pranab Mukherjee, the then External Affairs Minister, in 2007.[30] Mukherjee said some degree of healthy competition between the two countries was "inevitable", particularly in the area of trade and commence. But "we believe that there is enough space and opportunity in the region for both India and China to grow together," he added.[31] Describing its relationship with China as an "important determinant" for regional and global peace, India, said Mukherjee, sought all-round development of ties with China without allowing the outstanding differences, including the boundary question, to define the agenda.[32]

In July 2010, Chinese Premier Wen Jiabao also highlighted the importance of the relationship saying that China and India, as neighbours and large developing nations with the largest populations, enjoy not only profound historical and cultural origins but also broad common interests.[33] "A healthy, stable and dynamic

China-India relationship is of far reaching significance to the two nations, Asia and the whole world at large," he said.[34]

It has often been said that India's 'Look East' policy has been driven, at least in part, by an ineluctable rivalry with China.[35] Many believe that Japan, South Korea and Australia are all in search of a strategic tie-up with India as cooperation amongst them would be more effective in countering the growing Chinese influence in the Asia-Pacific. There is reason to believe that China too shares the same perception. It is true that from time to time dark clouds do appear on the China-India horizon.[36] It is also true that competition of a kind is reality and cannot be wished away. However, Sino-Indian relations, especially in recent years, have also been marked by a desire to enhance the prospects for cooperation between the two countries in various areas and see to it that the improvement in relations and the process of constant engagement do not founder the rock of deep-seated mistrust and negative mutual perceptions.[37]

Notwithstanding the trust deficit and mutual threat perceptions, India and China nevertheless are keen to put bilateral relations on an even keel. Given the thrust of this paper, it is pertinent to point out that both the countries, for example, realize the importance of boosting cultural ties to bring the two sides closer together. India has built a replica of the Sanchi Stupa with a Sarnath Buddha inside it near the historic White Horse temple, the first Buddhist temple in China in the Henan province, and hopes the Stupa will become a symbol of cultural ties between the two countries.[38] "There is a perception that India and China are distant in history with little in common. This temple is a reminder that we are actually quite close," said S. Jaishankar, India's ambassador to China.[39] China allotted a piece of land for the shrine inside the White Horse temple complex in 2005 in what was seen as a significant political gesture to revive the cultural relationship between the two countries. India's decision to participate in communist China's decision to enhance the importance of the historical temple is also a significant political move.[40] The export of Buddhist icons from India to China comes fourteen centuries after Chinese monk Hieuen Tsang crossed the Himalayas to travel across India and returned to China with important Buddhist texts.[41] Art historian Kapila Vatsayayan, who conceptualized the shrine in Henan, believes the shrine will enhance people-to-people contact between the countries and underline the importance of cultural contacts. "Only the cultural relationship survives history," she said.[42] Once opened to tourists and pilgrims, the shrine will become the most visible Indian presence in China and a symbol of shared heritage between the two countries.

India and Japan have decided to cement bilateral ties and implement their commitment to establish a 'Strategic Global Partnership'.[43] The leaders of the two countries agree on the importance of maintaining regular high level exchanges and strengthening their cooperation in regional and multilateral fora on numerous important issues. What cannot be overemphasized is that stronger Indo-Japan ties could help counter balance China's growing power in the region.[44] Japanese premier Yoshiro Mori's visit to India in August 2000 was the beginning of a new era in India-Japan relations. Since then the two countries have sought to strengthen bilateral ties through initiatives and programmes ranging from economic and cultural exchanges to defence and security.[45] The relationship has witnessed a remarkable enhancement in recent years, so much so that in 2007 the Japanese Consul General in Kolkata, Noro Motoyoshi, observed, "politically, in an attempt to add a new pillar of value-oriented diplomacy emphasizing universal values, Japan found in India a strategic partner with similar values and interests. Today a strong and dynamic India is in the best interest of Japan."[46] In August the same year, in a speech before a joint session of India's Parliament, the Japanese prime minister Shinzo Abe described India as part of "broader Asia" that spans "the entirety of the Pacific Ocean, incorporating the US and Australia."[47] Abe noted that these states comprise an "arc of freedom and prosperity" of "like-minded countries" that "share fundamental values such as freedom, democracy and respect for basic human rights as well as strategic interests."[48]

Japan directs thirty percent of its foreign aid to India and is the sixth largest FDI facilitator in India.[49] But our economic relationship is still far below its potential. Two-way trade (10.18 billion for 2007-08) has risen in the last few years, but still remains considerably low when compared with the China-Japan or even the India-China trade.[50] Similarly, Japanese foreign direct investment in India ill compares to its investment in smaller Asian countries such as Vietnam, not to mention China.[51] In April 2005, the two countries agreed to set up a Joint Study Group (JSG) for a free trade agreement (FTA).[52] The JSG in 2006 recommended a Comprehensive Economic Partnership Agreement (CEPA). Negotiations were launched in January 2007 covering trade in goods and services, investment flows, trade promotion and measures for promoting economic cooperation in identified sectors.[53] The recent surge in Japanese FDI in India (to the tune of $5 billion in 2008 against less than $ 500 million in 2007) indicates the increasing interest of Japanese investors in india.[54] According to a recent survey conducted by the Japan Bank for International Cooperation, India has become the most favoured investment destination for long-term Japanese investments.[55] Indian industry expects the CEPA to lead to greater flow of technology and investments from Japan into India.[56]

The main emphasis in this paper being on cultural diplomacy, brief comments about cultural affinities between India and Japan and about the recognition of the need for building bridges between the two cultures seem quite appropriate at this stage. While visiting Japan in 2006, Prime Minister Manmohan Singh underlined the importance of cultural diplomacy in bringing the peoples of the two countries together. The number of Indian restaurants in Japan has increased phenomenally, the Indian prime minister remarked proudly, underlining the new cultural camaraderie between India and Japan and the need for increasing people-to-people contacts between the two countries.[57] Tamil superstar Rajnikant, popularly known in Japan as 'Odori Maharaja' (The Dancing Maharaja) has mesmerised the Japanese with his machismo and flamboyance.[58] "I am delighted to hear the popularity of Odori Maharaja among young people here. Our children were delighted to see Odori Asimo – the dancing robot," said Manmohan Singh in his historic address to a joint session of the Diet, the Japanese parliament.[59] The remarks of the Indian premier were greeted with a burst of deafening applause. More applause followed when Manmohan Singh told his Japanese audience about the burgeoning popularity of Japanese cuisine in India. "I assure you that sushi and tempura are becoming popular in India," he said.[60] During the visit, the Indian Council of Cultural Relations, India's premier organ of cultural diplomacy, and the Japan Foundation signed a memorandum of understanding to improve cultural exchanges between the two countries.[61] Manmohan Singh and his Japanese counterpart Shinzo Abe also launched the year-long Festival of India in Japan to display the vibrance and creativity of Indian culture.[62] The two countries declared 2007 to be the India-Japan Friendship Year and the year of India-Japan Tourism Exchange. The two sides also hoped to substantially increase air connectivity between them to promote tourism.[63]

South Korea too has emerged as a major economic partner of India. Two-way trade which stood at $ 15.6 billion in 2008 is expected to grow by as much as $ 3.3 billion annually.[64] South Korea is one of the top foreign investors in India and the two countries have established a framework to facilitate further investment. Noteworthy in this connection is the signing of the India-Korea Comprehensive Economic Partnership Agreement (CEPA) on 7 August 2009. This agreement is expected to take India-Korea relations to a higher level and enhance India's presence in East Asia.[65] The reduction and abolitions of tariffs through the CEPA will result in an increase in trade and investment relations between two of the largest economies in Asia.[66] In a symbolic gesture that signifies the importance India attaches to East Asia, the South Korean president Lee Myung-bak was the chief guest at this year's Republic Day celebrations in New Delhi.[67] India and South Korea are partners in the ARF and the East Asia Summit. Coming to cultural ties between the two countries, it is relevant to quote Kim Jung Bae, president of the Academy of Korean Studies (AKS), who has recently observed, "The two countries are bound by close cultural ties, which may be traced back to the ancient past. Buddhism, India's unique gift to the world, facilitated exchange of ideas and served as a bridge connecting the two civilizations (Korea and India)."[68] Korean cultural presence is becoming increasingly noticeable in India's Northeast. Quite important in this regard is the diffusion of Korean popular culture and its impact, particularly on Manipuri society, through Korean satellite channel and movies.[69]

Let us now turn our attention to Australia. One will not fail to notice the steady upswing in bilateral ties. In 2008 the then Australian foreign minister Stephen Smith said that he wanted Australia to take its relationship with India to "the front line of its international partnerships."[70] Australia has strongly backed India's bid to join Asia Pacific Economic Cooperation (APEC) after the expiration of the 2010 moratorium on the group's expansion and also its bid to become a permanent member of the UN Security Council.[71] India, which has become one of Australia's leading trading partners, is Australia's fastest growing large trade partner. Two-way trade has grown a staggering tenfold in the last decade, and Australian exports last year grew fifty percent.[72] Ties between the two countries are indeed likely to get closer in the years to come. Rory Medcalf of the Lowy Institute observes, "Our nations are multicultural democracies, facing shared hopes and challenges in the Asian century."[73]

The Northeast in India's Look East Policy

India's Northeast naturally figures prominently in the country's 'Look East' policy. The region's advantageous and especially important position in our 'Look East' policy stems from the fact that it provides an important historical and cultural linkage between Southeast Asia and India.[74] At a seminar on 'India's Look East Policy – Challenges for Sub-Regional Cooperation' in Guwahati in 2007, the then external affairs minister Pranab Mukherjee emphasized the factor of location and said that considering the proximity India's Northeast has to Southeast Asia, the region could become the gateway to the neighbouring countries. "India is aware of the geo-economic potential of the northeastern region as a gateway to East and Southeast Asia. By gradually integrating this region through cross-border market access, the northeastern region could become the bridge between the Indian economy and what is beyond doubt the fastest growing region in the world," Mukherjee said.[75] The key concern is the development of the Northeast and the part our 'Look East' policy can play in the process.

Cultural Diplomacy and Look East Policy

Against the backdrop of the above discussion, let us now consider the importance of culture and cultural diplomacy, the richness of our cultural heritage, and the question as to how important cultural diplomacy is and should be in the formulation and implementation of our 'Look East' policy. Culture includes art, music, dance and drama, and is a whole way of life.[76] The culture of a nation finds its manifestation through language and art, philosophy and religion, education and science, films and newspapers, radio and television, social habits and customs, political institutions and economic organizations.[77] UNESCO at its 1982 Conference in Mexico had also adopted a holistic definition of culture.[78] Culture is an important factor in determining the status of a country in the community of nations.[79]

It is increasingly axiomatic today that the old calculations of "hard power" are no longer sufficient to guide a country's conduct in world affairs. "Soft power" has become much more important.[80] Former Indian minister of state for external affairs Shashi Tharoor defines "soft power" as the "ability of a country to attract others with its culture, social values and foreign policies.[81] Bollywood, Indian art, literature, fashion and cuisine, the values of Ashoka, Akbar and Gandhi, and the pluralism of our civilization constitutes our "soft power".[82] At a Technology, Entertainment, Design Conference in Bangalore in 2009, Tharoor said, "In today's world, it's not the size of the army that wins, it's the country that tells a better story."[83] Needless to say, a nation's cultural appeal would go a long way towards bolstering its "soft power". "India is and must remain a land of better stories", says Shashi Tharoor confidently.[84]

Cultural diplomacy would imply the use of the art of diplomacy in promoting culture, projecting a particular group to another, resulting in creating awareness of one another.[85] Such awareness leads to interaction among states and individuals. It would thus result in use of the instrumentality of culture in promoting a country's diplomatic interests in commercial, political and strategic fields.[86] The task of cultural diplomacy would be to produce understanding that goes beyond stereotyped images and to mould perceptions in a favourable way.[87] The Indian Council for Cultural Relations (ICCR) set up in April 1950 is India's preeminent instrument of cultural diplomacy. The ICCR has taken upon itself the twin tasks of promoting and interpreting abroad Indian culture in its widest sense as well as in establishing, reviving and strengthening cultural ties between India and other countries.[88]

India is culturally rich and powerful. On the occasion of the inauguration of the Rabindranath Tagore Centre in Kolkata in June 2008, the then external affairs minister Pranab Mukherjee referred to India as a cultural super power and said, "Our culture goes back to the dawn of time. It is distinguished by antiquity, continuity, refinement, diversity and an ability to assimilate the best from outside without losing its own inherent character and authenticity".[89] In the same speech Pranab Mukherjee highlighted the greatly increased importance of cultural diplomacy in today's world and referred to India's unique position to facilitate cultural interaction among nations.[90] While India may still have miles to go in its quest to be a global political power, the world indeed is already embracing it as a cultural super power. From Bollywood films and food to authors like Kiran Desai conquering the Booker street, brand India has seen a transformation of sorts.[91] No wonder, cultural diplomacy has evolved into a significant Track II and India is going all out to leverage this thrust now.[92] "Soft power", which is essentially the international influence a nation acquires when others are drawn to its culture and ideas, is being taken seriously by the South Block given the huge potential and the gains that may accrue.[93] Highlighting the importance of the Festival of India in Brussels in October 2006, Karan Singh, president of ICCR, said, "Earlier cultural diplomacy was considered peripheral, now the message is clear: soft power is important and the idea behind the festival is to project India as a plural multicultural society and to achieve the goals of political diplomacy."[94]

Two things about Indian culture stand out – its pluralistic nature and its composite character. People are getting more and more interested around the world both in the philosophy, in the Vedanta as well as in yoga and other spiritual practices. Buddhism, which originated here, spread throughout South and Southeast Asia.[95] What is noteworthy about our cultural expansion is that it was never done through the sword. It was done by sheer force of intellect and artistic merit.[96] That is why Thailand, Burma, Malaysia, Indonesia, Tibet, China, Korea, Japan all have had the influence of Hinduism and Buddhism.

Let us now cite a few examples of the diversity and richness of our culture. After Mecca and Medina Sharif, we probably have the largest Muslim shrines in the world. Our paintings go back to the frescos of Ajanta Ellora. The Taj Mahal, one of the wonders of the world, the Kailasha temple in Ellora built into solid rock or the great Jaina temple at Ranakpur – we have all these monuments. Dance is our great glory and so is music. Thus we have a very powerful heritage in every sphere of cultural activity.[97]

India has a long history of trade and cultural exchanges with East Asia. Trade links with East Asia stretch back two millennium to the Silk Road and Calicut emerging as a major trading port in South Asia.[98] Cultural and religious bonds date back to Emperor Asoka's spread of Buddhism beyond the sub-continent in the third century B.C.[99] Other notable periods of contact between pre-independence India and East Asia include the Kushan Empire, which built extensive trade networks with China, and the Chola Dynasty.[100] The exchange of pilgrims, explorers and traders continued until the onset of British rule over India in the eighteenth century.[101] It needs to be emphasized once again that India has ancient and enduring cultural links with Southeast Asia. French historian G.Coedes describes much of Southeast Asia and Indochina as 'Indianised' states, where two great civilizations of Asia, the Chinese and the Indian, merge and converge in unique harmony.[102] The largest Hindu temple complex in the world – Angkor Wat – is in Cambodia.[103] The largest Buddhist complex – Borobudur – is in Indonesia.[104] In Malaysia, the commander-in-chief is still called Lakshmana

– a remnant of the role played by Rama's brother in the battle of Lanka.[105] And in Indonesia, such words as 'sea' and 'ship' are recognizable for their Tamil roots.[106]

Not surprisingly India has actively used culture as an instrument of its 'Look East' policy. In 2007, while attending the India – ASEAN and the EAS Summits in Singapore, Prime Minister Manmohan Singh took the opportunity to set the stage for a productive cultural diplomacy in East Asia. He visited a special exhibition in Singapore that show-cased the rich history of the spread of Buddhism from Nalanda to different parts of East and Southeast Asia.[107] Among the many priceless exhibits donated by different collections in Asia was a relic of Buddha's bones sent by India and a copper plate that records the transactions between the Pala rulers in Eastern India during the eighth to twelfth centuries AD and the Srivijaya Kingdom in Southeast Asia.[108]

Unlike in the past when cultural diplomacy was largely viewed as India's veiled effort towards cultural dominance, the renewed thrust on cultural diplomacy has received genuine appreciation from the region.[109] Singapore prime minister Lee Hsien Loong has appreciated the growing cultural engagement between India and Southeast Asia. Indian cinema has always been popular in Southeast Asia.[110] India also has signed formal cultural agreements with a number of Southeast Asian countries – with Malaysia in 1978, the Philippines in 1969, Vietnam in 1976, Laos in 1994 and Burma in 2001.[111] Indian cultural centres are important platforms to promote India's cultural diplomacy in East Asia. There are such centres in Japan, Malaysia, Indonesia and Fiji. There are sub centres also, for example in Bali. The main activities of these cultural centres are to provide the local population an opportunity to learn about Indian culture.[112] Educational assistance forms another element of India's cultural diplomacy, offering the countries of the region opportunities to visit India, acquire education and learn about Indian culture.[113] Under the General Cultural Scholarship Scheme of the ICCR, more than fifty scholarships are provided to Southeast Asian countries. Technical assistance is also provided under the umbrella of Indian Technical and Economic Cooperation Programme.[114] An important aspect of India's cultural diplomacy is cultivating the Indian diaspora, over six million of them in Southeast Asia.[115]

Since the launch of the 'Look East' policy in the 1990s, India consciously avoided highlighting the deep cultural sources of its relationship with the region. There were good reasons for this attitude.[116] The earlier iterations of India's cultural diplomacy turned out to be disastrous. India's nationalist historians rightly drew attention to the newly discovered evidence at the turn of the twentieth century of the past interaction between the subcontinent and Southeast Asia.[117] They were utterly wrong, however in projecting the Southeast Asian kingdoms as India's "cultural colonies".[118] Independent India's early foreign policy initiatives on Asian solidarity were equally unsuccessful. The decolonised nations were not inclined to subordinate their emerging national identities to the notion of Asian unity; nor were there any takers in East and Southeast Asia for the Indian claim that it was the "mother of all civilizations" in Asia.[119]

A number of factors now allow India to craft a new cultural diplomacy and rebuild its soft power in East Asia.[120] At the same time, however, we should not forget that there are important tasks ahead and challenges to be met. It is particularly important to note that the initiative on cultural diplomacy has come from Southeast Asia. After all, it was the foreign minister of Singapore, George Yeo, who first promoted the idea of a new Asian university at Nalanda.[121] Thanks to Singapore's efforts, the Nalanda project is now on the agenda of the EAS. The celebration of the past is now very much part of an Asian renaissance. As the continent turns prosperous, expands its weight in global affairs, and embarks on building a regional identity, culture and history have inevitably acquired a new salience.[122] India is an integral part of Asia's heritage.

While reinventing its cultural diplomacy in Asia, however, India needs to focus more on the two-way interaction between South Asia and East Asian cultures and avoid the past crude emphasis on what India gave to the rest of Asia.[123] In many parts of Southeast Asia, domestic politics often prevents an acknowledgement of the common cultural past, let alone building on it. We should make it easier for these countries to explore, discover and preserve the shared history.[124] This would necessarily involve a return to greater cultural openness, which lies at the core of India's soft power tradition.[125] The road to rejuvenation of India's soft power in Asia lies though mutual cultural rediscovery. The rejuvenation should also include India's readiness to share its emerging strengths in technology and education.[126] C. Raja Mohan observes, "the new exphasis on culture and higher education does not imply that India's Look East policy is turning sentimental. It is based on a hard-headed assessment that reclaiming India's Asian past is necessary for establishing its role in the continent's political future ... If India does not rise to the occasion, Asia will inevitably drift towards a Sino-centric future. An India that seizes its opportunities will help anchor Asia in its richer and more diverse past".[127] One major challenge before India is revitalizing the 'Look East' policy. In another paper, emphasizing the importance of the task ahead, C. Raja Mohan cogently points out, "For nearly two decades now, the renewed engagement with Asia or the Look East policy has been the one enduring feature of India's external relations and one of New Delhi's more successful diplomatic initiatives. After being marginal to Asian economic and strategic affairs, India is now very much part of almost all the major regional institutions of Asia, including the East Asia Summit. *At the same time, it is quite clear that India's Look policy has hit a plateau and the conduct of India's relations with Asia has not been able to stay abreast of the region's strategic evolution. Without a rejuvenation of India's Look East policy, what we might have in the near future is a 'Chinese Century', rather than an 'Asian Century'."* [Emphasis added][128] Needless to say, a more effective cultural diplomacy is certainly one important avenue for rejuvenating our "Look East" policy.

India needs to develop new instrumentalities in leveraging its widely acknowledged soft power strengths. This would involve expanding and reorganizing India's cultural centres around the world.[129] Developing a solid public private partnership would allow India to fully mobilize its real cultural strengths that are in the private sector.[130] Facilitating contacts, both government-to-government and people-to-people, is one area that demands urgent attention, especially because India's claustrophobic security mindset has undermined the nation's natural advantages.[131] The government must move quickly to make it easier for citizens of other countries to tour, visit, study, research, or work in India.[132] While bilateral ties seem to be strengthening with East Asia, people-to-people connect seems to be minimal. The Malaysian prime minister Sri Mohmmad Najib Tun Abdul Razak did in fact admit this when he said, "for ties to be binding and meaningful, it is imperative to have the strongest people-to-people relationship".[133]

Conclusion

India still has a long way to go compared to how other major countries like the United States, the United Kingdom, Japan and China use cultural diplomacy as a tool of statecraft. The US, UK and Japan use the American Centre, the British Council and the Japan Foundation respectively to reach out to the target nations. China too has undertaken a mammoth expansion of its cultural institute named Confusius Institute with hundred branches and with a budget of $ 10 billion for it.[134] In comparison, until recently, India had only 22 cultural centres functioning under its missions abroad.[135] Of course, the ICCR opened seven new cultural centres in Asia in 2009 and is now planning many more across the continent, Europe and the Americas.[136] What is required is a cohesive and consistent policy to maximize the gains. For this the foreign office and the ministries of tourism and culture need to work with greater synergy.[137] The Ministries of Information and Broadcasting, Information and Technology and Human Resource Development all have to pool their efforts to concertedly promote India's public and cultural diplomacy.

The crucial responsibilities of the Ministry of Information and Broadcasting, the Ministry of Overseas Indian Affairs and the Ministry of Tourism of the Government of India deserve a special mention here. All India Radio is one of India's most visible media initiatives, broadcasting both nationally and abroad. Its external services, which aim to project a positive political and cultural image of India abroad as well as to connect with India's international Diaspora, reach over 100 countries in 27 languages with daily broadcasts.[138] The Directorate of Film Festivals of the Ministry of Information and Broadcasting, established in 1973, organizes and manages India's involvement in a number of international film festivals and cinema events.[139] The range of responsibilities of the Ministry of Information and Broadcasting include dissemination of information about India within and outside the country through publications on matters of national importance. The Publications Division serves as one of the leading publishing houses in India, producing books and journals aimed at highlighting India's cultural and political heritage.[140]

With an estimated 30 million Indians living abroad, particular attention has been paid to efforts aimed at encouraging dialogue in the international Indian community for the benefit of the nation's interests. The government has initiated a number of programmes focusing on outreach to Indians abroad.[141] Pravasi Bharatiya Divas or "Diaspora Day" is a major annual event that encourages the involvement of the Diaspora community in the development of their homeland.[142] In addition to Pravasi Bharatiya Divas, the government also hosts the Know India Programme (KIP) through the Ministry of Overseas Indian Affairs.[143] Last but not least, making the most of India's rich diversity, the government's Ministry of Tourism shapes tourism promotion according to the most appealing and interesting experiences India has to offer. Promoted sectors include Heritage sites, ecotourism, spiritual pilgrimages, and luxury vacations.[144] Spiritual experiences are particularly popular as a result of India's rich religious history and significance for Hinduism and Buddhism and the Ministry of Tourism draws on the appeal of religious sites and holy cities in targeted campaigns.[145]

Although the importance of cultural diplomacy needs no emphasizing yet again, two observations seem worth mentioning. In November 2009 in his valedictory address at an International Seminar on Changing Nature of Conflict, Shashi Tharoor said, "what is also required in responding to the changing nature of conflict is a dialogue of cultures."[146] The second observation is by Kim Jung Bac, president of the Academy of Korean Studies, who has recently said, "A political relationship or understanding between the two countries can have a future when it is anchored by education and cultural initiatives".[147] We must therefore widen and deepen our activities so that our role in cultural diplomacy becomes effective. Cultural diplomacy is no longer simply a luxury; it is central to our diplomatic experience and especially so because of our fabulous background in the arts, in culture, philosophy, religion, painting, in dance, music and in sculpture and our monumental heritage.[148] "Because of the fact that we are one of the few nations in the world that have been originators of great cultural traditions, cultural diplomacy can play an extremely important role".[149]

We conclude with the observation made recently by Karan Singh, President of ICCR, who has said, "Diplomacy is like the Ganga – Jamuna – Saraswati triveni. The Ganga is political diplomacy, the Yamuna is economic diplomacy and the invisible Saraswati is cultural diplomacy".[150] What clearly emerges from the above discussion is that looking east, India should rely on soft power,[151] though treading cautiously at the same time so as to make sure that the use of soft power does not turn out to be counterproductive. There is no gainsaying the fact that success in our 'Look East' policy and our foreign policy in general hinges in large measure on a judicious and calibrated use of cultural diplomacy.

ENDNOTES

1. For a discussion of these parts, see also the author's 'India's Look East Policy : Some Observations', in Rabindra Sen, Tridib Chakraborti, Anindya J. Majumdar and Shibashis Chatterjee (eds.), *Power, Commerce and Influence: India's Look Experience*, Lancers' Books, New Delhi, 2009, pp. 1-13.
2. The Look East policy partly owes its origin to the balance of payments crisis in 1991. The crisis and the ground that it provided for opening up the economy left India with little option other than responding positively to globalization. This meant accessing new markets. There was no other region of the world that had more vibrant markets than those in India's East. See, Amitendu Palit, 'India should continue to Look East', <http://www.eastasiaforum.org/2010/04/22/ india-should-continue-to-look-east/>
3. Indeed, India has maintained a relatively active diplomatic effort in East Asia. Satu P. Limaye, 'India-East Asia Relations: The Weakest Link, but not Goodbye', <csis.org/files/media/csis/pubs/0204qindia_easia.pdf>, p.9. India does indeed seem to be gradually figuring in geopolitical East Asian scheme of things. Beginning of 2010 saw India aggressively engaging major East Asian countries. Apart from state visits by leaders of South Korea, Japan and Malaysia, Indian Navy led 13 navies from the region in the Milan 2010 anti terror, humanitarian assistance and disaster relief exercise in the Indian Ocean. Madhurya Blog, <http://www.publicdiplomacyblog.com/2010/02/public-diplomacy-potential-for-india-in-east-asia>.
4. Ellen L. Frost, "India's Role in East Asia : Lessons from Cultural and Historical Linkages", *Research and Information System for Developing Countries* (RIS), New Delhi, Discussion Paper # 147, p.2.
5. *Ibid.*, p.3.
6. *The Telegraph* (Kolkata) editorial, January 12, 2001.
7. *Hindustan Times*, June 12, 2008; <http://www. hindustantimes.com/redir.aspx? ID = 4693 cfcd_a8b7-4326-boff-4e1b6908e87>.
8. "Shaping India's Foreign Policy to Stake Its Rightful Place in the Comity of Nations", Speech by Indian external affairs minister Pranab Mukherjee at the Defence Services Staff College, Wellington, January 22, 2008. See *Strategic Digest* (Institute for Defence Studies and Analyses, New Delhi), vol.38, no.2, February 2008, p.171.
9. *The Times of India*, September 25, 2007.
10. *The Statesman,* November 22, 2007.
11. *Ibid.*

12. Shankaran Nambiar, "India and ASEAN : an FTA and beyond", <http://www.eastasiaforum.org/2010/01/21/ india-and-asean-an-fta-and-beyond/>.
13. *The Statesman,* November 28, 2004.
14. *The Statesman*, November 29, 2004.
15. *Ibid.*
16. *Ibid.*
17. *The Economic Times*, November 29, 2004.
18. Seema Gaur, "ASEAN – India Ties Entering a New Phase", *Viewpoints* (Institute of South East Asian Studies, Singapore), October 8, 2003; <www.iseas.edu.sg/viewpoint/sg30oct03.pdf>, p.1.
19. Salman Haidar, 'Looking East', *The Statesman*, November 26, 2000.
20. Gaur, *op.cit.*
21. A.N. Ram, "India's Foreign Policy in the Asia-Pacific : Contemporary Issues", *Area Studies* (Centre for Southeast Asian and Pacific Studies, Sri Venkateswara University, Tirupati), vol.1, no.1, January – June, 2007, p.23.
22. Ram, *op.cit.,* p.24.
23. Gaur, *op.cit.*, p.2.
24. *Ibid.* For the detail of India's security concerns influencing New Delhi to seek a cooperative and mutually beneficial relationship with ASEAN, see, Arabinda Acharya, 'India and Southeast Asia in the Age of Terror : Building Partnerships for Peace', *Contemporary Southeast Asia*, vol.28, no.2, 2006, pp. 297-321.
25. Gaur, *op.cit.,* p.2.
26. Rajiv Sharma, "India's ties with Japan, ASEAN steadily improving", *The Tribune*, April 28, 2007; at <http://www. tribuneindia.com/2007/20070428/main7.htm>.
27. Frost, *op.cit.*, p.1.
28. C. Raja Mohan, "Look East Policy : phase two", *The Hindu*, October 9, 2003; at <www.hinduonnet.com/2003/10/09/ stories/2003100901571000.htm>.
29. *Ibid.*
30. *The Statesman*, September 15, 2007.
31. *Ibid.*
32. *Ibid.*
33. *News from China* (Embassy of the People's Republic of China, New Delhi), vol.xxii, no.7, July 2010, p. 8.
34. *Ibid.*
35. Raja Mohan, *op.cit.*
36. The row over the recent Chinese refusal to give a visa to an Indian Army general because he was commanding troops in Jammu and Kashmir is a case in point.
37. Sounding a note of caution, Prime Minister Manmohan Singh has very recently remarked, "There is a new assertiveness among the Chinese... So it's important to be prepared". But he also added it was his firm belief that the world was large enough for India and China to "cooperate and compete" at the same time. See, *The Times of India*, September 7, 2010. Also noteworthy in this context is the observation made by the Indian ambassador to China, S. Jaishankar. "Both of us today have an interest in ensuring that nothing happens to constrain our development", Jaishankar said.. "An emphasis on competition is not in the interests of either China or India." See, *News from China*, vol.XXII, no.8, August 2010, p.31.

38. Saibal Dasgupta, "China temple to be mark of cultural ties", *The Times of India*, April 25, 2010.
39. *Ibid.*
40. *Ibid.*
41. Saibal Dasgupta, "Stupa gift for China as Buddha smiles on ties", *The Times of India*, April 25, 2010.
42. *Ibid.*
43. *The Statesman*, November 22, 2007.
44. Geethanjali Nataraj, "India and Japan : Increasing interest, declining inflows", <http:/ /www.eastasiaforum.org/2009/09/09/india-and-japan-increasing-interest-declining-inflows/>, p.2.
45. Amit Singh, "India and Japan: poised to enter a new era", <http://www.eastasiaforum.org/ 2008/12/13/india-and-japan-poised-to-enter-a-new-era-of-economic-relationship/>, p.1.
46. *The Statesman*, December 14, 2007.
47. Chietigj Bajpaee, "India rediscovers East Asia", *Asia Times*, October 31, 2007; <http:/ /www.atimes.com/atimes/south_ Asia/IJ31Df01.html>, p.3.
48. *Ibid.*
49. Amit Singh, *op.cit.*
50. Geethanjali Nataraj, *op.cit.*
51. *Ibid.*
52. Amit Singh, *op.cit.*
53. Ibid.
54. *Ibid.*
55. Geethanjali Nataraj, *op.cit.*
56. Amit Singh, *op.cit.*
57. <http://www.indianews.com/asia/20061214/32560.htm>.
58. *Ibid.*
59. *Ibid.*
60. *Ibid.*
61. *Ibid.*
62. *Ibid.*
63. *Ibid.*
64. Editorial, "Korea-India ties", 26.1.2010; <http://www. asianewsnet.net/news.php ? id=9768 & sec=3->.
65. Pravakar Sahoo, "India-Korea CEPA : A step in right direction"; <http://www.eastasia forum.org/2009/09/15/ india-korea-cepa-a-step-in-right-direction/>, p.1.
66. *Ibid.* p.2.
67. Madhurya Blog, *op.cit.*
68. *The Times of India*, February 10, 2010.
69. Otojit Kshetrimayum, "I Like Korea" "Korean Cultural Diffusion in Manipur", <http:www.e-pao.net>features.
70. Patrick Walters, "Australian securities with India strengthened", *The Australian*, June 24, 2008; at <http://www.theaustralian.news.com.au./story/0, 25197, 23912274-25837,00.html>.
71. *Ibid.*
72. Rory Medcalf, "It's A Natural Alliance", *The Times of India*, May 14, 2010.
73. *Ibid.*

74. For a discussion of the case of Tai-Ahoms of Assam, see, Papori Phukan, "Cultural Tourism in the Look East Policy", *Institute of Peace & Conflict Studies* (New Delhi), Article No.2515, March 14, 2008; <http://www.ipcs.org/article_details.php?article No=2515>.
75. See <palashspeaks.blog.co.uk/2007/10/07/ cbi_calls_for_ control_on_cybernetwork-n~3099734>.
76. P.S. Sahai, "Cultural Diplmacy: India in Singapore"; at <http://www.diplomaticmonitor.org/codia/feature01.html>, p.1.
77. *Ibid.*
78. *Ibid.*
79. *Ibid.*, p.2.
80. <http://in.answers.yahoo.com/question/index?qid = 20070311222740AA 5 DEHS>
81. Shobhan Saxena, "How to be a cultural superpower", *The Times of India*, November 22, 2009; <http://timesofindia. indiatimes.com/home/sunday-toi/special-report/How-to-be- a-cultural superpower>, p.2.
82. <http://in.answers.yahoo.com/question/index ? qid = 20070311222740AA 5DEHS>.
83. Saxena, *op.cit.* p.2.
84. *Ibid.*
85. Sahai, *op.cit.*, p.2.
86. *Ibid.*
87. *Ibid.*
88. For the objectives of the ICCR see, *ibid*, p.3.
89. *Bharat Bichitra* (A High Commission of India Publication), Vol.4, Issue 4, June 15, 2008; <http://www.hcidhaka.org/ fortnight/20080515.pdf>.
90. *Ibid.*
91. Saurabh Shukla, "Soft Power", *India Today*, October 30, 2006; <http://www.india-today.com/itoday/20061030/ diplomacy.html>,p.1.
92. *Ibid.*
93. *Ibid.*
94. *Ibid.*
95. President's Inaugural Address at Azad Bhavan, 1 September 05; <http://www.iccrindia.org/inaugural.htm>, p.1.
96. *Ibid.* See also, Frost, *op.cit.*, p.3.
97. President's Inaugural Address at Azad Bhavan, *op.cit.*
98. Bajpaee, *op.cit.*, p.1.
99. *Ibid.*
100. *Ibid.*
101. *Ibid.*
102. See, A.N. Ram, "Historical Perspectives"; <http://www.india- seminar.com/2000/487/487%20ram.htm>, p.1.
103. T.V.R. Shenoy, "Eastward Ho!", <http://www.rediff.com/ news/2000/dec/14flip.htm>, p.1. For other examples of Indian influence which spanned across a huge region, see Frost, *op.cit.*, p.9.
104. Shenoy, *op.cit.*
105. *Ibid.*
106. *Ibid.*
107. 'India-ASEAN Summit : PM puts forward proposals for better ties", November 26, 2007; <http://news.indiamart.com/ news-analysis/india-asean-summit-p-17372.html>, p.2.

108. *Ibid.*
109. Pranav Kumar, "Contours of India's Cultural Diplomacy in Southeast Asia", *Institute of Peace & Conflict Studies*, New Delhi, Article No.2559, May 6, 2008; <http://www.ipcs.org/ article_details.php ? article No.=2559>, p.1.
110. Yogendra Singh, "Bollywood in Southeast Asia"; <http://ipcs.org/article/southeast-asia/bollywood-in-southeast-asia-2734.html>, p.1.
111. Pranav Kumar, *op.cit.*
112. *Ibid.*, p.2.
113. *Ibid.*
114. *Ibid.*
115. *Ibid.*, p.1.
116. C. Raja Mohan, "Soft power, hard facts"; <http://indianexpress.com/news/soft-power-hard-facts/ 240943/0>, p.3.
117. *Ibid.*
118. *Ibid.*
119. *Ibid.*
120. *Ibid.*
121. *Ibid.* For the Nalanda Project see, S.D. Muni, "Nalanda : a soft power project", *The Hindu*,August 30,2010; <http://www.thehindu.com/ opinion/lead/article604248.ece ? homepag...>; and P.K. Gautam, "The Upcoming Nalanda University", *Institute for Defence Studies and Analyses*, August 31, 2010; <http://idsa.in/idsacomments/The Upcoming Nalanda University_pkgau…>. S. D. Muni in his paper cited here points out that the idea of reviving the glory of Nalanda was first mooted by President A.P.J. Abdul Kalam in February 2006 during his official visit to Singapore.
122. C. Raja Mohan, "Soft power, hard facts", *op.cit.*
123. *Ibid.*
124. *Ibid.*
125. *Ibid.*
126. *Ibid.*
127. *Ibid.*, pp. 3-4.
128. C. Raja Mohan, "Diplomacy for the new decade"; <http://www.india-seminar.com/2010/605/ 605_c_raja_ mohan.htm>, pp.6-7.
129. *Ibid.*, p.10.
130. *Ibid.*
131. *Ibid.*
132. *Ibid.*, pp. 10-11.
133. Madhurya, Public Diplomacy Blog, *op.cit.*
134. Shukla, *op.cit.*, p.2.
135. *Ibid.*
136. Saxena, *op.cit.*, p.1.
137. Shukla, *op.cit.* p.2.
138. <http://publicdiplomacy.wikia.com/wiki/india>, p.3.
139. *Ibid.*
140. *Ibid.*, p.4.
141. *Ibid.*, p.5.
142. *Ibid.*
143. *Ibid.*

144. *Ibid.*, pp. 5-6.
145. *Ibid.* p.6.
146. *Strategic Digest* (Institute for Defence Studies and Analyses, New Delhi), vol. 39, no.12, December 2009, p.1451.
147. *The Times of India*, February 10, 2010.
148. President's Inaugural Address at Azad Bhavan, *op.cit*, p.1.
149. *Ibid.*
150. Saxena, *op.cit.*, p.1.
151. See, Baladas Ghosal, "Eastern Promises", *The Times of India*, November 2, 2009. Also see, Baladas Ghosal, "Some New Thoughts on India's Look East Policy", *Institute of Peace and Conflict Studies*, Issue Brief, No.54, October 2007.

15

Japan and East Asian Security

Rajaram Panda

Security issues did not dominate Japanese foreign policy prominently until recently, as the Japan-US security alliance provided Nuclear umbrella to Japan's security. Japan was free to concentrate on its economic development activities without bothering much in security matters. The ripple effect of Japan's growth strategy, as epitomized by the flying geese pattern of economic development, led to the emergence of new growth centers in South East Asia, Taiwan and South Korea. Though the US continues to remain the predominant sole superpower, its preeminence has diminished to some extent. Coupled with this, the rise of China and its ever-expanding spread of strategic reach much beyond its geographical borders, has injected some element of concern and anxiety in Japan. The growing anxiety in Japan coincides with the political transition in which the power is now transferred from the Liberal Democratic Party (LDP) to the Democratic Party of Japan (DPJ).

There is also a change in foreign policy perspective under the DPJ dispensation, which is oriented towards Asia. This Asian orientation in the foreign policy of Japan is a pointer to the fact that Japan is likely to review its relationship with the United States. Japan is likely to strive for a more independent foreign policy. In this paradigm shift, while Japan's relationship with China is likely to be redefined, the security order in Asia is also likely to undergo some change.

The rise of China, both economically and militarily, is a subject of discussion in academic discourses in the Asian capitals. There always lurks a perceived fear about China's rise. Viewed from China's perspective, much of these fears may be misplaced. This view would argue that China is cognizant of outsiders' feelings about its own growth, and therefore if China does not take corrective measures, such a feeling will lead to other countries coming together as a common front against China. China may not rejoice such a prospect. This will lead China to pursue a policy of greater tolerance and accommodation. How Japan responds to China's rise in the context of securing East Asian security will be one aspect of this paper.

The other aspect of the paper in the context of East Asian security is how to manage North Korea's nuclear proliferation activities. The underground nuclear tests conducted by North Korea in April and May 2009 threatened to disturb the fragile peace in East Asia. North Korea has walked out of the Six Party Talks (SPT), with no sign of its return lurking in the horizon. The US peace overtures towards North Korea have not yielded the desired results. Security analysts draw disturbing scenarios. The positive scenarios such as resumption of the negotiations and stalled talks, adoption of a carrot and stick policy, continuance of talks with one step forward but again one step backward, and so on do not point towards any permanent solution.

The wildcard scenario, however, projects the collapse of North Korea as thereby severely impacting the security scenario in the region. This scenario projects immediate serious consequences in the influx of refugees both to China and South Korea and the problems associated with this. How China and South Korea will be able to cope with such a situation when that arises remains uncertain. Reunification is yet another scenario that can be drawn but seems unlikely. In the event of both the Koreas reunified, where do the nuclear materials in North's possession finally land up is another worrying factor. If the South is able to manage the collapse of the North and shoulders successfully the rebuilding process and takes control of the nuclear materials in North's possession, what will be impact of this on countries like Taiwan and Japan? The immediate projection of such a development is that both Taiwan and Japan will exercise their option of going nuclear. In such a situation, how Japan will address the issue of East Asian security in the changed environment is another aspect of this paper. It needs to be mentioned here that some of the issues will be speculative and may not be very realistic.

What Concerns Japan?

In the Japanese political discourse, a new element of dynamism is seen in which Japan seems to be more confident, ambitious and better prepared to face the emerging challenges. A resource deficient country, Japan is dependent on overseas supplies of critical raw materials to sustain its economic growth. Also, much of its manufactured goods are transported by seas to overseas markets. Therefore, securing sea lanes of communication (SLOCs) is very important for Japan's economic prosperity. In view of the increasing threat from piracy to maritime trade and terrorism at sea, the vulnerability of Japan's economy is exposed. Japan alone is not competent to address such critical issues.

The second critical issue that confronts Japan stems from its pacifist Constitution. In particular, Article 9 of the Constitution severely limits Japan's capacity to play an active role in securing maritime trade. This calls for cooperation with the navies of other friendly countries. Therefore, both the issues of maritime trade and reforming the Constitution are important issues for Japan. Japan is aware of the fact that if it undertakes constitutional reforms that would enable it to play an active role to ensure maritime security single-handedly, the repercussions would be far reaching. Because of the historical legacy, Japanese actions would raise suspicions and might be seen as destabilizing developments in Asia.

Maritime Security

Japan is an archipelago, a maritime nation by definition. From time immemorial, Japanese people have sensed a great romance with the sea filled with surprises. Its prosperity and security are entirely dependent upon the ability of ships to move freely over the seas. True, the Japan-US alliance is the lynchpin of East Asian security, but Japan faces some dilemmas as the US urges Japan to demonstrate greater self-reliance and autonomy in security affairs. Seen differently, US preeminence as the sole superpower has shown signs of diminishing. From Japan's side, there is a desire also to be more independent of the US, though this seems unlikely in the near term.

This argument does not mean to suggest that the US would abandon Japan in times of crisis. Nevertheless, it has dawned on Japan that some sort of preparedness to meet contingencies is desirable. Finding ways to ensure the security of vital SLOCs is indeed a challenge to Japan.

As said, Japan is heavily dependent on energy imports from the Persian Gulf. While the import dependency, for example, of the US and the European Union remains diversified and therefore the risk is distributed, Japan cannot enjoy that luxury. Japanese vulnerability will be thoroughly exposed if any exporting country adopts a mercantilist approach with a view to control both transport routes as well as energy supplies in order to dominate sources of energy.[1]

Japan has realized that if it wants to demonstrate a pro-active stance towards its security, it should craft a permanent, national commitment, enshrined in law, to Japan's Maritime Self Defence Forces (JMSDF) participation in security operations, guarding safe passage of ships on the open ocean. It is a national embarrassment that Japan has not been able to maintain an uninterrupted JMSDF presence in the Indian Ocean in support of Operation Enduring Freedom's naval contingent.

Importance of the Malacca Straits

As mentioned, almost 80 per cent of the oil and 20 per cent of the ships bound for Japan pass through the Straits of Malacca, and therefore protection of the

SLOCs is of utmost importance and concern for Japan. The strategic import of the Straits of Malacca can be gauged from the fact that safety of the SLOCs is crucial for many countries in the region whose foreign trade is sea borne.

The Straits of Malacca, located between the east coast of Sumatra and the west coast of Peninsula Malaysia, stretches for about 520 miles. The linked Straits are the shortest route forming the main seaway between the Indian Ocean (via the Andaman Sea) and the Pacific Ocean (via the South China Sea). It is the shortest route for tankers trading between the Persian Gulf and the East Asian countries. The Straits of Malacca is a critical and strategic waterway, every year carrying more than a quarter of world trade and almost all oil imports to Japan and China.

The volume of traffic averages about 250 ships on a daily basis. Out of this, 36 per cent are oil tankers. About 3.23 million barrels of crude oil and refined products are transported from the region en route to Japan through the South China Sea. Approximately 80 to 85 per cent of Japan's oil imports pass through the Straits, protection of which is a perennial concern for Japan. For more than 1,000 years, trade, religion, culture, civilizations of India, China and the Muslim world and of the Europeans have flowed through the Straits of Malacca.

Despite the seas of East Asia being among the busiest in the world in carrying a substantial portion of the world trade, these seas are relatively ungoverned, and therefore the future stability of the maritime security remains always uncertain. In view of the strategic congruence of other emerging economies such as China and the ASEAN countries, a lot of importance is attached to strengthening the navies of these countries to tackle the menace from pirates and terrorists. Though Japan is keen to play a role in ensuring maritime security, its capacity to demonstrate naval strength remains constrained by the pacifist Constitution.

Security Interests and the MSDF

The sea is the worksite of the Maritime Self Defence Force (MSDF). Maintaining maritime security is a top priority for Japan. Maritime defence is extremely important for Japan's survival. Japan faced external threats in the past, which came from the sea. Indeed, Commodore Perry reached the Japanese shore and opened the country to the outside world. A major item in the Japanese diet – fish – comes from the sea. Japan's fishing fleet, therefore, needs to be protected and therefore has important security implications. The post-War economic development process again underscored the importance of maritime commerce, and thus maritime security emerged as a matter of serious concern for Japan. Not only critical raw materials must reach Japanese ports through the sea to feed the rising demand of the domestic industries, but also Japan's export industries depend on access to sea transport to carry goods to overseas export markets. Any disruption in sea traffic would cause a devastating blow to Japan's economic future. Japanese defence planners are, therefore, grappling with the issue of ensuring maritime security.

As one of the three wings of the SDF, the MSDF's – the naval wing – mission is to defend (Japan) from maritime invasion and to secure the safety of maritime traffic around Japan.[2] The JMDF's primary jurisdiction lies outside of Japan's territorial waters, which are protected by the Maritime Safety Agency.

Japan's military presence in the sea, known as the Maritime Self Defence Force and not "Navy", is not Japan's own making. In response to the war in the Korean peninsula, Japan was advised by the Supreme Commander of Allied Powers (SCAP), led by General Douglas McArthur, to create the SDF. But Article 9 of the Constitution that was drafted and imposed by the SCAP on Japan also prevented Japan from using force offensively. As such the role of the JMSDF is dedicated to "not becoming a military power that might pose a threat to other countries."[3] This does not mean to suggest that Japanese MSDF is weak. It has a powerful presence in East Asia. Though China is strengthening its naval capability recently, the position of Japanese navy vis-à-vis its neighbour is quite strong.[4] It has a long record of overseas training and holds joint exercises with allied navies. This makes it the most cosmopolitan of Japan's armed forces.[5]

The role of the MSDF has perceptibly changed in the post-September 11 security environment, and it has emerged as a responsible force capable of operating in a wider geographical range. The dispatch of JMSDF support ship to the Arabian Sea in 2001 to support the US-led invasion of Afghanistan was indeed "epoch-making."[6] Japan is also strengthening its naval fleet, enhancing MSDF's ability to operate in distant waters.[7]

Recent developments suggest that "Japan is moving away from its pacifist past towards a more hard headed and outward-looking security posture characterized by a greater willingness to use the SDF in support of its foreign policy and defence interests."[8] Dupont further argues that this "shift is evolutionary, not revolutionary, but it is gaining momentum and represents a defining watershed in Japan's post war security policy. However, there is little likelihood of a reversion to old style militarism."[9] While Japan will be prepared to defend its territory in the event of external attack, it is extremely unlikely Japan is ready to become a "normal" state. The public opinion is unlikely to approve such a course in the new term. However, if developments in its neighborhood such as in North Korea going fully nuclear compel Japan to review its options, public approval might be reversed.

Constitutional Constraints

Article 9[10] of the Constitution puts severe limitations on Japan's prospects for becoming a "normal" state. One might assume that given Japan's vulnerability, it should not be difficult for Japan to reverse its self-imposed limits on exercising military power. This is clearly not the case. A non-Japanese is unlikely to appreciate the extraordinarily detailed administrative and constitutional restrictions on what may be considered normal defence activities in most other countries. The Japanese peoples have accepted the clauses of Article 9 as the guiding principles that Japan as a nation will continue to deny itself the right to use aggressive force. The pacifist spirit has been embedded into the Japanese psyche so intrinsically that it has become a kind of national creed. Thus, Article 9 has remained untouched and as sacrosanct.

This position is unlikely to remain sustainable for long. There have already been subtle reinterpretations of the Constitution, and the original spirit is already diluted to some extent. The rationale of restricting the use of force in defence of national interests is being questioned. If the cry becomes louder, Japan might find itself confronted with new security choices. At the moment, what would be the role of Japan in positioning itself in a new security environment is difficult to predict. What one can hazard, however, is that the East Asian security will be reordered and a new kind of power equilibrium will emerge.

Already, the Constitution has undergone incremental interpretations with a view to adopt a more robust defence policy, without tampering with the language as such but diluting the spirit. This is a shrewd move on the part of Japan to weaken Article 9 and build up its defence preparedness without annoying its neighbors who continue to retain war time memories. If Japan openly abandons Article 9, its war time adversaries might revisit history. That would be a disturbing prospect for future East Asian security order.

The importance of Article 9 of the Constitution can be measured from the fact that it has never been amended since 1947 when Gen. McArthur drafted and imposed it on the Japanese people. In contrast, Germany, which adopted a similar pacifist constitution after World War II, has amended it over 40 times to facilitate military cooperation with its allies.[11] In Japan's case, even to think of revising the Constitution was a taboo until recently when there is now greater acceptability to talk about it.[12]

If, however, Japan gets ready with comprehensive constitutional reform, while not abandoning Article 9 in letter and spirit but considerably weakening its spirit further, Japan would have enhanced its security profile greatly. In such a scenario, what would this mean to Asia in terms of profile and activities?

The immediate enhancement of its security role will be seen in the deployment of its naval capability to secure its maritime commerce. Japan will be seen with a greater involved role in ensuring East Asian maritime security. This means that there will be approved political will domestically that will reflect in major reconstruction of the legal and philosophical foundation upon which that will be built.[13]

Responses from the Region to an Assertive Japan

The responses in the region to Japan's enhanced security profile will be mixed with both hope and anxieties. In South East Asia, Japan has a lingering image problem despite its low key foreign policy and billions in aid that it has disbursed in the region. As Japan enhances its defence profile, it will lead to suspicions and revive painful memories of its militaristic past. Japan has, therefore, preferred a multilateral approach by joining other countries in the region, and has shunned a unilateral approach to address regional issues. At the same time, South East Asian countries look at Japan with hope. They know that Japan can play effectively a crucial role in balancing Chinese power and prevent the Middle Kingdom from asserting its historical domination over the region. While Japan will be aware of the regional sensitiveness, and some attitudinal barriers are unlikely to go so soon, any attempt by Japan to acquire nuclear weapons even in response to, say, North Korea going fully nuclear, will be a frightening proposition and will be vehemently opposed.

As regards the response in South Korea, Japan is likely to be seen as a benign power, but at the same time unlikely to forget the traumatic experience of Japanese occupation in the previous century. The abductee's issue that bedevils Japan's relations with North Korea and the recent underground nuclear test conducted by North Korea threatens Japan's security. However, the Japanese response to North Korea's nuclear weapon development programs may upset South Korea. In such a scenario, military competition between Japan and South Korea for regional ambitions would not be unthinkable.

As regards China, China is already strengthening its military capabilities and occasional belligerent utterances make other countries feel uneasy about what China's real future intentions are. Yet Sino-Japanese ties, though growing strong economically, may see some hiccups if Japan's security postures drastically change. Like the Koreas, China does not forget the past experiences and Japanese atrocities in Nanking. The anti-Japanese demonstrations in April 2006 in some Chinese cities threatened to undo the strong economic links that are developed between the two. Though few in China believe that Japan will abandon its security alliance with the US, others hold the view that an independent Japan is unlikely to be unfriendly to China. There are still others who hold the view that Japan would attempt to make up the security deficit by increasing military spending and developing nuclear weapons.[14] Some Chinese strategists hold the view that if Japan is allowed to move from a disarmed country to a normal country, Japan will inevitably make the next leap from normal country to aggressive militarist power.

As China is poised to overtake Japan as the world's second largest economic power, and the "rise" of China has emerged as the fashionable topic of academic discourse and op-ed articles in many regional capitals, China is likely to perceive

Japan as part of a larger American strategy to "contain" China and prevent reunification with Taiwan. China is likely to see the promotion of "Chinese threat" in many Asian capitals as an excuse to justify Japanese military buildup. Here, the statement of the Ozawa Iichiro, the elder statesman of the DPJ in April 2002 which took power from the LDP in September 2009 is noteworthy. Ozawa said: "Japan can easily have thousands of nuclear warheads. In fact, we have enough plutonium in use at nuclear power plants for three to four thousand warheads. If that should happen, Japan would not lose (to China) even in military terms."[15] Some degree of Chinese paranoia on Japan may be acceptable because of the past experiences, but to use this as a leverage to browbeat Japan limitlessly may not be acceptable to Japan. As Michael Yahuda observes, while the Chinese have condemned every instance of Japanese assertiveness, it is not clear what Japanese role would be acceptable to China's leaders other than one (in which Japan) is politically and strategically quiescent until such time as presumably it would be overshadowed by China.[16]

Nuclear Issue in North Korea

The nuclear issue in North Korea has injected a criticality to the security environment in East Asia. When the SPT began in 2003 as the new approach to the re-emerged North Korean nuclear weapons problem, it raised the specter of hope. It looked as if North Korea was a responsible actor and would respond to the plea of the SPT to dismantle its nuclear program and cooperate with key parties in the post-crisis aid programs. Initially, the SPT functioned as the mechanism to avoid referring the case to the UN Security Council. With North Korea conducting underground nuclear tests in May 2009,[17] the second time in three years when it had successfully conducted a similar test in October 2006, the situation changed. The test of May 2009 came less than two months after North Korea launched a long-range missile Taepodong-2 into the Pacific, on the same day when President Barack Obama was making a lofty speech in Prague calling on the world to move towards eliminating all nuclear weapons.

The reactions from major world capitals were strong and one of condemnation. Then reaction from Japan was the strongest. Being the only country in the world which has been a victim of nuclear bombs, to have a nuclear state in its neighborhood is the most frightening proposition for Japan.

The US also accused North Korea of supplying missile and missile technology to Iran and nuclear technology to Syria.[18] The nuclear test reflected North's attempt to shift the agenda of any future negotiations to arms control instead of denuclearization. It is also believed that North Korea is a source of nuclear proliferators. Its nuclear nexus with Iran, Syria, Pakistan and even Myanmar are worrying to the world.

The developments in North Korea make peace in East Asia are very fragile. Pyongyang could heighten tensions in the region by adopting the following measures. First, carry out more nuclear tests. Though its technical skills have improved, it still needs to make its weapons small enough to be mounted on a warhead. Some experts, however, say that North Korea has already created nuclear warheads for medium-range Nodong missiles that could strike South Korea and Japan, and has stockpiles of medium-and-short-range missiles.[19]

Then again, there is information that Pyongyang is providing small research reactors to Myanmar. Though the likelihood of Pyongyang providing nuclear assistance or devices to non-state terrorist groups like Al Qaeda is less probable, the risk of non-state actors getting their hands on North Korea's nuclear material or technology is a concern. This is because North Korea has made it known that it is willing to sell anything to anybody as it is desperate to earn revenue because of the pathetic economic situation.

Though several scenarios can be drawn about the future of North Korea impinging East Asian security, the wildcard scenario is the collapse of North Korea. The greatest threat in this worst-case scenario is where does the stockpile of Weapons of Mass Destruction (WMDs) go and who controls these? If the lesson from Iraq is any guide, finding out the exact location where the WMDs are stored would be the real problem. There is no information available about the location of the North's stockpile or facilities beyond the Yongbyon nuclear complex. At the moment, North's nuclear infrastructure is kept under extreme control and therefore there is no possibility of any unintentional nuclear leakage to potential proliferators – countries or terrorist groups – outside the country. However, if an internal power struggle erupts, or if the central authority disintegrates, the possibility for leakage of know-how, nuclear technology, fissionable materials or even weapons could dramatically increase.[20] In this kind of end-scenario, prior planning will not work. "Planning policies based on an expected collapse of North Korea are unlikely to succeed."[21]

The collapse may also be triggered by external factors: Apart from denial of external economic assistance, the generational change and growth of markets may fuel discontent, which the North Korean regime might find difficult to manage. The contagion theory popularized after the demise of the Soviet Union that rocked the Eastern European allies did not reach North Korea as Pyongyang was able to avoid the pitfall because of limited economic reforms in the early 1990s, such as the establishment of farmers' markets. This time, Pyongyang, sitting in a veritable volcano, will not be able to withstand the irresistible forces that would be unleashed by the failing economy and rising expectations of the people. Food shortages will fuel discontent.

The impact of the North's demise would be huge on its neighbors. South Korea will launch almost immediately on the process of political consolidation of the newly unified Korean state. There could be resistance from the North Korean army or special operation units. Seoul would also have to cope with the massive humanitarian dislocations that could spill over to its territory. The US will back South Korea in this process of unification and foster greater stability in the region.

China's interests would clash with that of South Korea and the US. Because of strategic consideration, China would oppose if the US tries to establish bases in the North Korean territory or station troops in proximity to its borders. Beijing might also try to seize territory when political instability occurs, though may not try to fill the political vacuum all by itself. China might not lose any opportunity to extend its influence in the region and seek UN intervention just to deny South Korea any extra advantage, thereby preventing unification. Like South Korea, China will also be wary of refugee problems as an exodus of North Korean refugees into its territory will radically increase the number of ethnic North Koreans, who later may demand autonomy from China's central government. China's main interest would be to have some economic control in northern part of Korea in cross-border trade and investment, particularly in major infrastructure projects.

As regards Japan, it will feel threatened by the possibility of China establishing a stronger position of influence on the Korean peninsula or the possibility that a unified Korea could "go nuclear". Debates in Japan to exercise the nuclear option may be intensified and willy-nilly Japan might move towards becoming a "normal" state.

None of the major players having a stake in North Korea and Asian security – the United States, Japan and China – would opt for North Korea to collapse. North Korea's political and economic systems are unsustainable. Its aggressive behavior is alienating all potential friends and making things worse. The 'enemies' of North Korea are as much afraid of its collapse as its leaders are. No one seems to be prepared for what would happen if North Korea really collapses, but if it does happen, things would be more difficult to manage, let alone solve. Ignoring things would be as dangerous as delaying addressing the issue. South Korea is not prepared for a regime collapse because it would unleash a torrent of refugees and saddle Seoul with colossal reunification costs, as the continuing domestic costs of German unification attest.

China's role in reigning North Korea seems to be critical to addressing the North Korean conundrum. Barack Obama and his aides ought to enlist Beijing's influence on Pyongyang. Obama is already saddled with the problem of enlisting Beijing's support to grapple with other major challenges such as climate change and the global financial crisis.

The regime founded by Kim Il-sung after World War II was largely a creation of Moscow, but it was China that entered the Korean War in support of North Korea. It has become North Korea's leading patron since the Soviet Union's collapse. China's influence in North Korea has further deepened after the conservative government assumed office in South Korea in 2008.

Beijing might be much worried about the possible repercussions if North Korea collapses. A sudden withdrawal of aid might precipitate a possible collapse, sending refugees across the border and leaving its weapons up for grabs. Though China might not be much worried that it could itself be the target of North Korea's weapons, its more realistic concern may be the North Korean threat will set off a military build up in Japan, South Korea and Taiwan. Such a scenario would endanger what China would value most – stability.

Those who hold this argument are of the view that North Korea's aim in developing nuclear weapons is mainly political: avoiding the collapse of the regime and maintaining the status quo of a Korean peninsula divided at the 38th parallel. This school of thought believes that Pyongyang might opt for a strategic decision to abandon its nuclear program when it judges that survival of the regime is secured.[22] The other view is that notwithstanding the political aim of securing an assurance for regime survival, extracting economic aid and maintaining status quo with the aim of making North Korea a nuclear weapon state would be the real goal.[23]

China Factor

Viewed in the perspective of East Asian security, the rise of China is both a challenge and an opportunity. If analyzed in the context of maintaining power equilibrium in the Asia-Pacific, China's rise is a challenge to most Asian countries. At the same time, China's method of achieving economic growth with its authoritarianism firmly in place has a spin-off effect, which has contributed to the economic well-being of other countries in the region. This is an opportunity to keep China engaged in the Asian affairs and accord the crucial role of a responsible stakeholder.

Like Japan, China too is heavily dependent on the Straits of Malacca for energy transportation from the Middle East. Approximately 60 per cent of China's crude oil imports originate from the Middle East. It is expected to rise to 75 per cent by 2015. Having realized the strategic vulnerability, China wants to have a preponderant say in controlling the Straits as China realizes that whoever controls the Straits of Malacca can have a stranglehold on the energy route to China.

The criticality of the SLOCs guides China to secure the Strait from hostile foreign naval forces. SLOCs arouse different response strategies amongst different countries. For a military analyst, the SLOCs are related to the maritime instruments of power, and maritime geography becomes the pivot on which forces must be deployed. To a politician, SLOCs signify the state of relations with countries located along the sea routes. For an economist, it is just the shortest and most economical travel between the two destinations. As sovereignty issues also crop up, accommodating different perceptions and national interests of countries having a stake on the safety of the SLOCs becomes very important. In particular, accommodating China's interests in a multilateral framework as a responsible stakeholder is indeed a huge challenge.[24]

Recent statements by the Chinese leadership raise concern in Asian capitals about its real intentions. As said earlier, it is poised to be the world's second biggest economic power soon after replacing Japan. It has a stupendous foreign exchange reserve of $2.4 trillion in 2009, an increase of $453 billion over the preceding year.[25] It has become a financial, economic and geopolitical reality of surpassing significance. Two-thirds or more of the reserves are estimated to be held in dollars. Though China holds US treasury bonds to the tune of $1 trillion, it has the capability to "dump" the dollar and dethrone it as the world's major international currency. That, of course, would amount to a declaration of economic war and China is unlikely to do so.

Apart from China's growing economic might, its military might is swelling as well. Its military modernization program has caught the notice of the world. In 2010, its military budget rose by just 7.5 per cent, the first time to fall below 10 per cent since 1989. This could be because China wants to allay international concerns about its rising power. Much of its spending remains secret and it is believed that Beijing's real military spending is at least double the announced figure. A 2009 Pentagon report estimated China's total military spending to be between $105 billion and $150 billion but is still dwarfed by that of the US, which has about $719 billion in outlays in 2010 for national defence.[26]

Its strategic influence is even spreading towards South Asia. China is developing port facilities in Pakistan, Bangladesh and Myanmar, and is planning to build a railroad line in Nepal. These are worrying India as China expands its sphere of influence by surrounding India with a "string of pearls" that could eventually undermine India's preeminence and potentially rise to an economic and security threat.[27]

As China strengthens economically and militarily, it extends the sovereignty issue to Japan, India and Southeast Asia by claiming island territory that belongs to Japan, land that belongs to India and sea territory that some Southeast Asian countries say belongs to them. China is capable of raising the scale of claim that could exacerbate emotive nationalism.[28]

East Asian security is rendered fragile when China makes maritime claims, which covers about 3 million square km, mostly in two areas – the South China

Sea, where Beijing's claims overlap mainly with those of Vietnam, the Philippines and Malaysia, and the East China Sea, where its claims are contested by Japan. Though China has described these claims as "indisputable" or "inalienable" sovereignty, it has not described the claims as "core" national interests and therefore open to talks. This, however, has not prevented China from reinforcing its presence, influence and strength in various ways in or close to these disputed zones. Analysts describe the Chinese strategy as "creeping assertiveness", in which China gradually assembles the sinews of power that could eventually be used to enforce its claims.

Conclusion

Developments in North Korea and China's aspiration to be a global power severely limits Japan's role to do its bit for peace in East Asia. While various scenarios can be drawn about Japan's future in response to future developments in both North Korea and China, Japan is likely to remain embedded in its alliance relationship with the US. Though the US position as the predominant power has diminished to some extent, there is not another power to replace the US in the near term. China is of course an aspiring power to be comparable to the US, but the hiatus between the two in power projection capability is huge and is unlikely to be bridged in the near term.

US analysts have taken note of the recent publication of the book titled "The China Dream" by PLA Senior Colonel Liu Mingfu in which he urges China to "sprint" towards becoming the world's most powerful state. The book states that China and the US are in "competition to be the leading country, a conflict over who rises and falls to dominate the world". Liu calls for China to build the world's strongest military and move swiftly to topple the US as the global "champion". The book's thesis contradicts those of former President Jiang Zemin and other Chinese leaders who said China's rise to prominence in the 21st century would be peaceful. Though the book was published after calls by other Chinese military officials to punish the US for policies towards Taiwan, US criticism of China's lack of Internet freedom and US support for the exiled Tibetan leader Dalai Lama, the significance of the book published by the Chinese military must not be overlooked.

China's ultimate competitor could be the US. Whether China will succeed in overtaking the US, both economically and militarily, in the next decade or so is difficult to say. It is hugely difficult for China to maintain its growth rates consistently for the next decade. China is likely to get bogged down in handling domestic strife for quite some time. In order to divert attention, it would make noise periodically but the strategic balance in East Asia is unlikely to be altered drastically in the near future. Amidst occasional pinpricks, no country will allow any regional dispute stemming from claims to territory or resource, etc from exploding into a major crisis. Economic prosperity is in the interests for all and this realization has already dawned on all the stakeholders.

ENDNOTES

1. "Security and Strategic Challenges in Asia: Prospects of Japan-India Cooperation", *ORF Seminar Series*, vol. 1, Issue 2, August 2008, p. 6.
2. Japanese Maritime Self Defence Force, "Mission of JMSDF", http://www.mod.go.jp/msdf/formal/english/index.html
3. http://www.globalsecurity.org/military/world/japan/jda.htm
4. Peter J. Woolley, *Japan's Navy: Politics and Paradox, 1971-2000* (Boulder, CO: Lynne Rienner, 2000), p. 83.
5.. Woollet, "Japan's Navy: Politics and Paradox", p.1.
6. Toru Ishikawa, There are no borders at Sea:, (2004) *Proceedings 128*, no.6, pp. 70-73.
7. Alan Dupont, "Unsheathing the Samurai Sword: Japan's Changing Security Policy", Lowy Institute for International Policy, Lowy Institute Paper 03, 2004, http://www.globalsecurity.org/military/world/japan/jda.htm. Also see, Rajaram Panda, "Japan Beefs Up its Naval Capability", Issue Brief, 5 January 2010, http://www.idsa.in/issuebrief/JapanBeefsupitsNavalCapability_rpanda_050110
8. Dupont, "Unsheathing the Samurai Sword", p. vii.
9. Dupont, "Unsheathing the Samurai Sword"
10. Article 9 reads: 9(a) "Aspiring sincerely to an international peace based on justice and order, the Japanese people forever renounce war as a sovereign right of the nation and the threat or use of force as means of settling international disputes", and (b) "In order to accomplish the aim of the preceding paragraph, land, sea, and air forces, as well as other war potential, will never be maintained. The right of belligerency of the state will not be recognized."
11. Mayumi Itoh, "Japanese Constitutional Revision: A Neo-Liberal Proposal for Article Nine in Comparative Perspective", *Asian Survey*, (2001), Vol. 41, No. 2, p.311.
12. For an exhaustive review of the constitutional revision debate and opinion of different school of thoughts, see John Byington, "Japanese Constitutional Reform and East Asian Maritime Security", 12 April 2005, The Fletcher School, Tufts University. http://fletcher.tufts.edu/research/2005/byington.pdf
13. Byington, "Japanese Constitutional Reform and East Asian Maritime Security", p. 44.
14. On this debate, see Denny Roy, Stirring Samurai, Disapproving Dragon: Japan's Growing Security Activity and Sino-Japan Relations, Asia-Pacific Center for Security Studies, 2003, Occasional Paper Series, http://www.apcss.org/Publications/Occasional%20Papers/OPStirringSamuraiRoy.pdf, pp.4-5.
15. *Sankei Shimbun*, 7 April 2002, p. 2.
16. See, Michael Yahuda, "Ihe Limits of Economic Interdependence: Sino-Japanese Relations, pp. 162-185, in Alastair Lain Johnston and Robert S. Ross, eds:, *New Directions in the Study of Chinese Foreign Policy* (Stanford: Stanford University Press, 2006) pp. 463. http://books.google.co.in/books?id=DCihrQEdPzAC&pg=PA162&lpg=PA162&dq=Michael+Yahuda+on+Sino-Japanese+Relations&source =bl&ots=0wIbpm7m QW&sig=l_amFEq86XjJUauNIajNbL2NMR I&hl=en&ei=y7apS4eYCIi3rAfssN2kAg&sa=X&oi=

book_result&ct=result &resnum=2&ved=0CAkQ6AEwAQ#v=onepage&q=Michael%20 Yahuda% 20on%20Sino-Japanese%20Relations&f=false

17. Pranamita Baruah, "Japanese Vulnerabilities increase Following North Korea's actions", 23 June 2009, http://www.idsa.in/strategiccomments/JapaneseVulnerabilitiesincreases followingNorthKoreasactions%20_PBaruah_230609
18. See, Patrick M. Cronin, ed. *Double Trouble: Iran and North Korea as Challengers to International Security* (London: Praeger Security International,2008), pp. 255.
19. "How big a threat is North Korea?", http://www.csmonitor.com/2009/0528/p06s01-wosc.htm?print=true
20. Also see, Joel S. Wit, "Four Scenarios for a Nuclear South Korea", US.Korea Institute at SAIS, *Working Paper Series,* February 2010, WP 10-01, http://uskoreainstitute.org/bin/s/g/USKI_WP10-01_Wit.pdf
21. Joel S. Wit, "Four Scenarios for a Nuclear North Korea", 20 November 2009, http://www.eai.or.kr/type/panelView.asp?bytag=p&code=eng_report&idx=8936&page=3.
22. Hideshi Takesada, "North Korea's Nuclear Weapons: The Ultimate tool for Unification", *in North Korea's Nuclear Issue: Towards Peace and Security in Northeast Asia*, NIDS International Symposium on Security Affairs 2007-08, Tokyo, p. 97
23. Takesada, "North Korea's Nuclear Weaponss" p. 98.
24. P.K. Ghosh, "Maritime Security Challenges in South Asia and the Indian Ocean: Response Strategies", (mimeo) 18 January 2004.
25. Robert J. Samuelson, "China's $2.4 trillion grip on the global economy", *The Washington Post*, 25 January 2010, http://www.washingtonpost.com/wp-dyn/content/article/2010/01/24/AR2010012402299_p...
26. Michael Wines and Jonathan Ansfield, "China says it is slowing down military spending", *The New York Times,* 4 March 2010, http://www.nytimes.com/2010/03/05/world/asia/05china.html?ref=world&pagewanted=print
27. Vikas Bajaj, "India Worries as China Builds Ports in South Asia", *The New York Times,* 16 February 2010, http://www.nytimes.com/2010/02/16/business/global/16port.html?ref=world&pagewanted...
28. Michael Richardson, "Assuaging China's expanding 'core' concerns", *The Japan Times,* 14 March 2010, http://search.japantimes.co.jp/print/eo20100314mr.html

PART V

INDIA AND THE SOUTH PACIFIC

16

Australia's Engagement with Asia: A View from India

Manmohini Kaul

Australia's foreign policy in recent times has been marked by deepening relations with the Asian countries. This is reflected through its comprehensive approach towards the "new regionalism" in Asia. As a result of its realist policy of "constructive engagement," Australia is now accepted by the regional countries as a key player in the emerging new "Asian Architecture." The actual pattern of Australia's foreign policy has developed in phases through its links with outside powers, within the existing global environment. This can be better understood if one traces the recent genealogy of Australia's foreign policy.

Overview

Australia's foreign policy provides an excellent example of the "alliance" policy that grew out of Australia-US defence and trade relations, and operated within the limits imposed by the requirements of US foreign policy. It did not mean that it was controlled or directed by the United States, but that there was a genuine coincidence of interests and shared attitudes between the Australian political elite and the US Government. Though it took shape during the late forties and fifties in the atmosphere of the politics of the era of the Cold War, it acquired a certain flexibility in the course of time. By the time Menzies term ended in 1972 and Whitlam's government was inaugurated, the decision makers in the Australian government had started feeling the need for a change, however slight, in their country's foreign policy.

It was only when the end of the Cold War was in sight that striking improvements were made in Australia's relations with the newly industrialised economies (NIEs) of East Asia and Southeast Asia. In the late 1980s, important steps were taken to economically integrate Australia into the Asia-Pacific region through initiatives like the Asia Pacific Economic Cooperation (APEC) of 1989. In addition, strategic and political considerations were a major objective in Australia's policy formulation in building linkages with East Asia, Southeast Asia and South Asia especially India. "Australia, long concerned with its status as an isolated nation on the periphery of world politics and commerce, found itself in the fortunate position of being on the rim of the most dynamic region on earth."[1]

Australia's trade patterns reflected this change; the shift was from the west to the east, with East Asia emerging as its main trading partner. Being a trading country, Australia has pursued economic relations with those countries that are economically advantageous to it, irrespective of their political hue or their record of human rights violations. Critics like Noam Chomsky point out that Australia, in spite of being vocal on human rights violations, is more interested in economic gains than its professed human rights concerns. Australia's intervention in East Timor is more attributed to the abundance of oil and gas in the Timor Sea than to altruistic considerations.[2]

The demand for natural resources from East Asia has enormously benefited Australia; it is a crucial supplier of energy to economic powers like China, Japan and India. Coal (39%) and iron ore (30%) were Australia's top exports in 2009. According to preliminary data from the Australian Bureau of Statistics released on 3 February 2010, China has overtaken Japan as Australia's largest export market for merchandise goods. (Japan was Australia's largest market for the past 43 years).

Three key considerations stand out as an explanation for this deepening of relations between Australia and Asia. One, there are dramatic changes taking place in Asia which is shaping the emerging security and economic architecture. Australia's destiny is inextricably linked with these changes. Two, Australia, despite obvious differences, shares with some of the countries like Indonesia, Japan, South Korea and India many common perceptions on order, stability and co-operation in international relations. Three, there are shared values of democracy and multiculturalism and the belief in the "new geopolitics" of interdependence and "new regionalism."[3] By means of economic opportunities and strategic interests in Asia, Australia has pragmatically and effectively implemented its policy towards Asia. It is no longer regarded as the "odd man out" and is now accepted as a "creative middle power.[4]

Forging Alliance with the United States

In the fifties and sixties, particularly with security challenges emanating from Southeast Asia, Australia's policy was to keep its "great and powerful friends" committed to maintaining a military presence in East and Southeast Asia. Post

World War II, Australia's first priority was to prevent states that were potentially threatening from gaining access to the region. Sharing common security perspectives with the United States, Australia entered into a strategic partnership with the US. The ANZUS Treaty of 1951 was part of this strategy, and its main aim was to ensure a US commitment to defend Australia and New Zealand, against a resurgent Japan, primarily with World War II in mind.

However, in time it became the cornerstone of Australian foreign policy and remains so even in the 21st century. Through the ANZUS treaty, Australia is able to get access to US military intelligence and military equipment. Explaining the relevance of ANZUS, Camilleri observes: "Quite apart from its contribution to Australia's defence, the ANZUS pact was but the military expression of a common cultural heritage, including a common language, common aspirations and kindered institutions and legal systems. The philosophical and organizational foundation of the two societies made for comfortable and effective policy co-ordination in the military, political, commercial, cultural and scientific fields."[5]

On 8 September 1954, Australia became a member of the US led now defunct South East Asia Treaty Organization (SEATO). Its members included Australia, New Zealand, Pakistan, France, Great Britain, and the United States. Ironically only two countries from Southeast Asia – Thailand and the Philippines, became its members. The main aim of the treaty was to erect a bulwark against the Communist offensive as perceived by the outbreak of wars in Korea and Vietnam. While collective arrangements under the auspices of the United States were being finalized, important developments like the Bandung Conference took place in the nonaligned camp of Asian – African world. Ultimately, SEATO was disbanded in 1977 when it lost its relevance after the American defeat in the Vietnam War.

On all major international issues, Australia continued to support the United States. Practical considerations dictated this alliance relationship. As partner of the western alliance system, Australia helped Britain in putting down the communist insurgency in Malaya in the 1950s and 1960s, and sent troops in 1965 to help Malaysia against Indonesian confrontation. In 1971 the Five Power Defence Arrangement (FPDA) was established, consisting of Malaysia, Singapore, Australia, New Zealand and Britain.

In sum, the mainstay of Australia's foreign policy during the 23 years of conservative rule was its close alliance with the United States, which resulted in the signing of ANZUS and SEATO. The doctrine of "forward defence" formed the anchor of the country's weltanschuaang, resulting in Australia's participation in wars in Korea and Vietnam. Britain's withdrawal from the east of Suez in 1967 and the Nixon doctrine of 1969 brought home to the Australian political elite that self-reliance was the need of the day. In addition, it was also felt that close relations with Asia were essential to Australia's economic and trade interests, because after all, Britain's own economic interests were being guided by the economic integration taking place in its neighbourhood. As major policy changes took place in Australia's foreign and domestic policy in the late 1960s, the immigration laws were relaxed.

Towards a Regional Role

It was finally in 1972 that the Labor Party under Gough Whitlam put an end to the White only immigration policy and Asians were allowed without the restrictions imposed by the earlier policy. The White Australia Policy was a reminder of the hated apartheid policy of South Africa, and with the political elite realizing that Australia's economic and physical well-being lay with Asia; multiculturalism replaced the policy of assimilation. According to Macintyre: "The Whitlam government recast nationhood to remove official discrimination against non-British migrants and prohibit all forms of discriminatory treatment on the basis of race and ethnicity. Assimilation was abandoned as incompatible with an increasing diversity that was now celebrated for its enrichment of national life. As monoculture yielded to multiculturalism, so the recognition of difference became an aid to the removal of disadvantage."[6]

The Whitlam period (1972-75) although short, was significant for the autonomy displayed by Australia in its foreign policy. There were at least five noteworthy changes which were introduced. First, a stop was put to Australia's participation in the Vietnam War. Second, France was taken to the International Court of Justice in protest against the conduct of nuclear tests in the South Pacific. Third, cultural agreements were signed with Asian countries. Fourth, the "White only" policy was removed, leading to Asian immigration. Fifth, a more active role for Australia in Asia was established.[7]

With the return in 1975 of a Liberal government to power under the leadership of Malcolm Fraser, Australia's foreign policy reflected both continuity and change. The government, while aware of geographical imperatives and the need to establish an independent self reliant identity in the region, became excessively preoccupied with Soviet motives, especially its "designs" in the Indian Ocean. Australia had been alarmed when in November 1978 Hanoi signed a treaty of friendship and cooperation with the Soviet Union and also allowed the Soviets to lease the Cam Ranh Bay naval base.[8] The Soviet occupation of Afghanistan in 1979, further pushed Australia policy makers towards direct engagement with Cold War politics.

The Labor government that followed in 1983 under Prime Minister Bob Hawke took significant steps to establish a regional role for Australia. During Hawke's second term (1987-91), a number of developments such as the end of the Cold War, disintegration of the Soviet Union, post Mao China pursuing open door economic policies under Deng, regional developments in Cambodia and

Vietnam, increasing hesitation on the part of the great powers to intervene in the ASEAN countries, and development of successful regional cooperation allayed Australian fears of regional instability and led it to redefine its security concerns in Southeast Asia. Also, steps were taken towards institutional cooperation with the emerging Asian economies.

There was a new vigor and desire to present an "Australian identity" which would be different from the past projection of Australia as an isolated outpost of a civilization that was alien to its neighbours.[9] The Policy of Multiculturalism was adopted officially in 1972; however, it was only in 1987 that a positive step was taken to create a permanent 'Office of Multicultural Affairs' (OMA). In 1989, a National Agenda for Multicultural Australia was put in place giving a formal focus to the Multicultural ideology.

These policy decisions however, did not affect relations with the US. In fact, Hawke nurtured this connection, as it was felt that Whitlam's government failed to be re-elected because of the downgrading of relations with the USA.[10] It was during his administration that APEC was initiated and established. Many observers felt that the ostensible reason for its formation was to keep the US engaged in the region. The Australia-US alliance is epitomised by the joint Australian and US defense facilities that are crucial to both. The US is able to maintain communication with its nuclear submarines through these facilities. In Cockburn Sound (Western Australia) American nuclear armed submarines are stationed for nearly four month in a year. Some argue that this violates the South Pacific Nuclear Free Zone Treaty of 1985 (Treaty of Rarotonga), which clearly states; "there would be no stationing of nuclear explosives devices in the South Pacific."[11] The Australian government maintains that it does not allow permanent stationing and only access to its ports is allowed, which is consistent with the provisions of the treaty.[12]

Although Australia took back control of the North-west Cape in 1990, the US planes continue to conduct test flights over the Indian Ocean. Besides, American naval ships are allowed to visit Australian ports. Joint military exercises are a part of the defence cooperation between the two countries. For Australian policy makers, the US presence continues to guarantee security in the fast changing security scenario in the Asia-Pacific.

Comprehensive Engagement

It was in the late 1980s that a coherent conceptual approach towards Australia's security interests was developed. This epistemological rupture in Australia's foreign policy thinking found most dramatic expression in the Dibb Report of 1986, the 1987 Defence White Paper and the 1989 Ministerial Statement by Foreign Minister Gareth Evans. The Dibb Report started an intense domestic debate in

Australia *vis-a-vis* its defence policy. The Report analysed the Australian defence force structure and called for self reliance in defence.[13] The Report identified Southeast Asia and the Southwest Pacific as areas of primary strategic concern to Australia. The White Paper, using the Dibb Report as a springboard, supported the Report's emphasis on self reliance. The Foreign Minister's Statement clearly spelled out the principal security needs of Australia which were based on "Comprehensive Engagement" with Southeast Asia.[14] He explained: "If we can manage to develop a substantial and mutually beneficial range of linkages with the South East Asia region, then the motivation and intention to threaten us will be minimized. The linkages will do more to save us from threats: they will strengthen us and our partners."[15] The Statement laid out Australia's long term goals in Southeast Asia based on "comprehensive engagement" with countries of the region: "comprehensive" in that there should be many elements in the relationship, and "engagement" because it implies a mutual commitment between equals… Through these we should seek to convey a common message: our desire to be a full fledged partner, and the value of interaction with us."[16]

Since then the "engagement with Asia" has been central to Australia's foreign policy, and over the years it has grown in scope. The successive government of Prime Minister Paul Keating (1991-96), went about implementing the ideas postulated in this document by taking significant steps to establish a regional role for Australia. Realising the need to be part of the economic growth and regional integration taking place in the region, Australia chose to project an outward looking policy complemented by skilled diplomacy. The response from most of the ASEAN countries was positive albeit for occasional bilateral irritants. There was a marked convergence of strategic and security interests as seen in the successful conclusion of a Security Agreement with Indonesia which was signed on 18 December 1995. This was the first security agreement that Indonesia had signed with any country.

In Keating's successful relationship with ASEAN countries, Malaysia stood out as an exception. The unrestrained scathing comments by the Australian media regarding Prime Minister Dr Mahathir's rule were seen by him as a deliberate attempt to malign his government and leadership. In addition, Keating too made critical remarks which further alienated Mahathir from what he saw as 'white Australia' looking down on "Asian values." His response was to keep Australia out of his plan of East Asian Economic Caucus which he said was going to be a "Caucus without the Caucasians."[17] Other Asian leaders like those in Indonesia "found criticism by the Australian press a sign of disrespect. The preoccupation with human rights was an indication that the white outpost was still wedded to Western values."[18]

In spite of these irritants, which had the potential to derail bilateral relations, vigorous pursuit of Multiculturalism under the Keating administration did help improve Australia's image in Asia. During his term, Asian migration continued to grow. Moreover, 60 percent of Australia's trade was now with Asia and Asian investment in Australia was developing rapidly. The Australian Education Industry had discovered a lucrative market in attracting fee paying Asian students, and the tourism industry benefited by attracting tourists from Asian countries.

Approach towards Regionalism

When the Liberal Coalition government came to power in 1996 under John Howard, questions were raised regarding his approach towards foreign policy goals. Traditionally the Labor and Liberal parties represented competing ideologies: with the Liberal Party being regarded as less progressive than the Labor Party on economic, political and security issues. However, it was obvious from the beginning that the Howard administration would not want to change the status quo whereby Australia had emerged as an important middle power in the Asia-Pacific region.

The conceptual framework laid down by the Labor government basically continued unchanged, although Prime Minister Howard reaffirmed his country's ties with Europe and the USA. Thus, the Coalition government's major policy priority was to strengthen relations with the United States, which it felt had been neglected at the cost of turning "Australia into an Asian country" by his predecessor. It was explained in the 1997 White Paper that "closer engagement with Asia does not require reinventing Australia's identity or abandoning the values and traditions which define Australian society. Australia draws unique strength from the interaction of its history and geography."[19]

It was deemed that the presence of the United States helped in maintaining the balance between various powers in the region. The Defence White Paper of 1994 stated, "Increasingly, as we seek security in and with Asia, we will value our alliance with the United States not just for the contribution it makes to Australia's own defence, but also for its broader contribution to regional security."[20] The divergence in Keating and Howard's approach became apparent in the latter's pursuit of Multiculturalism. Howard's conservatism was underlined when soon after assuming office, he put the separate departments of Immigration and Multicultural Affairs together. In January 2007, he renamed the department by omitting multiculturalism from it and calling it the Department of Immigration and Citizenship.[21] Although he assured his Government's commitment to Multiculturalism, it was obvious he "generally took a position in favour of a more integrated than a 'multicultural' Australia."[22]

If one were to impartially evaluate the eleven years of Howard administration, one can assess it at two levels. At one level, Australia's economic and trade relations with Asian countries particularly with East Asia and ASEAN expanded; at the second level its " continuation and most recently, an intensification of its alliance with the United States."[23] This is seen in its decision to participate in the Iraq war in 2003, which compromised its image as a truly independent country, especially among the Muslim countries of Southeast Asia.

Howard received many brick bats during his term, and it was even held that the 'White Australia Policy' had been revived by the conservative Prime Minister. These negative assessments were based on Howard government's intervention in East Timor, sending of troops to Iraq, refusal to sign the Kyoto Protocol, the policy of "Pacific solution" towards the Middle East refugees, the maltreatment of illegal immigrants in the detention centers, and the alleged harassment of Asians, particularly Muslims after 9/11 and the Bali bombings.

Howard's fiercely pro-US foreign policy, along with common socio-cultural beliefs, did compromise Australia's image in the region. Howard is quoted to have remarked that Australia and the US had shared values and attitudes and that he was a great believer in "that you should have close relations with the countries closest to your own."[24] The principal detractor of Australia was Prime Minister Mahathir Mohamad who did not mince words when he stated, "We see Australia as some sort of transplant from another region with the same thinking as the transplanted entity."[25] The decline in relations with Malaysia and Indonesia turned Australia towards China for lucrative trade and economic engagement.[26] A year after assuming office Howard went to China on an official visit in 1997. Since then, relations with China have remained steadfast.

In spite of paradoxes, contradictions and anomalies, to be fair to Prime Minister Howard, the foreign policy as it unfolded during the long years of his government did "reflect the emerging realities" in Asia. The Howard government was witness to many dramatic events in Asia, such as the Financial Crisis of 1997-98, the ensuing political turmoil in Southeast Asia, the return of democracy in Indonesia, the emergence of the ASEAN+3 process, the increase in nontraditional threats, the fight against terrorism, the rise of China and India and emergence of new Asian regionalism. Even if contradictions continue to exist in Australia's foreign policy, much of the bilateral and multilateral relationship is being shaped by the process of globalization.

Relations with Southeast Asia

Dramatic improvements in bilateral relations with Southeast Asian countries happened during the last seven years of Howard's term; many Australian analysts felt that Howard was more comfortable with bilateral relations than with multilateral relations. The key factor underlying growing ties were based on the realization that they needed to review their strategic options in the new political landscape emerging in the region and their shared security interests in the profoundly transformed international strategic environment, especially after 9/11. The safety of the sea-lanes and their choke points like Malacca straits were crucial in leading to Joint naval exercises.

Except for the major misunderstanding over the Timor issue, no Australian Prime Minister can afford to alienate Indonesia permanently. The geographical proximity of Indonesia makes it imperative for Australia to work towards a secure and stable neighbourhood. "Less than 150 kilometers separate them at closest points."[27] As a policy of appeasement towards Indonesia, Prime Minister Hawke on 22 August 1985 had announced Australia's recognition of East Timor as an integral part of Indonesia. In April 1986, relations between the two became somewhat strained as a result of an article by David Jenkins in the Sydney Morning Herald of 10 April 1986. Jenkins had alleged the involvement of the Suharto family in business deals. However, the major low point in the relationship was reached when Australia led a UN multinational force in East Timor. Rizal Sukma observed: "Many Indonesians take the role of Australia in mobilizing world support for a UN mission in East Timor as evidence of a hostile external environment and of the unfriendly intentions of extraregional powers."[28] Australia relations improved with the end of East Timor crisis in 1999. There was a new warmth in the relationship, especially after Indonesian President Susilo Bambang Yudhoyono came to power in October in 2004 (he was reelected in 2009).[29] Immediate help by Australia during the Tsunami disaster in 2004 was appreciated by the Indonesian government. With the improvement of relations, a new security agreement known as the Lombok Treaty was signed in November 2006, with Indonesia on the island of Lombok in Indonesia. However, the Treaty only came into force in February 2008 under the new Labor Prime Minister Kevin Rudd. The Treaty is expected to strengthen security cooperation in defence, law enforcement, counter-terrorism, maritime security and emergency preparedness.[30]

The new thinking in Australia includes understanding of an emerging economic and military capability of not just Indonesia, but also of other ASEAN states as well. In fact, Southeast Asia is of crucial concern to Australian defence planners. It is feared that a conventional armed attack on Australia in strategic terms, can come mainly from South East Asia as it was seen during Second World War. From a national security perspective, Australia wants a stable Southeast Asia. If for example the Straits of Malacca are closed for some reasons, Australia is immediately affected. It would mean that the traffic plying between the Indian Ocean and the Pacific will have to be diverted via the South of Australia, leading to security and environmental problems.[31]

With Malaysia, relations also improved after Prime Minister Mahathir retired in 2003. The then new Prime Minister Badawi put an end to the acrimony of the past, and recast the bilateral relationship into a mutually beneficial relationship.[32] However, of all the countries in Southeast Asia, the bilateral relationship with Singapore is one of the most comprehensive. Singapore is Australia's largest trading partner in ASEAN, and is its fifth largest trading partner globally. Australia has increased its trade links and defence cooperation with almost all ASEAN countries. The rise of terrorist activities in Southeast Asia has given a new dimension to the threat scenario as evinced from the Bali and Jakarta bombings. There is a need to combat terrorism in cooperation with each other; therefore Australia has signed counter-terrorism MOUs with Indonesia, Malaysia, Thailand, Cambodia and Brunei. Maritime security is of paramount importance to this trading Asia Pacific nation with stakes in the safety of Indian Ocean. Efforts are being made to cooperate and coordinate in strengthening security with the maritime nations in the contiguous region.

Australia, since 2000, has vigorously pursued closer economic ties with the ASEAN states. By then the region was showing signs of recovery from the after effects of the financial crisis, and what is more two Asian countries – China and India, had emerged as crucial partners of ASEAN. Australia, not willing to be left behind, introduced a number of initiatives that would accelerate its own participation in the economic integration process of East Asia. In fact, the two way trade between Australia and ASEAN has increased over the years. With growing economic trade relations, institutional links too have grown vastly, giving an opportunity for better understanding of each other's needs.

The much delayed FTA between Australia and ASEAN was due to Prime Minister Mahathir's objection in 1995 and 2000. He "used the consensus rule to block ASEAN from opening negotiations with Australia on a free trade agreement."[33] Once Mahathir was no longer at the helm of affairs in Malaysia, progress was made towards the signing of an FTA. A strengthening of economic relations led to the fruitful development of intra-regional trade and linkages. Although the FTA negotiations started in 2005, it was finally signed in Cha-am, Phetchaburi, Thailand on 27 February 2009. It established the ASEAN-Australia-New Zealand Free Trade Area (AANZFTA Agreement). Through the AANZFTA Agreement, ASEAN, Australia and New Zealand effectively create a free trade area of over 600 million people with a combined GDP of US$ 2.3 trillion.[34] According to Australian official source: "AANZFTA is Australia's first multi-country (plurilateral) FTA. It was the first time Australia and New Zealand have been involved jointly in negotiating an FTA with third countries. It was the first time ASEAN has embarked on comprehensive FTA negotiations covering all sectors including goods, services and investment, intellectual property simultaneously. And, the agreement is the most comprehensive trade agreement that ASEAN has ever negotiated. The ten ASEAN countries have a population of 570 million people, third after China and India and a combined GDP of estimated at around

US$1 trillion, second only to China in emerging Asia. As a group, ASEAN is a larger trading partner for Australia (16 per cent) than any single country, including Japan (13 per cent), China (12 per cent) or the United States (11 per cent). However ASEAN attracted only a modest 5% of Australia's foreign direct investment as at December 2007."[35] In recognition of their growing role in the emerging East Asian architecture, Australia and New Zealand, along with India, were included in East Asia Summit (EAS) in 2005,

Engaging China and India

China

The framework for a bilateral economic relationship with China has been the 1973 Trade Agreement between the Government of Australia and the Government of the People's Republic of China. The signing of a successive agreement in 1988, the Agreement on the Reciprocal Encouragement and Protection of Investments, facilitated economic cooperation leading to strong commercial links. Besides, in order to further develop linkages with each other, regular dialogues were held between Australia and China. Prime Minister Howard visited China many times; in fact, it almost seemed he was going back every year. The visit by the then Chinese President Jiang Zemin in September 1999 was "the first ever visit by a Chinese head of state."[36] These high level visits demonstrate the importance both the countries attach to the evolving mutually beneficial relationship.

In 2009, China emerged as Australia's largest trading partner, and its investment in iron ore and natural gas plus "its strong import demand has helped Australia to avoid global recession."[37] China's spectacular economic growth, its emergence as Australia's largest merchandise trading partner, and the range of commercial opportunities available for both the countries have all contributed to substantial growth in the bilateral economic relationship. The FTA may get signed in the immediate future; after all, a detailed joint feasibility study on Australia-China Free Trade Agreement was completed way back in 2005.[38] "Two-way merchandise trade has grown from A$113 million in 1973, just after the establishment of diplomatic relations, to A$78.2 billion in 2009. China is Australia's largest trading partner, with total trade (goods and services) in 2009 valued at A$85.1 billion, an increase of 15.1 per cent over the previous year."[39]

Despite the economic enmeshment of China in the region, there is a growing perception that China's phenomenal economic and military rise may not remain benign. This perspective is shared by some leading influential experts in Australia as well. They warn about the growing profile of China in Australia. The Australian Defence White Paper of 2009 also expressed a certain degree of nervousness at China's economic and military might.[40] Besides, Australia continues to regard the

South China Sea dispute and the Taiwan issue as potential flashpoints. The recent aggressive posture by China in the South China Sea, and growing bilateral tension between China and Japan is seen as the beginning of instability in the region. According to some security experts in Southeast Asia, this "China fear" has resulted in several Southeast Asian countries setting up their own defence purchases, raising the prospect that territorial disputes in the South China Sea could turn violent.[41] Australia is equally concerned, and is pleased at the positive response to the emerging reengagement of the US with the region. There seems to be convergence of views in ASEAN, Japan and South Korea, that in order to prevent emergence of a "hegemonic power" in Asia, the US and Russia must be included in the EAS. China is not unaware of these views gaining ground and some of the recent political comments from China, during Indian Prime Minister's visit to Japan, Malaysia, and Vietnam in October 2010, reflect Chinese "vulnerability." However, with "strong commercial links," Australia treads carefully in order not to unnecessarily annoy China.

India

Competition between India and China will continue, especially for overseas markets and energy supplies. India's growing economic integration with the region is welcomed by Australia and helped its membership of Pacific Islands Forum (PIF) in 2002. This has helped India build linkages with the South Pacific Island states, which have not really been a focal point of India's foreign policy until now. All efforts are being made by China to enhance its visibility among the island nations. Perhaps to balance China's presence Australia is encouraging India to play a significant and constructive role in the economic development of these 'micro states'.

John Howard's harsh criticism of India's nuclear tests is no longer of any consequence. Today, Australia-India relations have strengthened at bilateral and multilateral levels. Commonality of interests, shared values and membership of some of the leading forums and organizations have helped further consolidate the mutually beneficial relationship, in the 21st Century. This achievement is particularly laudable when only a few decades ago they were embroiled in the quagmire of Cold War politics that distanced them from each other. Australia's White Paper of 2003 on foreign and trade policy stressed India's importance to Australia. It stated: "India's weight in international affairs will continue to grow, as will Australia's economic relationship with India".[42]

India's growing strategic partnership with the United States has had a positive fall out on India-Australia relations. The bombings in Bali in 2002 and again in 2005 have raised the question of Al-Qaeda penetration of Islamic organizations in Southeast Asia. India is now seen as a natural partner by Australia in fighting these "asymmetrical wars" and maintaining stability and peace in the region. The relationship at the diplomatic and strategic levels got energised when Howard visited India in 2000, and also with the first India-Australia Strategic Dialogue of 30 August 2001. Joint naval exercises are being conducted, even though in the not too distant past India's naval reach was viewed with suspicion by Australia. Many initiatives have been taken like the MOU on Defence Cooperation. India and Australia conducted joint naval exercises as part of the Malabar exercises in 2007. Earlier in 2004 the navies of the two countries had cooperated in relief efforts in the aftermath of Tsunami disaster. India's foreign and defence policy response towards Australia is based on cooperation and constructive engagement, and with the current enthusiastic atmosphere, Indian policy makers have responded positively to Australia seeking a greater defence link with India. In the long-term interest of both the countries, the emerging partnership is vital and so is the growing convergence on issues concerning security and trade.

The engagement between the two countries has been further helped by the many high level bilateral visits. Visits at Ministerial, Parliamentary and official levels from the Union Government and State Governments are a regular feature in Indo-Australian relations. The much anticipated Strategic Partnership agreement was signed when the then Prime Minister Kevin Rudd visited India in November 2009. It was Australia's growing linkages with India that helped its inclusion in 2009 as an observer in SAARC.

At the economic level, trade between India and Australia has grown annually over the past 5 years at around 30%. For the fiscal year 2007-08 India ranked 6th in Australia's export market with a share of 5.2% in terms of overall exports; its rank as an import source was 24th, with –0.8% market share in Australia's total imports; India ranked 11th as Australia's overall trading partner in 2007-08. India's share of Australia's total trade was 2.9% in 2007-08.[43] Although India's trade and economic relations with Australia have increased tremendously, this is of course significantly lower than the two-way merchandise trade between Australia and China.

A number of initiatives are being taken to facilitate and accelerate the process of economic integration and it is accepted that FTA between the two countries will be signed soon.

It has to be underlined that the closer engagement with India happened during Howard administration. It was during his visit to India in 2006, Howard showed his willingness to sell uranium to India. There was expected warmth towards Australia as a result of Howard's India policy. When his successor Kevin Rudd came to power, he decided to retract from Howard's position and refused to sell uranium unless India signed the NPT. The growing relations with rising powers China and India is a pragmatic culmination of Australia's realist foreign policy towards Asia. However, it appears that between China and India, Australia is inching towards the former due to its "voracious appetite for Australian resources," which means that money is rolling in.

From APEC to APC

The Kevin Rudd era would be known for the right moves that he made on assuming office. He signed the Kyoto Protocol, apologised to the indigenous people for the stolen generation policy, announced the withdrawal of troops from Iraq, promised to revive the policy of multiculturalism, and strengthened relations with Southeast Asia, although much of it got lost in translation.[44] His obsession in promoting his proposal for Asia Pacific Community (APC) kept him uselessly occupied during most of his brief rule. It is perhaps a coincidence of history that it is Labor Party that is associated with initiating new forums for cooperation. In 1989 Prime Minister Hawk initiated APEC and when Prime Minister Kevin Rudd brought Labor Party to power after a long rule of Liberal Coalition government, he initiated APC.

APEC was initiated by Australia in 1989, seeking to promote economic cooperation and free trade in the Asia-Pacific region. Today it has 21 members and they account for approximately 40% of the world's population, approximately 54% of world GDP and about 44% of world trade.[45] Steps were taken in 1994, to set goals at a meeting held in Bogor, Indonesia. The Bogor Goals aimed for free and open trade and investment in the Asia-Pacific by 2010 for industrialised economies and by 2020 for developing economies.[46] Inspite of these high goals it has set for itself its achievements have been few. It has many critics pointing out that "ASEAN states considered the US and APEC less than helpful and sympathetic during the Asian financial crisis."[47] Their difference in perception resulted in competition "between two different visions of the future of APEC, i.e. between a Western neo-liberal model and an East Asian state – involved model…"[48] Moreover, in assessing APEC's achievement some scholars are of the opinion that it definitely "needs a new identity" if it is to succeed.[49]

Perhaps had it been ASEAN-driven, APEC may have proved more effective and dynamic. The EAS would have fallen to differences due to the growing tension and irritants among the +3 countries. It is ASEAN's centrality in EAS that it has not lost its focus and is heading slowly but steadily towards regional integration.[50] Instead of strengthening the existing structures, both APEC in the past and more recently APC roused the suspicion of Southeast Asian countries. There were concerns in the ASEAN regarding hidden agendas and a plan to weaken ASEAN through APC initiative. They could not understand the need for APC when regional cooperation was thriving under the existing forums like ASEAN, ARF, ASEAN+3, and the new process of EAS.[51] Prime Minister Kevin Rudd tried to reassure his critics when he stated that Asia was his top foreign policy objective and his proposal of Asia-Pacific Community was in keeping with this intention. According to Rudd "there was no single institution in the Asia Pacific region with a membership and mandate to address comprehensively both economic and strategic challenges. The purpose of Australia's APC initiative is to launch a process of dialogue – a regional conversation – to make a start on collectively designing an overarching and effective regional architecture, and on engendering a stronger sense of the need for a region-wide will to work and plan cooperatively and plan cooperatively and in a coordinated fashion as possible."[52]

However, he was not able to convince the ASEAN countries to support his initiative. It received from most ASEAN leaders like the much reported "cool response" of Indonesian President Susilo Bambang Yudhoyono on his visit to Australia in early 2010. With the widening of EAS to include the US and Russia, APC seems to have lost its relevance and justification.

Future Trends

In these evolving paradigms, Australia will continue to remain constant in its engagement with Asia. There is too much at stake to do otherwise. The Australian public too recognises that the 'tyranny of distance' from Europe and other major world centers had become the "advantage of proximity" to Asia.[53] At the same time there would be instances of racism raising its ugly head due to the presence of some elements in its white population who do not like the changing landscape of Australia.

These apprehensions will not discourage the successive governments in Australia from pursuing multiculturalism, as it is an advantageous tool for forging links with Asia. From ASEAN to the EAS, Australia will continue to be seen as a valuable partner. Australia's engagement with China is mutually beneficial to be derailed by any one issue, unless something drastic happens within the domestic realm of China. An economic partnership will remain critical to both. Keeping its national interest in mind, Australia is reaching out to the other rising power India and is seeking a wider comprehensive engagement and strategic partnership.

The American-Australian alliance system will remain the key pillar of its foreign policy. That the alliance continues to be robust is evinced from the regular holding of military exercises. In 2007 Australia and the United States launched their biggest joint war games, involving 27,500 troops backed by a US aircraft carrier and a number of ships and planes.[54] Australia supports ANZUS Treaty and continues to share the global perspective with the US, the alliance remains imperative to Australia's security formulations in the Asia-Pacific. In the complex emerging security environment, Australia's standpoint on the greater US visibility in the region is now being shared by most ASEAN countries. The balance of power however much decried, is back in force as seen from the growing membership of

EAS. For some time now the US with its preoccupations elsewhere has been having a low profile in the region, with China's recent belligerent posture in the South China Sea it is fervently felt that there is a need for American presence, a perspective shared by Vietnam, a former foe turned friend. However Australia will continue to tread very carefully in not giving the impression of being a "part of 'contain China' effort."[55]

ENDNOTES

1. Hall Hill, *East Asia: Australia's Asia-Pacific connections* (Economic Division, Research School of Pacific and Asian Studies, ANU, Canberra, 1994), pp. 2-3.
2. See http://www.thirdworldtraveler.com/Pilger_John/Born_Tears_DV.html
3. Paul Bowles, "ASEAN, AFTA and the 'New Regionalism'," *Pacific Affairs*, Vol. 70, No. 2 (Summer, 1997), pp. 219-233.
4. A term used by former Prime Minister Kevin Rudd. According to him ".It means acting in partnership with our friends in the Asia Pacific region in organisations including APEC, the ASEAN Regional Forum and the East Asia Summit. It also means acting in partnership with the United Nations across the range of pan-global challenges from climate change, the Millennium Development Goals and the continuing challenge of nuclear weapons proliferation. In all these domains, Australia intends to prosecute an active, creative, middle power diplomacy in partnership with the community of nations." *http://www.radioaustralia.net.au/programguide/stories/200803/s2201195.htm*
5. Joseph A. Camilleri, *Australia's Predicament in the Nuclear Age* (Melbourne, Macmillan Australia, 1987), p. 18.
6. Stuart Macintyre, *A Concise History of Australia* (Cambridge University Press Cambridge 2004), p. 237.
7. Henry S. Albinski, "Australia and US. Strategy," *Current History*, April 1982, p. 150.
8. See Russell H. Fifield, "ASEAN: Image and Reality," *Asian Survey*, Vol. 19, No. 12, Recent International Developments in Asia (Dec., 1979),pp. 1199-1208Published by: University of California PressStable URL: http://www.jstor.org/stable/2643965
9. Robert J.O' Neill, "Australians' Perception of Threats to their Security" in Charles E. Morrison, ed., *Threats to Security in East Asia-Pacific* (Honolulu,1983), p. 185.
10. Dennis Phillips, *Ambivalent Allies* (Ringwood, Victoria, 1988), p. 62.
11. For the text of SPNF Treaty see Ramesh Thakur, *In Defence of New Zealand: Foreign Policy Choices in the Nuclear Age* (Boulder, Colorado, 1986), pp. 219-31.
12. Ramesh Thakur, "A Nuclear-Weapon-Free South Pacific: A New Zealand Perspective," *Pacific Affairs*, Vol. 58, No. 2 (Summer, 1985), pp. 216-238.
13. For details see Man Mohini Kaul, *Pearls in the Ocean: Security Perspectives in the Southwest Pacific* (UBSPD, New Delhi, 1993), pp. 92-94.
14. Ibid.
15. Ibid.
16. Ibid.
17. http://www.mofa.go.jp/announce/bulletin/jk10_gai.html
18. Stuart Macintyre, No. 6, p. 259.
19. "In The National Interest: Australia's Foreign and Trade Policy," *Department of Foreign Affairs and Trade White Paper (Canberra: AGPS, 1997).*

20. "Defending Australia: Defence White Paper 1994," *Department of Defence*, (*Canberra, Department of Defence, 1994*), pp. 10-11, 15.
21. Derek McDougall and Kingsley Edney, " Howard's way? Public opinion as an influence on Australia's engagement with Asia,1996-2007," *Australian Journal of International Affairs* April 2010, Vol. 64, No. 2, p. 219.
22. Ibid, p. 218.
23. William T.Tow, " Asia's Competitive" Strategic Geometries" The Australia Perspective", *Contemporary Southeast Asia*, 2008, Vol. 30, No. 1, p. 28.
24. Briendan O' Connor, "A Perspectives on Australian foreign policy, 2003", *Australian Journal of International Affairs*, June 2004, Vol. 58, No. 2, p. 208.
25. Ibid, 215.
26. Micheal Richardson, "Australia-Southeast Asia relations and the East Asian Summit" *Australian Journal of InternationalAffairs,* September 2005, Vol. 59, No. 3, p. 353.
27. T.B. Millar, *Australia in Peace and War* 2nd ed (Australian National University Press, Botany, NSW, 1991), p.184.
28. Rizal Sukma, " Indonesia and Regional Security: The Quest for Cooperative Security" inSee Seng Tan and Amitav Acharya, ed., *Asia-Pacific Security Cooperation: National Interests and Regional Order* (M.E. Sharpe, Armonk, New York,2004)p.82
29. Ibid. p. 355.
30. http://www.aseanaffairs.com/page/australia-indonesia/security%20pact%20australia,%20indonesia%20sign%20lombok%20treaty
31. Stuart Mc Millan, "The View from Wellington" in T.B. Millar, ed., *International Security in the Southeast Asian and South West Pacific Region* (St Lucia, Queensland, 1983), p. 197.
32. Micheal Richardson, No. 26.
33. Ibid, p. 352.
34. Performance Reporting, Section 2, DFAT Annual Report, 2009 –10, Department of Foreign Affairs and Trade, http://www.dfat.gov.au/dept/annual_reports/09_10/DFAT-AR0910-02Performance.pdf
35. http://www.dfat.gov.au/trade/fta/asean/index.html
36. Australian Government Department of Foreign Affairs and Trade, *Australia-China Free Trade Agreement: Joint Feasibility Study* (Canberra, 2005). p. 12.
37. "Australia," Country Report, October 2009, *The Economist Intelligence Unit*, p. 5.
38. Ibid. pp. 1-141.
39. http://www.china.embassy.gov.au/bjng/relations2.html
40. For details see http://www.defence.gov.au/whitepaper/docs/defence_white_ paper_2009.pdf
41. http://www.fpif.org/articles/an_emerging_trend_in_east_asia
42. "Australia's National Security: A Defence Update," Commonwealth of Australia, 2003, http://merln.ndu.edu/whitepapers/Australia-2003.pdf
43. http://www.financialexpress.com/australia/section1_story4.html
44. See Lina A Alexandra, " New Leadership in Australia Compassionate Policy and Creative Middle Power Strategy," *The Indonesian Quarterly*, 2008, Vol. 36, No.2, pp. 138-152.
45. http://www.apec.org/apec/about_apec.html
46. Ibid.
47. Josef Yu-Shek Cheng, "The ASEAN-China Free Trade Area: genesis and implications", *Australian Journal of International Affairs*, June 2004, Vol. 58, No. 2, p. 265.
48. Ibid, p. 274.

49. Soogil Young, Economic "Integration and Asia's New Role in the Global Economy," in Nagesh Kumar. etall ed., *Asia's New Regionalism and Global Role: Agenda for the East Asia Summit,* (Singapore, RIS and ISEAS,2008), p.15.
50. William T. Tow and Chin Kin Wah,ed *ASEAN India Australia: Towards Closer Engagement in a New Asia (*Institute of Southeast Asian Studies, Singapore2009*)*P.27
51. Ibid.
52. Kevin Rudd, "Towards an Asia-Pacific Community," *Asia-Pacific Community Sydney Conference,* 2009, http://www.apc2009conference.org/site/concept.php
53. Hall Hill, No. 1, p. 2.
54. http://newsinfo.inquirer.net/breakingnews/world/view/20070618
55. Kaushik Kapisthalam, " Australia and Asia's rise," *Australian Journal of International Affairs,* September 2006, Vol. 60, No. 3, p. 374.

17

Understanding Issues in India-Australia Relations

Ganganath Jha

Australia, located in Asia, has a democratic system, developed infrastructure and high growth rates. It has a vast territory and GDP per capita of $30,331.[1] It carries immense influence in APEC (Asia-Pacific Economic Cooperation) and is projected as "America's Sheriff" in Asia.[2] Being the strategic partner of the US through ANZUS and various defence treaties, it has been supporting the latter in fulfilling global strategic objectives. Whether it was a war against Taliban, Iraq or Vietnam in the historical past, Australia assisted the US with men and materials. Attaching importance to relations with Asia hardly got much attention. Although Australia was a member of the Southeast Asia Treaty Organization (SEATO) and treated that region as important for its security, its relationship with India remained confined to a diplomatic level. The politics of Cold War and the lack of proper understanding of the perspectives and policies kept the two alienated from each other as far as closer security and economic relations were concerned.

Although India is a democratic nation with a glorius past and distinct civilization, it did not attract Australian attention. As a critic of the policy of containment of communism and founder of the NAM (non-aligned movement), India's policies differed with Australia, which supported containment and alignment system. When India decided to modernize its navy, Australian opinions were not complimentary. When India got a nuclear submarine on lease from the Soviet Union in 1987, Australian strategic thinkers began to question India's motives in the Indian Ocean region. When India conducted its nuclear experimentation at Pokhran in May 1998, Australia condemned it. However, mutual appreciation is always expressed in the playground of cricket, wherein Australian strategies and style of play are discussed in millions of household in India. Indian players like Tendulkar and Gavaskar are praised in Australia and Bradman, Chappel, Warne and others are adored and praised in India.

It is desirable that India and Australia should come together to forge strategies to face the challenges of terrorism, climate change and sustainable development. Australia as a part of Asia, should understand the concerns of the countries in the region without any discrimination. As India and Australia were governed by the British colonial masters, India expected a better deal from Australia in the post-colonial period, but the developments were not conducive for closer relations. Great Britain, which had been shaping the policies of Australians before the Second World War, believed in the theory of "White Men's Burden" for centuries. Dominated by the people of British origin, Australians also believed in that theory.

The dynamics of the Cold War in the post-1945 era saw Australia strongly on the side of the western world. Australia supported the US with dedication through its alliance in SEATO and ANZUS. When the Cold War came to an end, India introduced structural changes in its economic system and foreign policies. There was an increasing urge to cooperate, in relations with ASEAN countries, Australia and New Zealand after economic liberalization. This region was given priority under the policy of India's Look East. The response of the Australians towards Indian overtures were slow, but both viewed each other as potential partners.

Unfortunately, a major asset to promote relations-Indian students in Australia-who could prove the decisive factor to influence policy decisions in both countries, are unhappy with the treatment they have received by the Australians. Indians were treating Australia as the best destination for professional, technical and managerial training for decades, but the experiences in the past one year have frustrated them. They have been physically tortured in certain areas and attackers are indulging in racial abuses. Although the country is multicultural with a democratic set up, the administration has been unable to curb the activities of rowdy elements of the society.

In 2009-10, a series of violent attacks on Indian students in Melbourne and Sydney generated shockwaves in India. The Indian families whose children were studying in Australia became totally disturbed. They began to advice their sons and daughters to come back to India with or without procuring the certificate. Australia had 465,000 foreign students, of which 90,000 were from India.[3] The international student market in Australia, worth $15.5 billion a year,[4] (third largest export industry behind coal and iron ore) got a severe jolt. A Survey of Victoria University, Ballarat University, Swinburne University, Australian Catholic University and La Trobe University showed that there were slump in the number as a result of abandonment of the courses by Indian students. Abizer Merchant, the acting Director of La Trobe University's international office, said in August 2009 that Indian students' enrolments for next year were set to halve to 300, following a dramatic drop in enquiries and applications since the attacks in May and June. What has aggravated the situation is the Indian media making it sound like racism rather than opportunistic crimes.[5] He added further that Australia needs to rebuild its brand in India but… it is going to take years."[6]

Abizer Merchant is right in his observations. Similar views have been expressed by John Cameron of Australian Catholic University, who said that enrolment of Indian student's applications for 2010 was down by 45 per cent nationally and 31 per cent in Victoria. Amit Menghani, President of the Federation of Indian Students of Australia, remarked that a lot of students are saying they are in fear and, once they are done with this semester, it is most likely that they will be going back. He was blunt in saying that the police, universities and the state government had done little to improve the safety of Indian students.[7]

Thus, those sections of Indian society trying to go abroad for higher studies are looking towards the US and Britain as their safer destinations. Those who have suffered attacks are talking about racism after their return and the intelligentsia perceive the arrogance of Australian society in the backdrop of "White Men's Burden." Thus the environment for cooperative relations has been disturbed. It is thus necessary to recognize irritants in our relations and amend ties for better tomorrow.

Indian Diaspora

The Indian diaspora has been playing a significant role in the United States and Britain in influencing policy decisions at the highest level in relations to India. However, as far as Australia is concerned, the role of the Indian diaspora is limited. There are 30,000 nonresident Indians (NRIs) and 160,000 persons of Indian origin (PIOs) in Australia. Amongst the PIOs, 40,000 migrated to Australia from Fiji and 10,000 from Uganda, Kenya, Tanzania, South Africa, the UK and Malaysia.[8] It is a reality that a large section of PIOs have lost touch with India and are ignorant of speaking Indian languages. Nevertheless, they will like India-Australia relations to be consolidated if that objective have the support of their political masters.

The composition of PIOs suggest that they are multicultural. Initial migrants were 3000 who arrived Australia after 1860 to look after the imported camels. Thereafter Punjabi Sikhs and Punjabi Muslims went to Australia as agricultural workers, hawkers and traders. Their concentration was on the north coast of New South Wales. Another group of migrants went after 1930 as labourers in sugar plantations and banana cultivations. Immediately after Indian independence, a section of Anglo-Indians migrated to Australia, and after 1966 when the "White Australia policy" was abandoned, there was a marked rise in Indian migration to Australia. From 75,00 in 1947 to 14,167 in 1961 to 29,212 in 1972, the number started growing.[9] In the 1990s, a number of professionals like computer and software experts, engineers, doctors, accountants, etc, went to Australia to enhance their career prospects and subsequently stayed back. This section of migrants is highly competitive and skillful. They inadvertently challenge their counterparts with their performance and excellence and their achievements on occasions are disliked by some who nurse the idea of affirmative action for whites without changing the laws of the land.

John Connell has analysed the position of Indians in Australia under the title "Neither Indian nor Australian.... Contemporary Indian Migration to Sydney." He has observed the following: "While Indian migration to Australia has become complex, bound up with the certainties and uncertainties of life in a rapidly growing world city, where over 30 per cent of the population were born overseas, it is very much a recent phenomenon. A quarter of a century ago the number of Indians in Australia was few and one of the most significant clusters, the Sikhs of Woolgoolga in northern New South Wales were for away from the general public eye. Other migrants from Southern Europe were much more important. Yet at the start of the 21st century Indian migration had altered the face of parts of some of the larger cities and an exotic nation had become a little more familiar and commonplace."[10]

John Connell has argued that the skills that Indians bring with them to Australia are not always used, and there has been a substantial skill loss. This has long been evident in the health sector and taxi driving. Indian doctors who apply for the post of lecturer have more than one degree. Again train guards, restaurant owners and workers have more than one degree. IT graduates are working at petrol stations and driving taxis. Indians are struggling, and they are hopeful that if they survive a difficult situation, better opportunities will come in the future.[11]

The hardship of the Indians are compounded when they hear the news of race attacks. The Times of India reported on 15 April 2010 that a brutal attack on an Indian student in Melbourne left him with a severely damaged left eye, a broken nose and sore ribs. The person known as Bhardwaj was waiting for a tram when two Australians asked him to hand over his wallet. One of them punched him several times in the face while speaking "Go back to your own country."[12] On April 11, a person known as Dharmendra Singh was found dead by the roadside. Regarding the prevailing situations, Gautam Gupta, Secretary, Federation of Indian Students in Australia (FISA) said that Indian students are now confused and concerned about their safety in the absence of definite assurances from the police. Many students and Indian families are no longer stepping out of their homes after dark.[13] This year there is a drop of 50 per cent in the number of Indian students who come to study in Australia compared to last year. Gupta said further that Victoria's Chief Commissioner of Police, Simon Overland had said that Indians should keep a low profile and should look as poor as they can. Since then most Indian students are keeping a low profile. They fear for their life and safety. Many have left and gone out of Melbourne.[14]

The attacks on account of race however, is not the end of the road for multiculturalism in Australia. The government in Australia is concerned to resolve the plight of the Indians. However, the experience of the last one year have shown that other ethnic groups i.e., Chinese, Vietnamese or Africans are not targeted for attacks. Indians have been suffering and it is the failure of the system that the discrimination is visible. The office of Multicultural Affairs in the Prime Minister's office and National Multicultural Advisory council have proved ineffective as far as assuring justice and equal opportunities to the Indian segment of Australian population.

Multiculturalism

The multiculturalism was evolved in 1972 to gain an Asian identity for Australia. Geographically located in Asia, Australia wanted to forge wide fraternity with the countries in the region. However, it is a daunting task to change the mindset of Australians, particularly of the people of European origin towards Indians. After all, Britain was the colonial master of Indians, and India had remained enslaved for centuries. It is difficult for them to digest that Indians can compete against them in academic and professional areas. It is due to mindset of these people, that the question arises as to why Australians want to redefine their country as Asiatic or Pacific. V.N. Khanna has rightly observed that it is a western country, having western culture and therefore the part of the Western world."[15] Gary Dean has said that Australia's early history was dominated by British outlooks and interests, reflecting the immigrant population that was overwhelmingly of British stock. Australia was a mere home away from home, a far-flung outpost of the Empire. The hearts and minds of most Australians were rooted in the pastoral English countryside, even for those who had never put their foot in Europe. In virtually every realm of life, social, cultural, political, Australians looked to London for guidance and support.[16]

Gary Dean has also noted that Australia's unique historical circumstances have led to the development of a certain set of attitudes and characteristics that underlie its foreign relation's behaviour. Among other characteristics, there has been a dependency syndrome, first with Britain and then with the US, an acute sense of geographic isolation from the European cultural heartlands, a corresponding sense of threat from Asia, and an attempt to identify and project an Australian identity to the outside world.[17]

Geographic realities have however compelled Australia to evolve a policy to gain an Asian identity. When Bob Hawke became the Prime Minister in 1983, he established a high powered committee under Paul Dibb to suggest policies for greater engagement with Asia. Dibb's Report, for the first time attached due importance to Asia. It was the period of Bob Hawke, that Indian Prime Minister Rajiv Gandhi had paid an official visit to Australia in 1986. His visit was considered very useful in understanding Australian opinion, but there was no qualitative change in the relationship. There was a campaign against the Soviet Union in 1986-87 for fishing deals with Vanuatu and Kiribati. Australians, like the Americans, were afraid that this would help the Soviets in establishing their strategic foothold in the region. Both opposed the deal, and because India was strategically close to the Soviets, it was denied any opportunity to build strong relations.

However, there was a positive impact on Indians to go to Australia after Rajiv Gandhi's visit for higher studies. As the "White Australia Policy" had been abolished and Asians were encouraged to come, Indians liked to stay back. In 1987, there was a military coup in Fiji and more than 40,000 Indians migrated to Australia. Thus there was an apprehension that if the volume of Indian arrivals would continue on the same level, the cartographic balance of Australia would change. Although those migrants were Fijian nationals, but they were also ethnic Indians. They were allowed to come to Australia to help the latter in establishing an Asian identity, but their immigration inadvertently generated communication gap.

John Ray, a commentator of Australia's non-white immigration policy[18] has summarized the reasons for the changes in the "White Australia" policy and they are the following:

1. Australia is too culturally isolated and inward looking;
2. Our policy angers other (Asian) nations;
3. We have a moral obligation to help the suffering humanity of Asia in every way we can;
4. Any form of discrimination on racial grounds is, in principle, morally offensive;
5. The gain to Australia would be greater than the loss even in purely material terms;
6. Racism is evil and we should force everybody to become non-racists.

John Ray considered those arguments one by one and found them faulty and inappropriate. He candidly argued that "the best place to help Asians is in Asia. One could even argue that importing a tiny minority of the Asian population into our midst (into what is, for them, an alien society) would be counterproductive to the welfare of both the individuals concerned and the countries concerned. What I want to do instead of this however, is to challenge the basic premise that we are under a moral obligation. I would contend that the entire conception of Right and Wrong here involved is faulty."[19]

On the other hand, J.J. Smolicz has observed that "Australia's success in bringing together people from well over 100 ethnic backgrounds has undoubtedly been greatest in the sphere of political democracy. Virtually all new comers who arrive on resident visas, have no criminal record and wish to be naturalized, are accepted into citizenship."[20] Australia may be regarded as a laboratory for multiculturalism, because of the way it has managed its internal pluralism, especially in relation to the settlement of ethnically diverse immigrant groups.[21]

Smolicz in the same article tried to define who is an Australian and what may be described as their core values. The answer is "only Australians of Anglo or Celtic origin are to be counted as Australians, while all those Australian citizens of minority ethnic background are viewed as 'other' or 'ethnics', i.e., not 'fair dincum Aussies' and therefore less than Australian. They may all have political rights as citizens, but because of their cultural and ancestral distinction, they are not identified by the majority as being part of the Australian nation. Somehow, in the popular mind, the majority identifies itself with the whole of the nation so that it is only possible to be an Australian in an Anglo-Celtic way."[22]

The multiculturalism is not to alter the core values of Australian society. It is to influence their attitudes in the due course of time. D. Gopal has cited the opinion of two Australian scholars, namely John Passmore and Alison Broinowski that Australia espoused variations of the hybrid cultural identity.[23] Australia's identification with Asia will not make it any less European either despite its proximity to Asia.

When Paul Keating succeeded Bob Howke in December 1991, he made it clear that Australia had no intention of redefining itself as an Asian nation. On 8 December 1993 he declared that Australia is not and can never be an 'Asian Nation. In his final foreign policy speech as Prime Minister on 17 January 1996, Keating said that he never believed that Australians should describe themselves as Asian or that Australia is or can become part of Asia.[24] Thus we find contradictions in the views of Australian leaders on the issue of multiculturalism and Asian identity. However, the use of race cannot be discounted in the calculations of power politics.

Bilateral Relations

India and Australia are the two important nations of the Asia-Pacific, but they were not close to each other in the post-1945 era due to several factors. The most important constraint was the politics of the Cold War. Australia supported the containment drive of the US and the western world. On the other hand, India supported the Soviet Union and the socialist world. Robert Menzies and his counterpart Jawaharlal Nehru differed on the ongoing politics of third world. Menzies was loyal to the global interests of the western world whereas Nehru was leading the struggle against colonialism of the western world. Menzies used to think that India was not yet fit for self-rule and this had annoyed the nationalist leaders in India.[25]

India and Australia soon displayed differences in approaches to regional security. When the Southeast Asia Treaty Organization was proposed, India opposed it. When Australia was awarded the Trusteeship position of Papua New Guinea, India expressed its reservations.[26] Thus when the issue of accession of Kashmir to India was discussed, Australia had strong reservations.[27] Australia, as defence partner of Pakistan, showed solidarity with the latter. All these developments had disturbed the very foundations of our bilateral relations at the outset. Again there was controlled economic system and nationalization drives in India which restrained business relations with Australia believing in the principles of market economy.

India started the process of economic liberalization in the post-cold war era. Hence Australia-India Council came into existence in 1992 and National Centre for South Asian Studies was established in Melbourne in 1993. The interactions for promoting trade, investment and security relations started but all these efforts were jolted when India conducted nuclear experimentation at Pokhran in May 1998. Prime Minister John Howard condemned it saying it was 'an ill-judged step' that would have damaging consequences for security in South Asia and globally.[28] His Foreign Minister Alexander Downer called the tests 'outrageous acts perpetrated by India.'[29] In the aftermath of the tests, Australia withdrew its High Commissioner from New Delhi. Australia imposed severe sanctions on India including suspension of ministerial and official level visits and defence relations, and cancellation of naval ship and aircraft visits, officer exchanges and other defence related visits. India also reacted in response and decided to severe all military ties with Australia. Indian reaction was "who is Australia to decide about India's security concerns?"[30] Australian response to Pokhran II encouraged all the old negative images of Australia in India with adverse implications on evolving bilateral relations.

Australian reactions to certain developments at the regional level are difficult to be understood. When colonel Rabuka led a military coup to oust popularly elected government in Fiji, its reactions were subdued. It remained a mere spectator, when a chunk of Fijian people were torchered and persecuted. Indo-Fijians faced racial discrimination and their houses, shops and temples were destroyed. But when India conducted its nuclear experiments in 1998, Australian reactions were to snap economic and defence relations with India. China, Pakistan and North Korea have also conducted nuclear experiments but Australian reactions to those experimentations have not been at the same level. Australians are giving an impression that the Chinese are very responsible nuclear power and conveniently ignore the reality that China has been supporting the nuclear proliferation of Pakistan and North Korea. Yet another example of Australian reactions which baffled the countries in the neighbourhood was in 2002 when a group of terrorists assisted by Jemmah Islamiyah, bombed the tourist resorts in Bali (Indonesia). This event was of utmost concern to Indonesian security system but Australian leaders including Howard added to the concern by saying that Australia will support pre-emptive strike against the terrorists in Indonesia. Australian involvement in East Timor referendum in 1999 had already annoyed Indonesians in the past, but when Australia talked about pre-emptive strike to nab the terrorists unilaterally, Indonesian response was strongly against it. The entire ASEAN group disapproved Australian policy of pre-emptive strike.

The severity of Australian condemnation or opposition are often out of all proportions, but they change if the US decides a different course of action. When US President Bill Clinton visited India in March 2000, Australia also began to change. Foreign Minister Alexander Downer visited New Delhi subsequently to announce resumption of defence ties. The Defence White Paper (2000) mentioned the strategic importance of India. Defence Update (2005) recognized the strategic and economic importance of India.[31] When Japanese Prime Minister Shinzo Abe said that Japan, Australia, India and the US had shared security concerns and they should express their security and strategic concerns in the multilateral setting, the proposal looked attractive. India was enthusiastic about the proposal but China was unhappy. But when there was a change of the government in Japan and Australia, the new government in Canberra unilaterally announced Australia's withdrawal from such quadrilateral framework. This withdrawal was enough to please the Chinese and others who disliked India-Australia relations to prosper.[32]

Uranium Factor

Indo-Australian relations have faced setbacks under the leadership of Kevin Rudd. As the leader of opposition in 2007, he had vowed to tear up any nuclear deal with India in case of his victory in the elections and when he came into power he reversed the decision of sale of uranium to India which had been proposed during Howard's leadership. In January 2008, Kevin Rudd refused uranium deal on the ground that India was not a signatory of Nuclear-non-Proliferation Treaty (NPT).

Although it is the discretion of a sovereign country to sign a deal or refuse it, but in the case of uranium deal, Australian attitudes were discriminatory and provocative. Australians were happy to supply uranium to China, which has been clandestinely supporting nuclear installations of Pakistan and North Korea. India on the other hand, is not supporting proliferation by a third party, but willing to use it for power generation and energy requirements. It is this reason that the US agreed to sign civilian nuclear technology deal in 2006. But such arguments were not enough to Change the opinion of Rudd towards India.

There is a wide scope for enhancing trade and investment relations between the two countries but there is lack of understanding and confidence building on both sides. If Australia is unable to extend due respects to India, if they continue to ignore Indian sensitivities and if they continue to carry "White Men's burden", proper environment for bilateral relations will continue to elude us.

There is limited trade and investment relations. India exports textiles and clothing, engineering goods, chemicals and related products, and leather products. India imports coal, transport equipments, wool, non-ferrous metals, dry fruits and pulses. India ranks 12 in Australia's exports and 23 in imports. On the other hand, investment relations are in telecommunication and information technology (IT) sectors on a limited scale.[33] This is natural because Prime Minister Kevin Rudd's Asia policy have proved China-centric. His first visit abroad after taking over Prime Ministership was to China.[34] Dilip Padgaonkar has said that many of Rudd's foreign policy pronouncements have echoed that of Chinese. He believes that the solution to the Afghan crisis lies in the stabilization of the entire region. The way to stabilize it is to make Kashmir an independent state. Once the Kashmir dispute is settled along these lines, Australia would support India's bid for a permanent seat in the UN Security council and agree to sell uranium to India.[35] Such ideas are soothing not only to Chinese ears but also to Pakistan. It is clear that Rudd is least bothered about Indian sensitivities while expressing his unrealistic opinions which cannot be considered diplomatic.

Despite setbacks, India is trying to engage Australia in a sustained dialogue regarding commercial and strategic matters. There is a consensus amongst the policy makers that Australia is important for India's economic and security interests in the region. Australia is in a position to fulfil India's energy security needs. Besides the cooperation and coordination of the two are required for combating terrorism and sea piracy. Prime Minister, Manmohan Singh, HRD Minister, Kapil Sibal and former Prime Minister Atal Bihari Vajpayee have on many occasions spoken about the need for cooperation with Australia. Pragmatic leaders in Australia have underlined the importance of India in world affairs. Richard Woodcott, former Secretary of the Department of Foreign Affairs have spoken on 2 April 2010 that India has a rapid growth rate and vibrant democracy.[36] He emphasized the complimentary character of the economies of India and Australia in several areas, i.e, resources, agriculture, service and renewable and clean energy technology etc. Thus closer cooperation are bound to be mutually beneficial. It is a reality that there is common strategic need for maintaining the security of sea lanes to facilitate the smooth transport of oil and other commodities. Both are concerned about issues of maritime security like smuggling of small arms, drug trafficking and illegal migration.[37] Both are interested in securing Indian Ocean region as zone of peace and prosperity. Besides, the terror outfits of Jemmah Islamiyah, Taliban and others can be effectively tackled with regional efforts including the support of Australia. The ARF had been established to address the security related problems in the region and both India and Australia were associated with this, but its achievements were too little. The workshops on the Spratlys and South China Sea under its auspices gave its focus on one side of the region. Many issues which were considered contentious were kept under the carpet. Australia, under the stewardship of Rudd, became China-centric. ASEAN became embroiled in resolving financial crisis (1997-98) and Indian concerns about regional security remained a voice in wilderness.

There is a growing naval presence of the Chinese in the Pacific and Indian Ocean. China has claimed sovereignty over South China sea, which extends up to Indonesian shores. Its naval presence at Paracels and the Spratlys are legitimated because it claims entire South China Sea. China on the other hand, has established bases at Coco and Hanggii (Myanmar) and thus it is well entrenched on the two sides of ASEAN. It is reported that China is in a position to stop the movement of ships in the Malacca Straits.

Again Chinese presence in the Indian Ocean have been intensified in recent years. Besides its presence in the Andamans, China has built bases at Gwadar (Pakistan) and Hambantota port (Sri Lanka). Thus South Asia has been encircled. China has naval agreements with Seychelles, Mauritius and Myanmar and its navy is patrolling Indian Ocean region as well. China may be an emerging super power but adjoining states have to protect their national interests, their sovereignty and integrity. Visionary leaders in India and Australia have to think about their common concern and come together for substantive cooperation, for preventive diplomacy and confidence building.

Endnotes

1. Barry Turner (2008) (Ed.), the Statesmen Yearbook, London, Palgrave, Macmillan, p. 7.
2. President George W. Bush Visited Australia in 2003 when he called Australia America's "Sheriff" in the region, See Stephen Blank, "Australia; A Sheriff with a strategy", 2003 Asia Times Online Co. Ltd., content @a time.com
3. Mark Russell (2009), "Slump in Indian Student numbers", *The Age, Melbourne* 30 August.

4. Ibid.
5. Ibid.
6. Ibid.
7. Ibid, Also see Dan Harrison (2009), "Indian Student Visa Requests Decline", The Age, 19 September.
8. L.M. Singhvi (2001), Report of the High Level Committee on the Indian Diaspora, New Delhi, ICWA, December, pp. 278-79.
9. Ibid, also see Peter Mayer and Purnendra Jain (2008), "More than cricket? Multiple Dimensions of Australia's Relationship with India", a paper presented at the 17th Biennial conference of the Asian Studies Association of Australia in Melbourne, 1-3 July 2008.
10. John Connell (2004), Neither Indian Nor Australian? Contemporary Indian Migration to Sydney", in Karan Singh, Ed., India and Australasia, New Delhi, Shipra Publications, p. 190.
11. Ibid, p. 201.
12. *The Times of India*, 15 April 2010.
13. Ibid.
14. Ibid.
15. V.N. Khanna (2002), "Australia and the Western World", in D. Gopal ed., Australia in the Emerging Global Order, Shipra Publications, New Delhi, p. 92.
16. Gary Dean, "Australia's Place and Influence in Asia," http.//www.okusi.net/garydean/works/OZIn Asia.html., p. 1.
17. Ibid, also see Henry S. Albinski (2000), Issues in Australian Foreign Policy, "*Australian Journal of Politics and History*", Vol. 46, No. 4, pp. 536-57.
18. John Ray (1974), "In Defence of Australia's Policy towards Non-white Immigration", in JJ Ray ed., conservatism as Heresy, Sydney ANZ Book, p. 1.
19. Ibid.
20. J.J. Smolicz (1997), "Australia: From Migrant Country to Multicultural Nation", *International Migration Review*, Vol. 31, No. 1, Spring, p. 171.
21. Ibid.
22. Ibid, pp.176-77.
23. D. Gopal (2002), "Australia's Perceptions and Policies in the Emerging Global Order: An Overview", in D. Gopal ed. Australia in the Emerging Global Order, New Delhi, Shipra Publications, p. 7.
24. Gerard Henderson (2003), "World Order from the old to the new", Australian Journal of International Affairs, Vol. 57, No. 1, November, pp. 478-79.
25. Peter Mayer and Purnendra Jain, n. 9, pp. 2-3.
26. Ibid.
27. Ibid.
28. Shanta Nedungadi Varma, "India and Australia Towards Forging a Dynamic Relationship", in D. Gopal ed Australia in the Emerging Global Order, n. 23, p. 260.
29. Ibid.
30. Manmohini Kaul (2002), "India-Australia Relations: A Critical Survey", in D. Gopal, n.23, pp. 220-34.
31. Peter Mayer and Purnendra Jain, n.9, pp. 9-10.
32. Ibid, p. 10 (Quadrilateral framework was to include India alongwith the US, Japan and Australia).

33. Madhu Bala (2002), "Australia-India Trade and Investment Relations in the 1990s", in D. Gopal, n.23, pp. 235-48.
34. Dilip Padgaonkar (2010), "Violence on the Wane: India and Australia must now quickly find common ground to promote their Mutual interests, *The Times of India*, New Delhi, 19 April.
35. Ibid.
36. Kapil Sibal, India's HRD Minister in his recent visit to Australia has proposed India-Australia Education Council, for broadening the scope of bilateral cooperation especially in the education sector, which is likely to bring together government, academia, business and industry to boost cooperation, *The Times of India*, 23 April 2010.
    Earlier Deputy Prime Minister of Australia, Julia Gillard had paid a visit to New Delhi from 21 August to 3 September 2009 and announced that a new institute, known as Australia-India Institute will be established at University of Melbourne and the government will provide eight million dollars, to strengthen and sustain bilateral relationship between Australia and India. This institute will be a joint project of University of Melbourne, La Trobe University and the University of New South Wales. For details see Media Release "The Hon Julia Gillard MP Deputy Prime Minister, Australia-India Institute to Strengthen International Ties, Parliament House, Canberra, 7 August 2009.
37. S. Uttam Kumar Jamadhagni and C S Anuradha (2003), "Indo-Australian Strategic Framework: Possibilities for the new Millennium", *Journal of Indian Ocean Studies*, Vol. 11, No.1, April, pp. 24-33.

18

India-New Zealand Relations: From Compatibility Conundrum to Constructive Engagement in the 21st Century

Pranav Kumar and Sarika Malhotra

> "The relationship between the two has traditionally and always been warm if distant, based on our shared language, Commonwealth membership and love of cricket. But massive advances in the years since have made the distance between the two ends less of a barrier. Trade and tourism have flourished and new significant links in education and science have been established. Both governments are undertaking negotiations towards a free-trade agreement, which has the potential to further enhance business opportunities for both countries. While I am not party to these discussions, I believe the diaspora could be crucial to the success of such a free trade agreement. Members of the diaspora will clearly be key players in business and trade relationships and the New Zealand government is actively seeking their input on expanding its dealings with India".
> (Anand Satyananda, Governor General of New Zealand, 8th January 2011, Speech at Pravasi Bharatiya Diwas, New Delhi)

India and New Zealand live in geo politically different conditions. India, with a population of more than one billion, is situated in South Asia. South Asia is one of the most populous and connected regions of world. On the other hand, New Zealand is spread over 268,680 sq kms, with an estimated population of 4.381 million and is situated in the South West Pacific Ocean, 1600 km East of Australia. Hence, geographically New Zealand remains isolated from mainland Asia. With the promotion of its national interest New Zealand is also committed to a stable and peaceful international environment. Hence, New Zealand's foreign policy goals are to safeguard its interest through diplomacy and bargaining and at the same time play a constructive role for world peace. To facilitate its goal, New Zealand has been an active member of major multilateral and regional organizations. New Zealand is a member of many international and regional organizations, for example the UN and all its specialized agencies, WTO, OECD, APEC, ASEAN+6, PIF, ARF, Cairns Group, and many others. Owing to its staunch opposition to nuclear weapons, it is no longer an active member of the ANZUS. New Zealand and India were the colonies of British Empire. The history of relationships between these two countries' relations go back to the time of the British Empire. Although there were some initial tensions after independence, the relations evolved and became stronger over time as the Commonwealth became the underlying bond between the two nations. New Zealand's early uneasiness in dealing with India's republican status within the Commonwealth and its active role in the NAM made India less important in New Zealand's foreign policy, and the nuclear issue marred the bilateral relationship for a long span. For a substantial period the personality factor of leaders has played an important role in India-New Zealand relations. For example, due to a personal friendship between Rajeev Gandhi and David Lange, the relationship grew stronger. However any relationship driven by the personality factor is prone to many ups and downs. In the last two decades, India is emerging as a major global player in both an economic and strategic sense. This has led to the dawn of a more consistent relationship between these two countries.

Evolution of India-New Zealand Relations

During colonial times, India and New Zealand interacted as colonies under the same imperial power. This interaction was important to know and understand each other. "Within this imperial structure of exchange, consumer goods from India, such as rum, tobacco, tea, rice and curry powder regularly found their way into New Zealand in the 19th century, and New Zealand's timber were shipped off to India to pay for these exports."[1] After India's independence, it was this imperial connection that shaped the Indo-New Zealand relationship, which was not without its share of initial tension. As India became independent, New Zealand's Prime Minister Peter Fraser welcomed the new nation and persuaded Jawaharlal Nehru to remain in the Commonwealth. But India's decision to become a Republic did not go very well. Fraser felt uncomfortable with the idea, as he believed that the presence of a republican India would weaken the traditional bonds of the Commonwealth. Therefore at the Commonwealth Conference of 1949, when London was prepared to bend the rules to accommodate a republican India in the Commonwealth, it was only Fraser who opposed the move. However, when this opposition failed, he accepted the change in the structure of the Commonwealth and subsequently had good relations with Nehru.[2]

But after Fraser, when a nationalist government came to power, it had much less sympathy for a socialist India under Nehruvian leadership. Nehru's policy of non-alignment was neither understood nor appreciated in New Zealand, which was gradually moving towards the anti-communist camp under the leadership of the United States, ultimately signing the ANZUS treaty in 1951. Particularly in 1950-51, during the Korean War, Nehru's policies came under criticism, as India, unlike some other Commonwealth countries, refused to be involved as a belligerent in this conflict. New Zealand's adherence to the Colombo Plan and her ambivalent attitudes to the Bandung Conference of the non-aligned nations in 1955 revealed her fear of communism and suspicion of the non-aligned movement. The situation improved with a Labour Prime Minister, Walter Nash in office (1957-60). Asia once again figured prominently in New Zealand foreign policy. Although Nash's attention was occupied more by South-east Asia, he maintained a warm friendship with Jawaharlal Nehru, visited New Delhi in 1958, and contributed $1 million for the foundation of the All India Medical Institute. But before these overtures could go further, India became embroiled in two wars – one with China in 1962 and the other with Pakistan in 1965. New Zealand's anti-communist position led her to lend support to India during her China war, and this was gratefully acknowledged by Prime Minister Indira Gandhi, when she visited New Zealand on 27-29 May 1968. However, it was not until Norman Kirk's tenure as the Labour Prime Minister (1972-74) that the relations acquired any substance.[3]

When the West Pakistan genocide began in East Pakistan in 1971, Kirk was one of the very few Western leaders who had raised a voice of protest, doing so as the Chairman of the Asian Bureau of Socialist International. In December 1973 Kirk embarked on an Asian tour, which included Indonesia, Singapore, Malaysia, India and Bangladesh, and was one of the first Western Statesman to visit the war ravaged country, and India had good reasons to be grateful. Kirk was given an extraordinary warm welcome in his five day state visit to India. At the end of Kirk's visit, Indira Gandhi expressed the appreciation of her government for the new outlook and attitude of New Zealand. The joint communiqué that was issued expressed their support for the Middle East Peace Talks and making the Indian Ocean 'a zone of peace'. It also expressed firm support for an immediate and permanent cessation of all test explosions of nuclear weapons. Kirk talked about the prospect of a South Pacific Nuclear Free Zone. He promised more aid to India and agreed to explore possibilities for bilateral trade and close cooperation in the fields of education, agriculture, medicine and animal husbandry.[4]

This was followed by an Indian official delegation visiting Wellington in March 1974. However, Kirk's efforts did not lead to a substantial leap in bilateral relations, as within four months of the premiere's visit, India experimented her first nuclear explosion on 19 May 1974, a move that was fiercely criticized by New Zealand's media. By contrast, the government's response was more cautious and reflected a greater understanding of India's position. On 22 May, in his first public statement on the issue, Kirk said that New Zealand understood India's desire for the peaceful use of nuclear energy and respected India's scientific capability and resources that went into this experiment. He also expressed faith that India would not manufacture nuclear weapons.

The fallout of the nuclear controversy was that India almost completely disappeared from the radar of New Zealand foreign policy, at least for some time. The next Labour Prime Minister Bill Rowling outlined his government's foreign policy in Asia in 1975; India was nowhere in that long policy document.[5] Then, as a National government came to office at the end of 1975, there was a distinct shift in focus in New Zealand's foreign policy – from Labour's emphasis on morality and idealism to Sir Muldoon's preference for trade and alliance with the United States. India became irrelevant to this new policy. From the time of the New Delhi meeting of the Commonwealth Asia Pacific Regional Leaders (CHOGRM) in 1980, Muldoon's relations with India and the Commonwealth had been deteriorating over the Springbok Tour and other issues.

However, India began to figure in New Zealand headlines again when in early 1982 Muldoon decided to close down the New Zealand High Commission in New Delhi. He announced on 16 February that the New Zealand mission in New Delhi along with the consulates in Toronto and the Port of Spain would be closed to reduce the cost of the Ministry of Foreign Affairs by 3% as a part of general cost cutting measure for all government departments. Muldoon branded the New Delhi mission as the 'least productive', as trade with India was declining. The Indian government did not reciprocate the measure; it announced that it understood the financial difficulties of the New Zealand government and hoped that the mission would soon be reopened.[6]

In his 1983 New Delhi visit for the next CHOGRM, Muldoon managed a disappointing outcome in the form of 'New Delhi statement on economic action,' the formation of a consultative group, which would consult as appropriate and report to the Commonwealth Finance Ministers' meeting at Toronto the following year. In December 1983 Muldoon's government decided upon a step that would take the diplomatic relations between two countries to an all-time low. It proposed to sell the land in the exclusive Chanakyapuri area of New Delhi, which had been given to New Zealand twelve years before by the government of India to build the chancery building. The Indian government objected to the sale and proposed to buy back the lease whereas the New Zealand government argued that the lease document gave it the right to do what it liked with the property. The proposal badly hit Indo-New Zealand relations. Ultimately, under concerted pressure the National government decided not to go ahead with the sale. After the elections in July 1984, Indira Gandhi sent a warm congratulatory telegram to David Lange, and Lange announced that the New Zealand mission in New Delhi would be reopened as soon as possible. By the end of September it was known that Sir Edmund Hillary would become the High Commissioner in New Delhi and the mission would be opened by the end of December at the latest. On October 4, Lange went to New Delhi on a 36 hour visit and formally announced the appointment of Hillary and discussed with Indira Gandhi a wide range of international issues. The period of David Lange's prime ministership was indeed the high point of Indo-New Zealand bilateral relations. His friendly overtures managed to heal some of the emotional wounds inflicted by Muldoon's actions. The high point of this cordiality in the India New Zealand relationship was certainly Rajiv Gandhi's visit to New Zealand in October 1986. The visit resulted in the signing of a double taxation treaty and the New Zealand/India Trade Agreement. Under its provisions, a New Zealand-India Joint Trade Committee was formed, and it has continued to meet regularly since its first session in New Delhi in 1987.[7]

What followed was another low point in the Indo-New Zealand relations with the second Indian nuclear explosion in May 1998, and immediately after the explosion, the New Zealand High Commissioner in India was recalled. Thereafter there were visits made by science and technology ministers from both sides as well as by the Indian Minister of Commerce Murasoli Maran. External Affairs Minister Jaswant Singh paid a visit in 2001 to put forward India's justification for the nuclear tests. In 2003 the Indian government christened a road in honour of Sir Edmund Hillary.[8]

If historically the peak period in the Indo-New Zealand relationship was the Lange period, though the growth had been modest, it was, of course, the result of initiatives taken by successive labour-led governments since 2000, despite China being at the centre of New Zealand's Asia Policy. At the high point of this initiative was Prime Minister Helen Clark's visit to India in 2004 – exactly twenty years after Lange's first official visit. Clark's visit was clouded by the nuclear controversy even before it began. A story in the Hindustan Times quoted her as saying that during her visit to India she would raise questions about Kashmir, take a strong position in expressing New Zealand's displeasure at India's nuclear programme, and urge signature of the Nuclear Test Ban Treaty. Clark immediately refuted the report, and both she and Indian Prime Minister Manmohan Singh tried to move past this controversy. Singh announced that India had a close, very cordial relationship with New Zealand. This visit, he hoped, would give this relationship a more solid content.[9]

In recent times the number of visits between the two countries has also gone up. From the Indian side notable visits include, November 2006 Finance Minister

P Chidambaram, in April 2007 Special Envoy of Prime Minister Ram Saran, in May 2008 Minister of Commerce Kamal Nath, in April 2010 Minister for Human Resource Development Kapil Sibal, in June 2010 Minister for Overseas Indian Affairs Vayalar Ravi, in February 2010 visited Rahul Gandhi as the inaugural Sir Edmund Hillary Fellow. From the New Zealand side visits include Phil Goff, Minister of Defence, Disarmament and Trade visited India in April 2007, followed by Deputy Minister Michael Cullen in September/October 2007, Governor General Anand Satyanand in September 2008, Tim Groser, Minister of Trade and Conservation in February 2009. Dr. Richard Worth, former Minister for Internal Affairs visited India in February 2009 leading a delegation of India Trade Group.[10] The growing number of official visits between the countries is an indication of how the relationship is on the threshold of breaking old stereotypes and finding meaningful engagement.

Economic and Trade Relations

"Trade is the economic life blood of most small states and New Zealand is no exception."[11] This fact is evident from the importance given to trade and economic relations in New Zealand's foreign policy. Incidentally, the ministry of trade and foreign ministry are clubbed together in New Zealand as the Ministry of foreign affairs and trade. For a long time New Zealand was primarily linked and dependent upon England for trade. The direction of trade and economic relations of New Zealand has undergone a fundamental shift in last three to four decades. Till 1970s, New Zealand was highly dependent on 'Mother England' in terms of trade relations. Due to Britain's entry in to European Economic Community in the early 1970s, New Zealand was forced to diversify its economic relationship with other countries. The Indo-New Zealand Trade Agreement was inked in October 1986 and so was the Agreement on Avoidance of Double Taxation.[12] By the 1990s, there was a realization about the economic rise of East Asia. Due to proximity New Zealand's trade linkages developed mainly with Southeast Asia, Japan, Korea and China.

However, the economic rise of India in post 1990s, with economic liberalization and globalization, has caught the attention of New Zealand's policy makers and traders alike. On the part of India, with the adoption of Look East policy in 1990s, India became more proactive in East Asia and the Pacific. India became a part of the ASEAN Regional Forum and East Asia Summit. It is very clear now that "India's interest extends to the pacific island states and in 2003 India became a dialogue partner of Pacific Forum."[13] This new awareness of India's potential can be well gauged from the remarks of Foreign Minister Phil Goff in 2001, "The Indian market, is now at its most open for 50 years." During the Lange period, trade between the two countries was only $99 million each way. Since then things have certainly moved, although rather slowly. In 2005 New

Zealand's exports to India increased to $194.4 million and India became the 25th biggest trading partner.[14] There is a coherent pattern of growth in trade relationship between two countries now. Although in terms of volume and percentage of trade for both the countries, India-New Zealand trade is not prominent. But have realized the potential of growth and are on the verge of finalizing the Free trade agreement between the two countries.

For the year ending June 2009, India was New Zealand's 13th largest export destination, up from 23rd largest export destination the previous year. It was also New Zealand's 24th largest overall trading partner, with bilateral trade valued at over NZ$1 billion for the first time last year.[15] According to ministry of commerce, India, during the year 2008-09 and 2009-10 there had been a consistent increase in trade by little over 23 per cent. But still New Zealand's share in India's total export is 0.142 per cent and New Zealand's share in India's total import is 0.173 per cent for the year 2009-10.[16] New Zealand does not figure in India's top thirty trading partners.[17] In terms of items India's main export to New Zealand consists of medicines, petroleum oil, jewelry, diamonds etc. The main items of export from New Zealand to India are coal, wood, butter/butter oil, milk powder, wool etc.[18] Coal, unprocessed logs, wool, scrap aluminum and sheep skin leather make 80 per cent of New Zealand's trade to India.

Trade Status

S.No.	Year	2005-06	2006-07	2007-08	2008-09	2009-10
1.	EXPORT	141.90	495.52	158.82	188.62	255.17
2.	% Growth		249.21	-67.95	18.76	35.28
3.	India's Total Export	103,090.53	126,414.05	163,132.18	185,295.36	178,751.43
4.	% Growth		22.62	29.05	13.59	-3.53
5.	% Share	0.14	0.39	0.10	0.10	0.14
6.	IMPORT	216.63	265.50	335.94	423.74	499.21
7.	% Growth		22.56	26.53	26.14	17.81
8.	India's Total Import	149,165.73	185,735.24	251,654.01	303,696.31	288,372.88
9.	% Growth		24.52	35.49	20.68	-5.05
10.	% Share	0.15	0.14	0.13	0.14	0.17
11.	TOTAL TRADE	358.53	761.03	494.76	612.36	754.38
12.	% Growth		112.26	-34.99	23.77	23.19
13.	India's Total Trade	252,256.26	312,149.29	414,786.19	488,991.67	467,124.31
14.	% Growth		23.74	32.88	17.89	-4.47
15.	% Share	0.14	0.24	0.12	0.13	0.16
16.	TRADE BALANCE		230.02			
17.	India's Trade Balance	-46,075.20	-59,321.19	-88,521.83	-118,400.95	-109,621.45

An aspect of world trade to undergo substantial change in the fifteen years after 1990 was services. New Zealand had a major interest here, particularly in the new services trade of tourism and education.[19] In line with this overall trade trend, there is a steady growth in the trade of services between India and New Zealand. The Civil Aviation Agreement between India and New Zealand was signed in August 1997. An MoU on Scientific and Technical Cooperation was between ICAR and Horti Research of New Zealand was signed in March 1998. Agreement between India and New Zealand for cooperation in the area of Technology was signed in December 2001. An MoU between Indian Institute of Carpet Technology (IICT) and the Wool Research Organisation of New Zealand (WRONZ) was signed in May 2003.[20]

"India is one of New Zealand's fastest growing education markets, now the fourth largest for New Zealand. There were 8,673 international fee paying students from India in New Zealand in 2009.[21] These days the Indian students are not only going for higher education but also for School education. New Zealand is emerging as an attractive destination for Indian tourists. And even Bollywood is being attracted towards New Zealand. "26,111 Indian tourists visited New Zealand in March 2010 with an estimated total spending of NZ$ 100 million (up from 16,000 in 2004, moving from 19th to 9th place)".[22]

New Zealand-India Free Trade Area – A study of the import and export basket of New Zealand and India signals that these two economies are complementary to each other. Hence there is a considerable potential to increase the trade relationship between the two countries. This can be achieved through the mechanism of a CECA/FTA. A CECA/FTA will bring down the tariff and trade barriers and increase the GDP of both the countries. In pursuance of these objectives New Zealand and India agreed to undertake a joint study to understand the implications of a free trade agreement in 2007. The objectives of the study, which was conducted by a joint study group of officials from both the countries, were to review the bilateral relationship, identify the strategic and economic benefits that can be derived from Closer Economic Cooperation Agreement/Free Trade Area, and discuss the issues that would need to be included in an FTA negotiation. The recommendations and conclusions of the study have been approved by the New Zealand and Indian governments.[23] Following this the first round of negotiation between India and New Zealand took place in Wellington in April 2010 and the second round was held in New Delhi in August 2010. The governor General of New Zealand, Anand Satyananda commenting about FTA said, "It will be of great benefit to both the countries if the free trade agreement, talks on which started last year, comes about."[24]

Strategic Dimensions of the India-New Zealand Relationship

The Defence White Paper released by the New Zealand government in the first week of November 2010 spells out the security perception and priorities for New Zealand in coming decade. This is probably the first time that India finds an important place in the authoritative statement of New Zealand's security perspective. The White Paper acknowledges that "India's growing economic power will give it a stronger voice in the region and internationally. New Zealand's engagement with India both bilaterally and in regional institutions will continue to expand".[25] However at the same time the White Paper is cautious about the emerging environment around India in South Asia. It says "Relations between states in the subcontinent will remain fraught. The possibility of miscalculations leading to military conflict has been heightened by the actions of violent non state actors. Conflict would have a serious impact on the region, and would intensify the threat from international terrorism. Confidence building measures should be supported."[26]

Here there are three important aspects. First, New Zealand finds the need to expand relationship with India in coming decades due to the increasing status of India in international politics. Second, New Zealand sees the problems in South Asia both from state and non state sectors. Third, it finds a role for itself in terms of peace and confidence building in the region. This strategic outlook of New Zealand marks a gradual shift in New Zealand's perception towards Asia and India. It will be pertinent here to analyze first the strategic outlook of New Zealand with a background of its national interests, historical experiences and strategic culture. Second, elaboration of India's strategic objectives in the South Pacific in general and New Zealand in particular. Third, an effort to figure out where both the countries fit in each others 'scheme' of things for coming decades. And then identify the pattern of growth in the strategic relationship between India and New Zealand.

As per the CIA Fact book, 2010, New Zealand is situated in the far South Pacific in 'isolation' with no land boundaries. It has a coastline of 15,134 km. The small state of New Zealand does not perceive any direct security threat to its borders, and hence its military expenditure remains below 1 per cent of its GDP. In terms of military expenditure to GDP, New Zealand ranks 135. This apparent sense of non threat to security is derived from the isolated but peaceful neighbourhood of New Zealand. New Zealand has no major dispute with any nation, it was never involved in direct military war on its borders or defending its territories, there is no civil unrest or any terrorist attack till now.

If we examine security and defence policies of New Zealand in retrospect, we find that after its independence it was identifying its national interest and security with that of Britain. But after the Second world war, New Zealand's perception about its security started changing, and hence its relationship with other countries. "Three factors generated a much more independent sense of national interest. First, there was a gradual realization that Britain was no longer in a position to defend New Zealand in military terms. Doubts had surfaced with the British defeat in Singapore. So, the ANZAC defence pact was concluded. Second, the Cold War propelled both Australia and New Zealand in to ANZUS treaty in 1951. Third, with Britain joining to EEC in 1973, New Zealand needed new markets and trade links."[27]

Wellington has generally adopted a policy of alliance to safeguard its security interests. However at the same time a concern for independence in foreign policy has led to taking independent actions on its own. New Zealand has always identified its security interest with Australia and has joined itself in a collective security mechanism. However, New Zealand feared the dominance by Americans, and it was also wary of bringing the Cold War to New Zealand shores. The growing anti nuclear sentiment and policies in terms of banning nuclear powered ships to New Zealand ports led to the suspension of the US security guarantee in 1986. New Zealand believes that its direct security interest lies in the defence of the South Pacific and Australia. By the turn of the millennium even South East Asia emerged as an important unit in New Zealand's defence thinking. Apart from this, 99 per cent in volume and 90 per cent in value of New Zealand trade is seaborne.[28] Hence New Zealand has an active interest in securing sea lanes of communication. Being a small nation oriented towards trade and development, New Zealand always supports a peaceful status quo with secure regional environment. To achieve its defence objectives New Zealand relies on alliance and collective security mechanisms. As, it is impossible for a small nation to project its power and safeguard its interest outside its region, hence it primarily supports multilateral forums and a less conflictual and more peaceful world. This is evident from New Zealands' policy on disarmament and arms control (especially nuclear disarmament), active role in UN peacekeeping, and a larger participation in multilateral forums. In last two decades "there is a growing recognition among NewZealanders that they live in Asia pacific and slowly but surely New Zealand is being locked in the Asian economic grid." Now New Zealand no longer "seek security from Asia, they now seek security in Asia by means of cooperative security and economic arrangements in the region."[29]

With a population of more than one billion people, an economy which comes in top five world economies, and a formidable military, India is an aspiring power. India's domestic and international security environment is totally different from New Zealand. The historical baggage of wars and contemporary regional environment of instability and insecurity emerging from both state and non state actors shape India's perception in terms of threats, challenges and rivalries. To achieve its long term objective of being a major power in world affairs, India needs to transcend the regional barriers and match upto other rising powers. Here, India needs to identify and secure its interest in every part of the world. In the post-Cold War era, the Asia Pacific has emerged as a key to achieving India's economic and strategic objectives in many ways. This was put on paper in the name of 'Look East policy'. Through Look East policy India tried to reorient its political and diplomatic energy towards Asia pacific in general and Southeast Asia in particular. India sensed the opportunity and need to play a larger role in Asia pacific in the new post cold war environment. Hence, she tried to deepen its scope of relationship with countries of this region and at the same time tried to be the member of multilateral forums emerging in this region. India's involvement with ASEAN and its membership of EAS can be viewed in this framework. Although India's policy does not stop at the borders of Southeast Asia, rather it extends to South Pacific including Australia, New Zealand and other pacific states, India also achieved observer status in Pacific island forum. This was a clear indication of India's growing interest in that region and vice versa.

Although there has been no historical or direct strategic linkages connecting India and New Zealand to build a partnership but "the emerging shape of Asia pacific region could push them together into a partnership to promote regional stability through cooperative security. India has the opportunity to play a historic role in shaping the future of Asia, and New Zealand could play a similar catalytic role in south west pacific."[30] New Zealand wants a peaceful engagement with all major and emerging powers in Asia pacific, and India wants trade and investment relations with South Pacific. India and New Zealand both have a common interest in coming together against emerging threats of global terrorism and other problems of global warming. Another important area of strategic cooperation lies in safeguarding the Sea Lanes of communication, especially in Indian Ocean. Maintaining peace and tranquility in this region which is a major transiting zone would benefit trade of both countries.[31]

Political Dimension of India and New Zealand Relationshp

Drawing on shared history, India and New Zealand have much in common – the English language, parliamentary democracy, a broadly similar legal system with an emphasis on rule of law, commonwealth ties, a fondness for cricket, and admiration for the late sir Edmund Hillary.[32] Despite these similarities, New Zealand India relationship has been inconsistent, issue based and personality driven. Generally labour party of New Zealand marks a friendly relationship with India and nuclear issues mark the difference in opinions. However with the economic and political rise of India, and changing view in New Zealand regarding

Asia, the relationship between the two countries seems to take a defined path with similar objectives. A new phase of deeper engagement commenced with the visit in 2004 of then Prime Minister Helen Clark. The visit represented something of a water shade as it was at that time that New Zealand really began to look at, and think about the relationship differently.[33] Now there is an increase in the number of high level visits from both sides. These growing numbers of visits are an indication towards growing interest in both the countries to develop and deepen the relationships. In May 2010 New Zealand opened a consulate general office in Mumbai.

There are also some bilateral treaties in force between New Zealand and India, the earliest of which date back to 1963, covering a range of areas including air services, double taxation and wool purchasing. In addition, there are bilateral arrangements on agriculture, plant quarantine, information technology, education and science and technology. An MoU on Cooperation between the Indian Council of World Affairs and the New Zealand Institute of International Affairs has been signed in November 2008. In 2010 two agreements were signed in education sector. One, an education cooperation agreement and two, an MoU between Indian Council of Cultural Relations and Victoria University of Wellington, New Zealand for short term chair in India's international relations or Indian politics.[34]

India and New Zealand share a similar world view about the stability and prosperity of Asia pacific region. Both are members of ASEAN regional forum (ARF) and East Asia Summit (EAS). There is a growing coordination and cooperation through these multilateral forums. For New Zealand multilateralism remains the foremost instrument of foreign policy. And in last two decades India has also realized the potential of multilateral forums and consequently has increased its participation. New Zealand and India are active members of Commonwealth of Nations.

These days the relationship is also cemented through a growing people to people contact. The contact is mainly realized through the means of education, tourism, sporting links, cultural links and growing number of Indian diaspora in New Zealand. We have already explained the increasing interaction in tourism and education sectors. There are about 110,000 people of Indian origin in New Zealand. They mainly hail from Gujarat and Punjab and are concentrated in Auckland, Hamilton, Wellington and Christchurch. Most of them are engaged in grocery business and dairy farming. There are also several professionals including doctors, professors, engineers, computer experts".[35] The name of cricket player's Jiten Patel and Deepak Patel are prominent among Indian diaspora. The contribution of the Indian diaspora in New Zealand is commendable and their role in bilateral relationship has been acknowledged by the New Zealand leaders. The Governor General Anand Satyananda observed that the "success of the Indian community here (NZ) in fostering positive inter community relations will ensure there is a solid foundation upon which to foster and strengthen our inter-country relations".[36]

Apart from these there is a growing cultural and sporting link between the two countries. Sir Edmund Hillary was posthumously awarded second highest civilian award of India 'Padma Vibhushan' in January 2008. The respect for Sir Hillary is common in both the countries. And this was a symbolic gesture from the Indian government to respect the great New Zealander. The Indian community in New Zealand plays an important role in strengthening cultural ties. The Asia New Zealand foundation organizes highly successful annual Diwali festival in Auckland and Wellington to celebrate the Indian festival of lights. The New Zealand international festival of Arts has also featured Indian artists.[37]

Despite growing areas of cooperation and similarity of world view on many issues, India and New Zealand remain estranged on nuclear issues. New Zealand has a coherent track record of anti nuclearism. This was marked by David Lange's decision to ban nuclear powered ships to visit New Zealand. Naturally, when India conducted its nuclear tests in 1974 and 1998, New Zealand's reaction was highly critical of India. In the NSG voting for India specific exemptions, New Zealand's hard line anti nuclear policy were initiating."[38] New Zealand advocating that India should sign the CTBT and other non proliferation treaties in order to get support for its nuclear installations were discriminatory. However India's denial to do so remains an irritant in India New Zealand relations. But India expects that New Zealand will understand the strategic concerns of India and at the same time take in view the non-proliferation record of India in this case.

The problem of divergence of views also relate to technology innovation and access or mobility of labour. The issue of agricultural production and trade could also potentially become a wedge between the two.[39] There has been dispute regarding India's maintenance of quantitative import restrictions on a wide range of agricultural, textile and industrial products. This issue was taken to WTO disputes Settlement system by New Zealand in 1997.[40] The government of New Zealand believes that India's average tariff overall is 11.9 per cent but this varies markedly across sectors. High tariffs on items of interest to New Zealand, particularly agricultural and value added products continue to restrict our exports. In recent years, however, India's average applied tariff rate has reduced in line with its tariff policy and WTO commitments. India's employment of non tariff barriers, particularly sanitary and phyto-sanitary (quarantine) barriers, have also restricted new Zealand exports to India.[41] New Zealand wants India to address these issues. Convergence is likely to emerge in future from augmenting cooperation through multilateral fora and bilateral engagements.

ENDNOTES

1. Sekhar Bandyopadhyay, "India and New Zealand: A sixty-year roller coaster," *New Zealand International Review*, New Zealand Institute of International Affairs, July 2007.
2. Ibid.
3. Ibid.
4. Ibid.
5. W E Rowling, 'New Zealand and the Asia/Pacific region,' *NZ Foreign Affairs Review*, Vol. 25, No. 2, 1975, pp. 3-16.
6. Sekhar Bandyopadhyay, "India and New Zealand: A sixty-year roller coaster," New Zealand International Review, New Zealand Institute of International Affairs, July 2007.
7. Ibid.
8. Jha Pankaj (2009), India-New Zealand Relations: From Estrangement to Engagement, Institute of Defence Studies and Analysis, New Delhi.
9. Sekhar Bandyopadhyay, "India and New Zealand: A sixty-year roller coaster," *New Zealand International Review*, New Zealand Institute of International Affairs, July 2007.
10. High Commission of India, Wellington, New Zealand:Background, Accessed on 23/10/2010, www.mea.gov.in
11. Nixon, Chris and Yaabsley, Johan (2007), New Zealand trade and Trade Policy, in Alley Roedric (ed.), New Zealand in World Affairs, IV, google books, http://www.googlebooks.co.in, p. 152.
12. High Commission of India, Wellington, New Zealand: Background, Accessed on 23/10/2010, www.mea.gov.in
13. Bano, Sayeeda and Paswan, Nawal (2010), India New Zealand Trade and trade potentials: recent experiences and future opportunities, paper for the 51st annual conference of New Zealand Association of Economists, University of Auckland Business School, 30 June.
14. Sekhar Bandyopadhyay (2007), "India and New Zealand: A sixty-year roller coaster," *New Zealand International Review*, New Zealand Institute of International Affairs, July.
15. GoNZ (2010), India Information Paper, http://www.mfat.govt.nz/Countries/Asia-South-and-Southeast/India.php
16. Government of India (2010), New Zealand Country Data, Export Import bank, Department of Commerce, Accessed on 25/10/2010, http://commerce.nic.in/eidb/iecnt.asp; EXIM data, 2010
17. http://www.infodriveindia.com/Export-Import/Trade-Statistics/Trading-Partners.aspx, Accessed on 10/11/2010.
18. GoNZ (2010) India Information Paper, http://www.mfat.govt.nz/Countries/Asia-South-and-Southeast/India.php 2010
19. Nixon, Chris and Yaabsley, Johan (2007), New Zealand trade and Trade Policy, in Alley Roedric (ed.) New Zealand in World Affairs, IV, google books,http://www.googlebooks.co.in
20. High Commission of India, Wellington (www.mea.gov.in)
21. Government of New Zealand (2010), New Zealand India FTA-Background information – NZ ministry, Ministry of foreign affairs and trade, Accessed on 23/10/2010 http://www.nzembassy.com/india/relationship-between-new-zealand-and-india/business-and-trade
22. GoNZ (2010), India Information Paper, http://www.mfat.govt.nz/Countries/Asia-South-and-Southeast/India.php

23. GoNZ (2010), India Information Paper, http://www.mfat.govt.nz/Countries/Asia-South-and-Southeast/India.php
24. http://epaper.timesofindia.com/Default/Scripting/ArticleWin.asp?From=Archive&Source=Page&Skin=ETNEW&BaseHref=ETD/2011/01/17&PageLabel=12&EntityId=Ar01201&ViewMode=HTML&GZ=T).
25. Government of New Zealand (2010), Defence White paper 2010, Ministry of Defence, Wellington, New Zealand, Accessed on 04/11/2010, http://www.defence.gov.nz. p. 31.
26. Government of New Zealand (2010), Defence White paper 2010, Ministry of Defence, Wellington, New Zealand, Accessed on 04/11/2010, http://www.defence.gov.nz. p. 31.
27. Patman, G. Robert (2005), Globalization, sovereignty and the transformation of New Zealand Foreign Policy, Working paper no. 21/05, Victoria University of Wellington, New Zealand.
28. Thakur, Ramesh (1999), New Zealand: the security and tyranny of isolation, in Booth,Ken and Todd, Russel (eds) Strategic Culture in the Asia Pacific Region, Macmillan Press Ltd. London, 300.
29. Ibid, 312.
30. Shahni, Varun (2007), New Zealand, India and the emerging Asian order, *New Zealand International Review*, July, Wellington, New Zealand.
31. Jha Pankaj (2010), Reconfiguring India-New Zealand Relations, in Jha Pankaj and Panda Rajaram (eds) India and New Zealand Emerging Challenges, Institute of Defence Studies and Analysis, New Delhi, 173.
32. GoNZ (2010), India Information Paper, http://www.mfat.govt.nz/Countries/Asia-South-and-Southeast/India.php
33. Holborow, Rupert (2010), India New Zealand relations: perspectives from New Zealand, in Jha Pankaj and Panda Rajaram (eds) India and New Zealand Emerging Challenges, Institute of Defence Studies and Analysis, New Delhi, 157.
34. High Commission of India (2010), Brief on New Zealand,Wellington, http://www.mea.gov.in/meaxpsite/foreignrelation/new_zealand.pdf
35. Ibid.
36. Jha, Pankaj, n. 31, p. 176.
37. GoNZ (2010), India Information Paper, http://www.mfat.govt.nz/Countries/Asia-South-and-Southeast/India.php
38. Jha, Pankaj , n. 31, p. 171.
39. Shahni, Varun (2007), New Zealand, India and the emerging Asian order, *New Zealand International Review*, July, Wellington, New Zealand.
40. Jha, Pankaj , n. 31, p. 171.
41. GoNZ (2010), India Information Paper, http://www.mfat.govt.nz/Countries/Asia-South-and-Southeast/India.php

Index